tear here

The Complete Idiot's Refe

Your Home Theater—What Belongs,

Though the cocoon we create at home with television is at least partially responsible for our country's epidemic obesity and intellectual vacuity, the advantages of owning your own collection of movies, flicks, and films for home viewing are innumerable. The problem at this moment in the history of visual technologies is that there are a number of competing formats for collecting, transmitting, transferring, and viewing movies, and they're all pretty good.

The Formats

- **Film.** Collecting actual film (in 16mm or 35mm) requires special care and some real expense for the films themselves. Still, real purists collect celluloid because, at its best, nothing yet takes its place for pictorial clarity.
- **Videotape.** It has the advantage of having been around for more than two decades now, so there are more movies released on this format than on any other. It has the disadvantage of having the poorest image quality of any format now widely available.
- **Compact disc.** Despite its famously compact size, the current problem with the CD is storage space—it's simply not big enough to hold a significant amount of high-quality digital video.
- **Laser disc.** Laser discs have plenty of storage for high-quality video, but you can't record on them, and they haven't become the format of choice for the rental or purchase market. Laser discs are probably on their way out as more and more companies switch to DVD.
- **DVD.** DVD technology is very good and is about to get better and cheaper. DVD disks are the same size as CDs, so they fit in everything from computers to CD wallets and storage towers. Because computers are now being shipped with CD-DVD drives, you can easily play DVDs on them. Though recording on DVD is prohibitively expensive for consumers, recorders will probably come down to an affordable price pretty soon.
- **Internet download.** It is now possible to download all kinds of films—legally and otherwise—from the Internet, from three-minute experimental projects to feature films. The Internet is probably the real wave of the future, but not yet. Download times are enormous, hard-drive and other computer system resource drains are huge, and there are considerable legal problems (Napster, anyone?). Soon, though, larger telephone bills will be a small price to pay for all the added access.

The Equipment

The three basics of any home theater will be the viewing source, the viewing mode, and sound. Other considerations include amplifiers, space constraints, and, of course, cost.

- **Viewing source.** In the end, if you can't have 'em all, we suggest a good super-VHS deck and a DVD player because, finally, there are a lot of movies on videotape, and DVDs are the coming thing.

The Equipment (continued)

- **Viewing mode.** If you can afford it, *CRT* (cathode ray tube) projection is a terrific way to go. This is a video projector, not a television set. You project from the back of your room, or perhaps suspend it from the ceiling. The big advantage is the size of its picture, which can dwarf the largest big-screen television. Next, we recommend *large-screen television* because it gives the next-best impression of the big screen. *HDTV* is not yet worth the expense if you are just watching cable TV because most programming is not done in high-resolution format yet. It is also not very compatible with DVD technology at the moment. But higher-resolution TVs may in the future be a better idea if you are investing in DVD technology.
- **Sound.** Most television speakers are not good substitutes for a nice speaker-amplifier system. A good present technology is six-speaker Surround Sound, so that those aliens can sneak from behind you on your left and creep to the front right of the room. The six speakers include two fronts, a center, two rears, and a powered subwoofer. The home-theater room itself should not be "live." You should not be able to hear sound reverberate too much; when you clap you should not hear an echo. Thick and padded carpeting helps. So does lots of comfortable furniture. And curtains. If you have the dough, acoustic absorption products are also available. The room should be large enough so that speakers can be placed comfortably far apart in relation to each other and to you.

The Most Important Film Credits and What They Mean

Art Director The person responsible for the look of a film's sets; also responsible for their construction.

Assistant Director Helps break down the script and make decisions about the shooting order.

Associate Producer/Production Manager Actual administrator for the daily operations of the film.

Best Boy An apprentice to the gaffer or key grip.

Camera Operator/Second Cameraman The technician actually operating the movie camera.

Casting Director Actually picks the "talent," or actors who will appear on-screen.

Cinematographer/Director of Photography The person who literally brings the director's vision to light.

Continuity Clerk Ensures that the actions and look of the talent from one shot to the next is consistent.

Dolly Grip Operates the dolly, a wheeled and motorized platform on which the camera is placed for "dolly" or "tracking" shots.

Executive Producer Administrator in charge of the business end of production such as raising money for the budget.

Foley Artist Invents the sound effects that are dubbed onto the visuals.

Gaffer The chief electrician responsible for lighting the set.

Key (or Head) Grip The person on the set in charge of the other grips. Grips are in charge of all physical work except electrical.

Line Producer/Production Manager Oversees the day-to-day operations of a film's production.

Location Manager Person who finds locations at which to shoot.

Producer The chief administrator for a film.

Production Designer The person who decides how the film is going to look, based on the needs and vision of the director and the script.

Screenwriter The craftsperson who writes the scripts.

Second Unit Director Directs the film crew ("second unit") that photographs sequences for which the director and principal actors are not required.

Sound Designer Oversees all aspects of sound recording for a film project.

Stunt Coordinator Determines where, in the film script, stunts will take place.

Supervising Editor The person in charge of film editing in post-production.

Unit Photographer The still photographer who takes publicity photos on the set for the film.

Visual Effects Supervisor The person who oversees the team that actually creates special effects.

Wrangler The person responsible for the animals acting in front of the camera.

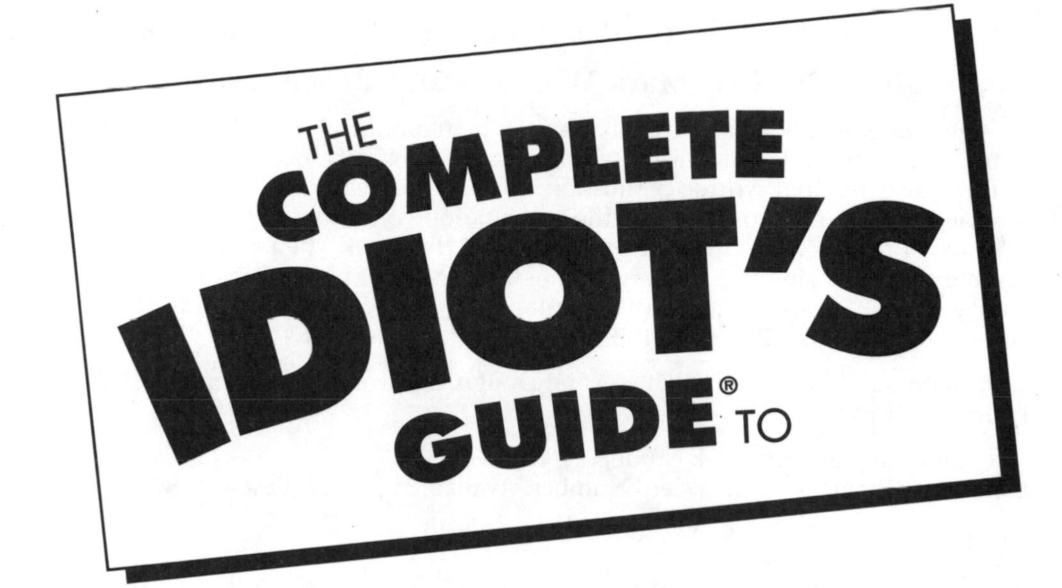

Movies, Flicks, and Film

by Mark Winokur and Bruce Holsinger

A Pearson Education Company

This book is lovingly dedicated to Anna Brickhouse and Katherine Eggert.

International Standard Book Number: 0-02-863988-x
Library of Congress Catalog Card Number: Available upon request.

04 03 8 7 6 5 4 3

Interpretation of the printing code: The rightmost number of the first series of numbers is the year of the book's printing; the rightmost number of the second series of numbers is the number of the book's printing. For example, a printing code of 01-1 shows that the first printing occurred in 2001.

Printed in the United States of America

For marketing and publicity, please call: 317-581-3722

The publisher offers discounts on this book when ordered in quantity for bulk purchases and special sales.

For sales within the United States, please contact: Corporate and Government Sales, 1-800-382-3419 or corpsales@pearsontechgroup.com

Outside the United States, please contact: International Sales, 317-581-3793 or international@pearsontechgroup.com

Publisher
Marie Butler-Knight

Product Manager
Phil Kitchel

Managing Editor
Cari Luna

Senior Acquisitions Editor
Randy Ladenheim-Gil

Development Editor
Michael Koch

Production Editor
JoAnna Kremer

Copy Editor
Faren Bachelis

Illustrator
Kevin Spear

Cover Designers
Mike Freeland
Kevin Spear

Book Designers
Scott Cook and Amy Adams of DesignLab

Indexer
Amy Lawrence

Layout/Proofreading
Angela Calvert
Svetlana Dominguez
Steve Geiselman

Contents at a Glance

Contents

Foreword

What other form of entertainment could ever be all the things to us that film is? Movies are at once elitist and populist, highbrow and low, sweeping in scope and intimate in nature. When we sit in a darkened theater or bring home a box from the video store, we take it for granted that the combination of actors and writers and director and hundreds of other people and pieces is one of limitless possibility. No wonder they call it the dream factory. Anyone who has ever cried at *Old Yeller*, quoted *Monty Python and the Holy Grail*, or argued heatedly whether *Titanic* ruled or sucked knows how pervasive the influence of the movies is in our lives.

Today, more than ever, we're not just consumers of cinema but connoisseurs. We subscribe to entertainment magazines, order up the Independent Film Channel on cable, we know what a back-end deal is and who took home the audience award at Sundance. So what do we need to read this book for? Aren't we all seasoned scholars already?

As the pretentious, Francophile film students say, *au contraire*. Film, as you're about to discover, is a great big interdisciplinary world—incorporating twentieth-century history, multiculturalism, business theory, and artistic technique. And while a lifetime of moviegoing has probably taught us that we can be devoted fans whether we study film or not, even things we think we're experts on are improved with a little extra knowledge. Think of this, then, as a *Kama Sutra* of cinema, a means of stretching our eyes and ears and ultimately, our minds, in ways we never thought possible.

As we journey, chapter by chapter, through the history, process, genres, and interpretations of film, we unlock new and deeper ways to enjoy not just the movies but the craft behind them. And unlike Dorothy's deflating exposure of the man behind the curtain in *The Wizard of Oz*, each new thing we learn about the workings of cinema only adds to our awe at its magic. Plus, authors Mark Winokur and Bruce Holsinger have helpfully thrown in an array of trivia and behind-the-scenes stories, perfect for impressing a date or stumping a cineaste. You know the subtitle-loving, Eisenstein-worshipping snobs who can always be overheard pontificating in the local arthouse-cum-coffee shop? We need never be intimidated by them again. But the best reason to study film, of course, is for nobody's benefit but our own.

Whether our taste runs to *A Day at the Races* or *A Nightmare on Elm Street*, when we become informed, critical moviegoers, we find something to fall in love with every time the houselights go down. To understand cinema is to bask in the glory of the human imagination. Happy reading—and more important—happy viewing!

—Mary Elizabeth Williams

Mary Elizabeth Williams is a critic for Salon.com and the host of Table Talk, Salon's reader community. A film school survivor, she's written for *The New York Times*, *The Nation*, and other publications. She thinks *Citizen Kane* is overrated. So sue her.

Introduction

You've always loved the movies. Who hasn't? Whether browsing new releases at Blockbuster or sneaking away for a matinee at the local multiplex, you're a bona fide cinema junkie. But when it comes to talking intelligently about the history, technology, and artistry of the medium you love, you're at a total loss. Truffaut? Parallel montage? Art direction? Those "film people" might as well be speaking Swahili.

It's not too late! *The Complete Idiot's Guide to Movies, Flicks, and Film* will help you navigate your way across the vast visual ocean that is film. Everyone knows how bewildering the subject can be, of course. After you get past the Hollywood basics, the 100-year history of the movies confronts you with a hopelessly steep learning curve.

What exactly is *film noir,* and how do I know it when I see it? When my sister-in-law gushes about the "great cinematography," what am I supposed to say? Can I learn to live with subtitles when all I want to do is grab the latest Schwarzenegger? I know Warren Beatty's work, but who was the Czech director receiving that lifetime achievement award at the Oscars a while back? These are just a few of the questions you'll find answered in this book.

Why This Book?

Scanning the movies and film section at your local chain bookstore is a little like standing in front of the pasta section at the grocery store. A search on Amazon.com for books containing the word *movies* yielded 1,342 titles. *Flicks* got only 12 hits, but *cinema* got 3062, and *film* yielded—get this—*11,217* titles! With so many books on film to choose from, how are you supposed to know which one to buy? More specifically, what sets this book apart from the crowd, and why should you take it home with you today?

Let's start by telling you what this book is *not* going to do. First off, we're not going to make you read a dense, 40-page chapter on French silent film that you'd never remember the details of anyway. Too many of those big, intimidating "history of world cinema"–type tomes, while wonderful for the serious scholar, aren't very useful for the beginner. They're loaded with too much information, and given your busy schedule, you just don't have the time to sit down with a dense, three-columns-per-page scholarly essay on the impact of new sound technologies on the 1940s Norwegian film industry.

Nor is this *Complete Idiot's Guide* an encyclopedia of film. Though we've included a glossary of terms from our "Filmophile's Lexicon" sidebars in Appendix D, we aren't going to make you slog through an alphabetical list of 10,000 actors, actresses, directors, producers, technical terms, and so on.

Finally, unlike those thousand-page video guides describing every one-star flick under the sun (in eight-point type, no less), this book gives you a selective guide to finding what you like—and discovering what you *could* like if you only knew where to look, from 1920s French poetic realism to John Ford's classic Westerns to the Taiwanese

"New Cinema" of the '70s and '80s. In short, the book you're holding in your hands right now provides an entertaining, user-friendly how-to manual for the aspiring filmophile.

Film, the authors believe, is like fine wine: A little knowledge acquired during a few weeks can lead to a lifetime of cultivation, pleasure, and enrichment. *The Complete Idiot's Guide to Movies, Flicks, and Film* will quickly become the one book you'll always want next to your VCR.

What You'll Find in This Book

As you can tell from the table of contents a few pages back, we've organized *The Complete Idiot's Guide to Movies, Flicks, and Film* with your convenience in mind. The five parts of the book will take you from industry and production basics through the history and aesthetics of American and foreign film. Along the way you'll find many how-to-watch tips, helpful hints for honing your interpretive skills, and some guidelines for putting together your home theater and your own film library.

Part 1, "What Is Film?" introduces you to the film industry: the business, the personnel, and the process of making a movie from start to finish.

Part 2, "A Brief History of (Mostly American) Film," takes you from the "prehistory" of the movies through the golden age all the way to present-day Hollywood and independent film.

Part 3, "The Hundred Languages of Foreign Film," provides something of a whirlwind tour through selected foreign film traditions. We hope you'll find these chapters especially helpful in orienting you on the great global tour of world cinema you're about to take.

Part 4, "The Aesthetics, Technologies, and Artistry of Film," is the most technical part of the book. But we hope you'll find the chapters (on camera movement, directing, lighting, sound, editing, and so on) easy to read and even fun. With any luck, you'll soon be able to use them to help spot some of the intricate ways films are actually put together on the set and in the editing room.

Part 5, "Becoming a Filmophile—For Life," takes you on a guided tour of film theory before applying everything you've learned in this book in an in-depth reading of a single film, the silent Expressionist masterpiece *Nosferatu.*

While we're pretty proud of the book you're holding in your hands, we'd never pretend it's a definitive reference work on world cinema. In our first appendix, you'll find a helpful list of further readings that will point you to more great books on movies, flicks, and film. Appendix B gives you a rundown of some of the major North American film festivals (in the United States and Canada), while Appendix C provides just a few URLs for movie-related Web sites we'd recommend your taking a look at. Finally, the long glossary at the end of the book gives you a thumbable reference guide to the most important terms used in our book.

A Little Something Else!

In each and every chapter that follows, you'll come across four different kinds of "sidebars," as we in *The Complete Idiot's Guide* business call them: sets of terms, definitions, hints, warnings, and so on that are set apart from the main text in their own shaded little areas for your convenience. Here they are:

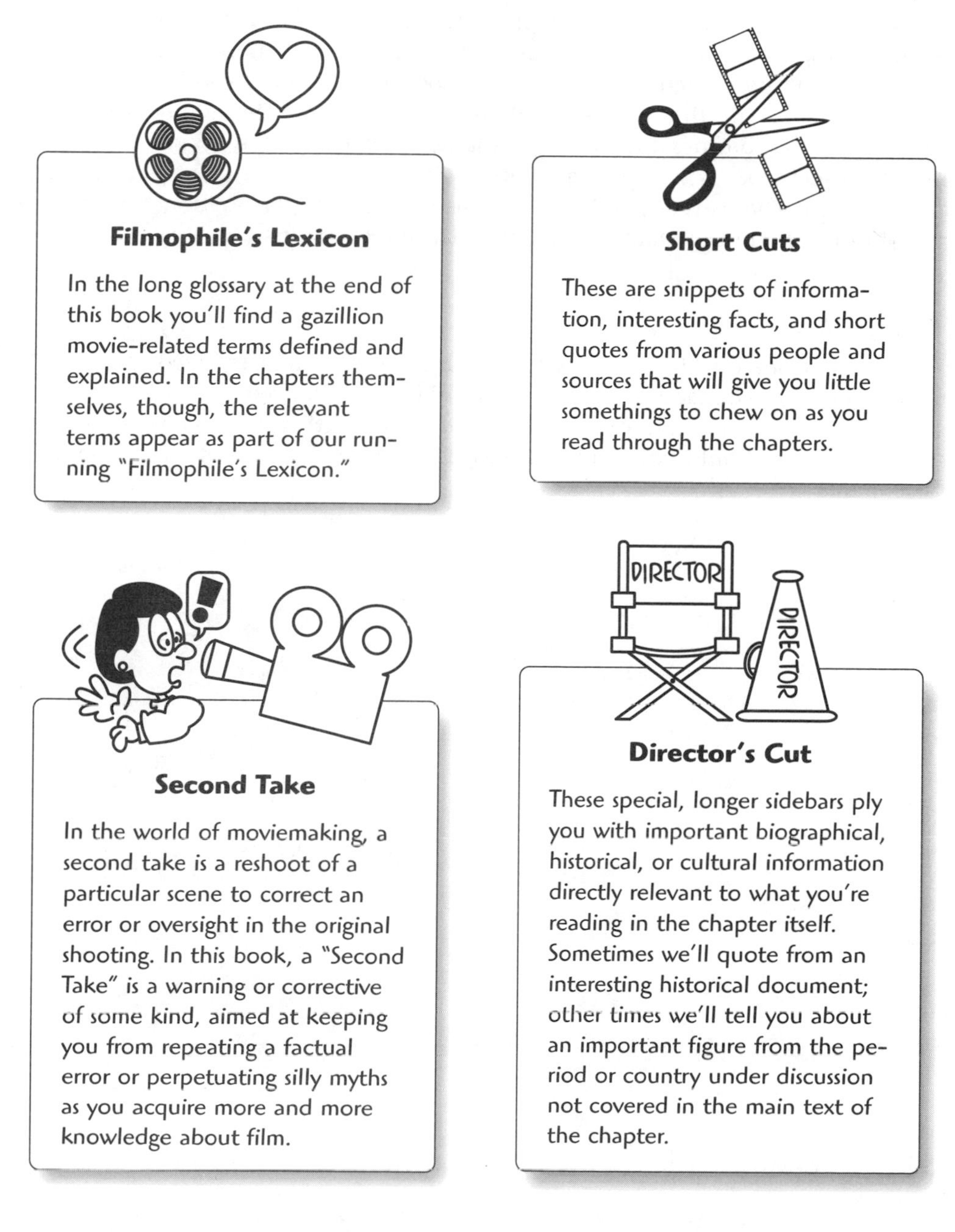

Filmophile's Lexicon

In the long glossary at the end of this book you'll find a gazillion movie-related terms defined and explained. In the chapters themselves, though, the relevant terms appear as part of our running "Filmophile's Lexicon."

Short Cuts

These are snippets of information, interesting facts, and short quotes from various people and sources that will give you little somethings to chew on as you read through the chapters.

Second Take

In the world of moviemaking, a second take is a reshoot of a particular scene to correct an error or oversight in the original shooting. In this book, a "Second Take" is a warning or corrective of some kind, aimed at keeping you from repeating a factual error or perpetuating silly myths as you acquire more and more knowledge about film.

Director's Cut

These special, longer sidebars ply you with important biographical, historical, or cultural information directly relevant to what you're reading in the chapter itself. Sometimes we'll quote from an interesting historical document; other times we'll tell you about an important figure from the period or country under discussion not covered in the main text of the chapter.

Acknowledgments

First and foremost, we would like to thank Katherine Eggert and Anna Brickhouse, who generously tolerated the stress and deadlines involved in this project and without whose support our writing of this book would have been impossible. Two Boulder, Colorado, coffee shops—Vic's on Broadway and Penny Lane on Pearl—made the writing process vaguely social by providing friendly atmospheres for laptops and harried academics. Randy Ladenheim-Gil of Alpha Books, Michael Koch (our developmental editor), Sheree Bykofsky (our agent), Howard Mandelbaum of Photofest, Brodie Austin, Barry Dougherty, Jean-Pierre Trebot, David Underwood, Manu Ghaffari, Bruce Kawin, Ilisa Barbash, and Lucien Taylor came through to help us bring in this book in good order and on time. Finally, we would like to acknowledge Campbell Brickhouse, who was born at about the same time as the project (though conceived somewhat earlier), and who gave us inspiration, perspiration, and other kinds of moisture during many of our authorial think sessions.

Part 1

What Is Film?

This part introduces you immediately to some basic ways of thinking about movies. Chapter 1 helps you begin to distinguish between some different kinds of flicks, and provides you with routes for enjoying all sorts of films. Chapter 2 takes you through the typical production process from A to Z. Chapter 3 lets you in on some basic but important information about the film industry, while Chapter 4 explains who does what, and generally gives the lowdown on all those jobs listed in the film credits.

Chapter 1

Flicks, Movies, and Films: Developing Distinction

In This Chapter

- Acquiring a sense of distinction
- Honing your movie-watching and film-analyzing skills
- Comparing and contrasting films

While we were researching and writing this book, our friends, colleagues, and skeptical family members asked the same two questions: "Are movies today worse than they were in the golden age of Hollywood?" and, "Are foreign films inherently less commercial and more 'artsy'—and therefore of greater quality—than American movies?"

When Is a Movie a Film?

These are impossible questions to answer with any degree of certainty, of course. On the one hand, if you look at the sum total of American films made in any given decade, whether the 1920s or the 1990s, you'll find a much greater percentage of bad, banal, uninteresting, and poorly directed movies than you will of good, skillful, well-written, satisfying ones. The same holds true of foreign versus American films: For all its aesthetic leadership in the medium, Paris has produced just as many awful flicks as Hollywood.

The problem is that good, well-received, or money-making movies from America's past are much more likely to have survived the ravages of history to end up on the shelves at your local video store. And only those European films that certain distribution executives feel can "make it" in the American market will go through the expensive process of subtitling, international licensing, and export across the Atlantic.

Filmophile's Lexicon

Throughout this book we'll be throwing dozens of important movie terms at you from our "Filmophile's Lexicon." These first four, though, shouldn't be taken as hard-and-fast definitions: They're entirely subjective, we use them interchangeably at times, and you'd do best to think of them as flexible, malleable, and always up for grabs.

Movie: The general, nonjudgmental term for any run-of-the-mill motion picture.

Flick: A movie with no artistic aspirations whatsoever that's made purely for entertainment's sake.

Film: A motion picture whose age, artistry, budget, or nationality distinguishes it as a culturally significant work (thus the most subjective term of all!).

Cinema: The motion picture industry at large; movies, flicks, and film in general.

Director's Cut

Today's great directors know how to learn from the past, and so should you. Over the main door of our university's library is an inscription that reads, "He who knows only his own generation remains always a child." Pretty harsh, but it's true in a fundamental way: Without learning from history you'll never achieve a sufficient understanding of the present in which you and everyone you know live.

Nevertheless, one of the purposes of this book will be to help you develop a sense of distinction: a sensitivity to the differences between standard-fare movies and aesthetically challenging films. So pay attention as we take you through three cinematic subcategories that subsequent chapters of this book will examine in more detail.

Old Movies

As you'll see throughout Parts 2, "A Brief History of (Mostly American) Film," and 3, "The Hundred Languages of Foreign Film," we're very keen to hook you on silent-era cinema, whether American, European, or Asian. "Why bother?" you might be asking. "Why should I spend so much time learning about ancient movie history when I could be casting my net more widely in the present? And given how much contemporary stuff is out there that I'll never have time to see anyway, what's the point of delving so deeply into film history?"

To be frank with you, that's a little like asking why you should bother taking in the Louvre while on a visit to Paris when there are so many great nightclubs to visit!

In this book we've stressed films that were made sometimes as much as 60, 70, or even 80 years ago, from D. W. Griffith's epochal *The Birth of a Nation* (1915) to the *benshi*-narrated films of pre–World War II Japan to the postwar New Wave of 1950s France. Today's great directors stand at the end of a rich and enduring tradition of worldwide filmmaking that they have inherited as an integral part of the medium they've mastered. It's up to you to learn how to watch their films through the historical lens this book will teach you how to develop.

Second Take

This book is not asking you to go out and become an expert on Eastern European Cold War dramas, or to master the cinematic art of post-Maoist China. While we have our own preferences, the whole point of this book is to serve as a selective guide to finding the kinds of movies that *you* like, and to encourage you to expand your horizons beyond the usual Blockbuster new releases fare.

Foreign Films

"It's a foreign film." This simple sentence is enough to send chills of anticipated boredom and entrapment down the spines of many American moviegoers. At the end of a hectic work week, you want a fast-paced thriller with a clearly unfolding plot, or a chick flick that you don't have to work very hard to understand. The *last* thing you want is a 1950s Romanian art film with white subtitles that hardly stand out against the too-bright background anyway.

Fair enough. But you wouldn't have picked up this book in the first place if you weren't at least willing to give foreign film an honest try, right?

But don't take our word for it. To whet your appetite for foreign film, the next time you're in the video store (this evening after dinner, say), pick up a 1959 picture by French director Jean-Luc Godard called *Breathless* (the French title is *À Bout de Souffle*). We'll have more to say about this movie in Chapter 11, "French Revolutions," but for now keep in mind that it's one of the hallmark works of an aesthetic movement in post–World War II French film called the New Wave. Sounds pretty dull, huh?

Second Take

When you go out to rent *Breathless,* be sure to request the 1959 Godard version. There's a 1983 Jim McBride remake starring Richard Gere that you'll definitely want to avoid (and besides, it doesn't count as a foreign film!).

Don't bet on it. *Breathless* is actually a complex, absolutely gripping and very fast-paced story of cops and robbers, car theft, love, and betrayal. We guarantee you'll be left "breathless" by this classic French movie and salivating for more.

Foreign films such as *Breathless* and the dozens of others discussed in the following chapters are wonderful as movies in their own right. Just as importantly, though, they open windows onto other cultures in ways that no other medium can. They have served as some of the most important means of cultural exchange during the last century, providing a form of ambassadorship between the nations of the world in which you now have the opportunity to participate yourself. Don't chicken out!

Filmophile's Lexicon

An **avant-garde** is a group of artists or intellectuals that develops innovative, experimental, or radical concepts and aesthetic changes in an art form.

Director's Cut

Stan Brakhage is an American experimental filmmaker now based at the University of Colorado. Though he has a loyal following and is generally regarded as a great film artist, his pictures (like those of many avant-garde filmmakers) employ styles and techniques that will probably prevent his oeuvre from ever being assimilated into commercial movie-making.

Avant-Garde Cinema

Speaking of chickening out, you'll also read quite a bit in this book about some of the various *avant-garde* film movements that have characterized the last century in world cinema. As you'll soon learn, though, many films that were loosely considered "avant-garde" in their own day—D. W. Griffith's *The Birth of a Nation,* to use the most notable example—became quite run-of-the-mill once their techniques were absorbed into mainstream cinema.

Whatever the case, it's crucial to cultivate an appreciation of the avant-garde as part of the learning experience you get out of this book. The avant-garde film is inextricably rooted to the intellectual history of its moment; you can learn quite a bit about the history of ideas in general if you push yourself to pay attention to the artistic, aesthetic, and political statements being made in *any* film you watch, whether avant-garde or not.

This can be very difficult to do, of course. In an age when many of our politicians speak knowingly and contemptuously of a "cultural elite" in Washington and Hollywood, it's easy to fall prey to this kind of widespread anti-intellectualism. Don't let yourself! Insist on your right to interpret any movie you watch in as rigorous and intelligent a way you can. After all, the filmmakers were thinking hard about how to put the picture together, and it's the best compliment you can pay an avant-garde director to allow his or her film to challenge your mind!

Taking in a Movie vs. Watching a Film

Sounds simple, right? When you "take in a movie," you drive to the local multiplex, buy a bag of popcorn, and settle back into a comfortable reclining seat in preparation for two hours of innocent escapism. When you "watch a film," you fight for parking on the campus of the local college, university, or public library, get handed a brochure describing upcoming films in the "Paraguayan Cinema Since 1970" series or some such, and sit craning your neck for three hours in an impossibly uncomfortable folding metal chair as a half dozen beret-wearing grad students with goatees murmur knowingly at every incomprehensible snippet of dialogue.

The "flick" you'd watch in the multiplex would be something like *Die Hard* (1988), a cliché-ridden but fun-as-hell romp featuring Bruce Willis, explosions, and truly badass special effects. The "film" you'd likely see in the film series would be something along the lines of Orson Welles's *Citizen Kane* (1941), a classic and artistically innovative work with complex psychological themes highlighted by brilliant technical feats of camera work, sound, and mise-en-scène.

Die Hard: *The classic flick in which things explode.*

This kind of image is one of the main stumbling blocks keeping many people from becoming real aficionados of film. So many of our students have complained that learning too much about the aesthetics, economy, and theory of film "ruins" the movies for them. Quite simply, they say, we're trying to "intellectualize" too much, losing sight of the simple enjoyment that the movies can provide.

Let's get this out on the table right now: The things you'll learn in this book will *enhance* your enjoyment of the movies, not detract from it. Once you become educated about, say, the role of cinematography in the "look" of a film, or the crucial process of editing in the final phases of production, or the fascinating perspectives to be gained through a psychoanalytic approach to interpreting the pictures you watch, you'll be amazed at how much more you get out of each and every trip to the theater. By the end of this book, we hope you'll no longer completely accept the venerable distinction between "flicks" and "films." Though it's an important distinction to be aware of (and in fact we use it regularly in the following pages), we want you to regard every flick you watch as a film that you can unpack, analyze, and interpret to your heart's content.

Citizen Kane: *The classic film with literal and figurative depth.*

How to Watch a Flick as If It Were a Film

"But why?" you're probably wondering. "What's wrong with just sitting back and letting yourself have a good time without worrying about all that film stuff?"

Absolutely nothing. Sometimes (in fact, many times) an escape from your daily routine is exactly what you want out of a trip to the movies, and we don't want to discourage you from having a good time. But as Socrates put it, the unexamined life is not worth living. If you don't spend at least some time questioning the world around you (and our world is a media-saturated one in which movies are one of the central pastimes of a vast portion of the populace), your experiences of any art form—literature, painting, film—will be woefully impoverished.

"Entertainment"

We're not saying that you need to bring this book with you every time you go to the movies. God forbid! Rather, what we hope you'll do is question the very notion of "entertainment" itself.

When you're being entertained, what exactly is happening? Why is one scene in a movie so enjoyable and the next not? What's happening in your brain when you laugh, and what's happening in the broader culture when an entire audience laughs? Why do certain movies succeed and certain others fail? Is it simply because some are "good" and some are "bad"?

We want you to have a good time at the movies, but we also want you to be just a little bit suspicious of your own enjoyment. Never take it for granted that the pleasure you're taking in any given movie is entirely innocent—it almost never is!

Didacticism

Now for an example. Take a picture like Alexander Payne's *Election* (1999), a very clever, independently directed film that featured Reese Witherspoon and Matthew Broderick in a black comedy/satire that won rave reviews. On the one hand, this movie is clearly part of a subgenre of well-done high school flicks from *Fast Times at Ridgemont High* (1982) to *Dazed and Confused* (1993). It's fun to watch, no doubt about it.

But as Peter Biskind cleverly pointed out in *The Nation* not too long ago (in the April 3, 2000, issue on independent film—worth reading, by the way), if you think about this film in light of our last presidential election, its cultural resonance becomes loud and clear: Reese Witherspoon's Tracy Flick is Al Gore, who's been preparing for an election practically since infancy; Paul Metzler, the dumb but well-meaning jock, is George W. Bush, who bummed around drinking beer and giving wedgies to younger fraternity brothers before settling down and deciding politics was for him. *Election* even has a Ralph Nader figure in Tammy Metzler, who runs as an "anticandidate" opposed to the high school version of the two-party system.

While *Election* was made quite a while before the election itself, isn't it a lot more fun to watch the movie with this uncannily right-on-target interpretation in mind?

What we're encouraging you to do, then, is to view films as what literary critics call *allegories,* texts in which the surface meaning of the story will always refer to elements of the larger political, ethical, religious, or social context in which it appears. Most movies contain clear cultural messages, whether intended or unintended, that you can discover after just a little bit of reflection.

Filmophile's Lexicon

An **allegory** is a work that employs fictional figures or characters as symbols of wider cultural, political, moral, or religious values in order to express a particular viewpoint concerning contemporary society.

As a final example, think about *Fatal Attraction* (1987), a box-office smash that featured Glenn Close as a psychotic stalker who has an affair with

Michael Douglas and makes his family life a living hell. *Fatal Attraction* was one of the defining and most successful thrillers of the 1980s, and few would dispute its value as well-done entertainment.

But if you think about this movie allegorically—that is, *if you interpret this flick as a film* and take its cultural effects seriously—a not-so-innocent picture emerges: released in the penultimate year of Ronald Reagan's presidency, *Fatal Attraction* clearly embeds a direct, virulent, and by any measure misogynist attack on the single, sexually autonomous female. Glenn Close's adultery-inducing character is killed off at the end by Douglas's wife, a stay-at-home mom played by Anne Archer, in a gesture that eliminates the working, urban, sexual feminine threat and confirms the sanctity of the nuclear, bourgeois, suburban family.

Short Cuts

Fatal Attraction didn't originally contain that happy, Anne-Archer-blowing-away-Glenn-Close-in-the-bathtub ending. If you check out the director's cut video you'll find the director's original, and much darker, vision of how this narrative of threatened bourgeois life was supposed to end!

If you think we're "reading too much" into *Fatal Attraction,* consider this: Virtually every element of the film serves this ultimate antifeminist goal. The mise-en-scène includes Close's apartment in the meat-packing district of Manhattan, where flames circle ominously around the hanging corpses of butchered animals; the soundtrack, in its brilliant use of scenes from Italian opera, serves to construct Glenn Close as an icon of the sexually aggressive woman doomed to die; and it's no mistake that Anne Archer begins showing up five years later as the wife of Harrison Ford's Jack Ryan in a series of adaptations of Tom Clancy novels (*Patriot Games,* 1992; *Clear and Present Danger,* 1994), confirming her place in America's cultural memory as a symbol of wifely loyalty and family values.

Short Cuts

Another convincing interpretation of *Fatal Attraction* that a number of scholars have made views the film as an AIDS allegory told from the right-wing point of view: If you're unfaithful, sleep around, and have sex in unsavory places with unsavory people, you may just die as a result.

Some Examples to Contrast

Before going on to the next chapter, take a night or three to compare and contrast some of the pairs of movies we've listed below. We've chosen pictures with similar themes, topics, or plots to illustrate the often striking differences between so-called "films" and so-called "flicks." We hope you'll view both pictures in each pair with the same critical eye to make this exercise worthwhile.

- *Election* (directed by Alexander Payne, 1999) versus *Porky's* (directed by Bob Clark, 1981)

Payne's witty look at power, desire, and the politics of education in America's high schools shows that the same themes treated in the inexplicably popular *Porky's* 18 years earlier can be examined with intelligence, compassion, and smart humor rather than adolescent crudeness.

- *The Hunger* (directed by Tony Scott, 1983) versus *John Carpenter's Vampires* (1998)

  Here we have two vampire flicks, the first featuring Catherine Deneuve, David Bowie, and Susan Sarandon in a complex and multilayered psychological struggle; the other a schlocky, low-camp disaster that takes almost no risks in its glossy portrayal of the undead.

- *La Femme Nikita* (directed by Luc Besson, 1990) versus *Point of No Return* (directed by John Badham, 1993).

  The Bridget Fonda–starring American adaptation dumbs down the French original with not a hint of self-consciousness; *Nikita* featured Besson's brilliant directing coupled with an offbeat, nervous hilarity that *Point* simply couldn't manage to reproduce.

- *Twelve Monkeys* (Terry Gilliam, 1995) versus *Armageddon* (Michael Bay, 1998).

  Both of these were Bruce Willis science fictiony/futuristic vehicles. But where *Armageddon* settled for a typical hero-against-seemingly-unstoppable-forces-of-nature story-line that virtually defined predictable, the vision of apocalypse in *Twelve Monkeys* included a sophisticated approach to time and a psychological depth that *Armageddon* couldn't touch with a 10-foot pole.

- *Down By Law* (Jim Jarmusch, 1986) versus *The Fugitive* (Andrew Davis, 1993).

  We loved *The Fugitive* (who didn't?), but we thought we'd put this weird pairing on the list so you can think about each film's treatment of "the law" as an institution. Which do you find more complex and/or convincing?

- *Boyz N the Hood* (John Singleton, 1991) versus *New Jack City* (Mario Van Peebles, 1991).

  Though released in the same year, these two films couldn't contrast more drastically in their treatments of contemporary urban decay, poverty, and violence. While *New Jack City* settles for a *Miami Vice* aesthetic of glamour transported to Manhattan, Singleton's *Boyz* works diligently and brilliantly to create a mode of realism suitable to the ravaged streets of South Central Los Angeles.

Remember: These are just our opinions about the movies described and contrasted above. And whatever you do, don't take our work for it! If you put down *The Complete Idiot's Guide to Movies, Flicks, and Film* with one lesson in mind, let it be that you're just as qualified as we are to judge the artistry, technique, and political content of any film you watch!

The Least You Need to Know

- Despite the hundreds of books available on the subject, *The Complete Idiot's Guide to Movies, Flicks, and Film* is uniquely useful and organized for the smart beginner.
- Movies, flicks, and films are separate categories that nevertheless need to be seen in relation to one another.
- Any flick can be watched, unpacked, and analyzed as if it were a film.
- All movies of whatever genre, period, or nationality contain hidden messages or arguments about the society that produced them.

Chapter 2

"Lights, Camera, Action!"

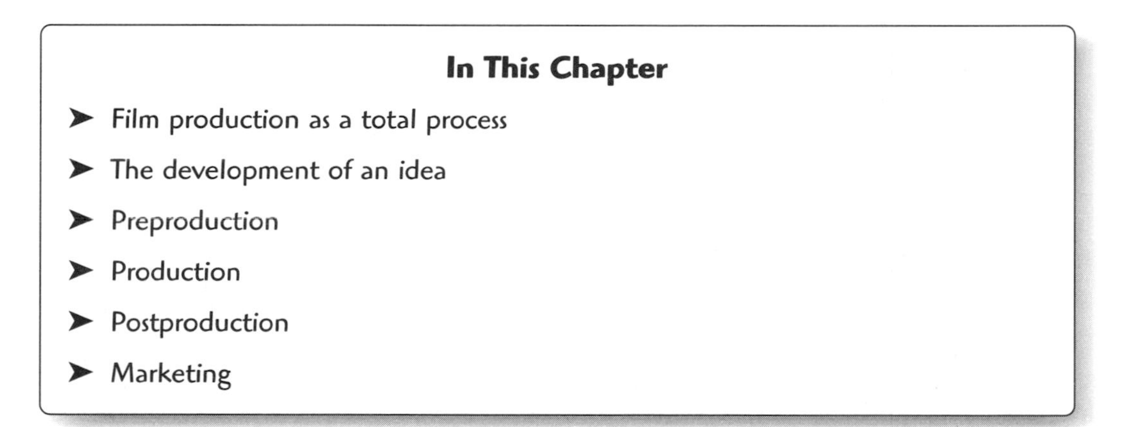

In This Chapter

- Film production as a total process
- The development of an idea
- Preproduction
- Production
- Postproduction
- Marketing

So how does a film get made? What are the basic elements of making a film? This chapter will describe the entire movie-making process, from beginning to end.

There Are Many Ways of Making Films

If we have considered the question at all, most of us assume that there is a standard mode of film production. This book in fact often seems predicated on the stability of the various jobs in the movies and of the division of labor and the technology. We have this sense because, for many years, the movies our culture produced did come largely from a single, monolithic process: the studio system. In fact, though the studios do not operate like the assembly lines they once were, those assembly lines have left a legacy to be copied or resisted, but never ignored.

Today there is actually no single way or set of ways to correctly go about making a film, so this chapter is in a sense nearly impossible to write. (Of course this won't stop us.) First, there are more sectors in filmmaking than there once were. The most conspicuous sectors are Hollywood feature films, independent films, and foreign films. The latter two kinds of film have slowly garnered an increasingly significant audience interest since the 1950s, when the old studio system began crumbling.

Further, the old studio model, though still present in a kind of ghostly way (MGM still exists, though it's more an oversight agency for various projects than a factory now). Studios can't exert the same kind of authority over stars and directors that they could in the "golden era." The talent now has free agency, and is now forming its own production companies.

So it is important to remember that the model we are giving you here is hypothetical, if logical. This model has five parts, which we shall briefly define here:

- **Development.** From idea to signing of contracts.
- **Preproduction.** All the technical matters that can be settled before shooting.
- **Production.** The actual shooting of a film.
- **Postproduction.** The technical portion of filmmaking that turns raw film into finished product.
- **Marketing.** The process of getting the finished product to its audience.

Development: Birth of a Notion

Development includes all stages from the germ of the idea to the hiring of the talent, and includes fundraising, screenplay drafts, and initial location scouting.

Ethel, I Have an Idea: The Story

Typically, a feature film's genesis is the story. The story can come from a variety of places. Sometimes it is the director's own idea. The stars of *Good Will Hunting* (1997), Matt Damon and Ben Affleck, also wrote the piece. Sometimes studios will vie for the rights to an already-famous book. (The recent battle for the rights to the phenomenally successful children's book *Harry Potter* comes to mind.) Some stories come from contemporary headlines, like *Boys Don't Cry* (1999), which was based on the life of a woman killed in Nebraska for passing as a man.

One truism bouncing around Hollywood for the past 50 years is that it's easier to make a great film from a potboiler or second-rate novel than it is to make a great movie from a great work. Some of the most legendary films to come out of Hollywood—*The Caine Mutiny* (1954), *The Thin Man* (1934), *The Shining* (1980), *The Big Sleep* (1946)—come from novels that dated quickly, or literary genres like horror or detective fiction often thought of as less "serious" than, say, psychological novels. On the other hand, some real clunkers have been made from literary works: *A Midsummer Night's Dream* (1999), *Oliver!* (1968, a musical adaptation of *Oliver Twist*), and *The Big Sleep* (1978), for example.

Directors and adapters seem to have a better time of it when they aren't being reverential. Many critics liked *Clueless* (1995) as an adaptation of *Emma* better than they did the more authentic adaptation because it managed to be as funny as Jane Austen really is. There are exceptions to this rule. John Ford's film version of *The Grapes of Wrath* (1940) is almost as great as Steinbeck's novel.

One favorite Hollywood gambit is the remake. When in doubt, redo an earlier successful film. For some critics this is okay, simply akin to the Renaissance tendency to repaint the same religious subjects over and over. We are a little less sanguine, believing that an era in which there are too many remakes generally reflects a film industry with too much money and too few brains. Most of the time the remake is less interesting than the original. Despite the color photography and the hipper-than-thou transformation of the lead from a cook to a photographer, the 1995 remake of the 1954 Billy Wilder film *Sabrina* is less biting and critical of the mores of the idle rich. In fact the color photography makes the story seem mindlessly sunnier than the noir photography of the original does. Another example is of course the remake of *The Big Sleep,* which can't really touch the Bogart and Bacall original.

A related phenomenon is to remake a foreign version of a film. This has also been a popular trend of late. Fellini's *Nights of Cabiria* (*Le Notti di Cabiria*) (Italy, 1957) was remade as *Sweet Charity* (1969). The French films *Boudu Saved from Drowning* (*Boudu sauvé des eaux*) (1932), *Breathless* (*À Bout de Souffle*) (1960), *The Tall Blond Man with the One Black Shoe* (*Le Grand Blond avec une Chaussure noire*) (1972), and *La Cage aux Folles* (1978), were all remade as, respectively, *Down and Out in Beverly Hills* (1986), *Breathless* (1983), *The Man with One Red Shoe* (1985), and *The Birdcage* (1996).

If someone tries to market an original screenplay, but is not directing it herself, she will probably try to acquire an agent. Agents try to maintain contacts in the film industry so that they can get into

Director's Cut

In the last decade, American filmmaking has seen a boom in the television show remake business: *The Fugitive* (1993), *The Flintstones* (1994), *The Brady Bunch Movie* (1995), *McHale's Navy* (1997), and *My Favorite Martian* (1999), to name a few. Hollywood hopes to capitalize on the nostalgia of the baby boomers for the shows of their youth. If not precisely productive of original work, this strategy seems to work just fine at the box office.

Short Cuts

Writers, to paraphrase Rodney Dangerfield, don't get no respect. With some conspicuous exceptions, they tend to be the least valued member of the creative team. An old Hollywood joke goes something like this: How do you tell the really dumb but ambitious rising star? He or she is the one who sleeps with the writer.

studio literary departments to hawk their wares. Often, as a door-opener, the whole script is not submitted. Rather, a 10-page treatment of the script is offered around the studios. If interest remains, the whole script is submitted. The script can go to a director or producer, who then tries to sell the idea to a studio who funds the project; or it can go to the studio first, who then assembles producer and director itself. Still another route is for the agent to actually buy a story and hire someone to do a screenplay. After this point, the original writer may be out, or may be retained to work on the screenplay.

Director's Cut

The two quirkiest remakes of late have been *Psycho* (1998), which attempts to reproduce Hitchcock's 1960 masterpiece shot for shot, and *Twelve Monkeys* (1995), an offbeat sci-fi homage to an avant-garde film by Chris Marker: *La Jetée* (France, 1962).

Magic and Mud

The next phase involves secret negotiations, insider trading, savage industry back stabbing, and much calling in of favors. This is the negotiating phase, when it's determined which creative team does which film. Hollywood negotiations are murder. Stars scramble to catch plum roles, directors scrabble to land plum films, producers scrabble for plum funding sources, fruit wranglers scrabble to land plums, and so on. The budget is also decided during this negotiation process, and distribution and advertising are considered. During this process, the producer is expected to bring the project together. Probably the least bloodletting occurs in companies owned by the creative staff: LucasFilm, Industrial Light & Magic, and so on.

Preproduction

After the dust has settled, the business of making a film actually begins. Preproduction is the stage at which war plans are formed: The rest of the crew and cast are hired, the shooting schedule is planned, and so on. Again, the producer is very active here. The director is now playing an increasingly large role in determining how the film is going to be shot.

Storyboarding

Either during or after the negotiations, others—generally the director and writer—are figuring out how to get from script to shooting script. The process can be tighter or looser. Some directors try to leave room for on-site improvisation. Others don't. Alfred Hitchcock, for example, had more or less entirely planned out the shooting of his films before the first camera setup.

The storyboard is an essential part of this process. It is the narrative of the film in pictures, a sort of flow chart showing how one shot derives from the former shot and gets to the next. It can be more or less detailed, perhaps providing cues for sound (dialogue and/or music) and for character motion.

The feeling of Contract negotiations: film still of board meeting of gangsters from Dick Tracy *(1990).*

Scripting

The screenplay will probably have gone through a dozen drafts by this point. (This is why there are sometimes so many writers in the credits.)

Location, Location, Location

Since the 1950s and the influence of the Italian Neorealists and the French New Wave, American filmmakers have tended more and more to leave the studio for the realism of the great big world. As with most other decisions, the consideration is partly economic and partly aesthetic. Toronto is not only a cheaper city to shoot in, it looks more like 1940s Los Angeles than Los Angeles does.

During or after the storyboard stage, the filmmakers consider the best locations to shoot. In the studio or on location? If on location, which city? If San Francisco, which locales? Does the director want to shoot famous landmarks (as in just about any Hitchcock film), or does the filmmaker want a location one block away from the tourist traps (Jim Jarmusch's *Stranger Than Paradise* [1984], for example, which takes place a couple blocks off of Memphis's Beale Street, on a very seedy street)? At some point, the location scout is sent out to figure out the best places to set up camp.

Technical Concerns

Preproduction is also the moment at which many of the various creative technicians begin work: costume designers, production designers, modelers, sound designer, and so on. Sets are now constructed. The music director will begin working on a score and incidental music for the film, though this job may still be going on straight through postproduction, because it is intimately tied to the sound "mixing" process. The special effects department must begin creating effects before, alongside, and after the principal photography has taken place. These days that department is often a digital effects crew.

Short Cuts

There are brilliant exceptions to this tendency to save money by leaving the studio. Eschewing both economic considerations and a traditional realist aesthetic, Francis Ford Coppola built Las Vegas from the ground up in *One from the Heart* (1982), rather than shooting his film in the real Babylon in the desert.

Most of the creative staff have to figure out how to coordinate their products with the story. If the filmmakers are really trying to produce a masterpiece, they will try to coordinate music, set design, special effects, costume, decor, and other aspects of the mise-en-scène before the shooting begins. Lower-budgeted flicks will make this a postproduction concern. If the film is an adaptation of the eighteenth-century romantic comic swashbuckler *Tom Jones* (an actual and absolutely corking 1963 British film), will the music be romantic, comic, or swashbuckling? Will it be harpsichord music or something more contemporary? If comic, how well will it match with the austere but opulent eighteenth-century interiors?

To which mood should the actors respond: the comic or the romantic? Will the director stay in the studio, or will he use those terrific "stately homes of England," manors, estates, manses, palaces, and county seats the British have managed to keep alive since at least the Elizabethan era?

If on location, will the director use ambient, natural lighting (as in the eighteenth-century period film *Barry Lyndon* [1975]), or will he bring in big spots to liven things up?

Production design, costume, and decor are all carefully delineated in sketches and models before shooting. Though the largest part of the comedy of *Austin Powers: International Man of Mystery* (1997) may be in lead comic Mike Myers, much of the comedy is simply in the anachronistic 1960s clothing and decor: the mod suits and the modular chairs.

The Big Production

Okay, this is the part that budding thespians dream about: the moment when the movie is actually filmed. As it turns out, this part can be incredibly boring for actors, who are sometimes surprised to see how exciting their movie can be, when their only memory was of sitting around and waiting. A lot.

Actually, this is the director's big scene. With any luck, her studio and producer have bowed out of the process at this point and remain simply presences who provide material and solve administrative problems.

This is also the shining moment of the location crew, all those people you will be reading about in Chapter 4, "Gaffers, Grips, and Gofers: The Personnel."

Behind the camera on location in the Arizona desert filming Universal's comedy Lady in a Jam *(1942) is seen Irene Dunne (sitting, center) dressed for a scene in the film.*

The Breakdown Script

After the storyboard and shooting script, the breakdown script is probably the most important document the director has on hand. Generally assembled by the assistant director, it lists all the equipment, props, and other paraphernalia necessary for shooting each scene in the film. It helps the director figure out how to schedule the shooting schedule in advance, and to be completely prepared as each scene comes up, so that she can stay within the shooting schedule.

Principal and Other Photography

Really another name for the whole course of production itself, principal photography is the actual process of shooting the major sequences. It is called principal photography because, after the roughly assembled film is examined, the filmmakers may decide that ancillary photography may have to be done.

Before, after, or at the same time the principal action is being filmed, the second unit is filming establishing and other accompanying shots, perhaps with doubles for the principal actors.

This is the moment in which seemingly minor but key decisions are made moment to moment about how to shoot a sequence, scene, or shot. We believe that the tautest drama is behind—not in front of—the camera. Where does the lighting go? How are actors supposed to move in relation to the camera, the set, and each other? How intimate or grand is the set supposed to be? What last-minute additions will not later spoil the continuity?

Production ends when the director says, "That's a wrap. Go home."

Postproduction

Postproduction takes place in the time from "That's a wrap" to "delivery" of the finished film print. It includes the various kinds of editing—in sound and celluloid—we discuss in the more technical chapters. (See especially Chapter 23, "Making the Cut: Film Editing," and Chapter 24, "BOOM! The Sonic Side of Film.")

Editing

Chapter 23 details the technical process of editing. Here we are just going to mention that the director and editor do not normally decide on the final cut. Probably the best-known example of the studio's prerogative is *Blade Runner* (1982). The studio decided that the story was too difficult to follow, so they added a film-noirish voice-over narrative by Deckard, the futuristic detective (Harrison Ford). The studio also tacked on a kind of happy ending after the more ambiguous one created by director Ridley Scott. We know this because the "director's cut" of *Blade Runner* was released on laser disc a few years ago, so that fans of the film could decide which they liked best. Since then, there has been an avalanche of "director's cut" video releases, often simply proving that the director and the studio are equally insipid and clueless.

Independent filmmakers, of course, have much more control over the final cut.

Sound Mix

After the music is composed and recorded, the postproduction dubbing is finished, and the special sound effects are created, the sound mixer assembles all these tracks together so that they sound right when projected to an audience. The sound mixer cleans up the various tracks, making absolutely sure there is no audible ambient noise (unless such noise is part of the plan). The crowd noise decreases in volume as the romantic couple speaks to each other on a crowded street. The music swells and peaks as the space cowboys defeat the bad guys.

To Market, to Market, to Market We Go

This stage of filmmaking is the one that people consider the least, but that is precisely as important as the others.

Part of the marketing process is testing the film with audiences, to make any changes that might be necessary. The most famous method is the sneak preview, in which, after viewing a film, audiences will be asked questions about how much they enjoyed the film. If the audience response is lukewarm or negative, the film goes back to the editing room, or even back for additional shooting.

Hopefully, the producer has lined up a distributor in the preproduction stage. If not then, this is often the last moment at which distribution can be obtained, when a film is freshly made. It is the unfortunate fate for most independent films to end up on the shelf without ever having had a real shot at a large—or even a small—audience.

Some Films Worth Viewing

These films concentrate on the process of trying to make a film.

- *Will Success Spoil Rock Hunter?* (1957). Jayne Mansfield takes on the media industry.
- *Nickelodeon* (1976). Peter Bogdonavich's comedy-drama about trying to make silent movies in the shadow of D.W. Griffith.
- *The Kentucky Fried Movie* (1977). Hilarious satire of our expectations of how films—and commercials and television—are made.
- *The French Lieutenant's Woman* (1981). A great but very loose adaptation of the John Fowles novel. Unlike the novel, this movie is a meditation on making a period (nineteenth-century) film.
- *Soapdish* (1991). While this film is about television soap operas rather than movies, it's a hilarious vision of how the backstabbing and infighting works for every aspect of the entertainment industry.
- *Watermelon Woman* (1996). In this absolutely stunning fiction feature, an African American lesbian filmmaker makes a film about a lesbian African American actress.

The Least You Need to Know

- The process of making a film varies, depending on the kind of film being made.
- The standard Hollywood filmmaking process includes five steps: development, preproduction, production, postproduction, and marketing.
- Each stage of the process requires its own set of experts, but the producer is present in most phases of production.
- The director is all-powerful in the actual production of the film, less so in the postproduction process.

Chapter 3

From First Fidelity to First Run: Film Economies

In This Chapter

- The economy of the primitive film industry
- Film economics in the classical era
- Production, distribution, exhibition
- Star salaries
- Foreign film funding
- Money and independent films

In 1998 Hollywood's box-office receipts totaled $6.8 billion. Because movies are a major industry and an expensive instrument as well as an art form, money has almost always been of vital importance in determining the meaning of the medium, from Leland Stanford's bet about how horses run—and his 1872 hiring of Eadweard Muybridge to photograph galloping horses. (See Chapter 5, "The Earliest History of the Movies," for the whole story—to the latest megamerger that results in a major studio being owned by a multinational megacorporation. Who provides the dough? Who takes it? How is it distributed? How do investors recoup their investments? What strings are attached?)

We'll treat this chapter a little like a murder mystery, "following the money" from its various sources—banks to fertilizer salesmen—in an attempt to discover how the meaning of films is in part determined by who funds them. We'll examine the three basic modes of moving money: production, exhibition, and distribution. We'll look at the different sources and methods for funding in different countries, with special reference to countries with different economies and therefore different ways of viewing films. Finally, we'll provide a list of films that take a look at the industry and economy of film.

The Economic and Industrial Setting: The Primitive Era

Why, between 1893 and 1914 (when commercial film went through its birth pangs), would anyone want to watch movies when they had opera, baseball, ballet, theater, dime novels, horseracing, boxing, and vaudeville? (I'm glad you asked.) The end of the nineteenth century coincides with a peaking in industrialism in the developed countries, especially in England, France, Germany, and the United States. This industrialization meant, first, that the technology was available for making pictures move (discussed at greater length in Chapter 5).

But for this discussion, it's more important to remember three things about the industrial revolution:

- The urban working classes, composed in the United States significantly of immigrants, African Americans, and children, were working in the factories for 10 to 12 hours a day. For these people, there was less time and not much money for entertainment.
- Industrialism gave the middle classes a greater amount of leisure time and disposable income.
- The pace of everyday life for everyone was generally increased, in the same way that today we think of computers as having speeded everything up.

Film was the entertainment response to these facts of industrial life. In its first incarnations as "mutoscopes" and "kinetoscopes," film appealed to thrill seekers who wanted—or only had time for—a few seconds of entertainment. As we discuss the economy of Hollywood, keep in mind that, even as the one-reeler becomes the 90-minute feature film, movies remain shorter and cheaper than the several-hour "legit" stage production of *Hamlet.*

Production, Distribution, Exhibition

The first public showing of film by the Lumière brothers cost one franc per patron (about 20¢). This first audience contained 35 spectators. However, within a month, the showings earned about 7,000 francs per week, and commercial film was born.

The Lumières were their own producers, distributors, and exhibitors. But these jobs would be quickly compartmentalized. One reason was that the closest popular-entertainment model—vaudeville—had, in the previous century, divided the workload in roughly this fashion. Also and as we'll discuss later in this chapter, government intervention prevented the film producers from gaining too great a control over distribution. Further, the widening appeal of cinema in several countries made international distribution a rather taxing process. But perhaps the principal reason was that, by the 1920s, each task had become incredibly complex, requiring specialized knowledge, sets of contacts, and mountains of legal issues. Ultimately, the film industry compartmentalized itself into three categories. *Production, distribution,* and *exhibition* are the Three Stooges of the film industry: distinguishable but inseparable.

Filmophile's Lexicon

Production: That part of the moviemaking industry that actually cranks out the product. In the golden age of Hollywood, production was principally associated with the big studios.

Distribution: The middleman of the business, distribution includes that part of the industry that gets the movie from the studio to the theater.

Exhibition: The branch including the theaters in which films are shown; the people and technologies involved in exhibition—projectors and projectionists, sound equipment, and so on.

Production

Of the three tasks, production is chronologically first: You have to make a film in order to distribute and exhibit it. At first, the inventors financed and showed their own films, even renting their own halls.

Getting Gold in the Golden Era

As the primitive era of film in the United States became the golden era, East Coast banks had a greater and greater role in financing film production. Because movies had become increasingly expensive to make in the first three decades of the twentieth century, filmmakers found themselves more and more seeking capital from outside sources. In 1903, the average one-reel film cost between $200 and $500. By the 1930s films could be priced in six figures. Today, the cost of feature filmmaking is astronomical. The total cost of *Titanic* (1997) was $265,000,000. We shall discuss star salaries later in this chapter, but it is worth mentioning that a hefty percentage of most widely distributed feature films today is not invested in production at all, but in star salaries, publicity, and advertising.

Director's Cut

Always a shameless self-promoter in classic American fashion, Thomas Edison not only cofinanced his own films, and tried to push any competitor out of the picture, he bought someone else's projector and then claimed it as his own in what film critic/historian David Cook describes as "a scandalous agreement whereby [Edison] would himself manufacture [the projector] and take full credit for its invention while Armat [the actual inventor] would be allowed a small plate on the back crediting him with 'design.'" You have to think of Edison as the Bill Gates of his day: brilliant, unrelentingly greedy, and power-hungry, and without many business scruples.

From early on, there were several financing routes. The studio could ask the distributors to advance money. Money was also borrowed from banks, and even loan sharks. Finally, the studios might issue stock in a public offering.

The moment that solidified this dependence of the movie industry on external capitalization, and put an end for several decades to autonomous Hollywood production, however, was the 1929 stock market crash, and the onset of the Great Depression. Initially doing well because people still wanted to go to the movies, if only to see resolvable versions of the Depression onscreen, the studios started going into receivership, requiring refinancing.

This dependence on financing had real consequences for the kinds of films that were produced. As the industry increasingly depended on financing through more traditional corporate capital routes, the early notion of the film artist—the D. W. Griffiths and the Eric von Stroheims—pursuing a personal aesthetic/social vision, disappeared, to give way to the industrially familiar assembly line mode of making films. The filmmaker became subordinate to the studio, which was answerable to the banks.

A related side effect of the increasingly high cost of film production was the subordination of the independent unit producer. Only a few managed to survive with their autonomy intact: David O. Selznick and Charlie Chaplin, to name two. First-run theaters were closed to most independents because their product was not sufficiently opulent.

Finally, though there was little direct connection between the financing banks and the artistic part of the filmmaking process, it is also true that Hollywood in the 1930s did not make films exploring the depths of the Great Depression, its causes, and, perhaps, realistic resolutions. The exceptions—films like *The Grapes of Wrath* (1940)—are often considered great exactly because they are fairly courageous exceptions.

Financing Now

When the studio system began to fail in the 1950s, independent producers and small production companies began springing up to take their place. Also, as the studios began hurting financially, they began to be bought up and to became subsidiary corporations. This tendency began in the 1970s. Sometimes in this global economy the takeovers have been international: Columbia Pictures became a subsidiary of Sony Corporation. It's almost impossible to discuss contemporary financing because it has become extremely variegated. Later in this chapter we will discuss the more limited issue of independent film financing.

The corporate takeover and merger history of one company can in some ways stand for all. Beginning life as an autonomous company, Warner Brothers was founded in the 1920s. At first an ailing studio, it finally bought out and controlled First National Pictures after its success with sound. However, in the late 1960s Warner Brothers changed hands twice, finally changing its name to Warner Communications in 1972. Time, Inc., merged with the company in 1989 to form Time-Warner, which was itself recently purchased by AOL, making Warner the subsidiary of a subsidiary.

Second Take

Not all profit is made at home; much of it has been realized abroad. American films have been so popular that various countries at various times have imposed quota restrictions to prop up the economic health of their own national film industries. Even countries with significant industries of their own have at one time or another formed such policies: the British and the French, for example.

Distribution

How does the "product"—the feature film—get from the filmmaker to the theater? Why do you need a "middleman" in the first place? How did this process start?

Primitive Distribution

Early on, production companies simply sold their prints to exhibitors, who then traveled around with their prints as itinerant showmen. This practice ended in part because it conflicted with the interests of theater-owners, who did not need to own a print because they changed their bills so much more often than the itinerants did.

Filmophile's Lexicon

Block booking was part of a larger move in the industry to bring all three segments of the industry under single ownership. So Paramount not only controlled some aspects of distribution, but also owned its own theaters (still called "The Paramount" in several cities). In economics this move of one industry into related industries is still called vertical expansion. In the United States, it was still considered a monopolistic practice.

So beginning in the early 1900s, middlemen sprang up, businessmen who bought prints from filmmakers and then rented them to exhibitors, pricing films according to production costs and popularity.

Block Booking

The most controversial mode of distribution began when, in 1916, Paramount began forcing theaters to lease several of the studio's films along with its most prestigious titles, effectively exerting control over the way its films were distributed. This practice was called *block booking*. Almost immediately, a group of exhibitors formed their own studio, First National Pictures (ultimately bought out by Warner Brothers) so that they, too, could profit by allying production and distribution. The practice ended in 1948 when the government intervened to prevent this essentially monopolistic practice.

Today, distributors remain an integral part of the film industry. Generally, they are the ones who hold the legal right to send out a film. You can't even rent an old 16mm film print (legally) to show to a film class without getting it from one of the distributors for whom this market is a specialty.

Exhibition(ists)

Of course you can't see a movie unless someone projects it. But there's more to this story. The medium in which the film is projected is part of the message. Why did we go from nickelodeons to picture palaces to drive-ins and beyond? What is the historical significance of these movie venues?

Nickelodeons

How could any writing about movies and money not include a bit on the exhibition practice whose root word means money? Though, from the very beginning, movie distributors tried to appeal to the moderately moneyed middle classes in venues like vaudeville houses, one of the earliest methods of exhibition—the nickelodeon—first appeared in working-class neighborhoods.

At the height of their popularity, there were thousands of nickelodeons in cities across the United States. The nickelodeon was not terribly fancy, much of the time composed of a simple store front with a screen, a projector, and chairs. The exhibits were also simple: a series of silent movies lasting only a few minutes apiece, with simple narratives and easily identifiable characters. And it all cost only a nickel.

In several ways these first movie theaters were the perfect response to their early audiences: They were easily accessible to working-class people (who would then not have to spend money and time on transportation). Because the movies were silent, they did not alienate an immigrant audience with difficult dialogue. Further, the movies were cheap. Also, they were a quick form of entertainment for an audience with no time. The whole bill took much less time than a contemporary feature film, and, because the short films ran more or less continuously, you could come into the exhibition at almost any point and leave after you'd seen the entire run once. It was the movie equivalent of the quickie. Finally, for moviemakers and exhibitors, the nickelodeon offered the possibility of huge audiences. Nickelodeons cost far less than most other forms of entertainment, but, unlike the audience for boxing or opera, the potential audience included just about everyone.

After the nickelodeon craze ended, exhibitionists in different decades tried to find ways of appealing to the changing tastes and modes of living of the middle classes. The following sections offer the principal means of exhibition in roughly chronological order.

Director's Cut

Even after the nickelodeon boom ended, the "flickers" were still much less expensive than other forms of entertainment. In Boston in 1909 a movie cost a dime, but a vaudeville show cost 50¢, "legit" theater was a buck, and the opera two bucks. We live under this economic rule today. Movies seem outrageously expensive at $7 or $8 a pop, but consider the $30 some baseball stadiums charge, or the hundreds of dollars you might pay to see a command performance of the current darling of opera tenor fans. The reason is fairly simple: Technologically reproducible events tend to be cheaper than live events because they *are* reproducible over and over with the aid of a single (so cheap) projectionist rather than a cast of dozens.

Movie Palaces

The seediness and down-market locations of many nickelodeons did not appeal to middle-class patrons. So exhibitors started spending money on big movie palaces in the hearts of major urban centers. Their decor was often wildly exotic, and the theaters sported names like Grauman's "Egyptian" or "Chinese." On entering the lobby of a palace, you were supposed to feel a bit as if you had just entered a movie. Or the Taj Mahal.

Of course films would no longer cost a nickel, but by the 1920s, when movie palaces were going up, the American economy was going great guns. Palaces even continued being built (albeit at a slower rate) during the Great Depression. Most have now been torn down, but some cities have chosen to restore their palaces as active historical landmarks.

Director's Cut

During the height of the Great Depression, when box-office receipts were faltering, exhibitors would try anything to get people back into the theaters. They would hold raffles for prizes like dish sets or other useful household items, and announce the winners during intermission. Talk about dinner and a movie!

Some examples of these great old movie palaces can be seen in cities across America today. The most famous of these is probably Mann's Chinese Theater in Los Angeles. It is more than 70 years old and is where the famous "footprints of the stars" in cement is located. But there is also Milwaukee's Egyptian, Chicago's Music Box Theater, and the United Artists in Detroit. Unfortunately, fewer exist than ought to because we have a tendency to tear down the old and replace it with particle board. One useful Internet site with information about preserving these great old theaters is www.mindspring.com/~kallym/palaces.htm.

Drive-Ins: Asphalt and Art

The 1950s and early 1960s saw the heyday of the drive-in movie (though they continue to exist to the present day). They became popular as Americans moved to the suburbs, and large tracts of land were available that were almost impossible for exhibitors to own in the middle of major cities.

The appeal of drive-ins was multifold: Parents could save money by paying for a single carload of kids and adults rather than for individual tickets. Teenagers could "make out"—or even get to "third base" and beyond—in the comfort of the back seat of Dad's roomy 1955 Chevy. And though the speaker system that you hooked on the side of your car was much more tinny-sounding than the sound system in a theater, the screen and its image were satisfyingly *huge*. Godzilla, Rodan, and other huge latex 1950s monsters would never roam the earth like this again.

A typical early drive-in.

Multiplex Madness

Though there has been a recent retro/nostalgic revival, most drive-ins are now defunct. Suburbia, small town, and city alike are now in the era of the multiplex cinema: theaters with two or more screens showing more than one film. Many older theaters have been converted into multiplexes by simply splitting the auditorium and screens into two or more separate units. More often, however, multiplexes are built from scratch in urban and suburban shopping areas, mainly malls.

At first modestly consisting of two screens, multiplex builders have recently become much more ambitious, with theaters boasting 30 or more screens. But we still wonder how it is that, with so many screens, all of America seems still to show the same eight films at any given time.

Stars' Bucks

Because the early flickers were considered a debased form of entertainment, actors often did not want their names associated with them in the credits. In the early 1900s a star actor's salary was very low relative to what it would be in the next decade, with the rise of the major stars like Charles Chaplin, Douglas Fairbanks, and Mary Pickford. Production companies were happy not to name the actors in the credits, lest they begin demanding more money. So, for example, Florence Lawrence was simply known as "the Biograph Girl."

Charlie Chaplin's salary is a good gauge of how early moviemakers learned a star's worth. Every time Chaplin moved to a new studio, his salary increased almost by simply adding a zero on at the end. Beginning at the Keystone studio for a three-figure weekly salary (itself pretty opulent for 1914), Chaplin moved to Essanay for

$1,250 per week, then to Mutual for $10,000 per week (and a bonus for signing). Finally, he became a partner in his own studio, United Artists. Quite a cost-of-living increase!

Photo of the United Artists producer/stars: Charlie Chaplin, Mary Pickford, and Douglas Fairbanks.

Independent Films Today

In the United States, films made outside the studio system (or the looser confederation that constitutes mainstream Hollywood today) have always had a harder time getting off the ground. In part this is because the industry has been so healthy that the government has not felt a need to step in to help out filmmakers in any significant fashion.

The downside of this absence of funding has been twofold: Independent production companies—*indies*—must spend a significant part of their time fundraising rather than making films. Also, their films tend to be much lower-budgeted than the Hollywood product because they do not have access to the same large funding sources.

Still, independent filmmakers get some funding from federal agencies like the National Endowment for the Humanities and the National Endowment for the Arts. (You know the NEA; it's that arts funding agency that Congress tries to shut down every year.) Private organizations like The MacArthur Foundation, The Rockefeller Foundation, Carnegie-Mellon, and the like, also finance projects they believe to be worthwhile.

Indies often have to finance and create very cannily and creatively. In making his debut film *El Mariachi* (1992), Robert Rodriguez spent only $7,000 for the entire project, which was shot in 14 days. Contrast that with Kevin Costner's *Waterworld* (1995), a big flop at $150 million. In making his most famous semiunderground film, *Putney Swope* (1969), Robert Downey Sr. got partial financing from a fertilizer company. Perhaps the most famous independent filmmaker, Ed Wood, got financing for the worst film of all time—*Plan 9 from Outer Space* (1958)—from an ex-Baptist minister who thought he would be producing biblical epics.

Filmophile's Lexicon

Indie: Short for independent production company, it refers to artists and their companies making films outside the Hollywood production industry.

Some independents simply max out their credit cards (and those of their parents) to get a film into production. Sometimes a filmmaker will make a five-minute trailer to send to funding sources to "push" his product. Young indie directors beg, borrow, and steal equipment, sometimes working on a feature film crew or university film-department project during the day, and then just "borrowing" equipment to shoot after hours or weekends.

Finally, because the Hollywood system has recognized that much talent comes from the indie pool, Hollywood scouts are now a major presence at independent film festivals—like Sundance—where indies strut their stuff.

Foreign Films

Some governments actively and usefully support their film industries. We have elsewhere discussed the involvement of various governments in the first half of the twentieth century: the Soviets and The Moscow Film School, the Italians and Cinecittà, and so on. The 1960s and 1970s were a sort of high point for government funding in several countries. For example, the Australian Film Development Corporation in the 1970s and 1980s jump-started a moribund industry, catapulting it into international prominence with films like *Picnic at Hanging Rock* (1975, directed by Peter Weir), *Walkabout* (1971, directed by the British Nicolas Roeg), *The Last Wave* (1977, also a Weir film), and so on. It helped begin the careers of directors like Peter Weir and Bruce Beresford.

Federal aid and co-involvement for young filmmakers from the 1960s on spurred Germany's "New German Film" movement, and consequently helping the careers of internationally famous and controversial directors like Rainer Werner Fassbinder, Wim Wenders, and Werner Herzog. The Canadian Film Board and the Canadian Film Development Corporation have been encouraging filmmakers since about World War II.

Unfortunately, when a country's filmmaking industry prospers under such financing, the federal help often disappears, and films start becoming more commercial. Australian filmmaking moved from a cinema with the social bite of *Breaker Morant* (1979) to highly enjoyable and completely empty-headed flicks like the "Crocodile Dundee" films.

Some Films About the Film Industry

Though few filmmakers would approach the subject of money in film for fear of boring their audiences, these films try to take you behind the scenes of filmmaking in such a way that you get a glimpse of how the money flows.

- *Boy Meets Girl* (directed by Lloyd Bacon, 1938). In old newspaper headline parlance: "Tiny Tot Pix Hit in Stix!" Jimmy Cagney and Pat O'Brien turn a baby into a child star. A perfect combination of greed and sentimentality.
- *Day for Night* (directed by François Truffaut, France, 1973). Romanticized vision of filmmaking in France. Good bits about insurance and financing woes.
- *Hollywood Shuffle* (directed by Robert Townsend, 1987). A biting film about the troubles an African American actor encounters in trying to break into movies. Not precisely about money, it is about what money allows and does not allow on screen.
- *The Player* (directed by Robert Altman, 1992). A terrifically satirical view of the power plays and sharklike behavior in the industry.
- *Ed Wood* (directed by Tim Burton, 1994). Still another outsider trying to break into Hollywood, but this time the outsider is perhaps the worst filmmaker of all time.
- *Get Shorty* (directed by Barry Sonnenfeld, 1995). A comic look at where the moviemaking money comes from.
- *Bowfinger* (directed by Frank Oz, 1999). Hilarious account of shoestring director trying to make a film with a major star without letting him know he's in the film.

The Least You Need to Know

- The film industry consists of three major branches: production, distribution, and exhibition.
- Film arose as a popular entertainment in part because it was a cheap and fast amusement.
- Though difficult to show a direct connection, the kinds of films made are in part determined by who owns the means of production.
- Each era has its own favored mode of exhibition: the nickelodeon, the movie palace, the drive-in, the multiplex, and so on.
- Foreign and independent films are often financed differently, often depending on state funds or parents' credit cards, because they do not have the same access to major sources of credit.

Chapter 4

Gaffers, Grips, and Gofers: The Personnel

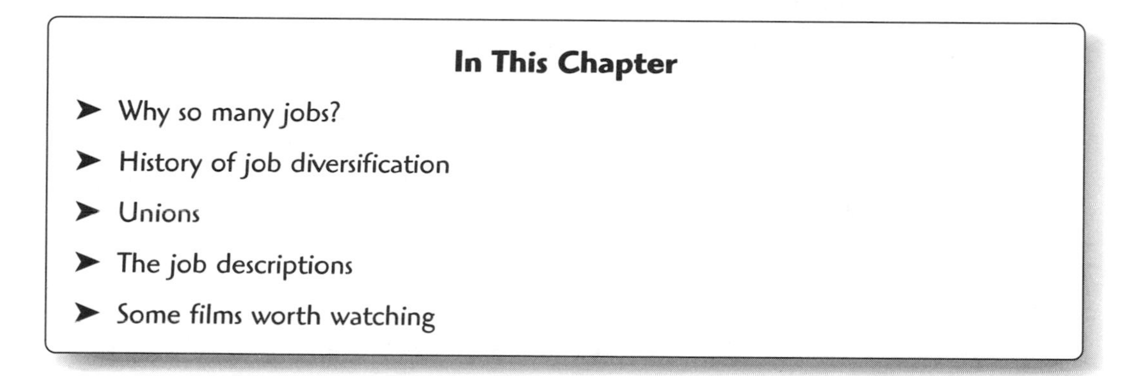

In This Chapter

- Why so many jobs?
- History of job diversification
- Unions
- The job descriptions
- Some films worth watching

Who the heck are those people in the opening and closing movie credits? At one time we all thought a gaffer was an elderly, talkative, alcoholic inhabitant of a pub. *Whose* best boy, exactly (the gaffer's?), and what makes him best? Are there other boys who are just okay?

Depending on which critic you read, or which filmmaker you read about, film is almost always either a "corporate" or a "collective" endeavor. In other chapters we have discussed the people at or near the top of the corporation/collective: the bankers, the studio heads, the best and most famous directors, and so on. (See, for example, Chapter 3, "From First Fidelity to First Run: Film Economies," and Chapter 9, "Staying Afloat in the Hollywood Mainstream.") The people in this chapter are the unsung: the workers, technicians, and grunts without whom a film could not be made.

Though we will say a word about these kinds of jobs in other countries, the vocabulary and definitions in this chapter are largely derived from American cinema.

Mystifying Movies

In a way, we don't know what the "dolly grip" does because movies don't want us to; they "mystify" us, making us believe that they magically appear. As one theory has it, understanding the "means of production" of film would destroy the illusion that film simply *is,* that it exists as anything other than the brief fulfillment of our fantasy lives. This reasoning is why some viewers are afraid to learn anything about the movies: It will destroy the illusion on which pleasure depends.

However, for better or worse, reminding us that movies are created artifacts doesn't necessarily work against our movie-going pleasure. Think of movie musicals, which are constantly showing us how musicals are made ("Gee, let's put on a show!"). Or television specials titled *The Making of Whichever Overbudgeted Spectacle Broke Box-Office Records This Month.* Or the outtakes at the ends of some movies like *Being There* (1979). These moments capture audiences by giving them the feeling that they are being "let in on" moviemaking secrets.

So this chapter contains the secret for decoding the credits at the beginning and the end of films. We have left out the most obvious job descriptions— "mouse wrangler" should be obvious if a little odd—as well as the jobs discussed elsewhere (in the technical chapters on sound, editing, and camera work, for example). Movies can be magic, but they require an enormous amount of intelligence and labor from an enormous number of people.

Employment History

Originally, the hundreds of jobs that now exist in filmmaking were done by one or two people. For the Lumières at first, the writers and directors were also the cinematographers; they also edited and exhibited their own films. Méliès performed some of his special effects "in the camera," while filming. Even later, some filmmakers retained a large measure of control over the creation of their own films. As we have discussed elsewhere (see Chapter 20, "Director's Cut: Calling the Shots"), even in the 1930s Charles Chaplin wrote, directed, produced, scored, and starred in his own films. Even today, some independent film directors have to do a large measure of the work themselves because there simply is not enough money for a full film crew.

But the tendency for greater diversification inevitably arose as a result of two influences. First, movies were invented and flourished in an industrial society very much committed to the idea of the assembly line: a series of people each of whom performs a specialized task that results in the production of an artifact or service with the greatest possible speed and efficiency. So the camera operator ultimately separates from the editor because it is more efficient for one person to know one job well. (Though more efficient is not always the same as more aesthetically desirable.)

Second, as film moved from the one-reeler to the feature, and as the technology of film became so complicated that it was almost impossible for a single person to understand the techniques of each category of work, more people were required to produce a movie. The job subcategories split again and again, until the camera crew could include literally dozens of people. New categories were created: dialogue coaches during the introduction of sound, for example.

Unions

Because we are talking in part about the grunts of the studio system, it's worth spending a moment on the labor organizations that represent them.

The First Unions

As in other industries, the first organizations in the film industry proper were really more like craft guilds and benevolent societies, created as learning and service organizations meant to maintain high standards of quality within each craft. Early organizations formed in the 1910s and 1920s included the Friars Club for actors (still very much alive and kicking), the Screen Club, the Reel Club, the Static Club (for cameramen), the Actors' Equity Association, and the Photoplay Authors' League. At the end of the 1920s, the International Photographers, the cinematographer's union, became affiliated with the AFL (American Federation of Labor).

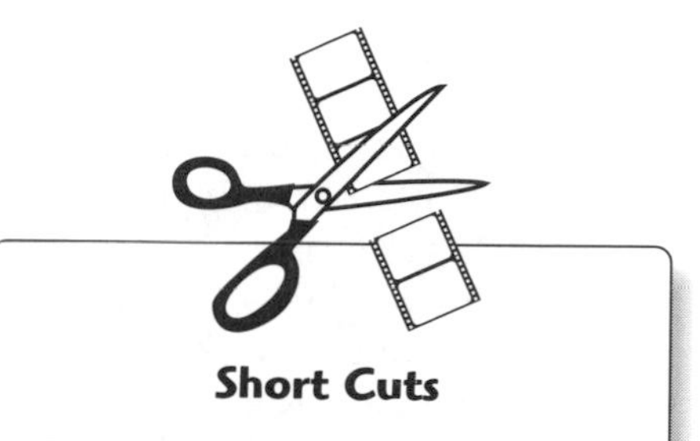

Short Cuts

The early show business fraternal organizations were themselves based on models that varied from the Harvard Club to ethnic and immigrant *landsmanschaften*, or benevolent societies.

Photo of early Friars Club membership; this fraternal organization was one model for many later industry unions.

(The Friars Club.)

In fact, one of the first uses of commercial film in the United States was to break up a strike in the vaudeville industry. Vaudeville theater and circuit owners projected short films in place of the live acts that were not going on. It worked: The strike was broken.

The first film union in the United States was organized by theater projectionists in the first decade of the twentieth century. IATSE—the International Alliance of Theatrical Stage Employees—arose as one of the most independent and comprehensive labor organizations in Hollywood. Originally organized for projectionists, IATSE came to represent many other crafts as well.

IATSE's best moment came in 1933. As a consequence of the Great Depression, the studio bosses insisted on across-the-board pay cuts of 50 percent for anyone making more than $50 per week, though no one saw these moguls mortgaging their own Beverly Hills homes. While most other sectors of the industry—actors and directors, for example—accepted the cut, IATSE did not. Instead, it threatened to send its people out on strike. The producers backed down but did not forget this negation of their authority. In the meantime, a few months later, writers got together and formed the Screen Writers Guild. Writers became some of the most activist workers in the industry. Some, like Dalton Trumbo, were severely punished for this activism during the McCarthy Era.

Unions in the McCarthy Era

Because of such successes, and despite the fact that Hollywood unions were often "proproducer," which is to say very cozy with the studio bosses, the studios were always afraid of the power of the unions, and tried several ways to contain them or break them up.

Short Cuts

As an example of union repression, the founding of the Conference of Studio Unions in 1941 for those craftsmen not yet well represented was almost immediately marred by accusations that the organization was "Red." Its authority was as a consequence much weakened.

The McCarthy era was named for the most famous red-baiter of the times, Senator Joseph McCarthy; it designates an historical moment in history during which Congress and the House Un-American Activities Committee (HUAC) abrogated the Constitution by criminalizing political affiliations, making it essentially criminal to belong to the Communist Party. This was a terrific moment for breaking up unions in Hollywood. Historian and critic William Triplett sees the studios' willingness to go along with the HUAC as a way of controlling movie unions, because unions were viewed as suspiciously procommunist by American conservatives. The most visible targets of the HUAC—people like Ring Lardner Jr.—tended also to be members of the Screen Writer's Guild or other Hollywood unions. Anticommunism turned out to be simply another kind of very hypocritical and destructive union-busting.

I'm Stickin' to the Union—Not: Labor Today

Film industry unions still exist, of course, and studios don't normally try the same overt union-busting tactics of yore. Still, like other American industries, Hollywood often attempts to cut costs by evading both local taxes and union salaries by sending productions abroad: to Canada, to Central and South America, and so on. In the last few years, for example, Vancouver has become a major production center for American film. Brian De Palma's *Mission to Mars* (2000) was shot there. And just as American blue-collar workers are outraged at the disappearance of their jobs, so Hollywood workers are taking steps to bring this business back to the United States, including lobbying for tax cuts for California filmmakers.

As terrific as the idea of independent filmmaking is, it is sometimes also a way of getting around union workers. It is only possible to make a film for four figures (*El Mariachi*, 1992) if you don't use high-quality and relatively high-cost union labor.

Second Take

Before completely embracing the technology that creates realist characters digitally (as in *Star Wars: Episode I—The Phantom Menace* [1999]), it is important to remember that some critics perceive this technology as a potential threat to actors' livelihoods. Technology as scab labor.

The Job Descriptions

Here is the list of the most high-profile jobs (not covered elsewhere) in the Hollywood system:

- **Art director.** The person responsible for the look of a film's sets, he or she is also responsible for their construction.
- **Assistant director.** Most of the time this is an administrative position rather than truly directorial. The assistant director helps break down the script and make decisions about the shooting order.
- **Associate producer/production manager.** 1) The next-in-charge of a film after the producer. Depending on the relationship with—and the working style of—the producer, the assistant producer can have a greater or lesser

Second Take

Though there are union and industry definitions of the various employments, because these are not civil service jobs, and so not carefully delineated, sometimes one title covers a number of different kinds of responsibilities, depending on the way a particular studio, producer, or director defines the position. A gaffer can be an electrician and/or a location scout. Sometimes jobs overlap, as in the case of the art director and the production designer.

say in creative as well as administrative decisions. 2) The actual administrator for the daily operations of the film.

- **Best boy.** 1) A person in charge of the paperwork for administering the head grip's or gaffer's crew. Can take care of timesheets, salaries, and so on. 2) The head grip's or gaffer's gofer. An apprentice to the gaffer or key grip. So called because he (or now she) is the "best" person available for the job.
- **Boom operator (or boom man).** The technician who handles the boom microphone and its paraphernalia, making sure that it is in position to record sound to the best advantage. Requires a steady hand to hold the mike over the heads of the actors.
- **Cable person.** This person makes certain the sound cables are efficiently and inconspicuously placed.
- **Camera operator (or second cameraman).** The technician actually operating the movie camera. Of course, this person is under the careful supervision of both the director and the director of photography.
- **Carpenter.** The person whose crew physically builds the set.
- **Casting director.** Often in collaboration with the director and/or producer, the person who actually picks the "talent," or actors who will appear onscreen. This means not only the stars, but supporting players, bit players, and so on. At one time studio employees, most casting directors now work independently, though often regularly with the same directors and producers.
- **Cinematographer (director of photography).** This is the person who literally brings the director's vision to light. Sometimes the cinematographer is almost as responsible for the look and feel of a film as the director. It is impossible to think of *Citizen Kane* (1941) without Gregg Toland, or Charlie Chaplin films without Rollie Totheroh. Other major technicians—art directors and gaffers, for example—consult with the cinematographer who, with the director, actually decides on mood, angles, and composition.
- **Compositor.** Really one of a host of computer programmers now involved in film production, the compositor creates layers and textures for the film image in order to lend it a greater impression of reality.
- **Computer animator.** The computer programmer in charge of digitally creating special effects that will be transferred back to celluloid. Images can be transformed live-action sequences, or completely computer-generated.
- **Construction coordinator.** Answerable to the art director, the construction coordinator is responsible for the actual construction of the film set.
- **Continuity clerk (continuity girl, script girl, script supervisor).** Traditionally a woman, this person makes sure that, if an actor is walking toward the sun in one shot, he is walking in the same direction in the next shot, though the

camera may be set up at a different angle. Or, if there is a cat in the room in one shot, that cat is still scratching up the furniture and coughing up hairballs in subsequent shots.

- **Dolly grip.** The technician who operates the dolly, a wheeled and motorized platform on which the camera is placed for "dolly" or "tracking" shots.
- **Executive producer.** As the job title suggests, an executive, and administrator in charge of the business end of production, issues such as raising money for the budget. Rarely involved in the day-to-day operation of the film, the executive producer may be involved in the business of several productions at once.
- **Gaffer.** 1) The chief electrician, responsible for lighting the set. 2) More generally, the technician who makes the set run smoothly, from scouting locations to streamlining the set. Legend has it that the term originally applied to the European carney who herded, or "gaffed," audiences into the circus tent.
- **Grip.** 1) A jack-of-all-trades on the set, responsible for physically moving and setting up equipment, sets, and so on. The "muscle" on the set, the grip must also be able to do a bit of carpentry. 2) The grip is in charge of all physical work except electrical.
- **Key (or head) grip.** The person on the set in charge of the other grips, or the crew of workers.
- **Lamp operator.** Person in charge of operating film lamps.
- **Lead man.** The set scrounger, responsible for finding objects to make the set more atmospheric or realistic.
- **Line producer (production manager).** This executive oversees the day-to-day operations of a film's production.
- **Location manager.** The person who finds locations at which to shoot.
- **Mixer.** The sound technician who assimilates—or "mixes"—sounds together for each of a film's sequences, determining the relative values (volume, pitch, and so on) of the background music, dialogue, ambient noise, and so on.
- **Model.** The actor filling in for close-ups of a portion of the principal actor's body; a "body double."
- **Modeler.** Originally, a technician who makes the small-scale models that are photographed as if life-sized. Now more often applied to the computer programmer who creates 3-D digital images that are then transferred to film.
- **Nursery man.** The worker who provides the appropriate plant life for a scene.
- **Producer.** The chief administrator for a film; the producer's duties can vary widely. The producer is at the beginning of the process: buying the rights to the original book on which a movie is based. He or she considers various "treatments" of the original "property," selects the director, and consults on creative

aspects and budgets. Sometimes the producer has little visible effect on the product. Other producers, like Arthur Freed at MGM, are almost auteurs themselves.

- **Production designer.** The person who decides how the film is going to look, based on the needs and vision of the director and the script.
- **Prop man (property master).** The property man keeps track of, cares for, and places the props on the set.
- **Publicist.** Promotes films and stars through press releases, publicity events, contacts with newspapers, distribution of publicity stills, and so on. This job overlaps with that of the public relations executive. The "unit" publicist publicizes a particular film.
- **Screenwriter.** The craftsperson who writes the scripts. The writer may adapt a literary work, produce an original script, or revise ("doctor") an already-existing script. Like most of the rest of filmmaking, screenwriting tends to be a collaborative effort.
- **Second unit director.** The director of the "second unit." The second unit is the film crew that photographs sequences for which the director and principal actors are not required.
- **Set decorator.** On instructions ultimately from the art director, the set decorator actually furnishes a set with the items that create the appropriate atmosphere and ambience: rugs, lamps, and potted palms.
- **Set dresser.** Related to set decoration, set dressing is the art of making the set look as if it has always been inhabited, rather than new and artificial.
- **Sound crew.** The technicians on the set responsible for audio recording. This crew is sometimes a single person: the sound man.
- **Sound designer.** The production designer for sound, the sound designer oversees all aspects of sound recording for a film project.
- **Special effects supervisor.** The special effects team is now most often an independent company rather than a division of a major studio, so the effects supervisor can be either an administrator or a supervisor of the day-to-day operations of the special effects team.
- **Stand-in.** Chosen for their physical resemblance to the main stars, stand-ins are the people who substitute in place of the stars during the often time-consuming process of readying the set for actual photography.
- **Stand-by painter.** The set's "touch-up" painter who makes any last-minute adjustments in the set's color and sheen, subduing glare or changing hues when necessary.
- **Story analyst/reader.** This is the person who considers whether a script or a literary property is worth considering as a film.

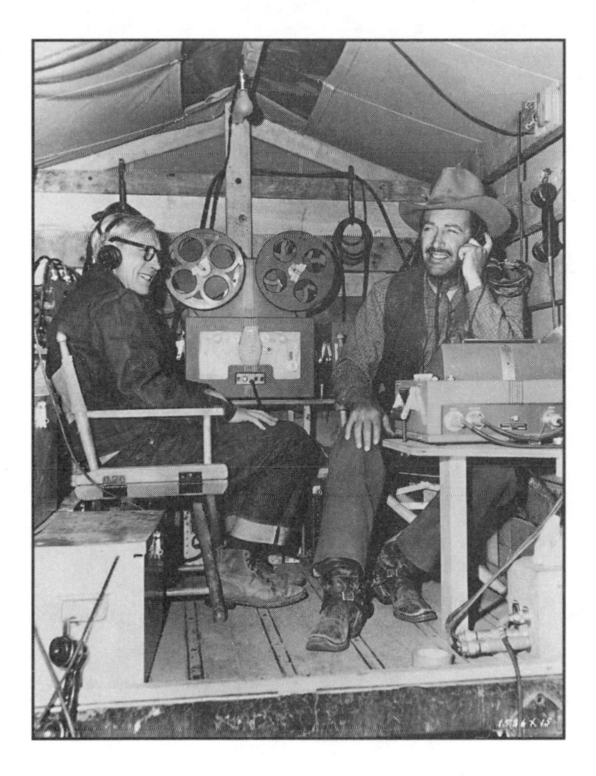

Robert Taylor listens in with sound technician Howard Voss in the special Sound Truck while on location for MGM's Westward the Women *(1951).*

- **Stunt coordinator.** Determines where, in the film script, stunts will take place.
- **Stunt person.** The stunt people take all those falls, dives, crashes, and punches that making a film "action-packed." The stunt person can play a distinct, if minor, character: the yeoman in the landing crew on the original *Star Trek* series you know is going to die upon landing on the hostile planet. Or she can double for the star in the automobile crash that no one could actually survive in real life.
- **Supervising editor.** The person in charge of film editing, this technician works closely with the director and, if budget allows, supervises a team of editors.
- **Swing gang.** The grunts who fetch and carry props and other equipment to and from the set.
- **Talent.** Vernacular expression of the people in front of the camera; the actors. Occasionally used ironically.
- **Unit.** The designation for the technical crew actually working on the set.
- **Unit photographer.** The still photographer who takes publicity photos on the set for the film.
- **Visual effects supervisor.** The person who oversees the team that actually creates special effects.

- **Wrangler (animal wrangler).** The person responsible for the animals acting in front of the camera, whether dogs, horses, mice, or fish. Cares for the animals. Job can overlap with that of the "animal trainer," who actually owns and prepares the animal for movies.

Films Worth Viewing

Since the decision about what films are produced get made in the end by the people who run Hollywood, there are not, as you might expect, many films about Hollywood unions. Still, there are some films about entertainment labor history that you might find intriguing:

- *Hollywood Shuffle* (1987). The underbelly of the Hollywood industry from the perspective of an African American actor trying to break into showbiz.
- *Singin' in the Rain* (1952). A specific if fanciful look at the technologies of early film.
- *The Front* (1976). This Woody Allen film (directed by Martin Ritt) gives a detailed sense of the difficulties Hollywood faced during the McCarthy era.
- *The First 100 Years: A Celebration of American Movies* (1995). A little too celebratory, and a little light on information, but this documentary does give some sense of the evolution of the job categories in Hollywood.
- *Cradle Will Rock* (1999). Though not about film, this movie gives a rather nice sense of the nastiness that characterizes American antiunionism.

The Least You Need to Know

- Because the process of making a movie became increasingly complex during the era of assembly-line manufacturing, filmmaking went from a job for one or two people to one that employed dozens—sometimes hundreds—of laborers.
- Though often overlapping with other jobs, each job category requires its own special technical skill.
- Originating in craft guilds and benevolent societies, unions became major players in the economy of Hollywood.
- Though historically very effective, unions have had a hard time of it in Hollywood, in part because of active opposition by the industry owners and in part because of competition from other countries for filmmaking business.
- The government—in the form of the HUAC—played a formidable role during the 1940s and 1950s in repressing Unions.

Part 2

A Brief History of (Mostly American) Film

In this part you will be exposed to the most influential and pervasive cinema (for better or worse) in the world. Think of the chapters as the various sections of a Disneyesque historical theme park. Chapters 5 and 6 are Jurassic Park, or the chapters about when silent films roamed the earth. Chapters 7 and 8 are Main Street, USA: They are about an era when film defined what America should look like. As the part about the major filmmakers themselves, Chapter 9 is sort of the Pirates of the Caribbean ride. And Chapter 10 is Fantasy Land. So, fasten your seat belts, it's gonna be a bumpy (if delightful) ride.

Chapter 5

The Earliest History of the Movies

In This Chapter

- The world's first films and the people who made them
- Crucial precedents and technological breakthroughs
- The birth of the cinematic experience
- Studios and directors in turn-of-the-century America
- D. W. Griffith and the triumph of narrative film

It was a dark and stormy night, but it was about to get a whole lot brighter.

The date: December 28, 1895, a Saturday night just three days after Christmas. The place: Paris, France, along the Boulevard des Capucines. A small sign stood on the walk outside the Grand Café, luring curious passersby down the stairs and into a brave new world of light, motion, and magic.

The first thing the small but stunned audience saw that night was *La Sortie des Oeuviers de l'Usine Lumière,* or *Workers Leaving the Lumière Factory.* It was simple, really. A pair of brothers, Auguste and Louis Lumière, had rigged up a projecting camera, which they'd invented and patented just months before, in front of the family's photographic factory in the industrial city of Lyons. Choosing their location and camera angle carefully, Auguste and Louis waited patiently until quitting time, then shot a few minutes' worth of film showing the factory's workers getting off from the afternoon shift.

Second Take

Don't be a francofool! *Lumière* isn't pronounced loom-ee-*ay,* as you might be tempted to say it, but loom-*yer.* In one of those fabulous filmic coincidences, the word itself means "light" in French.

Despite its workaday subject, the showing of *La Sortie des Oeuviers de l'Usine Lumière* was a truly revolutionary event, and that first modest shot of the factory gate opening is "moving" in more than one sense. The Lumière brothers had shown the short film months earlier to an audience of politicians and industrial leaders at a meeting of the Société d'Encouragement pour l'Industrie Nationale.

German scholars would quibble (Max and Émile Skladanowsky were busy in Berlin at around the same time). But most historians of film believe that the basement showing that night in the Grand Café represented the first successfully projected motion picture for a paying audience.

The history of world cinema had begun.

Film Firsts and First Films

Well, sort of. When the Lumière brothers opened their impromptu basement cinema at the Grand Café, they were pioneering a new way of experiencing and living in the visual world. Shots like this one, of a speeding train coming directly at the audience, were thrilling and unprecedented. At the same time, though, the evening was the culmination of a long tradition of experimentation with moving pictures. If Louis and Auguste Lumière were the Orville and Wilbur Wright of film, they were also the inheritors of a proud tradition of scientific and mechanical creativity and achievement that all but today's specialists have largely forgotten.

A head-on shot of a train from the Lumière brothers' L'Arrivée d'un Train en Gare de la Ciotat *(1895).*

Technically speaking, "motion pictures" have been around for centuries in a wide variety of forms. The technology has changed drastically during the past 100 years, but the basic idea is still the same.

Think back to those slow days in fifth-grade math. Do you remember the hundreds of little stick figures you and your friends would draw in the bottom corner of every right-hand page? Each page would depict the stick man in a slightly different position. The figure might be standing at attention on page 23, but by the time you got to page 134 he'd be up in the air, clapping his hands and clicking his heels. And when you gave the book to the girl at the next desk (when your teacher's back was turned, of course), she'd flip through the book at 20 pages a second, watching your stick man perform his crude gyrations.

Your math book worked on the same fundamental principle as even the most sophisticated present-day movies: the rapid, sequential presentation of still pictures or photographs to create the illusion of movement. Each page of your textbook corresponds to an individual "frame," or basic sequential unit, on a roll of film. You didn't know it at the time, of course, but you were an active preadolescent contributor to the history of motion pictures.

Before There Was Film ...

There's a big difference between line-drawings in a math book and *Erin Brockovich* (2000), of course—and Julia Roberts isn't the only one! Long before there was an actual film to be projected to a paying audience, there were dozens of experiments aimed at presenting images in motion for numerous commercial, financial, and political reasons. Though some devices were invented with an adoring public of visual consumers in mind, many of these ancestral techniques had little or nothing to do with entertainment. The century of Queen Victoria and the American Civil War saw a proliferation of oddball inventions aimed at making pictures "move."

Short Cuts

The great American director Francis Ford Coppola (of *Godfather* fame) established a small production company in San Francisco in 1969. In a bow to the prehistory of cinema, Coppola dubbed his company "American Zoetrope" after the nineteenth-century children's toy.

Following are just a few of the more important nineteenth-century precedents to film you should be familiar with:

- The **phenakisticope**, built by Joseph Plateau in 1832, employed a rotating disk covered in drawings and a mirror to simulate movement.
- The **zoetrope**, invented by William George Horner in 1834, was a Victorian drum-shaped

toy with sequential drawings or paintings around the inner surface. The drum was spun around as the user viewed the images through a narrow slit.

- The **kinematoscope,** invented by Coleman Sellers in 1861, employed a rotating paddle machine that showed sequential photographs mounted on individual paddles.
- The **phasmotrope,** first demonstrated by Henry Renno Heyl in Philadelphia in 1870, showed a rapid succession of still photographs of dancers in motion.
- The **zoopraxiscope** was Eadweard Muybridge's device for viewing his hundreds of sequential shots of animal movement.

The idea of motion pictures goes back to the ancient Greeks and Plato's allegory of the cave. And the camera obscura, the world's first projector, dates from the Renaissance.

The last two decades of the nineteenth century, though, raised the technology of motion pictures to a whole new level.

As these sequential shots demonstrate, all four hooves of Muybridge's "test horse" left the ground at the same time—a fact impossible to prove without the advent of photography.

Director's Cut

It all began, according to typically unverifiable cinematic legend, with a bet. In 1872, Leland Stanford, governor of California and founder of the university of the same name, made a wager with a friend that all four of a horse's legs leave the ground simultaneously at least once in its gallop cycle. In order to settle the matter, he commissioned Eadweard Muybridge, an English photographer interested in animal movement, to photograph a horse in motion. Muybridge rigged up 24 cameras along a stretch of fence, each of which was activated by a trip wire when the horse passed. The result was a striking series of photographs showing the most detailed imagery ever captured of an animal's movements.

By the way, as you can guess from the photograph, Stanford won his bet, if he ever made one—though at quite a loss: Legend has it that he spent 10 times what he won hiring Muybridge to prove his point!

The Big Breakthroughs

Like that of any technology, the history of film is in large part a history of problem solving—and the problems presented by motion pictures were formidable ones indeed. Muybridge had come up with an ingenious way to take photographs sequentially, but even he had to use dozens of cameras to do so.

For the small but growing group of inventors, scientists, naturalists, and others interested in motion pictures at the turn of the century, then, there was a series of pressing questions: How can we capture a sequence of images using a *single* camera? How can we record these images in a convenient form so we don't have to flip through Muybridge's 30-odd photographs every time we want to view the sequence? After we do record the sequence, what kind of device can we use to view it and allow others to view it? Similarly, how would the public ideally want to view motion pictures—through small, individualized peephole machines, or projected onto a wall or screen?

These were practical but confounding technological problems. Their solution is synonymous with the early history of film.

Mechanics and Movement

While Muybridge was interested in horses, the French inventor Étienne-Jules Marey, a doctor by training, was fascinated by birds, and particularly by the mechanics of avian flight. In 1882, Marey came up with the chronophotographic gun, an ingenious device that, unlike Muybridge's fence-sitting cameras, allowed him to record a sequence of images of birds in flight with a single camera. After the photographs were developed, he could view them in order and see the discrete stages of wing and body movement involved in flying.

By far the most significant American film pioneers, however, were the great inventor Thomas Alva Edison and his more obscure assistant, W. K. L. Dickson. Edison's longstanding desire to develop a device for recording and viewing motion pictures led him in 1876 to establish a lab in New Jersey dedicated entirely to the exciting new technology of film. After setting up his lab, Edison delegated the task of developing the new apparatus to his laboratory chief, Dickson, a British emigrant who deserves just as much credit as Edison for the birth of motion pictures in the United States. In fact, Dickson's expertise in the new medium inspired him to write what would become the world's first textbook on cinematography, *History of the Kinetograph, Kinetoscope and Kinetophonograph* (1895), coauthored with his sister Antonia.

Short Cuts

No one knows exactly where, when, and why the notion of "shooting a film" first originated, but it's a good bet that the phrase was more than a loose metaphor. Étienne-Jules Marey's "chronophotographic gun" resembled an AK-47 assault rifle: a gun that could be aimed up in the air at a flock of birds and "fired" when the camera operator wanted to put the birds on film. So when your know-it-all roommate coos over a "great shot" the next time you're watching a Hitchcock film, you can smile calmly and say, "Interesting choice of words."

Several years before the Lumière brothers perfected their projection apparatus, Edison and Dickson developed a group of closely related devices for recording and viewing motion pictures. The kinetograph (from the Greek words for "motion" and "picture") was the first bona fide motion picture camera. A roll of film was fed horizontally through its machinery, and the images that resulted were then fed through a kinetoscope, a viewing device that allowed the spectator to peer down through a long scope at the moving images below.

The *kinetograph* employed an ingenious clawlike apparatus to progress the film through its machinery. The claws grasped the small perforations on the sides of each frame, moving a 50-foot loop of film along at a rapid clip and allowing the entire sequence to be viewed continuously.

Despite the breakthroughs accomplished in Edison's laboratories, many film historians sneer at his customary designation as the "father of film." While the importance of Edison's achievements cannot be denied, Dickson was clearly just as important a figure in the development of the new technologies.

We think it's most accurate historically to think of the early history of film as a sometimes cooperative but often competitive effort among scientists, inventors, and artists around the world to find a new way of capturing and experiencing the moving image.

Second Take

Thomas Edison was a pretty smart guy. Among other gadgets, he gave us the light bulb, the phonograph, and the stock ticker—not bad for the son of a timber merchant. But the same Thomas Edison made one of the most notorious "wrong guesses" in the history of film: that the public would pay more to watch moving pictures through peepholes than they would to see large images projected onto a screen. Whoops!

You're Projecting, Louis!

Several months before Auguste and Louis Lumière shot *La Sortie des Usines Lumière* outside the family factory in Lyons, they attended an exhibition of Thomas Edison's kinetoscope in Paris. Peering through the scope at the tiny moving pictures below, the brothers became convinced that they could go one better by projecting the same serial images onto a large screen.

And they were right. The main difference between Edison's and the Lumières' devices is the difference between small and large. Rather than squinting through a narrow scope with one eye, the viewer of a Lumière film could sit back, relax, and take in a wall-sized spectacle without any physical discomfort. Another advantage over Edison's kinetograph and kinetoscope was the power source. While Edison (not surprisingly for the light bulb guy) insisted on using electric power for his devices, the Lumières used a hand crank device that made their machine much more efficient and portable—and, as a direct result, vastly more popular in the succeeding years.

Filmophile's Lexicon

The **cinematograph** (*cinématographe* in French) was a combination camera and projector first widely used by the Lumière brothers at the end of the nineteenth century. The **kinetophonograph,** an American invention, was a device capable of showing film and producing sound simultaneously.

The word *projection* is derived from the Latin *iacere,* "to throw," and this is probably the best way to think about the revolutionary impact of early film projection. Moving images were quite literally "thrown" onto a screen or a wall in front of an audience. We'll have more to say about the early experience of cinema later in this chapter, but for now just think about the difference between reclining on your couch looking through a kaleidoscope and lying in the grass watching a fireworks display.

Though it took decades to develop into its final form, the actual technology of projection is really

Short Cuts

Annie got her gun around the world in the 1890s. One of the most popular short films shown in Edison's kinetoscope parlors depicted the remarkable shooting abilities of none other than Annie Oakley—and another featured the Old West skills of William "Buffalo Bill" Cody.

Filmophile's Lexicon

The term **35mm,** or 35 millimeter, refers to the width or gauge of the celluloid film strip passing through a camera, editing machine, projector, and other equipment. George Eastman's first celluloid strips were 35mm with four perforations per side on each frame, which remains even today the industry standard.

quite simple. In order to project an image onto a surface, you need a light source in some kind of enclosed box as well as a narrow aperture, or opening. The light is refracted through the image and out the aperture in a narrow enough stream to prevent its diffusion. With any luck, the image will appear on whatever surface stands in front of the aperture.

Without projection, the history you're reading would be pretty short: There'd be no screen, no audience, no stars, no *ooh*s and *aah*s over beautiful shots—in short, no movies, flicks, or films for us to teach you how to enjoy!

Rolls and Rolls of Celluloid

A seemingly minor but absolutely crucial step in the progress of film was the widespread use of celluloid, a flammable but tough form of thermoplastic developed in the 1870s. Celluloid was superior to the old single photographic plates for any number of reasons, the most obvious and important of which was its flexibility. (Unlike the kinds of plastic used in, say, a milk carton, a spatula handle, or a steering wheel, thermoplastics like celluloid can be bent, folded, and rolled without losing their form or durability.)

It was George Eastman (of Eastman Kodak fame) who was initially responsible for the earliest use of celluloid film in the shooting of motion pictures. In 1889, Eastman came up with a pretty clever idea: perforating the sides of a roll of celluloid to allow it to be moved mechanically through a camera.

Eastman passed off the invention to Edison and Dickson, who in turn incorporated Eastman's design into their kinetograph and kinetoscope apparatuses. Just a few years later, the Edison team came up with the kinetophonograph, which combined this technology with a primitive but synchronized sound recording that the viewer could hear as he or she watched the film.

The rest, as they say, is celluloid history.

"The Illusion Is Complete"

Living as we are at the beginning of the twenty-first century, it's difficult, if not impossible, for most of us to imagine a world without film. But for the tens of thousands of people attending a film showing in 1900 for the first time, the impact of motion pictures was profound. The birth of the "cinematic experience," as it's been called, was swift, powerful, and all-encompassing, giving audiences around the world an utterly new relation to the image and its impact.

Even the inventors of film themselves were swept away by the fantasy world of motion pictures. Here, for example, is W. K. L. Dickson himself, Edison's trusty assistant, raving about the impact of his boss's brilliant innovations as demonstrated through the kinetophonograph machine (or "penny-in-the-slot," as it was popularly known):

> "Nothing more vivid or more natural could be imagined than these breathing, audible forms, with their tricks of familiar gesture and speech. The inconceivable swiftness of the photographic successions, and the exquisite synchronism of the photographic attachment, have removed the last trace of automatic action, and the illusion is complete. The organ-grinder's monkey jumps upon his shoulder to the accompaniment of a strain from 'Norma.' The rich strains of a tenor or soprano are heard, set in their appropriate dramatic action; the blacksmith is seen swinging his ponderous hammer, exactly as in life, and the clang of the anvil keeps pace with his symmetrical movements; along with the rhythmical measures of the dancer go her soft-sounding footfalls; the wrestlers and fencers ply their intricate game, guarding, parrying, attacking, thrusting, and throwing, while the quick flash of the eye, the tension of the mouth, the dilated nostrils, and the strong, deep breathing give evidence of the potentialities within."

Dickson and his wife published these words in the magazine *Century* in June 1894, and though they're undeniably self-promoting, they reveal something of the true magic of motion pictures.

By 1896, though, Edison was regretting his decision to forsake projection in favor of individual "peeping," and in April that year—just four months after the Lumière brothers' big splash in Paris—he began promoting his so-called "Vitascope" projector to American audiences. Edison and Dickson had already opened the world's first real film studio, *Black Maria,* in 1893, and the studio released dozens of short films to U.S. audiences during the following years.

Filmophile's Lexicon

Black Maria was Edison and Dickson's film studio; it was a hideous tar paper–covered structure that got its name from the New York slang term for a police van.

Cinema at the Century

The technological experiments with moving pictures performed by Edison, Dickson, the Lumière brothers, and others were quickly transformed into widespread commercial successes. Cinematograph parlors and kinetoscope arcades opened up all over the United States and Europe, and soon the great inventors of film were household names.

American popular culture would never look the same.

Filmophile's Lexicon

Nickelodeons were makeshift theaters—often set up in union halls, cafeterias, libraries, living rooms, and other public and private spaces—that became the first popular movie houses after 1905. There may have been as many as 10,000 nickelodeon houses in the United States by 1910.

The First Movie Monopoly

It wasn't all fun and games, however. In December 1908, Edison and a cohort of other industry leaders founded the Motion Picture Patents Company, which was basically a bunch of rich bullies set on keeping aspiring independent film makers out of the business. The MPPC legally controlled the technology and raw materials needed to make and show movies: the cameras, the projectors, even the rights to Eastman Kodak's celluloid roll of film. The history of American movies in the 1900s and 1910s is also a history of monopolies, antitrust suits, plotting, and scheming on the part of a few dozen studio heads, directors, and, increasingly, actors and actresses for public attention and money.

As the monopolistic grip of Edison and company started to loosen around 1910, the first independent American studios and production companies began to emerge. You've heard of some of them already—Fox, Paramount, and Metro Goldwyn, for example. Others, like Biograph, Famous Players, and Keystone, were eventually absorbed or bought out and no longer survive.

A direct result of this new proliferation of film companies was competition, and thus, of course, innovation. In the decade after 1900, moviemakers started experimenting with new techniques and longer films, and the first real artist-directors—Edwin S. Porter in the United States, Georges Méliès in France, Cecil Hepworth and George Albert Smith in Great Britain, and several others—staked their claims to fame on the strength of their creativity.

Seven Early Silents to Savor

Here's a list of seven films from the earliest part of this century that will give you a good look at some of the most important innovations in American and European moviemaking before World War I. All of them represent significant breakthroughs in editing, narrative technique, parallel action, and so on that you'll be able to see when you compare them with one another. We've picked titles available on video that your local specialty video store or university library should either own or be able to order without much trouble. (By the way, most of these are less than 15 minutes long, so you can probably watch all of them in one evening.)

- *The Big Swallow* (England, 1901), directed by James Williamson.
- *Le Voyage dans la Lune* (*A Trip to the Moon*) (France, 1902), directed by Georges Méliès.
- *The Great Train Robbery* (United States, 1903), directed by Edwin S. Porter.
- *Rescued by Rover* (1905), directed by Cecil Hepworth.
- *La presa di Roma* (*The Capture of Rome*) (Italy, 1905), produced by Filotea Alberini.
- *Aufgrunden* (*The Abyss*) (Denmark, 1910), directed by Urban Gad.
- *The Morphine Takers* (Denmark, 1911), directed by Holger Madsen.

In Chapter 6, "The Quiet Pleasures of Silent Film," you'll read more about the history of silent film—the directors, the producers, and the world's first movie stars. First, though, we need to tell you about a man who changed cinema history forever.

D. W. Griffith and the "Birth" of Narrative Film

"He put beauty and poetry into a cheap and tawdry form of entertainment."—Erich von Stroheim

"He" is David Wark Griffith (1875–1948), far and away the most important director in the history of film. The Prussian-born Stroheim, Griffith's student and awestruck follower, was repeating what the world already knew about the Kentucky-born doctor's son.

One of the odder characters in the early years of film, Griffith came from a poor Louisville family, took an early interest in the stage, and began his movie career as a writer and actor for Biograph, the Edison studio's main competitor in the first decade of the twentieth century. His 1908 directorial debut was *The Adventures of Dollie,* his last film *The Struggle* in 1931. Between these two, Griffith made some 500 motion pictures for Biograph and several other studies, including Reliance-Majestic, Triangle, and United Artists.

The Michelangelo of Film

Aside from the prolific number of movies he made in these years, what set Griffith apart from his contemporaries was the revolutionary artistry of his filmmaking. When we watch a movie today, we take for granted many of the innovations that Griffith integrated into mainstream directing: parallel action, crosscutting, the close-up, multiple camera angles, and so on.

Griffith's greatest and still most controversial work, *The Birth of a Nation* (1915), was the first film of significant length (12 reels) to achieve much of its impact from its editing. In other words, Griffith used the technique of crosscutting from one perspective or scene to another to heighten the visual impact and emotional intensity of the story he was telling. While many of the techniques Griffith employed had been used by other directors, he was the first to realize the true artistic possibilities of the medium. The camera became his paintbrush, and a whole new way of making movies was born.

An intimate shot of wringing hands and a battlefield panorama represent the richness and variety of Griffith's camerawork in The Birth of a Nation *(1915).*

Short Cuts

If you want a fascinating (and gossipy) glimpse at Griffith's life and art, check out the 1925 book *When the Movies Were Young,* written by none other than Linda Arvidson, Mrs. D. W. Griffith.

The two greatest aesthetic influences on Griffith's filmmaking were the novel and the drama. Like the great nineteenth-century novelists and playwrights, Griffith told his stories from multiple, interlaced viewpoints rather than from a single perspective; his choice of shots, camera angles, and so on reflected this newly flexible approach to directing and did much to make the long narrative film the standard-bearer of world cinema.

At the same time, Griffith departed from convention by abandoning the notion of movies as "filmed theater." Motion pictures before Griffith were filmed primarily in the "long shot": The camera was set up to shoot individual scenes from a single angle, and the actors and actresses entered or exited the scene as they would the stage during the performance of a play.

But Griffith changed all this. Rather than relying exclusively on long shots, he would construct his scenes by cutting back and forth between close-ups of individual actors, medium-range shots of small groups of people, and long shots of entire landscapes full of actors—as in *The Birth of a Nation,* in which a panoramic shot of a battlefield is immediately preceded by an intimate shot of two main characters.

When you watch today's epic movies like *Braveheart* (1995) or *Star Wars: Episode I—The Phantom Menace* (1999), you're seeing crystal-clear examples of Griffith's spectacular influence on the visual artistry of film.

D. W. and His Klan

When you get a chance (soon, we hope!) to watch *The Birth of a Nation,* you'll immediately understand why this Civil War epic remains one of the most controversial motion pictures of all time. The film's prejudiced portrayal of African Americans and frankly heroic depiction of the Ku Klux Klan was a problem even for Griffith's contemporaries, many of whom reacted with sharp criticism in newspapers around the country.

Interestingly, the film's release immediately increased membership in two national organizations: the NAACP and the Ku Klux Klan.

It's difficult to separate the aesthetics of *The Birth of a Nation* from its politics, and in fact we wouldn't even suggest that you try! Numerous innovative twentieth-century artists—including T.S. Elliot, Ezra Pound, and the list goes on—held political views that were, let's say, questionable at best. Just bear in mind that the first true masterpiece of American filmmaking carries with it a damaging legacy of racism and white supremacy that will always remain inextricable from its unparalleled contribution to the history of cinema.

Second Take

Don't be so fast to pooh-pooh the racism of *The Birth of a Nation* as a mere distraction from its artistry. Griffith based the scenario for the film on Thomas Dixon's *The Klansman,* a notoriously racist novel that raised the founders of the Ku Klux Klan to demigod status. In other words, Griffith knew exactly what he was doing!

The Least You Need to Know

- There is no single "father" of world cinema, though the Lumière brothers and Thomas Edison come as close as anyone.
- Numerous technological and conceptual advances made in the nineteenth century eventually gave rise to film as we know it.
- The early history of film is also a history of technological breakthroughs and problem solving.
- With the spread and popular success of cinema, the turn of the twentieth century gave birth to an entirely new way of experiencing the visual image.
- D. W. Griffith was the most important and influential director in the history of film, though his legacy is tainted with racism.

Chapter 6

The Quiet Pleasures of Silent Film

In This Chapter

- Learning to appreciate (and maybe even love) silent movies
- The rise of the studio system
- Hollywood and world cinema
- The great silent directors
- The genres in their infancy
- America's first movie stars

Although the full-scale introduction of sound into motion pictures would have to wait until the late twenties, the silent era gave its directors, actors, and producers ample room for artistry and innovation. The brief period from 1915 to 1927 was the golden age of silent film, an era that saw the beginnings of the movies as we know them today, from the "star system" that gave us Charlie Chaplin and Harrison Ford to the so-called "genre film," whether the silent Western or, ultimately, the contemporary urban slasher flick.

Learning to Love, Honor, and Cherish Silent Film

Okay, so you've just walked into your local video store, and all you want to do is stroll on over to the bright 'n' shiny new releases section and pick out the latest horror film, romantic comedy, or thriller.

It's understandable. You know you'll be getting a hi-fi, multisensory movie experience, complete with a soundtrack, a decent score, punchy dialogue, maybe even some clever sound effects, all of which you can experience through the three-foot speakers bookending your entertainment center. The movie will undoubtedly be in color, it won't be grainy or have subtitles you'll have to read, and as long as you can hear the TV from the kitchen you won't have to worry about missing anything when you jump up to make popcorn or grab a soda.

Why Bother?

They'd never admit it, but even the snobbiest film connoisseurs probably breathe a secret sigh of relief when their friends choose Charlie Sheen over Charlie Chaplin. Watching a silent film can be demanding: *The Birth of a Nation* and *Intolerance* are hard movies to sit through, and many other works from the era before sound test their modern viewers' patience in more ways than one.

Director's Cut

After the extraordinary success of *The Birth of a Nation* (1915), D. W. Griffith got just a tad overconfident. His next film, *Intolerance* (1916), didn't attract the massive audiences that had flocked to see *Birth.* Those who did see it were largely turned off by its narrative complexity, which presented story lines treating prejudice in four different historical eras separated by thousands of years. Worse yet, *Intolerance* cost Griffith—get this—$2.5 million *in 1910s dollars* to make, and it bankrupted him for the next few years.

This is not to say that the film isn't worth seeing; it's a truly spectacular work, and like *The Birth of a Nation,* it had a massive influence on the subsequent history of moviemaking. Yet it may have been the commercial failure of *Intolerance* that temporarily dimmed Griffith's star and made room for other directors to emerge onto the scene—some of whom would take American film in myriad new directions that Griffith himself could never have predicted.

But if you've never bothered to rent or attend a silent film—if you've never watched a tear stream slowly down Greta Garbo's cheek, or howled at Buster Keaton's comedic acrobatics—then you've been cheating yourself out of one of history's greatest sources of visual entertainment. The first three decades of the twentieth century witnessed the birth and initial development of an entirely new art form, one that too many of us have left by the wayside in our preference for the splashy flicks of the present.

Reasons to Shut Up and Watch

Here are five simple, practical, and economical reasons to start renting, attending, watching, and enjoying silent film tonight:

- Public libraries, colleges, and universities around the country often sponsor free or reasonably priced screenings of classic movies, including silent film; "John Barrymore Month" at the local community college will give you four cheap evenings of great cinema.
- "Old stuff" is usually a lot cheaper than new releases at the video store, meaning you can rent three or four tapes' worth of silent films for the price of a single Leonardo DiCaprio DVD.
- Once you've become accustomed to recognizing the demands that silent film places on actors, you'll have a better eye for separating the artistic wheat from the untalented chaff among today's stars.
- Many silent films (especially from the earliest years) are quite short, some of them less than 30 minutes long, allowing you to rent, say, three Lillian Gish films on one cassette—and master the major works of a single director in a few evenings.
- Today's great directors, from Woody Allen to Steven Spielberg, all know the early history of film like the backs of their hands, and they make constant visual references to silent classics in their own work—meaning the more you learn about the movies of the past, the more you'll get out of the movies of the present.
- Chaney, Chaplin, Keaton, Garbo, DeMille—these names are woven into the very fabric of American popular culture, an integral part of our nation's history that have important lessons to teach us even today.

Our job in this chapter is to show you just a little bit of what you've been missing out on, and encourage you to direct your cinematic eye a few decades further into the past than you're accustomed to. We guarantee you'll be glad you did!

Short Cuts

"Hollywood has no set physical boundaries. Many of the studios are located in other communities, some many miles away. It has always been and will continue to be a state of mind, a dream shared by millions, rather than a mere place where movies are made. And that's probably why it will never die."

—Ephraim Katz, *The Encyclopedia of Film*

Studio City

Ever been to Los Angeles? Believe it or not, in 1909 Hollywood was still a quiet little suburb on the outskirts of the growing metropolis. The country's film industry was still dominated by Edison and his cohort in the Motion Picture Patents Company (MPPC), the monopoly that kept most of its competitors out of the business through the early 1910s.

Things started to change, however, when the MPPC was dealt a devastating blow in an antitrust suit in 1915. At the same time, a small but talented group of independent filmmakers was emerging to challenge the conglomerate's creative throttling of American cinema.

One of the more important events in these years was the establishment of the short-lived Triangle corporation, founded in 1915 as a way of bringing together three (hence the name *Tri*-angle) of the country's hottest new directors: Thomas Ince, D. W. Griffith, and Mack Sennett. Though Triangle lasted only until 1918, it marked the beginnings of a new way of producing, making, and marketing motion pictures that other emerging studios would imitate with often resounding success.

Director's Cut

Surely you've heard of the Keystone Kops before. But unless you're over 60 you probably have no clue who or what they were. When Mack Sennett came to Keystone Studio in 1913, he began directing a series of comedy flicks that featured a band of incompetent police officers whose hilarious adventures delighted cinema audiences. In dozens of films through the middle part of the decade, the Keystone Kops bumbled their way into the nation's heart.

Though few of us have seen the Keystone Kops in action, their legacy lives on. In crucial ways, they're the direct ancestors of Barney Fife, Deputy Dawg, Jackie Gleason's pudgy sheriff in *Smokey and the Bandit* (1977), and hilariously incompetent lawmen everywhere.

The silent era's other important American studios included MGM, Inceville, Paramount, Fox, and Keystone, all of which forged their own identities as film production businesses and gave the public an ever-growing body of movies to consume and enjoy. As the small independents grew into major studios during the 1910s and '20s, an entirely new kind of entertainment phenomenon sprang up on the west coast. Rather than a disrespected and "tawdry" business, American moviemaking came into its own as a full-fledged industry—one of the nation's three or four largest by 1920. Not surprisingly, the changing shape of the new film economy brought with it unprecedented opportunities for those who knew how to manipulate it to their advantage. The first so-called "moguls," the money guys behind the scenes, pumped newfound wealth into their studios, and the system immediately opened itself up to widespread corruption, graft, and greed.

Short Cuts

In one of the brightly glaring ironies of film history, the early independent studios have now become the monopolizing monsters of our own day. Not entirely unlike Edison's MPPC (though admittedly with less success), a handful of massive production companies still attempts to control what movies are distributed to the nation's multiplexes, allowing only the rare independent film to make its way to the nonspecialty screen.

Many of the major studios are still with us today—though what's most interesting (and troubling) about their history during the last century is how little things have changed. As we'll see in later chapters, the culture of Hollywood in subsequent decades was characterized by the same struggle between major studios and smaller independents, who constantly strove to get their cinematic voices heard.

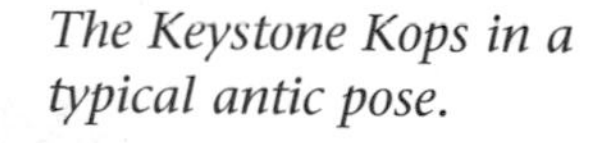

The Keystone Kops in a typical antic pose.

HollyWorld

With the outbreak and spread of World War I after 1914, the fledgling cinema businesses in most European countries suffered an inevitable downturn. With their economic and personal resources dedicated entirely to the war effort, France, Germany, England, and other nations had neither the motivation nor the financial means to spend on the movies, a form of popular entertainment still widely viewed as a glorified form of vaudeville.

Paradoxically, if there was one factor that would ensure the total worldwide dominance of the American film industry in this period, it was the country's continuing isolationism, which kept the United States out of the Great War for several years and, as a result, narrowly focused on its own industrial and commercial development. And some of the biggest beneficiaries of this inward-looking trend in American life were the studio heads bent on making the nation's film industry a global powerhouse.

The Giant Sucking Sound

A phrase coined by one of our own era's more entertaining politicians, Ross Perot, aptly sums up the relationship between Hollywood and the rest of the world during these years: "A giant sucking sound" could be heard around the globe during and after World War I, as Hollywood lured the world's greatest film talents away from their home countries and into the growing maelstrom of the American cinema industry. Some of the era's greatest cinematic artists came from abroad, enriching the U.S. film business while practically devastating their own country's much smaller versions of the industry.

Born in the USA ... Not!

Two of American silent film's most familiar and defining faces were in fact "imports" from other countries. Charlie Chaplin was born into an extremely poor London working-class family and had what many film historians have aptly called a "Dickensian" childhood. But during an American tour with a child dancing company he caught the eye of Keystone's Mack Sennett, and the rest of his career was spent in Hollywood. Greta Garbo, a Swedish peasant's daughter, made a few films in her native Stockholm before her discovery by an MGM mogul and subsequent move to New York.

The same holds true of foreign-born directors. Ernst Lubitsch made a number of fabulous films in Germany in the 1910s, including *The Eyes of the Mummy* (*Die Augen der Mummie,* 1918) and *The Oyster Princess* (*Die Austernprinzessin,* 1919), before coming to America and shooting his greatest commercial successes—*The Marriage Circle* (1924), *Kiss Me Again* (1925), and the later Garbo sound vehicle *Ninotchka* (1939), among others—for Warner Brothers and Paramount. Victor Sjöström abandoned the new but booming Swedish film business during the 1920s after making some of the true gems of early Scandinavian cinema, such as *Ingeborg Holm* (1913) and *The Sons of Ingmar* (1919); he, too, was seduced by the promise of wealth and fame in Hollywood, directing Lillian Gish in *The Wind* (1928), Lon Chaney in *The Tower of Lies* (1925), and Garbo in *The Divine Woman* (1928).

Ah, Garbo, shown here in her fame-launching picture The Torrent *(1926).*

So what does this "giant sucking sound" mean for the history of American film? Well, most of all it means that this history isn't strictly or even predominantly "American." While the moguls were working in Hollywood and buying up the world's cinematic talent, other countries were making crucial aesthetic and artistic contributions that made the industry into a dominant worldwide phenomenon. It was in these crucial years that the Hollywood studio system became a diverse, international, and global powerhouse.

New Directions

As we saw in the previous chapter, while D. W. Griffith changed movie history in 1915 with *The Birth of a Nation,* there were plenty of important and innovative American directors before him whose silent films are still worth tracking down. Thomas Ince, for example, was possibly just as influential as Griffith in his own time, and directors such as Jack Conway and Fred Niblo did much to make the action film a booming genre within the fledgling industry. The dozen-odd years following the release of Griffith's masterpiece represent a period in which directing per se came into its own as a unique mode of artistic production.

The Ones to Watch

It's well nigh impossible to pick and choose when the selection is so vast, but here's a representative checklist of 10 American (or Europe-to-America emigrant) silent directors from the early 1910s to the coming of sound in the late 1920s. We've given you the names of three films for each director, including acknowledged masterpieces, some more obscure gems, and two or three truly awful flicks (just for fun!).

If you make an effort to view these 30 movies during the next several months, you'll acquire a rich and broad knowledge of American filmmaking in the early part of the last century.

- D. W. Griffith: *The Birth of a Nation* (1915), *Intolerance* (1916), *Way Down East* (1920).
- Mack Sennett: *One Round O'Brien* (1912), *Mabel's Strange Predicament* (1914), *The Big Palooka* (1929).
- Ernst Lubitsch: *Rosita* (1923), *Kiss Me Again* (1925), *Monte Carlo* (1930).
- Buster Keaton: *One Week* (1920), *The Three Ages* (1923), *The General* (1927).
- William S. Hart: *The Man from Nowhere* (1915), *The Aryan* (1916), *Tumbleweeds* (1925).
- Thomas Ince: *A Manly Man* (1911), *The Alien* (1915), *Civilization* (1916).
- Cecil B. DeMille: *The Squaw Man* (1914; remade in 1918; remade for sound in 1931), *The King of Kings* (1927), *The Ten Commandments* (1923).
- John Adolfi: *A Man and His Mate* (1915), *The Burden of Proof* (1918), *Husband Hunters* (1927).
- Christy Cabanne: *Arms and the Gringo* (1914), *The Beloved Cheater* (1919), *The Sixth Commandment* (1924).
- John Ford, *The Iron Horse* (1924), *Lightnin'* (1925), *Four Sons* (1928).

Committing (to) Harry Carey: The Early Genre Film

"It's a romantic comedy—you know, chick flick."

"We're going to a slasher film. You'd hate it, Mom."

"Seen that new war movie yet?"

When we label individual movies like this—as horror, Western, screwball comedy, science fiction, musical and so on—we're identifying them by their *genre*. Genre is French for "type" or "sort," and it allows an individual work, whether a piece of literature, a musical composition, a television show, or a film, to be categorized in terms of its style, content, or form.

There are many reasons for labeling movies by their genre, the most important of which is predictability. The early studio heads knew that a new screwball comedy was practically guaranteed to draw so many viewers for a certain number of weeks to the nation's theaters. A war movie released at the height of American involvement in World War I would almost certainly draw a patriotic crowd of customers eager to watch the martial spectacle unfold on the screen.

The "golden age" of Hollywood, which you'll read about in the following chapter, marked the real triumph of the genre film. But like so much else from the later period, this crucial aspect of American moviemaking was anticipated in important ways in the decades before and during the war. Some "quasigenres," such as the serial film, didn't survive more than a decade or two and are now largely forgotten; others, such as the Western, exploded into vast traditions that have inspired countless directors and actors to produce their finest work.

The genres of narrative film whose seeds were planted in the silent era are many: the musical, the epic adventure, the melodrama, the war movie, the gangster/crime flick, and the list goes on. But there are two genres in particular that were identified practically from the get-go (and one of them by definition) as specifically American, and it's impossible to understand the nature and history of the genre film without paying more careful attention to these two varieties of early picture.

Second Take

John Ford, one of America's greatest directors, is known today for a series of great Western talkies starring such notables as John Wayne. On your way to Ford junkiedom, though, don't forget about his numerous silent films, which provide crucial background for understanding the development of his artistry.

Short Cuts

In one of the coolest self-referential moments in the history of the genre film, the final shot of John Ford's *The Searchers* (1956) depicts John Wayne turning from the camera and grabbing his left elbow in pain. The shot is a direct reference to a similar gesture often made by Harry Carey, the primary leading man of Ford's silent Westerns, and was probably meant to identify The Duke with this early star of the genre.

Film West, Young Man!

The Western, the quintessential American genre, begins with *The Great Train Robbery* (1903), which was shot on location in, uh, New Jersey. But soon production companies were traveling thousands of miles and shooting Westerns in Montana, Wyoming, and Colorado, bringing panoramic shots of the nation's most spectacular vistas to tens of thousands of East Coasters who had never made the westward trek. Actors and directors such as

John Ford, William S. Hart, Cecil B. DeMille, Hoot Gibson, Tim McCoy, Buck Jones, Harry Carey, and many others were responsible for making the Western an essential part of American culture throughout the early twentieth century.

Best of all, the Western is easily the most visually satisfying of the early genres. Watch a dozen Westerns from the 1920s and you'll be exposed to some of the most beautiful vistas ever captured on film, from the high plains of Montana to Colorado's Monument Valley, the rugged Rocky Mountain landscape that captured John Ford's imagination. There are literally hundreds, perhaps thousands of American Westerns out there to savor; and if you start with some of the tradition's silent gems—*The Battle at Elderbush Gulch* (1914), *The Squaw Man* (1914), *Firebrand Trevison* (1920), *The Sawdust Trail* (1924), and the list goes on—you'll be well on your way to acquiring a connoisseur's expertise in the genre.

Reel Funny

Film comedy began with the Lumière brothers themselves, whose *L'Arroseur arrosè* (*Watering the Gardener*, 1895) initiated movie slapstick. In the United States, figures such as the rotund actor John Bunny, director-producer Mack Sennett at Keystone, the great Charlie Chaplin and Buster Keaton, and Marion Davies (under the direction of King Vidor) created a comedic idiom that swept the world at lightning speed.

Major influences on the development of American film comedy included vaudeville, theater, and the circus, all of which contributed specific personnel, mannerisms, techniques, and scenarios to cinematic humor. The actress Marie Dressler came to Keystone after working for years on the New York stage, while Harold Lloyd toured with summer stock before making more than 100 "Lonesome Luke" action comedies with Hal Roach at Universal.

There are as many flavors of silent film comedy as there are of ice cream, so don't give up if it takes a while to find something you like!

Filmophile's Lexicon

The **trick film,** perhaps the earliest true film genre (and mastered by French musician-cum-filmmaker George Méliès), was a form of stop-action animation in which one figure (say, a horse) was switched for another (perhaps a lion) between frames, creating the illusion of shape-changing.

Silent Stars

The silent screen was filled with new faces every week, and one of the main attractions of the early cinema was the introduction of unknown performers into American culture. But there were a few actors and actresses in this era who simply dominated the cinema marquees, the gossip headlines, and the popular imagination.

The 1910s saw the emergence of what we now call the "star system," the studio-sponsored promotion, marketing, and featuring of individual films determined by the performers who starred in them. Before the public knew who she was, for example, Florence Lawrence was called simply "The Biograph Girl" after her appearances in Biograph-produced films. It took a publicity stunt by Carl Laemmle of IMPC to get her name known to her many fans; as a result, she became the first "named" movie star in the history of the medium.

After that things moved very quickly, and soon the public had dozens of stars' names on the tips of their tongues. As always, the list is too long to do any kind of justice to here, but we'll try to give you some sense of those names and faces that gave the history of entertainment whole new ways of experiencing laughter, beauty, and art in the early years of the last century.

The Best Medicine

Watching a Charlie Chaplin film at the beginning of the twenty-first century is like opening a time capsule, or peering through an opaque window onto another era. Alternately light and serious, poignant and flip, naive and wise, Chaplin's pale face could register the most cloying sentimentalism while conveying the seriousness of his films' subject matter with moving grace.

In commercial and business terms, Chaplin defined the twentieth-century movie star. While today's cinema superstars (Leonardo DiCaprio, Harrison Ford, Julia Roberts) can command tens of millions of dollars per film, Chaplin was so in demand around the world that his salary virtually *doubled* every time he switched studios.

In an age when *Dumb and Dumber* (1994) and *Road Trip* (2000) define the nation's comic tastes, it's sometimes hard to appreciate the purely gestural and expressive dimensions of silent comedy. But we guarantee it will grow on you if you allow it to.

Second Take

While the coming of sound ended or radically altered the careers of many silent stars, this wasn't true for Charlie Chaplin; in fact, *City Lights* (1931) and *The Great Dictator* (1940) were silent films that defiantly resisted the trend toward sound while reaping yet more commercial and critical awards for Chaplin.

A Thing of Beauty Is a Joy Forever

For the first time since Helen of Troy launched 1,000 ships to begin the Trojan War, the silent era transformed beautiful female faces into international commodities. While popular theater actresses had long attracted fanatical audiences, it was only with the joining of beauty and celluloid that the modern cult of the sublimely gorgeous movie star could truly emerge.

Charlie Chaplin as Adenoid Hynkel, a thinly disguised Adolf Hitler, in The Great Dictator *(1940).*

You gotta begin with Garbo, the Swedish star whose sudden appearance on the American scene was "torrential" in more ways than one. After MGM mogul Louis B. Mayer featured her in *The Torrent* (1926), her fate was sealed as audiences across the country became captivated by the Scandinavian goddess. Though she never won an Academy Award, Garbo received rave reviews for both her silent and her sound performances (for the latter, check out especially *Anna Karenina* [1935] and *Camille* [1937]), producing an aura of mystery and unwilling vulnerability that continues to define the ideal of cinematic beauty. (Whether Garbo could really act, though, remains an open question among film historians.)

If Garbo exuded statuesque expressiveness, the earlier actress Mary Pickford defined all-around movie-star sexiness for the silent era, playing a variety of roles that made her "America's Sweetheart" (and, for a few years, the nation's top box-office attraction) in the 1910s. More than a pretty face, however, Pickford exercised tight control over her career, carefully managing the personnel involved in her film and the public persona she projected to the world. In films such as *White Roses* (1910), *Madame Butterfly* (1915), *Stella Maris* (1918), and *Pollyanna* (1920, in which at 27 she played a 12-year-old!), Pickford displayed a stunning artistic adaptability coupled with a natural grace on the screen.

Film Acting as Art Form

When D. W. Griffith decided to cast Lillian Gish in *The Birth of a Nation* as the female lead, he was announcing to the nation what he had known for several years: that the young woman from Ohio was a prodigiously talented actress whose adaptability on the screen—a face that could register a pitiable fragility along with the most bitter strength—was simply astonishing. The collaboration between Gish and Griffith lasted roughly a decade, after which Gish went on to direct several of her own films and further consolidate her image as "The First Lady of the Silent Screen."

As much as any other silent star, Lillian Gish (whose sister, Dorothy, was also a talented actress) was responsible for the elevation of film acting to an art form. Though it might be controversial to say so these days, silent film simply made more demands on actors and actresses than the talkies ever would, creating the need for a brilliant coordination of face, eyes, and hands for every performance.

For better or worse, the silent era bequeathed to posterity the notion of the film actor as artiste. Some of today's film stars—Jim Carrey, Anthony Hopkins, Frances McDormand, Meryl Streep—truly deserve inclusion in the pantheon of film artists alongside Chaplin, Keaton, and the Gish sisters. Though many others rest on the laurels of name recognition and stock performances that never seem to change, this isn't anything new either!

Theda Bara, John Barrymore, Lon Chaney, Charlie Chaplin, Douglas Fairbanks, the Gish sisters, Keaton, Bessie Love, Wallace Reid, Gloria Swanson, Pearl White: Watch their films and you'll see why acting became the twentieth century's most visible and popular art form, a passionate medium of human expression unlike any other.

Director's Cut

Lon Chaney (1883–1930), "The Man of a Thousand Faces," was one of the greatest mimes in the history of the art form. One of his most dazzling talents was his knack for playing maimed, disfigured, or disabled characters with empathy and compassion. In films like *Treasure Island* (1920), *The Penalty* (1920), *The Hunchback of Notre Dame* (1923), and *The Phantom of the Opera* (1925), Chaney portrayed characters with missing legs, disabling humps, and disfigured faces without turning them into dehumanized monsters in the process.

Perhaps Chaney's primary motivation for such empathetic portrayals of disability was a personal one. Both of his parents were deaf and mute; rather than speaking and hearing, little Lon communicated with them instead through sign and sight. His parents' physical disability gave Lon Chaney and the history of cinema a repertoire of gesture and movement that remains one of film's most treasured gifts to the world.

The Least You Need to Know

- Silent film is still worth watching for dozens of reasons, not the least of which is that it's relatively inexpensive to rent and often beautiful to watch.
- The Hollywood studio system first emerged in the 1910s, quickly growing into an international behemoth that devoured much of the world's directorial and acting talent.
- The first great directors appeared in the same decade, creating a vast legacy of motion pictures that can (and should!) still be enjoyed today.
- The genre film—Westerns, gangster flicks, comedy, and so on—was also a product of the silent era.
- Film actors from Charlie Chaplin to Lillian Gish first became international stars during the silent period, and acting itself became a respected art form.

Chapter 7

Hollywood in the "Golden Age"

In This Chapter

- The coming of sound
- The triumph of the studios
- The director as auteur
- The Production Code and Hollywood's new morality
- Actors and actresses in the golden age

Bogie, Stewart, Cagney, Kelly, Grant, Hepburn: Their names are synonymous with Hollywood at its historical apogee. We can all pick out famous lines and quote them at will. "Here's lookin' at you, kid." "I have a feeling this is the beginning of a beautiful friendship." *"Stell-aaaaaa!!"*

It's easy to run off a list of classic lines, names, and titles and imagine that this kind of nostalgic recitation gives us a genuine glimpse at the golden age of American moviedom. But what was really important historically about this era were the underlying economic, commercial, and aesthetic forces that began to shape the industry as we know it today. The studio system that had arisen during the silent era quickly evolved into a worldwide economic power, while film genres established themselves as the primary means of writing, filming, and marketing the movies. These two factors—the triumph of the studio system and the consolidation of the genres—explain many things about Hollywood's golden age, from the specific directors who became famous and established their artistic identities to the stars who flourished within the boundaries of specific film genres.

Short Cuts

"The talkie has completely nullified the silent screen. This is entirely characteristic of the machine. A new machine (or process) does not merely *add;* it *replaces.* In most lines the replacement is gradual, but in the show business nothing can prevent the replacement from being almost instantaneous."

—*Fortune* magazine, 1930 (anon.)

"You Ain't Heard Nothing Yet!": The Coming of Sound

Silence is golden, but cinema wouldn't be nearly as lifelike without synchronized sound. Skip ahead to Chapter 24, "BOOM! The Sonic Side of Film," to read about film's sound pioneers and innovators. For now, just be aware of the immense psychological and artistic impact that the coming of sound must have had on the hundreds of thousands of cinema junkies around the nation and the world.

Long used to directing their primary energies toward watching a film, the average viewer now had to *listen*—and often quite carefully. With the full-scale introduction of sound, dialogue—and therefore entire plots—could be more complex and demanding. If the silent era represents cinema's childhood, the coming of sound brought the medium and the industry into a robust adolescence.

Studios and Their Identity

That the U.S. film industry flourished and assumed a central role in American popular culture during the Roaring Twenties was the result of many factors: the introduction of sound, new wealth generated by the country's powerful industrial base, the late entry of the United States into World War I, and a population boom in the major cities, to name just a few. That the industry survived and even thrived during the Great Depression of the '30s, when film attendance across the nation plummeted, is a testament to the permanent grip that cinema had established on the popular imagination.

Of course, the public itself was largely unaware of the larger social forces shaping the fortunes of its newly favorite form of entertainment. For most folks, the movies were, well, just plain fun. Accordingly, it was the job of the major studios to keep the masses entertained and happy during the many social upheavals between the Stock Market Crash of 1929 and Nazi Germany's surrender in 1945.

And they were well suited to the task. Beginning in the mid-1920s, the fledgling studios you read about in the last chapter went through a dramatic growth period that culminated in the 1930s with the utter dominance of the industry by the four or five biggest and most powerful.

But the studios in Hollywood's golden age weren't simply distribution centers for reels of celluloid. In fact, each studio had its own unique character, producing movies that reflected the tastes, prejudices, ideologies, and finances of its affiliated directors—and, just as important, those of its often quite idiosyncratic boss.

Money Plus Glamour Equals Movies (MGM)

The glitziest studio in the golden years was unquestionably Metro-Goldwyn-Mayer, more commonly known as MGM. Founded in 1924 when three smaller studios merged, MGM was headed during the twenties and most of the thirties by Irving Thalberg, its vice president in charge of production, who molded the studio into the most spectacular and desirable entertainment company on the planet.

Director's Cut

The medallion that surrounds the so-called "MGM Lion" (whose name was and is "Leo") is inscribed with a Latin inscription reading *Ars Gratia Artis*, or "Art for Art's Sake."

When audiences heard that roaring lion just before the credits, they knew they were in for some quality entertainment. Bankrolled by Thalberg, Louis B. Mayer (the real source of power at MGM), and a friendly relationship with the boys at Chase National Bank, MGM attracted the greatest talents in practically all areas of production, from Hollywood's most creative cinematographers and sound and lighting technicians to the era's most beautiful and talented stars. While Thalberg kept an iron grip on production, and Meyer became perhaps the most hated man in Hollywood, the studio created a warm 'n' fuzzy image of America that the nation gobbled up during a rough phase of its history.

Second Take

One of Irving Thalberg's first and most ruthless acts as head of MGM was his cutting of Erich von Stroheim's epic masterpiece *Greed* (1925) by almost 75 percent. When you watch the 140-minute version available on video, bear in mind that you're seeing a fraction of an originally seven-, eight-, or even, by some accounts, nine-hour film!

Aside from Greta Garbo, John Barrymore, and other holdovers from the silent period, the actors and actresses employed by MGM in these years included Cary Grant, Elizabeth Taylor, Clark Gable, Judy Garland, Spencer Tracy, Jimmy Stewart, Joan Crawford, Myrna Loy, Mickey Rooney—you name 'em! It was an impressive pantheon of cinematic talent, and the studio knew it, too, releasing movie after movie designed to feature the sweet, suave, sophisticated, wry, cynical, and naive faces it had introduced to an increasingly adoring public. So extraordinary was MGM's array of talent that the studio boasted that it possessed "more stars than there are in the heavens."

A list of MGM's movies during the 1930s and '40s reads like a "greatest hits" list of cinematic achievement: *Grand Hotel* (1932), *Dinner at Eight* (1933), *Mutiny on the Bounty* (1935), *The Good Earth* (1937), *The Wizard of Oz* (1939), *The Philadelphia Story* (1940), and, of course, that perennial favorite *Gone With the Wind* (1939), which was made by Selznick International and distributed by MGM. As you might guess, some of these films were breathtakingly expensive to make: Think of the Emerald City in *The Wizard of Oz,* or all those fires in *Gone With the Wind.*

But what distinguished MGM in these years was its incredible luck. A solid majority of its movies turned into money-makers for the studio, which flourished for decades as one of the world's entertainment leaders.

The Brothers Warner

It's an all-American story almost too good to be true. In 1903, four brothers—Albert, Harry, Jack, and Sam Warner—started a small nickelodeon house in the town of Newcastle, Pennsylvania. During the next 20 years the company slowly expanded; by the mid-1920s, the brothers were producing and distributing films of their own. The big break came in 1927, when the family owned and still quite small studio released *The Jazz Singer,* the first motion picture to feature synchronized music and dialogue.

Director's Cut

A comparison between two Warner Bros. films will give you a pretty good idea of the difference between MGM and its less illustrious competitor: While *The Wizard of Oz* features elaborate costumes, expensive sets, and an otherworldly feel created by an array of lighting gimmicks and fancy lenses, *King of the Underworld* portrays the gritty world of urban crime and corruption with skillful but no-frills camerawork and a bare-bones approach to cinematography and set design.

The full-scale introduction of sound was quite a gamble for the Warner brothers, who had invested considerable funds in experimenting with emerging sound technologies. But it paid off, and how! Within a few months Warner Bros. had become one of the nation's leading motion picture studios.

Unlike MGM, though, Warner Bros. wasn't a glam factory. In fact, what distinguished the studio's productions throughout the 1930s was their willingness to tackle the difficult social and cultural issues raised by the Great Depression. While Irving Thalberg was shelling out the big bucks on the Judy Garland escapist fantasy *The Wizard of Oz,* released in 1939, the same year saw Humphrey Bogart appearing in the low-budget Warner Bros. gangster flick *King of the Underworld.*

This is not to say that Warner Bros. didn't possess sufficient "star power" of its own: Bogart, Bette Davis, and, after 1943, Joan Crawford were among its featured faces, while the dashing Errol Flynn's adventure flicks—*Captain Blood* (1935), *The Charge of the Light*

Brigade (1936), *Dive Bomber* (1941), *Desperate Journey* (1942), *Uncertain Glory* (1944), and many others—kept the studio's coffers filled during the decade before and during World War II. But it's undeniable that Warner Bros. was the "workingman's studio," a far cry from the glitzy Establishment folks at MGM.

Sly as a Fox

The name of the Greater New York Rental Company might not sound so grand, but William Fox's realization that there was an enormous amount of money to be made in streamlined film distribution was the foundation for another successful launching of a major studio in the 1910s. Fox, a Hungarian by birth (and thus yet another European import bulwarking the U.S. film industry), started producing his own films in 1912.

By 1920, the Fox Film Corporation (which became 20th Century-Fox in 1935 after a merger) was producing movies featuring major and emerging stars such as the Mae West–like Theda Bara, Betty Blythe (*The Queen of Sheba* [1921]), and Tom Mix, a perennial favorite in Westerns. The studio also favored musicals and, anticipating one of the stranger cinematic phenomena of our own day, spent lots of time producing remakes of "old" movie classics.

Combining the sentimentalism of MGM with a flair for American nostalgia, Fox quickly established its role as a strong contender in the struggle to exploit the country's growing obsession with the movies throughout the 1930s.

Director's Cut

One of Fox's biggest coups was its successful luring of the popular director John Ford away from Universal in the early 1920s. What this meant in practical terms was that the studio would eventually employ Will Rogers, John Wayne, and other hard-hitting Western stars in some of their best roles. The child actress Shirley Temple was also a prodigious (and prolific) moneymaker for Fox.

Other Studio Stalwarts

While MGM, Fox, Warner Bros., and Paramount ruled the roost during Hollywood's heyday, other companies—Columbia, RKO, Universal, United Artists, to name the most important—established their own unique identities and contributed just as much to the culture of cinema.

The financially struggling RKO went into receivership at one point, but kept itself afloat with the dance musicals of Fred Astaire and Ginger Rogers

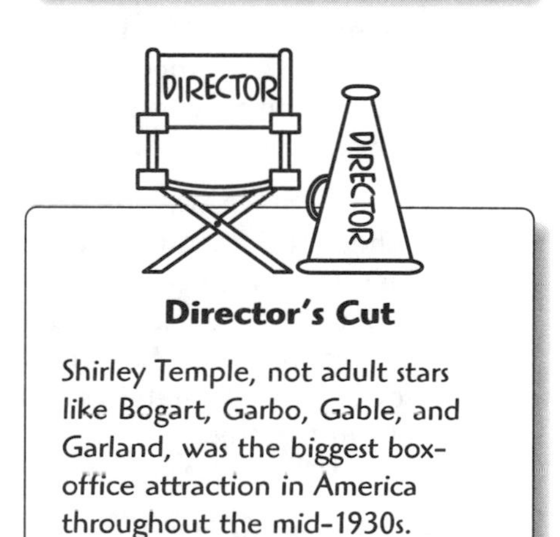

Director's Cut

Shirley Temple, not adult stars like Bogart, Garbo, Gable, and Garland, was the biggest box-office attraction in America throughout the mid-1930s.

as well as a brief stint with John Ford in the mid-1930s. The notorious Harry Cohn, who virtually defined the dictatorial mogul during these years, ran Columbia (founded in 1924) with an iron first, pilfered out-of-favor actors from other studios at bargain prices, and made lots of dough by producing the money-making films of Frank Capra and discovering the talents of Rita Hayworth. (The two most common nicknames Cohn was given by his employees were "Harry the Horror" and "White Fang"). And the always-struggling Universal weighed in with some of the earliest and most successful contributions to the emerging horror genre, including Tod Browning's *Dracula* (1931), starring Bela Lugosi, and James Whale's incomparable *Frankenstein* (also 1931) with Boris Karloff—yet another example of the crucial way in which the studios and the genres marched hand-in-hand across the golden age.

The Auteur Theory

As Hollywood's triumphant era was coming to a close in the early 1950s, the French director François Truffaut (see Chapter 11, "French Revolutions") published an article in a la-dee-da journal called *Cahiers du cinéma* outlining what came to be called the "auteur theory" of film aesthetics. According to this theory, it's the director—the auteur (oh-*tur*), from the French for "author" or other creative genius—who is the controlling artistic force behind any individual film. After Truffaut, the auteur theory became a buzz phrase among international writers on the cinema, who took up the idea and searched out individual directors' works among the massive studio-controlled legacy of Hollywood.

There are many, many problems with the auteur theory, which obscures the nature of film as a truly collaborative artistic enterprise involving dozens of contributors exercising their own particular kinds of talent and artistry—cinematographers, editors, set designers, actors, and so on. But it's no mistake that best director award still comes right before best movie award at the Oscars. Though it should be obvious from other chapters in this book that we think of film as a cooperative art form, the auteur theory is too ingrained in film history and criticism to ignore, and at least it gives us a convenient way to look back, as Truffaut's contemporaries did, at just a handful of the era's directors who were later claimed as auteurs.

D. W. Griffith was the first such director, of course, but he was followed by 20-odd others in the United States who seem to have been able to establish a unique artistic identity within the tight constraints of the studio system—no small task! George Cukor, Michael Curtiz, John Huston, Billy Wilder, a host of European directors (whom you'll read about in Part 3, "The Hundred Languages of Foreign Film"), and several others established directing as the most prestigious and respected dimension of filmmaking.

The Man Who Shot The Man Who Shot Liberty Valance

In Chapter 6, "The Quiet Pleasures of Silent Film," we warned you not to overlook the excellent silent films of John Ford, the Big Daddy of the Western. Ford is most famous these days, of course, for a handful of talkies that defined the classic genre film of Hollywood's golden age. Westerns aren't for everybody, and if you're one of those folks who can't stand the sight of a strong, silent cowboy gazing across the prairie grass or cantering through big sky country to a schmaltzy Go-West-Young-Man tune, these films may not be your cup of tea.

But even in terms of their basic visual impact, Ford's pictures are still stunning. Shot mostly on location and featuring spectacular vistas and landscapes while capable of the most sublime intimacy and detail, Ford's movies continue to captivate new viewers with their romance, pathos, and sheer elegance. With his many Westerns, Ford bulwarked the classic American genre film and preserved a unique image of the West for posterity.

For a representative sampling, treat yourself to a John Ford marathon one night by renting his so-called "Cavalry trilogy," which includes *Fort Apache* (1948), *She Wore a Yellow Ribbon* (1949), and *Rio Grande* (1950); or the four films (not one of them truly a Western, curiously enough) that won him best-director Oscars: *The Informer* (1935), *The Grapes of Wrath* (1940), *How Green Was My Valley* (1941), and *The Quiet Man* (1952).

What you're seeing in these films is vintage Americana, a visual spectacle that represents the most noticeable legacy of Manifest Destiny ("Go West, young man!") to the history of entertainment. Ford's films projected the enduring image of the western frontier as rugged, unforgiving, and cruel, while simultaneously peaceful, natural, and, in a crucial sense, American.

Sir Alfred, King of Suspense

By any measure one of the world's most influential, inventive, and beloved directors, Alfred Hitchcock began his illustrious career in his native England with a string of highly successful suspense films including *The Man Who Knew Too Much* (1934), *The 39 Steps* (1935), and *The Lady Vanishes* (1938), one of his very best. Though Sir Alfred's "British Period" (note the implicit comparison to Picasso) witnessed some of his finest work, however, he was quickly claimed by America upon his move to the States in 1939, and he made his most important later pictures in Hollywood.

Hitchcock's direction is characterized by dazzling camera technique, innovative special effects, and a flair for featuring the grotesque. For example, next time you rent *Psycho,* wait for that fabulous scene when Norman Bates is leaning over the table and talking to the sheriff. See his neck, how birdlike it looks when Norman takes little nibbles of his sandwich? This is vintage Hitchcock, who loved to transform the human body itself into a "readable" object that would reveal the inner motivations and mysteries of his characters.

Hitchcock was also perhaps the only truly great director who made a successful transition to television, the medium that would bring the film industry to its knees in the 1950s (see Chapter 9, "Staying Afloat in the Hollywood Mainstream"), with his popular *Alfred Hitchcock Presents* series between 1955 and 1962.

Anthony Perkins as Norman Bates in Hitchcock's Psycho *(1960).*

Hitchcock directed some true bombs, of course. Anyone who's sat through *The Paradine Case* (1947) or *I Confess* (1953) knows that the master's genius failed him at times. But Hitchcock remains one of the most revered masters of the cinema, a director whose pictures consistently joined artistic brilliance and mass appeal into a film legacy that remains unchallenged for its continuing hold on the vocabulary and imagination of the English-speaking world.

Filmophile's Lexicon

HUAC is short for House Un-American Activities Committee, a temporary panel in the U.S. House of Representatives that terrorized the U.S. film industry in the early 1950s by rooting out real and alleged Communists and attempting to cleanse the business of their allegedly seditious influence.

Of Casts, Commies, and Kazan

The 1999 Academy Awards show featured one of the great film industry controversies of the modern age. Who will ever forget that shot of Nick Nolte defiantly folding his arms and refusing to stand and applaud as Robert De Niro and Martin Scorsese presented a lifetime achievement award to the Turkish-born director Elia Kazan?

Nolte's arms were folded for a quite specific reason: In 1952, Kazan had testified before *HUAC,* the Commie-fighting Congressional committee, during its investigation of alleged Communist influences in the film industry. Unlike some of his less cooperative colleagues,

Kazan named names—and, as a direct result, got a number of actors, directors, and others permanently blacklisted and unable to find work in the business (for more on HUAC and the blacklist, see the next chapter).

We'll leave it to you to judge whether Kazan's politics influenced his films. But whatever your own ideological leanings, don't pass up a chance to watch some of the real gems of American filmdom, from the gritty realism of *On the Waterfront* (1954) to the sentimental Midwest depicted in *Splendor in the Grass* (1961) to the highly personal adaptation of his own novel, *America, America* (1963).

Kazan's greatest directorial gift was his ability to squeeze the greatest possible performances out of his actors, several of whom he truly "discovered" in career-launching ways. Marlon Brando was well known as a stage actor on Broadway, but it was Kazan who made him a movie star by directing his defining and Oscar-winning performance in *A Streetcar Named Desire* (1951). James Dean was another of Kazan's tough-guy leading men, earning an Oscar nomination for one of his only starring roles in a film, Kazan's *East of Eden* (1955), often described as the director's masterpiece.

Mr. Feelgood

When you think of all those one-good-idealistic-man-taking-on-the-corrupt-system flicks from the 1930s and '40s—*Mr. Deeds Goes to Town* (1936), *Mr. Smith Goes to Washington* (1939), and *You Can't Take It With You* (1938), to name just three—there's a good chance you're thinking of the work of Frank Capra, one of the golden age's most successful and popular directors. A Sicilian by birth who emigrated with his family to California early in life, Capra had a rough start to his film career, having directing credits stolen out from under him, getting fired a couple of times, and releasing some real flops in the late '20s.

But after he hooked up with Harry Cohn at Columbia Pictures, Capra's career took off. His films were notable especially for their idealism, which spoke to Americans surviving the Depression (and, later, living in a climate of war) and gave them something to hold on to as the world unraveled around them. Gary Cooper and Jimmy Stewart were among the leading male actors who made his films so successful (and Barbara Stanwyck's career took off after *Ladies of Leisure,* released in 1930), projecting images of the common man fighting

Director's Cut

Frank Capra's most famous and well-known film, *It's A Wonderful Life,* was a commercial and critical failure when it was released in 1946, dismissed as too sentimental and simplistic for moviegoers in the post–World War II 1940s. The reason you've probably seen it is that its copyright lapsed in the 1970s; since then it has become a Christmas season staple on television.

against seemingly insurmountable odds while maintaining a sense of human decency in the bargain.

It's true that Capra, unlike Ford, Hitchcock, and Orson Welles, is not known for having introduced any real technical, directorial, cinematographic, or other aesthetic innovations into film. But Capra won three best director Oscars for feature films and another for a documentary, *Prelude to War* (1942). His pictures gave the nation something it desperately needed during some hard times; for that reason alone he belongs in the pantheon of American film auteurs.

Second Take

Although Orson Welles is generally credited with the brilliant screenplay of *Citizen Kane,* one prominent critic, Pauline Kael, argued (quite controversially) in 1974 that the real kudos for the movie's script belong to Herman Mankiewicz, Welles's cowriter and fellow recipient of that year's Oscar for best screenplay.

"The Greatest"

Consult any list of the best movies of all time (ours, for example! Check out the "Reference Card" at the beginning of this book) and you're sure to see *Citizen Kane* (1941) at or very near the top. This is because *Citizen Kane* represents one of the very finest achievements in film directing. Orson Welles's acclaimed masterpiece featured innovative use of deep focus, voice-overs, multiple narrative perspectives, and an almost modernist story structure, along with flawless acting, a dynamite script, and unprecedented exploitation of the sound medium.

Welles was especially qualified to mess around with sound technology given his background in radio. His notorious broadcast of an adaptation of H. G. Wells's *The War of the Worlds* on Halloween in 1938 convinced half the East Coast that aliens from outer space were invading the country!

Short Cuts

The long opening shot of Brian De Palma's otherwise undistinguished *Snake Eyes* (1998), which pans skillfully around a boxing arena just before an assassination, was intended as a tribute to the opening scene of Orson Welles's *Touch of Evil* (1958).

Welles got into a bit of trouble when the publishing mogul William Randolph Hearst became convinced (probably correctly) that *Citizen Kane* was meant as a swipe at him and his notorious narcissism. Hearst's concerted effort to thwart the release of the film was only partially successful and actually did much in the following years to cement its reputation as such a bold experiment in filmmaking (in the end, even Hearst grudgingly admitted that it was a pretty good flick).

Welles never again achieved the success of *Citizen Kane,* spending the remainder of his career in conflict with studio heads and too broke to make films as quickly as he would have liked. Much of his time in the late 1940s and '50s was spent in Europe pursuing independent production, though he did return to Hollywood briefly to make *Touch of Evil* (1958). Among his other pictures we'd especially recommend this much later film, which has recently been reedited from surviving reels to reflect Welles's original vision. (If you're feeling especially ambitious you might rent both versions for the sake of comparison.)

The story of crime and corruption in a U.S.–Mexican border town, *Touch of Evil* opens with perhaps the most understatedly gripping scene of all time: one of the longest continuous shots that had yet been incorporated into a feature film. And if you're having one of those Welles weeks, don't miss *The Magnificent Ambersons* (1942)—though it, too, was reedited after Welles was done with it and now bears only a pale resemblance to the original.

Hollywood's Not-So-Secret Code

While the HUAC investigations and the morality of the 1950s would eventually exert enormous pressure on filmmakers, 1930s Hollywood had its own values watchdogs. In fact, one of the defining features of golden age Hollywood was its general adherence to the values promulgated in the Motion Picture Production Code (known to film buffs and historians simply as "The Code").

First published in 1930, The Code represented an unprecedented set of prohibitions against certain kinds of content in motion pictures: favorable presentation of adultery or other forms of sexual "deviance," the ridiculing of morality, justice, or religion, the detailed portrayal of brutal killings, morally ambiguous representation of the struggle between good and evil, even sympathy for the bad guys (or, as one provision put it, "*sympathy with a person who sins*").

Today certain sections of The Code read almost like parody (check out the accompanying "Director's Cut" excerpt about locations, for example, which contains some of the most hilarious writing in the history of filmdom—and, if enforced today, would eliminate about 90 percent of the movies out there!). But there can be little doubt that The Code had its intended effect. For years screenwriters, directors, and producers molded their work into a form that would be acceptable to Hollywood's moral police force. For better or worse, The Code created an atmosphere of self-censorship in American film that would last for decades.

Filmophile's Lexicon

The **Hays Office** was shorthand for the Motion Picture Producers and Distributors of America (MPPDA); the name derived from the MPPDA's first and most important head, Will H. Hays, who was primarily responsible for the writing and enforcement of The Code beginning in 1930.

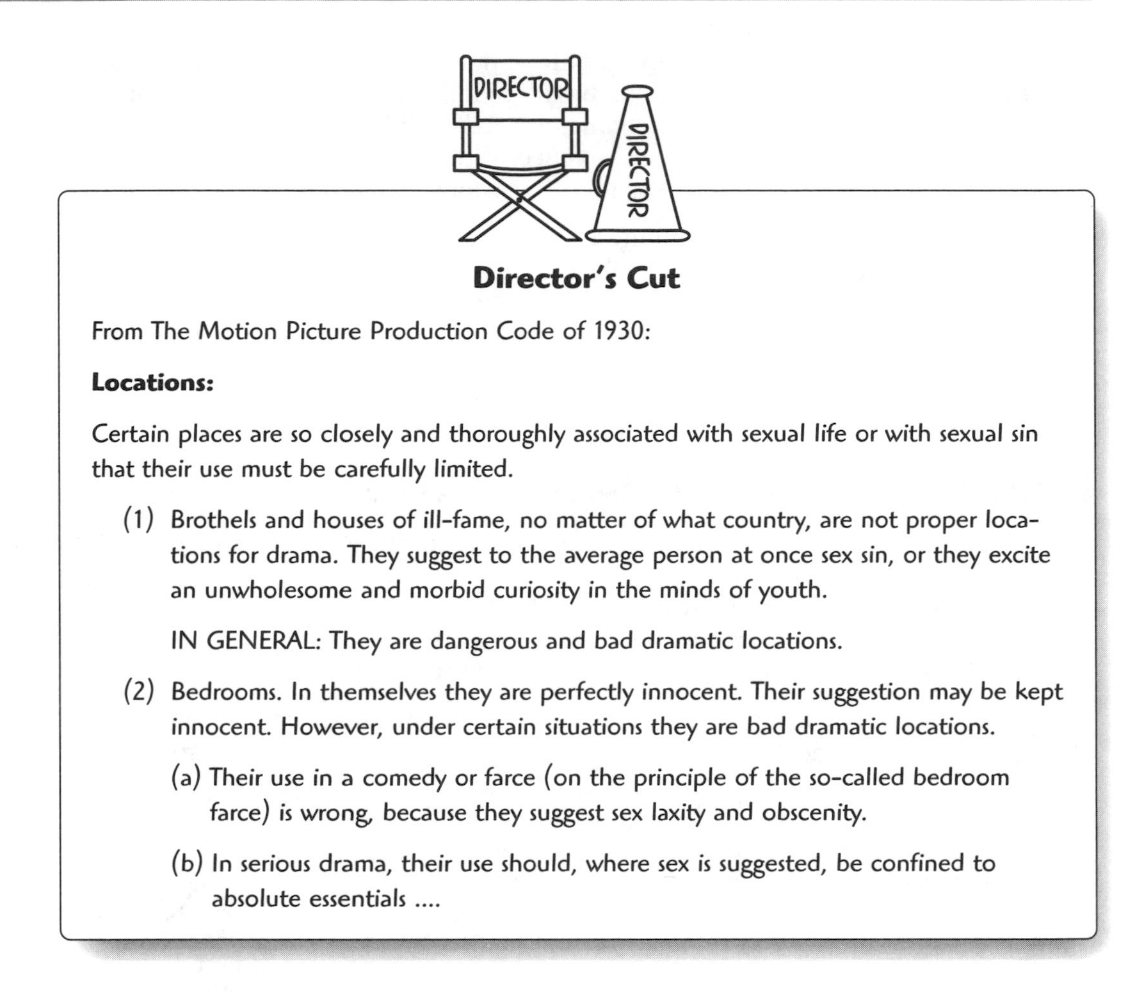

Director's Cut

From The Motion Picture Production Code of 1930:

Locations:

Certain places are so closely and thoroughly associated with sexual life or with sexual sin that their use must be carefully limited.

(1) Brothels and houses of ill-fame, no matter of what country, are not proper locations for drama. They suggest to the average person at once sex sin, or they excite an unwholesome and morbid curiosity in the minds of youth.

IN GENERAL: They are dangerous and bad dramatic locations.

(2) Bedrooms. In themselves they are perfectly innocent. Their suggestion may be kept innocent. However, under certain situations they are bad dramatic locations.

(a) Their use in a comedy or farce (on the principle of the so-called bedroom farce) is wrong, because they suggest sex laxity and obscenity.

(b) In serious drama, their use should, where sex is suggested, be confined to absolute essentials ....

Face Time: Actors and Actresses in the Golden Age

While the studios, the genres, the moguls, the directors, and The Code fundamentally shaped the culture of American cinema in the 1930s and '40s, few of us would deny that we still tend to think about and remember the era through its stars: the actors and actresses who brought the directors' visions to life. Burt Lancaster and Deborah Kerr rolling around on the beach in *From Here to Eternity* (1953), Rita Hayworth's bewitching smile in *Gilda* (1946), the laconic smirk of Robert Mitchum: The era speaks to us across the decades through the faces and voices of those who filled its screens and the nation's hearts with a quintessentially American longing.

In fact, there are so many great actors and actresses who symbolize this cinematic era that it would be impossible to do justice to even a fraction of them here, let alone give you four or five to choose from.

Rita Hayworth's dazzling smile from Gilda *(1946).*

Six Simple Star-Gazing Strategies

What we'll do instead is give you a few hints about how to get a feel for actors and actresses and their work, to become knowledgeable about the entire span of an actor's career rather than a few famous films everyone already knows.

- Go to the local public library and find a reference book containing a reliable and complete listing of your actor's or actress's films, organized by the years in which they were released (Ephraim Katz's *Film Encyclopedia* might be the most convenient, though there are many others that will suit).
- With a photocopy of the list in hand, highlight the films you've already seen and circle those you haven't.
- Choose three films from the list that you haven't seen: one from the very beginning of the star's career, a second from the middle years, and a third from among the last two or three films he or she made. Set aside a weekend to rent and view these three movies all at once. Repeat the same process the following weekend with three other pictures.
- While you're watching, think about your actor's visual style: Does he or she have any specific facial "ticks" that repeat themselves from film to film, or is each performance uniquely its own? Are there certain gestures, laughs, smiles, tilts of the head, eye-squints, tones of voice, and so on that the actor likes to

incorporate at certain moments? If so, do you think he or she does so consciously or unconsciously? Finally, what specific factors allow you to distinguish a good or just barely adequate performance from a truly great one?

- Choose your two or three favorite films from what you've seen. Now go back to the reference section at the library and identify a handful of films made by the same director during the same years but *not* starring your actor. Watching these films will give you a good sense of what's unique about your actor's idiosyncrasies during a specific time period, within an individual director's oeuvre, and so on, as well as how much the director had to do with the level of the performance.
- Start over. This time, though, repeat the entire process with a "minor" star—a brilliant character actor like, say, Hattie McDaniel (why not compare her films before and after *Gone With the Wind?*), or a B-movie star such as, well, Ronald Reagan.

Widening the scope of your star-gazing beyond the blockbuster hits and the marquee names will allow you to acquire a richer and more discriminating knowledge of American filmmaking in the golden age.

The Least You Need to Know

- The introduction of sound in the late 1920s fundamentally changed the culture and aesthetics of film.
- The 1930s were the triumphant years for the big American studios like MGM, Fox, Universal, and Paramount.
- The golden age solidified the genre film, making Westerns, horror flicks, musicals, and many others staples of American filmdom.
- The concept of the director as original artist or auteur arose along with the cult of the director.
- The Production Code of 1930 exerted a massive influence on the moral content of American movies.
- The art of acting became a respected and revered part of the culture of film.

Chapter 8

The Decline and Fall of the Studio Empire

In This Chapter

- *Singin' in the Rain:* a jaundiced view
- Television's challenges to the film industry
- McCarthyism and the Hollywood witch hunt
- The changing economy of American movies
- The rise of the independent producer and director
- Foreign influences on American filmmaking

"Greater commercial empires than that of Hollywood have crumbled and sunk beneath the sea."—Gilbert Seldes, *The Movies in Peril* (1935)

Seldes's words of warning, published in *Scribner's Magazine* just a few years into the era of sound, were truly prophetic. World War II was a boom time for Hollywood, with the industry churning out massive numbers of propaganda films and escapist flicks aimed at getting the nation through the long struggle in Europe and on the Pacific. In the immediate aftermath of the war, it seemed that the American film business was thriving as never before; 1946 was the most financially profitable year in movie history, and the future appeared filled with endless opportunities for further growth and unprecedented success.

But change was on its way—and, most immediately, the change was for the worse. In the decade following 1945, Hollywood was repeatedly hit by a series of social, political, economic, and artistic disasters that left the industry knocked on its heels as never before. If the golden age of American moviemaking (even during the Depression) was an era of growth, greed, and gold, the post–World War II years were characterized by equal measures of retrenchment, paranoia, and failure.

In order to understand the implications of these problems for the movies themselves, you need to learn to watch films from this period through the sometimes opaque lens of their historical moment. Let's begin by giving you a quick example of what we mean.

Singin' in the (Acid) Rain

On June 25, 1950, the North Korean army crossed the 38th Parallel and invaded the south, compelling Pres. Harry Truman to mobilize U.S. troops in what would come to be called the Korean War. The following April, Gen. Douglas MacArthur was relieved of his command of American troops fighting in Korea by President Truman, who was angered by MacArthur's public criticism of his administration's cautious approach to the war. That same month, after a controversial and internationally visible trial, Julius and Ethel Rosenberg were convicted of spying for the Soviet Union and sentenced to death. And in November 1952, the United States exploded the first hydrogen bomb at the Enewetak Atoll in the Pacific.

It was also in 1952 that Gene Kelly appeared in *Singin' in the Rain*. A lighthearted musical featuring Kelly's famous "rain dance" on a Hollywood street, *Singin'* was a dazzling commercial success, reaping accolades from the public and the industry alike for its silky-smooth musical numbers and its seemingly self-conscious narrative of the advent of sound in motion pictures (the movie is set in the late 1920s, just as sound was sweeping the industry). For many film historians, *Singin' in the Rain* remains the greatest movie musical of all time.

So what do the Korean War, MacArthur, the Rosenbergs, and the hydrogen bomb have to do with *Singin' in the Rain?* Absolutely nothing—and absolutely everything.

What's notable about this film, along with innumerable others from early 1950s Hollywood, is its success in avoiding any direct engagement with the momentous historical events that surrounded it. One of the messages of the mainstream Hollywood film from this period, and especially the wildly popular musical genre, is that entertainment can substitute for an analysis of or engagement with contemporary politics and world events. In this sense, *Singin' in the Rain* provides an ideal example of the kind of head-in-the-sand avoidance practiced by many American moviemakers during this era.

When Gene Kelly sings to the nation that he's "laughin' at the clouds so dark up above," it's easy to interpret those "clouds" as potent symbols of specific historical problems: as the thousands of American soldiers dying in the Korean War each month, as the threat of thermonuclear annihilation, as the nation's painful internal and external struggle with Communism. *Singin' in the Rain,* set decades earlier during the transition to talkies, is about the movie industry just before the Depression: The film looks back nostalgically at the 1920s and, in a quite literal sense, encourages its audience to use the movies to help them laugh at the daunting problems facing the nation and the world.

Gene Kelly's carefree umbrella dance from Singin' in the Rain *(1952).*

To "read" *Singin' in the Rain* this way might seem unfair. After all, it's just a flick, right? Why should we expect it to try to do anything more than entertain us?

Well, sure. And it would be an exaggeration to say that Hollywood avoided all engagement with difficult social problems during these years. Fred Zinnemann's *From Here to Eternity* (1953), for example, dealt with alcoholism, hazing, adultery, and low morale among the nation's soldiers on the eve of the American entry into World War II.

But like *From Here to Eternity,* most films that did tackle difficult subject matter were set in an era much earlier than the contemporary 1950s. And what's truly astonishing about the vast majority of mainstream films from this era is the sheer lengths to which they'll go not to do or say anything remotely controversial or unsafe. While the same era witnessed the rise of new independent producers and directors who faced society's ills head-on (see the list later in the chapter), for the most part the Hollywood studios studiously avoided the political arena even as the world was changing drastically around them.

Hollywood's Headaches (and HUACHes)

While the world at large was experiencing unprecedented conflicts and crises, Hollywood endured its own economic and cultural nadir. The factors that made post–World War II American filmmaking so troubled were many, though it's relatively easy to identify the most immediate and major causes of Hollywood's headaches. Between television and Commie-hunters, Tinsel Town stared hard at itself and emerged from the '50s with its reputation only partially intact. Here's why.

The Curse of the Little Black Box

For those of us living in the modern industrialized world, "going to the movies" is a social activity that involves getting out of the house, traveling to a specific kind of retail establishment, and sitting for two or more hours taking in a film projected through a dark theater onto a white screen in front of a (usually decent-sized) audience.

Director's Cut

"We are about to enter what can be the most difficult competition imaginable with a form of entertainment in which all the best features of radio, the theater, and motion pictures may be combined. Today there are 56 television stations on the air, with 66 additional stations in process of construction. The chairman of the Federal Communications Commission points out that by 1951 there may be 400 stations in operation. There are now 950,000 receiving sets installed, sets are being produced at the rate of 160,000 per month and next year that rate will be doubled. Soon there will be a potential audience of 50 million people or more.

Here we have the development that will change the whole entertainment business. Fifty million Americans will be able to sit at home and take their choice of visiting the ball park, the prize-fight matches, the wrestling bouts, the legitimate theater, and the motion pictures without stirring from their own living rooms. It is going to require something truly superior to cause them not only to leave their homes to be entertained, but to pay for that entertainment."

—Samuel Goldwyn, "Hollywood in the Television Age," *Hollywood Quarterly*, Winter 1949/1950

"Watching a movie," on the other hand, is most likely done at home (or at someone else's home). Per day, for every American who goes to a cinema to watch a film on screen, something in the neighborhood of *50* Americans rent a movie from Blockbuster, purchase a pay-per-view showing, or watch a movie broadcast on network or cable television. What this means is that only 2 percent of Americans enjoying a movie today, as you read this, will do so in a commercial theater designed for that purpose.

In 1950, that figure was almost 100 percent.

Most of the studio executives in early 1950s Hollywood knew at least on some level what was coming, though very few of them realized that the impact of television on the motion picture industry would be quite so immediate, lasting, and profound. Samuel Goldwyn, one of the founders of MGM, was one of the most prophetic, proclaiming as early as 1949 that "Motion pictures are entering their third major era. First there was the silent period. Then the sound era. Now we are on the threshold of the television age."

Goldwyn wasn't exaggerating. Television's effect on the film industry was hard, fast, and nasty. But the little black box was only one of Hollywood's postwar headaches.

HUAC and the "Hollywood Ten"

In the fall of 1947, as the nation reveled in its victory over world fascism, a group of prominent artists from the American film industry were hauled before the House of Representative's Committee on Un-American Activities, or HUAC. (This committee was the House's answer to Joe McCarthy's red-baiting Senate panel.) The "Hollywood Ten," as these film figures came to be known, included Alvah Bessie, Herbert Biberman, Lester Cole, Edward Dmytryk, Ring Lardner Jr., John Howard Lawson, Albert Maltz, Samuel Ornitz, Adrian Scott, and Dalton Trumbo. All of these artists—producers, directors, and screenwriters—refused to cooperate with HUAC in divulging their political affiliations; as a result, they were tried in federal court, convicted of contempt, and sentenced to a year in prison (only Edward Dmytryk later cooperated). Even worse, they were permanently "blacklisted" by the industry as Communist sympathizers or partisans, and their careers in American moviemaking were almost completely destroyed.

In 1951, HUAC began an even larger investigation of alleged Communist infiltration of Hollywood, hauling dozens of industry leaders in front of the committee and forcing them to choose between cooperating fully or being condemned as a Communist sympathizer, blacklisting anyone suspected of potentially subversive behavior. Friendly witnesses during this second round of hearings included Lee J. Cobb, Elia Kazan, Clifford Odets, Jack Warner, Louis B. Mayer, Adolph Menjou, John Wayne, and Gary Cooper. Unfriendly witnesses included Zero Mostel and, initially, at least, Humphrey Bogart, Lauren Bacall, and others. The Red Scare (shorthand for America's weird obsession with Communism during this era) devastated the American film industry, robbing it of many of its top talents and creating the lowest morale in cinema history. Given the anticommunist fervor of these years, it's not at all surprising that many Hollywood films, while not engaging the problem head-on, disguised a blatantly anti-Red message under seemingly innocuous plot lines, creating an often disturbing synchronicity between film and real life. For example, Gary Cooper (like Ronald Reagan) volunteered enthusiastically during the 1947 hearings to aid HUAC in its Hollywood witch hunt. A few years later, Cooper starred in Fred Zinnemman's *High Noon* (1952), a transparent (albeit quite entertaining!) piece of Cold War propaganda that depicts Cooper as sheriff of a small Western town battling the ever-growing forces of evil. *High Noon* was released at the height of the Korean War; it's pretty easy to see how the image of Gary Cooper "standing alone" against the forces of evil in the American West mirrors in miniature the larger American struggle against Communist North Korea in Asia.

Short Cuts

Some films were quite transparent in their red-baiting. One hilarious movie that you just *have* to rent one night is Leo McCarey's *My Son John* (1952), the story of a warm 'n' fuzzy '50s couple that begins suspecting its son of Communism. The angst-ridden familial struggle that ensues creates a real howler.

The nation's underlying anxieties about Communism are also clearly apparent in the newly popular horror and science fiction film (*Invasion of the Body Snatchers* [1956], *The Blob* [1958])—sort of "Communist from Another Planet," if you will; and, especially, in *film noir,* in which evil is imagined as hidden inside of the individual, just as larger sinister forces are hidden inside society.

Like The Production Code but in very different ways, the industry's and the country's protracted struggle against a Communist threat that it perceived as ubiquitous created a climate of fear, intimidation, moral superiority, and repression from which it took decades to recover.

Filmophile's Lexicon

Film noir (literally, "black film") is a term used to describe a type of picture that arose in the late 1940s featuring dark, pessimistic, stingy atmospheres, the gloomy underbelly of society, and the life-cheapening consequences of crime, corruption, and hopelessness.

Hollywood's Changing Economy

A third extremely daunting challenge facing Hollywood after World War II was a financial one. As a result of many related economic factors—shrinking audiences fleeing to television, famous stars demanding more money for each picture, and foreign embargoes on American films—the industry faced an unprecedented commercial crisis. The government's antitrust suits against the major studios resulted in a large-scale divorce of production companies from their lucrative theater holdings, and by the mid-1950s increasing production and distribution costs had virtually bankrupted some of the industry's former leaders.

This is not to say that all moviemakers were financially strapped; in fact, some studios, such as MGM, made more money than ever before in these years. But decline was inevitable, and American moviedom had some tough choices to make about the course of its future.

Flirting (but Coping) with Disaster

Confronted with unprecedented cultural, technological, and political challenges to its very existence, the American film industry had to act. That it did so mostly successfully is a testament to the continuing ingenuity of the business's leaders, who have always been adept at finding their way around the often formidable obstacles in their path.

A Wider View

One of Goldwyn's solutions to the television threat—essentially "if you can't beat 'em, join 'em!"—had its advantages. But many in the industry also believed that, for sheer visual spectacle and awe, the black box in the living room would never be able to compete with the big-as-a-house silver screen. To make the cinema remain a viable option, however, they felt strongly that some things had to change, and especially the ways audiences actually experienced an evening at the cinema. The result was a proliferation of new technologies aimed at heightening the sensual and experiential dimensions of the movies—though only a few of these "innovations" lasted longer than a few years or even months.

Director's Cut

Bwana Devil (1952), directed by Arch Oboler, was the first commercially released 3-D feature film. Its African setting hosts a series of attacks by angry (and hungry) lions upon a group of railroad laborers.

For example, 3-D movies, though seemingly full of promise in terms of their ability to add depth of field to practically any projected image, quickly fizzled out after their introduction in the early 1950s, though they've occasionally been revived for publicity's sake, as in *Friday the 13th, Part 3* (1982). Other experiments that now inevitably bring smiles to our lips include "pansensory" cinema, designed to appeal to more than the two senses of sight and sound employed by audiences taking in a picture. "Aroma-Rama" was invented by a guy named Charles Weiss and first used for a documentary about China, *Behind the Great Wall* (1959). In this system, the "scents of the Orient," as the film's perhaps less-than-brilliant makers claimed, were piped into the theater through the cinema's heating ducts so that everyone could smell what they were seeing.

The main TV-fighting project that did pan out in the end was the introduction of the wide screen and the technologies that made it possible. The first innovator here was Henry Chrétien, a French inventor who had developed the *anamorphic lens* in the 1920s.

Though there had been occasional experiments with the technique in the decades following Chrétien's initial invention of it, it was only in 1952 that Twentieth-Century Fox bought the anamorphic lens and, using the technology it relabeled as CinemaScope, began shooting films with much wider shots than ever before possible. The result was a new ability to fill a rectangular screen with an amazing horizontal array of images and thus to pack each shot with "more stuff": lovers could stand farther apart but still be shot in close-up during a quarrel, an action sequence could involve more characters doing more things, a wider and more detail-friendly gauge of film could be used in shooting, and so on.

Soon the other major studios were following in Fox's footsteps: Paramount's Vista Vision was a close second, followed by MGM's wildly successful Panavision and Super Panavision, which allowed filmmakers to use 65mm film (a very wide gauge) while eliminating distortion. The initial result was William Wyler's *Ben-Hur* (1959), the first movie shot with the new Super Panavision technique. That chariot race near the end wouldn't be nearly as exciting without the wide-screen anamorphic technology first developed by Chrétien. In fact, some video versions of *Ben-Hur* even switch to wide-screen format just for this scene, changing the viewing area on your television from a square to a rectangle in the blink of an eye!

Filmophile's Lexicon

Anamorphic lenses distort images in the process of filming them but straighten them out again during projection. An **anamorphosis** is any visual object, such as a painting (Hans Holbein's *The Ambassadors* [1533] is a famous example), in which a certain image comes into focus from a particular angle while remaining invisible or obscure from others.

Director's Cut

For his 1981 comedy and first feature film, *Polyester*, John Waters designed a scratch-and-sniff card in an experiment he called "Odorama" (perhaps in tribute to earlier experiments in cinematic sniffing such as Smell-O-Vision and Aroma-Rama).

The famous chariot race from Ben-Hur *(1959), shot in Super Panavision.*

But the black box had done its damage. Of course, television didn't kill the movies; today the American film industry (despite some recent negative signs) is as successful as ever, and few of us prefer sitting home on the couch to experiencing a first-week showing on a 30-foot screen. Nevertheless, the business had to go to great and often costly lengths to adapt to the new entertainment medium, even to the extent of releasing many films in "straight-to-video" format—the ultimate Hollywood heresy.

Second Take

One of the problems created by odoriferous cinema technologies was the issue of simply getting rid of scents after the relevant scene was over. How is the audience supposed to smell the fine Stilton cheese if wafts of methane remain in the air? This was a simple problem that created a real stumbling block for the proponents of Smell-O-Vision, Aroma-Rama, and the like.

Dodging the Red-Baiting Bullet

If mainstream Hollywood responded to television with technology and wishful thinking, it met HUAC with a fascinating mixture of revulsion, elusiveness, and propaganda. Some blacklisted artists continued to work in the industry, often secretly aided by sympathetic colleagues. For example, Dalton Trumbo came up with the story line for *Roman Holiday* (1953), the wonderful Hepburn-Peck vehicle directed by William Wyler, but the screenplay writer Ian McLellan Hunter fronted for him to keep him out of trouble. And Trumbo's original screenplay for Irving Rapper's *The Brave One* (1956) won an Oscar for the pseudonymous Robert Rich, deeply embarrassing the uptight industry.

One thing Hollywood didn't do, though, was actually deal with the HUAC problem in film itself. The first comedy on the subject didn't come out until 1976. *The Front,* starring Woody Allen as a pathetic front man substituting his name for blacklisted writers, is a hilarious must-see treatment of the industry's red-baiting that included a number of blacklisted personalities in its illustrious cast.

During the 1950s, though, comedy was one way precisely to *avoid* the issues that HUAC had brought to the surface. If the screwball comedies of the 1930s and early '40s dealt in a mystifying way with the Depression or World War II (think of Chaplin's 1940 performance in *The Great Dictator*), the 1950s stopped dealing in any critically overt way with just about any real social problems at all. Only a very small number of specifically designated "social problem" films dealt with anything substantive: Kazan's racial "passing" drama *Pinky* (1949) treated race relations in the South, for example, while the James Dean film *Rebel Without a Cause* (1955) grappled with the dissatisfaction and rebelliousness of contemporary youth.

Another glitzier way of submitting to the limitation on the amount of social criticism that could come out of Hollywood was simply to celebrate the limitations by purposefully avoiding any possibility of political entanglement. If serious issues were becoming increasingly taboo, especially in the early '50s, then one could celebrate in a self-conscious way the return to entertainment as a positive value rather than as criticism—and this is what films like *Singin' in the Rain* (and *Meet Me in St. Louis* [1944], *Take Me Out to the Ball Game* [1949], and so on) are all about. In fact, the musical as a genre celebrated light-hearted enjoyment and gay spontaneity as simply the best way to live.

Independence Days

This is not to say that post–World War II American moviemaking was all about saying nothing socially important—in fact, quite the contrary. While studio Hollywood suffered under the twin watchdogs of The Code and HUAC, a handful of more daring, largely independent producers and directors arose who would permanently change the moral face of American filmdom. A huge anti-trust crackdown on the industry enabled the "resurgence" of the independent filmmaker in the United States in the late 1940s and '50s, when directors and stars embarked on their own projects for which they created their own production companies—and thus paving the way for the "New Hollywood" of the 1960s and '70s (see Chapter 10, "The American Independent Film).

Mostly unaffiliated with or only temporarily under the control of the major studios, this period's filmmakers were the immediate forebears of the independent film extravaganza that began in the 1960s with Stanley Kubrick and Woody Allen and continues into our own day with *The Blair Witch Project* and *Boys Don't Cry*. Here are a few of these mavericks' names and films to watch out for from the 15 years following the end of the war:

- After being "unsigned" by Columbia in 1954, **Stanley Kramer** defined the early independent film artist but with mixed results; we recommend *The Defiant Ones* (1958), a racial drama with lots of twists, and *On the Beach* (1959), a tense drama about a group of Aussies waiting for the deadly fallout to arrive from a worldwide nuclear holocaust.

- **Otto Preminger** had a cushy deal with Fox but turned independent in the early 1950s and promptly made the intentionally Code-defying *The Moon Is Blue* (1953), the first Hollywood movie to use words like (goodness!) *pregnant, virgin,* and so on; in 1955 he came back with *The Man with the Golden Arm* (1955), which features Frank Sinatra as a heroin addict.
- **Nicholas Ray** directed James Dean in *Rebel Without a Cause* in 1955 just after releasing the send-up Western *Johnny Guitar* (1954), which featured Joan Crawford in one of her greatest roles as a raunchy barkeeper in the Old West.
- A true political and artistic maverick, **Samuel Fuller** (a cult figure even today) had Code-busting fun with the violent and seamier sides of life in films like *Fixed Bayonets* (1951), *Forty Guns* (1957), and *The Crimson Kimono* (1959).
- Born in Wisconsin, **Joseph Losey** was blacklisted from the American film industry after the 1951 HUAC hearings and so went to England, where he made such gems as *The Sleeping Tiger* (1954), *Finger of Guilt* (1956), *Chance Meeting* (1959), and, slightly later, *The Servant* (1963).
- German-born **Douglas Sirk**'s jaundiced view of American culture transformed the stock melodrama into cultural criticism with heavy doses of irony in *Magnificent Obsession* (1954), *The Tarnished Angels* (1958), and *Written on the Wind* (1957).

Second Take

Be sure not to avoid the work of the small but talented postwar American avant-garde, part of a worldwide underground cinema movement constantly in tension with the studio mainstream. The Santa Barbara–born experimental film icon Kenneth Anger made *Fireworks* (1947), *Puce Moment* (1949), *Inauguration of the Pleasure Dome* (1954), and other hard-to-find pictures decades ahead of their time, while James Broughton's *Mother's Day* (1948) and *The Happy Lover* (1951) feature visually arresting experiments in cinematography and camerawork.

Foreign Factors

One of the other important pieces of information you need to know about post–World War II Hollywood is the increasingly crucial aesthetic role of foreign film in the producing and directing of American movies. While the industry had greedily absorbed the world's cinematic talent during the silent era, beginning in the late '40s this process began to reverse itself. American producers and directors now began to look around at the cinematic world and were finally willing to learn from the techniques of other nations' talents without sucking them into the Hollywood vortex.

A critical factor in this increasing internationalization of cinema was the rise of the film festival. Directors such as Luis Buñuel, Japan's Akira Kurosawa, Sweden's Ingmar Bergman, and India's Satyajit Ray (you'll read all about these directors in

Part 3, "The Hundred Languages of Foreign Film") won awards at Cannes, Venice, and other important festivals, exposing their work to a much wider audience of critics and industry leaders.

Some of the economic factors we discussed earlier were also responsible for exposing American film personnel to foreign innovations. As a result of the sporadic economic embargoes against U.S. films throughout the 1950s, directors had to shoot their pictures more and more often in Europe, a process that culminated a few decades later: By the mid-1970s, *more than 50 percent of American movies were not being made in this country*—an extraordinary change from just 20 years earlier.

The Least You Need to Know

- Hollywood movies from the post–World War II era had a confusing and difficult relationship to world and national events.
- The arrival and spread of television in the early 1950s had devastating effects on the movie industry.
- The HUAC investigations demoralized American filmdom, while the declining financial fortunes of the major studios changed the nature of film production.
- Hollywood responded to the television assault with new technologies, including Panavision and CinemaScope.
- A host of independent producers and directors emerged as a result of the studios' difficulties.
- American moviemaking began to be influenced significantly by foreign film.

Chapter 9

Staying Afloat in the Hollywood Mainstream

In This Chapter

- Being a businessperson and an artist
- Defining insiders, outsiders, and players
- Who is outside the loop
- Listing the players and some of their films

This is not the chapter in which we discuss the best directors of all time, but the most visible mainstream filmmakers of *this* time (some of whom may be really good directors). The categories we are avoiding are the one-hit wonders, the legendary-but-recently-dead (Stanley Kubrick), and the independent directors (see Chapter 10, "The American Independent Film," for more information about these people).

With one or two ambiguous examples (is Terry Gilliam, of Monty Python fame, American or British? Who can tell? They're still trying to figure that one out for Henry James and T. S. Eliot), we are sticking to American directors, or at least directors working in the American film industry. Essentially, we are focusing on the box-office boffos: Hollywood or Hollywood-style filmmakers who are the hottest selling tickets right *now*.

Yes, But Is It Art?

The works of Michelangelo and Shakespeare are easy to figure out: Everything they did is art. Steven Spielberg's work is a little less traditionally straightforward to talk about this way. Okay, *Schindler's List* (1993) and *The Color Purple* (1985) are serious works, so they may be art. But what about *The Money Pit* (1986) and *Joe Versus the Volcano* (1990), not the most unforgettable works ever made, and for which he was simply the executive producer? Can you look at even these films seriously? (The correct answer is yes, because you can examine the meaning of anything produced by human beings.) Is it as rewarding to look at these films? And finally, how do contemporary Hollywood directors fit into the category of artist?

Second Take

We are a list-making, hierarchicalizing culture that always needs to know what's best. But ranking art—even (perhaps especially) popular culture art—doesn't work this way. What's better: da Vinci's Mona Lisa or Michelangelo's David? What's better: *The Taming of the Shrew* or *Citizen Kane?* The questions can make for fun conversation, but don't take them too seriously.

Who Really Decides What Films Get Made?

Though we will be discussing mainly contemporary directors in this chapter, it's important to remember that most of the real power is invested in the CEOs and other chief executives of the largest studios and ancillary corporations. Even after the erosion of the classical studio system in the 1950s and '60s, even after the various kinds of trust-busting in the twentieth century, even after the phenomenal salaries of stars and increasing visibility of directors, it is still the case that ideas follow money, and money is distributed by heads of corporations.

Again, there is no way to directly index the kinds of films made with desires of the CEOs at the top. The official story is always that a good idea eventually gets produced. But don't you wonder a little bit why, if that's the case, there seem to be so few good ideas in Hollywood and so much junk? Never mind whether films are too violent or sexual. (Try reading *The Odyssey* or the Bible all the way through sometime.) It's tough to find films that even have good dialogue. Our suspicion is that the illiteracy of much American film derives from the semiliteracy of businessmen who have no time or desire to read.

The essentially noncreative people who call the shots include the following:

- John Calley, chairman, Sony Pictures Entertainment.
- Michael Eisner, chairman-CEO, The Walt Disney Company.
- Alan Horn, president, Warner Brothers.
- Jeffrey Katzenberg, partner, DreamWorks (with Steven Spielberg).
- Ron Meyer, president, Universal Studios.
- Rupert Murdoch, chairman-CEO, News Corp., owner of Fox movie studio.

- Tom Rothman, president, Twentieth Century Fox Film Group.
- Alex Yemenidjian, chairman-CEO, Metro-Goldwyn-Mayer (MGM).

These people are mainly studio executives. They are considered the major power brokers in Hollywood at the present moment. But chief executives at talent agencies, parent companies, and other related industry corporations also wield power.

Filmophile's Lexicon

Insider: A person in the Hollywood system, either on the talent side or on the administrative or executive side.

Outsider: Someone not in the Hollywood loop. Often a term of contempt applied to people trying to get into the system.

Player: Someone with power in the Hollywood loop.

Creative People Who Call the Shots

The only real way, then, for the "talent" to exercise more or less complete control from beginning to end is to take over administrative and executive control. The most spectacularly successful examples of this strategy have, without doubt, been Steven Spielberg and George Lucas. We will discuss them at greater length later in this chapter, but it's worth noting here that part of their tremendous success is attributable to their founding of their own corporations, like Amblin Entertainment and Industrial Light and Magic. This strategy, when successful, helps solve the problem of the independent director who does not want to be in the system, but who then has to spend 90 percent of his or her time raising money, and 10 percent actually making a film. (This is no exaggeration.)

Sometimes the ownership is a headache for talent, as Francis Ford Coppola's on-again, off-again relationship with Zoetrope films demonstrates.

At an only slightly less grandiose level, many stars and directors opt to move in the producer's seat, again to gain more authority. This more ambitious talent includes Robert Redford, Jodie Foster, Martin Scorsese, Tom Hanks, and so on.

The essentially creative people who call the shots include:

- James Cameron, paradigmatic Hollywood director and producer.
- George Lucas, founder, Industrial Light and Magic, the premiere special (digital) effects company.
- Steven Spielberg, who controls DreamWorks film division.

Director's Cut

Cameron, Lucas, and Spielberg together are responsible for six of the top 10 grossing movies of all time. These are, in order, *Titanic* (1997), *Star Wars* (1977), *Star Wars: The Phantom Menace* (1999), *E.T.: The Extraterrestrial* (1982), *Jurassic Park* (1993), and *Return of the Jedi* (1983).

What Is a Hollywood "Insider"?

Some of the filmmakers we will be discussing or alluding to in this chapter are central players in the Los Angeles film industry (such as Barry Sonnenfeld), while others are marginal figures, having just arrived from the independent scene but hoping to make it with mainstream films. Some filmmakers have a mixed relation to the film industry in a variety of ways. Some, like Woody Allen, maintain more autonomy than many directors because they work on smaller budgets and so are less beholden to the stockholders. Others, like Scorsese, love Hollywood movies but are still mavericks and outsiders, despite the fact of having made hit after hit. A couple, like Terry Gilliam, make blockbuster hits and are big players, but are outside the Hollywood loop completely. (Gilliam is now a British citizen.)

This difficulty in determining who is a Hollywood insider is disturbing for supporters of the independent film sector. Many critics see the indies as being appropriated by mainstream producers and studios. For example, when the Sundance Film Festival was founded by Robert Redford in 1984, it was held in a little town in Utah, in part because Utah seems as far away from Hollywood in sensibility as Thailand. But the festival has turned out so many successful directors that studios and moguls from the Hollywood sector of the industry show up to scout the up-and-coming talent and whisk them away to La La Land and big studio contracts. Some directors, such as Quentin Tarantino, seek this out; others don't. Others, like feminist filmmaker Lizzie Borden, are ambivalent, liking the economic support but hating the creative constraints.

Who Makes It?

There is a historical irony in the fact that Hollywood is still white and male. As historians have recently been at pains to point out, the Hollywood film industry began (after the era of white-guy inventors like Edison) as a decidedly ethnic phenomenon. And women found great good places as professionals: directors, writers, and so on.

This occurred because establishment, post-Victorian America thought of the flickers as a vulgar, passing fad. On discovering they were wrong, Hollywood slowly became the same white male domain that the rest of corporate America was until the 1960s.

Today, minority representation in Hollywood works a little as it does in sports, where, though so many star players are black, very few are working in the front office in positions of managerial power. Though there are still a disproportionately small number of African Americans who get to be major stars (and fewer Latinos and Asians), the figures are somewhat better than they were 20 years ago. But ownership, production, and direction are still much more disproportionately white. It is of course difficult to say with absolute assurance what effect this has on films themselves, but it is still the case that films starring African American males are all too often still about violence, or sex, or sports.

Power and authority in Hollywood is still a masculine domain.

Miscellaneous Concerns

Power can be very brief in Hollywood, generally lasting about as long as your last hit. Three flops and you're out. Or even one really big flop.

From the 1960s to the 1980s, Hollywood was worried that its properties were being bought out by outside concerns. Sometimes the companies were American multinationals: Warner Brothers became Time-Warner. Sometimes the worry was xenophobic, as when the Japanese Sony Corporation started becoming interested in American filmmaking. But the history of Hollywood has been the history of outside funding sources from small investors to banks making films possible. Our sense is that a very insulated Hollywood executive elite gets worried about takeovers more from a worry about their own jobs than because of the health of the industry as a whole.

Director's Cut

Heaven's Gate (1980) director Michael Cimino was a star director until the box-office flop of this hugely expensive fiasco, which was universally panned and then pulled from theaters three days after its general release. It took years for him to resume a career, which never peaked again. Ironically, the film is actually a pretty good and serious drama.

Film industry power brokers are by turns worried and elated by the economic impact on the industry of cable television, the VCR revolution, the increasing sophistication of the internet, and other technological innovations. The largest concern is to take over some of these sectors before these sectors (especially the newer technologies) threaten to take over Hollywood.

The Categories

We will break up these Hollywood players into four camps:

- White guys.
- Women.
- Players of color.
- New kids on the block.

Most of these people have real executive as well as directorial power. Most for example have been producers of successful films at one time or another. Our apologies in advance for leaving out your own favorite director/producer. This list is representative rather than exhaustive.

White Guys in the Mainstream

Given the ridiculously exclusive state of the film industry, this of course would be the longest list of players, were it not for time constraints. The number of insiders we have to leave out because of space is ridiculous: Chris Columbus, James Brooks, Francis Ford Coppola, Richard Donner, Clint Eastwood, Scott Rudin, and Barry Sonnenfield, to name a very few. The following figures are essentially just directors we like.

Clint Eastwood shooting in the 1960s; For A Few Dollars More *(1965).*

Clint Eastwood shooting in the 1990s; Eastwood directing White Hunter, Black Heart *(1990).*

Woody Allen: Outsider Player

Born in 1935, Woody Allen, nee Allan Konigsberg, does not produce films, or spend much time in Los Angeles trying to be an insider, because that would take him away from his beloved New York. Nevertheless, he is a player in the best sense: He has arranged a creative life in which people pay him to make almost anything he wants. This happens because he makes critically acclaimed box-office hits on relatively modest budgets, because he is prolific, and because he brings his projects in on time. He also attracts major stars who seem to put aside their need for obscenely huge salaries just for the privilege of working with him. We're talking the likes of Drew Barrymore and Julia Roberts (*Everyone Says I Love You* [1996]), Billy Crystal (*Deconstructing Harry* [1997]) Hugh Grant (*Small Time Crooks* [2000]), Sean Penn (*Sweet and Lowdown* [1999]), and John Malkovich (*Shadows and Fog* [1992]). The combined usual salaries of these stars would put a significant dent in the French national debt.

Director's Cut

Woody Allen's films can often seem either to embody the profundity of his one-liners from *Annie Hall* (1977)—"Life is divided into the horrible and the miserable"—or to make fun of that same profundity—or ridicule that very profundity: "I was thrown out of college for cheating on the metaphysics exam; I looked into the soul of the boy next to me."

It probably doesn't hurt that Allen brings a touch of class to the film industry sadly lacking in this commodity. Though modest, his films are incredibly interesting to watch, especially influenced as they are by Fellini and Bergman. And they are little islands of brilliant dialogue in a sea of mediocrity. From *Annie Hall* (1977): "Don't knock masturbation. It's sex with someone I love."

George Lucas: Nostalgia Merchant

Whether making a film about the 1950s in the 1970s (*American Graffiti* [1973]) or a space opera set "in a galaxy long ago," Lucas sells an enchanted past of simple, old-fashioned American values. Luke's home farm may be on a distant planet, but it sure looks like Oklahoma from here. Born in 1944, Lucas is old enough to have experienced the 1950s, and young enough to interpret them for contemporary audiences. We believe that because American culture doesn't have much of a past in comparison to, say, the European or African continents, we buy it, along with popcorn, on Saturday nights. Lucas is marvelous at combining canny showmanship with a romanticized version of American life.

Even his primary company's name suggests business and romance: Industrial Light and Magic. This combination of sensibilities has been a sort of corporate Midas touch. He has also founded LucasFilm Ltd., Skywalker Sound, and American Zoetrope (with Francis Ford Coppola), all highly visible and influential companies. With these companies, and with the invention of THX sound, he has managed to stay in the Hollywood technological avant-garde.

Steven Spielberg: Commercial Artist

Okay, let's do the Spielberg list—some of the films for which he has been director, producer, or executive producer. The titles pretty much say it all: *Jaws* (1975), *Close Encounters of the Third Kind* (1977), *Raiders of the Lost Ark* (1981), *Poltergeist* (1982), *E.T.: The Extraterrestrial* (1982), *Back to the Future* (1985), *The Color Purple* (1985), *Empire of the Sun* (1987), *Who Framed Roger Rabbit* (1988), *Schindler's List* (1993), *Twister* (1996), *Men in Black* (1997), *Amistad* (1997), and *Saving Private Ryan* (1998). These are not all of Spielberg's films, just his best.

Like George Lucas, Spielberg founds companies; his DreamWorks and Amblin Entertainment have been successful and influential.

Spielberg specializes in two kinds of film: entertainment and uplifting entertainment, whether dealing with Nazis (*Raiders of the Lost Ark* and *Schindler's List*), issues of color and Technicolor (*Who Framed Roger Rabbit* and *The Color Purple*), or trial by water (*Jaws* and *Amistad*).

Women in the Deep End: A Shorter But Not Shallow List

Despite the fact that women are also underrepresented in the top positions at the front office, some do wield some serious—and seriously terrific—creative power. Here is the short list.

Jodie Foster: Foster Children Can Grow Up Happy

This magna cum laude Yale graduate received two Oscars before turning 30. Jodie Foster is smart, tough, and savvy, and a model for how to acquire authority in a male domain. Born in 1962, Foster began her professional career as a model at the age of two. (At three she played the Coppertone Suntan Lotion girl.) Though appearing in a few films and television shows early on, it was her role as the child prostitute in *Taxi Driver* (1976), for which she won an Oscar nomination, that catapulted her to almost immediate stardom.

She has moved from model and film prostitute to writing, directing, and producing. She directed, among other things, the commercial hit *Little Man Tate* (1991). She has been the producer or executive producer for a number of films, including *Nell* (1994), *Home for the Holidays* (1995), and *Waking the Dead* (1999). Foster currently has at least two more projects productions in the works or in the can: *Dangerous Lives of Altar Boys* and *Flora Plum.*

Director's Cut

Foster has perhaps had the oddest career as film icon of anyone on this list. The on-screen muse for killers Travis Bickle in *Taxi Driver* and Hannibal Lecter in *Silence of the Lambs* (1991), Foster made headlines in 1981, not for her movie career, but because she was the inspiration for John Hinckley Jr.'s, attempted assassination of President Reagan.

Barbra Streisand: Mental Yentl

Born in 1942, this funny girl has been a controversial power player. Sometimes hated, often loved for her outspokenness and assertiveness, we figure she is just a woman doing her job right because she has pissed off so many people. Her success is all the more remarkable because she does not conform to Hollywood notions of beauty and her musical success comes outside the conventional popular American genres: rock-and-roll and country-and-western.

Her success in Hollywood came after stints as nightclub singer, Broadway star, and recording artist. After a mercurial career with a phenomenal start (*Funny Girl* and *On a Clear Day You Can See Forever*), she had a rather lackluster decade. But she returned to successes in films, many of which she directed, wrote, or produced. Her acting, producing, and directing credits include an astonishing number of films, most hits, for a contemporary actor: *A Star Is Born* (1976), *Yentl* (1983), *Nuts* (1987), *The Prince of Tides* (1991), and *The Mirror Has Two Faces* (1996).

Director's Cut

Excerpt from speech given by Barbra Streisand at Harvard in 1995 on Congress's continued efforts to abolish funding to the arts: "So maybe it's not about balancing the budget. Maybe it's about shutting the minds and mouths of artists who might have something thought-provoking to say."

Ethnic Directors Making a Difference

Again, the number of African American players in Hollywood, though higher than at any period before the Civil Rights era, is still disproportionately small. The number of Asians and Latinos is smaller still. There are a few high-profile names, but not many: Mario Van Peebles, John Woo, John Singleton, the Wayans brothers, Robert Townsend, and so on.

Robert Townsend: Painfully Funny

Born in 1957, Robert Townsend produced two of his own films (and his biggest successes): *Hollywood Shuffle* (1987) and *Meteor Man* (1993). He also directs, acts, and writes films.

Townsend's films are a bit odd for most American audiences, first because they feature African American protagonists in nonstereotyped roles, and second because they tend toward the savagely satirical. The film that made him a player, *Hollywood Shuffle,* is especially funny and hard to watch, as it follows a paradigmatic outsider—a black actor trying to get work in Hollywood—from job interview to job interview. Especially painful to watch is a sequence in which an Ivy-League accented man has to try on a stereotypical inner-city pimp accent in order to get a part.

Mario Van Peebles

Born in 1957 to an illustrious filmmaker father, Melvin Van Peebles, whose *Sweet Sweetback's Baadasssss Song* (1971) is a raucously legendary bit of underground political filmmaking. Having graduated from Columbia University, Mario is more establishment-oriented, though his films still show a sense of political responsibility: *New Jack City* (1991) is about the violence, self-destructiveness, and hopelessness of inner-city drug culture. Van Peebles's films have recently tended toward the historical. Though a standard western, *Posse* (1993) is also about racial tension. *Panther* (1995) documents the history of the Black Panther Party, while *Sally Hemmings: An American Scandal* (2000) is about the affair between Thomas Jefferson and his slave mistress.

Gen X, Y, Z Filmmakers: New Kids on the Block

These babies were all born after 1969. They are players despite the fact that they inhabit a world in which the Vietnam War is ancient history and The Rolling Stones are a geriatric nostalgia group.

Ben Affleck and Matt Damon

I'm grouping these two as a team because they are: They were even childhood friends. They not only worked together as, respectively, producer and writer on the megahit *Good Will Hunting* (1997), but starred together in this film. After waiting by the phone for job offers, they simply wrote their own script, finally selling the idea to Miramax, which sold it in turn to Kevin Smith as executive producer and to Gus Van Sant as director. They also share producing and acting laurels for the upcoming *The Third Wheel.*

Paul Thomas Anderson

Born in 1970, the son of a voice actor and television horror-film host, Paul Thomas Anderson has produced and directed two big critical and commercial hits thus far: *Boogie Nights* (1997) and *Magnolia* (1999). His subjects and/or film style tend toward the quirky: *Boogie Nights* was about the porn industry in the 1970s and 1980s while *Magnolia* contained a huge cast and a difficult but brilliantly dramatic story, at the center of which is a dying man and his son and a miracle. Last heard, Anderson was negotiating with Miramax Films to make an eighteenth-century costume drama.

Kevin Smith

Smith is a cautionary tale about moving from independent filmmaking to Hollywood-style films. Audiences raved over the very low budget—and low-budget-looking—*Clerks* (1994). (There has even been a television cartoon series version of the film.) But, given a boost and more funds, he turned out the much-maligned *Mallrats* (1995) before finding his balance again with *Chasing Amy* (1997), and as one of the producers of *Good Will Hunting,* only to then turn in the ambitious but mixed *Dogma* (1999). Many critics and fans find everything he has done since being "discovered" less interesting than his initial efforts.

Some Films Worth Viewing

We could recommend you some films about filmmaking, but thought it best to give you the best films by some of the directors in this chapter. All the films listed here are blockbusters that still managed to be *about* something, demonstrating that films can be serious and fun:

- *Meteor Man* (directed by Robert Townsend, 1993). Inner-city schmo discovers he has superpowers, and ultimately overcomes not just crime, but community indifference to poverty and injustice.
- *New Jack City* (directed by Mario Van Peebles, 1991). Odd success because it is explicitly didactic in a mainstream culture that doesn't like to be taught lessons by its movies.
- *Schindler's List* (directed by Steven Spielberg, 1993). Noble attempt at depicting the Holocaust. Controversial because it concentrates on a handful of people

who survived, perhaps missing the point of the Holocaust, which is that people behave miserably, not nobly.

- *The Prince of Tides* (directed by Barbra Streisand, 1991). Nice unpacking of the insecurities behind some kinds of macho posturing.
- *Sweet and Lowdown* (directed by Woody Allen, 1999). Warm and funny and cynical, all in one. The waif is another Allen homage to Fellini, because she looks and acts just like Fellini's actor wife, Giuletta Massina.
- *Dogma* (directed by Kevin Smith, 1999). Mixed reviews because no one is comfortable with a comedy that savages the Catholic church.

The Least You Need to Know

- There are Hollywood insiders, outsiders, and players. The positions may be transitory, but they are carefully defined.
- In the end, you are an insider and a player if you have talent and access to money.
- The problem with the insider-outsider model is that it excludes the traditional outsiders: women and ethnic and racial minorities.
- To be a player rather than simply a "talent," you have to move from acting and directing to producing and administration.

Chapter 10

The American Independent Film

In This Chapter

- America's long history of independent film
- The African American "parallel" industry during the silent era
- The "New Hollywood" of the 1960s and '70s
- The 1980s and the mainstreaming of independence
- Independent film today

Chances are you've seen numerous independent films without even knowing it (much less trying!). If you accompanied those tens of millions of teenagers to a showing of *The Blair Witch Project*, or remember that bitchin' motorcycle chase in *Easy Rider*, you're already on your way. Acquiring a real taste for independents, though, requires a bit of history and a selective eye, both of which this chapter will provide.

A Brief History of American Independents

MGM, Paramount, Universal: You've read about America's studio empires and what their leaders did to forge a dominant force in world cinema, from the earliest pioneers like Griffith and DeMille to recent tycoons such as Spielberg and Cameron. Now it's time to cast your viewing net a little wider to take in some of the many alternative voices that populate the history of American film.

The Silent Era

Until 1994, only a few specialists knew anything about one of the most successful alternatives to the powerful Hollywood studio industry during the American silent era. The 1994 documentary *Midnight Ramble: Oscar Micheaux and the Story of Race Movies,* produced by Northern Lights, uncovered an extraordinary but neglected "parallel cinema," as it's often called, that allowed African American filmmakers to produce, direct, and star in literally hundreds of silent films. This was the cinema, for example, that launched the career of the great singer, lawyer, actor, and athlete Paul Robeson, who starred in his first film, Oscar Micheaux's *Body and Soul,* in 1925. Micheaux, one of the leading figures in black silent cinema, was also one of the most prolific American directors of the 1920s and '30s. Though many of his films are lost, his work is currently being recovered and rediscovered as a part of American filmdom in the early part of the last century.

Filmophile's Lexicon

Race movies were feature-length silent films with all-black casts that were made specifically for African American audiences, becoming the standard fare in early black cinema.

Filmophile's Lexicon

Midnight ramble refers to showings of late-night movies to African American audiences, who were largely segregated from whites-only daytime and evening film performances.

Though the handful of black-owned production companies never rivaled the major Hollywood studios in the quantity of films released, some of these corporations did make quite a dent in the silent distribution system. The Lincoln Motion Picture Company, the first organized exclusively by black filmmakers, was launched in 1916 by the actor Noble Johnson, quickly became the leading African American production company, and released its first feature, *The Realization of a Negro's Ambition,* in 1916. The story of a young black engineer who triumphs over discrimination in the oil industry, it was followed the next year by the longer feature *A Trooper of Troop K,* which narrated a real-life massacre of a company of black soldiers by Mexican bandits in 1916.

After the company's epic, ambitious, and expensive film, *By Right of Birth* (1921), failed commercially (in large part due to its failure to attract white audiences), the company folded, leaving behind a rich array of films only recently available on video.

Ironically, aside from the so-called race films being produced by a handful of black-owned production companies, the early history of American independent film is largely the story of the early pioneers who formed Hollywood itself. As we saw in an earlier chapter, the Motion Picture Patents Company, or simply The Trust, as it was known, virtually monopolized the production, distribution, and exhibition of

American silent film. It's weird to think of MGM, Paramount, and so on as the direct precursors of today's independence-minded filmmakers, but there you are!

Director's Cut

In Cheryl Dunye's clever, well-researched, and witty *Watermelon Woman* (1996), an African American lesbian filmmaker named Cheryl goes on a quest to find any information she can concerning the legendary "Watermelon Woman," a black actress who appeared as a compelling figure in numerous '30s "race movies" but left little trace in the historical record. Though Dunye invented the Watermelon Woman for the purposes of this film, Cheryl's pursuit of the elusive figure allowed the filmmaker to draw on her extensive archival research into the early history of African American film, providing a compelling look at a neglected chapter in American cinema.

The Sixties and Seventies: "The New Hollywood"

In 1969, a low-budget motorcycle flick called *Easy Rider,* starring Peter Fonda and Dennis Hopper as two Harley Davidson–riding cool guys in search of America, captured the imagination of a generation of the nation's youth. Directed by Hopper himself on a shoestring budget, *Easy Rider* was one of the first products of what came to be called the "New Hollywood," which was led by a wave of younger directors who overturned enduring industry conventions.

For one thing, the film lacked typical Hollywood hero-figures; Fonda, Hopper, and their "recruit," Jack Nicholson, were more like antiheroes, and rather than depict their motorcycle-riding as a sign of reckless delinquency, the movie crafted it into a quest for freedom. In technical terms, *Easy Rider* used jump cuts and forward flashes to transition between scenes rather than straight narrative sequencing; the acting was highly improvisational, drug use was glorified, and the effect of the film as a whole was a studied rebelliousness, a to-hell-with-convention attitude shared by director and characters alike. At the same time, *Easy Rider* was very self-conscious of its place in the history of

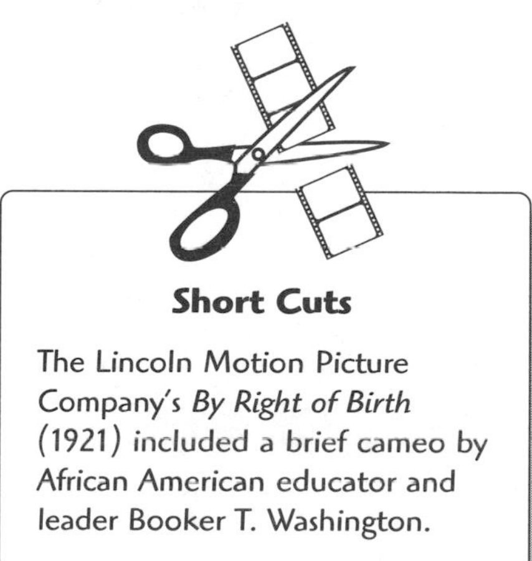

Short Cuts

The Lincoln Motion Picture Company's *By Right of Birth* (1921) included a brief cameo by African American educator and leader Booker T. Washington.

American film: One famous sequence of the bikers riding through Monument Valley at sunset was clearly meant to evoke the Westerns of John Ford with their pioneering spirit of independence.

What *Easy Rider* showed was that you didn't need millions of dollars and the backing of a major studio to make a thoughtful, successful, provocative film that lots of people would see. Indeed, with the final collapse of the studio system and a loosening of censorious restrictions on film content throughout the 1960s (see Chapter 8, "The Decline and Fall of the Studio Empire"), a new, younger generation of directors realized that the public was craving intelligent, convention-busting movies that would refute the '50s moralizing and McCarthyist politics that had suffused the era's cinema.

This was the *new* Hollywood, not the old, and suddenly innovation was everywhere: in Francis Ford Coppola's maverick company American Zoetrope, which released *The Godfather* in 1972 to enormous acclaim and success; in David Lynch's grotesque and six-years-in-the-making *Eraserhead* (1977), an enduring cult classic; in Mike Nichols's screen adaptation of *Who's Afraid of Virginia Woolf?* (1966), which made money precisely by rejecting Hollywood's polite constraints on obscenity; in Martin Scorsese's gritty vision of urban decay in *Taxi Driver* (1976), which catapulted America's most successfully anti-Hollywood director into the stratosphere; in John Cassavetes's harsh camera work and improvisational, off-the-cuff style in *Husbands* (1970); in the unforgettable performance of Divine in John Waters's groundbreaking *Pink Flamingos* (1972); in Stanley Kubrick's horrifying depiction of youth violence and nihilism in *A Clockwork Orange* (1971); and in the work of numerous other independent-minded directors.

Second Take

Most of what gets counted as "independent film" in the late '60s and '70s is specifically *narrative* film; the aesthetic avant-garde gets left behind more often than not. But long before the so-called indie revolution of the '70s and '80s, experimental filmmakers like Maya Deren (*Meshes in the Afternoon,* 1943), Kenneth Anger (*Escape Episode,* 1946), Curtis Harrington (*On the Edge,* 1949), Stan Brakhage (*Reflections on Black,* 1955), and many others weren't even thinking about their relationship to Hollywood as they crafted their own experimental and forward-looking contributions to art film.

Of course, many such films were financed and/or released by the major studios and production companies; it would be wrong to draw a strict line between the independents and the mainstreams in the 1970s. In the case of American cinema in this period, "independence" is often less an economic or commercial reality than a state of mind, a willful rejection of staid Hollywood conventions.

The Eighties and Nineties: How Much Success Is Too Much?

While flush with innovation in its own right, the 1970s set the stage for a veritable explosion of independent filmmaking in subsequent decades. With the rise of numerous film festivals nationwide and a flood of eager-beaver students into suddenly hip film schools (especially NYU and USC) in the early '80s, the venues for non- and anti-Hollywood filmmaking increased drastically—and with diverse consequences for the face of American film.

You'll often hear this complaint from today's avant-garde and experimental directors: Many of the so-called independent filmmakers getting so much public attention have used the label of independence simply as a launching pad into the Hollywood mainstream. They have a point. We won't name names here, but it's true that a number of directors hailed as politically or aesthetically avant-garde just 15 years ago have been virtually bought by the major studios, seduced by the extra millions to be earned through corporate funding and advertising tie-ins.

Second Take

Does size matter? Technically speaking, you could call *Star Wars: Episode I—The Phantom Menace* (1999), one of the greatest box office successes of all time, an "independent film." It was financed exclusively by George Lucas with all the money left over from the original trilogy in the '70s and '80s. In spirit, though, few would disagree that this movie is anything but an "indie." We'll leave it up to you!

Nevertheless, if you scratch away at Hollywood's slick '80s veneer (you know, *Wall Street* [1987], *Fatal Attraction* [1987], and so on) you'll find a host of popular and successful independent directors who steadfastly refused to surrender their creative and artistic control to the boardrooms of the moguls. We're thinking in particular of folks like the Coen brothers, Joel and Ethan, whose dark comedies like *Blood Simple* (1984), *Raising Arizona* (1987), and *Fargo* (1996) established them as leading American directors; Woody Allen, perhaps American cinema's purest contemporary auteur, whose dazzling success with the multiple-Oscar-winning *Annie Hall* in 1977 and numerous films during the '80s (*Hannah and Her Sisters* [1986]; *Crimes and Misdemeanors* [1989]) testifies to a unique creative relationship between a fiercely independent director and major-studio financing; and Jim Jarmusch, who has received countless offers of megabucks from the big boys but who has always refused to bend with films like *Stranger Than Paradise* (1984), *Down by Law* (1986), and *Mystery Train* (1989).

Short Cuts

At a fresh-faced 24 years old, John Singleton was nominated as best director at the Academy Awards for *Boyz N the Hood,* becoming the youngest filmmaker ever so honored.

The 1980s and '90s were also important years for several minority directors who managed to make their way into Hollywood's directorial club of rich white men. Spike Lee's visionary *Do the Right Thing* (1989) was a complex look at racial prejudice in Reagan-era America as well as a beautifully shot and brilliantly written piece of filmmaking. The Taiwanese-born director Ang Lee emerged as a major talent with his own well-received *The Wedding Banquet* (1993), *Eat Drink Man Woman* (1994), and *Sense and Sensibility* (1995), for which he received an Academy Award nomination. John Singleton's *Boyz N the Hood* (1991) garnered international praise for its harsh and unforgiving look at the consequences of urban youth violence.

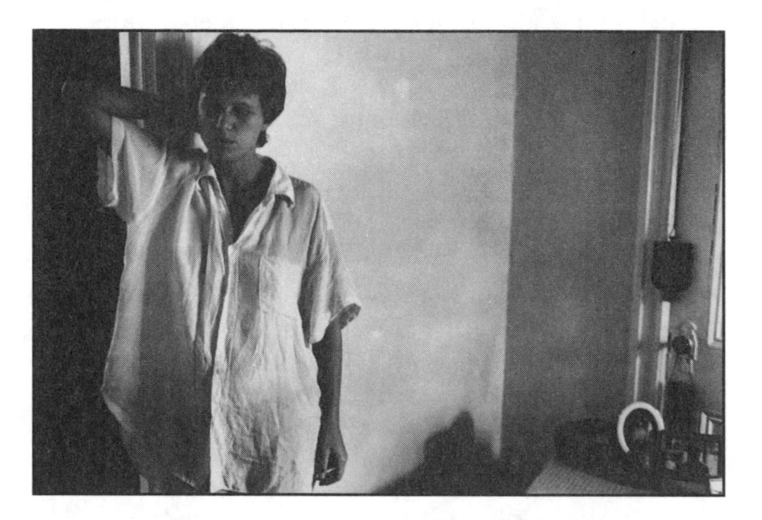

A gritty scene from Lizzie Borden's hard-hitting Working Girls *(1986).*

On the other side of the independent spectrum, the same year saw the release of Richard Linklater's ultralow-budget *Slacker* (1991), an immediate cult classic that helped define America's "Generation X" and did much to fashion the image of early '90s youth as confused, directionless, and apathetic. And Linklater's 1993 *Dazed and Confused* rivals *Fast Times at Ridgemont High* (1982) as the most hilarious and brilliant high school film ever made.

One of Richard Linklater's typical Gen-Xers in the ultralow-budget Slacker *(1991).*

The 1990s may also be remembered for what we'd call the "mainstreaming of independence." You can now subscribe to the Sundance Channel on cable, which brings some of the most innovative independent film into the comfort of your living room. Indie film festivals have sprung up all over the place, and already some of the nation's multiplexes are devoting a screen (albeit one out of 24 in some cases!) exclusively to film festival fare.

The Independent Scene Today

The last year of the twentieth century marked a significant turning point for the future of American independent film. If the '80s and '90s witnessed an increasingly difficult and fierce relationship between independent filmmakers and the major studios who sought to co-opt their more successful products, the first decade of the twenty-first (and we're prognosticating here!) may well be remembered as the turning point: the moment when independent filmmakers finally figured out how to beat the major studios at their own game and, ultimately, seized control of American cinema from the jaws of the media giants.

Hollywood Be(Blair)Witched

An overstatement, perhaps, but there were two films released in 1999 that signaled such a possible trend more than any others. The first, *The Blair Witch Project,* set a record for total box office receipts as a multiple of total production budget. Shot on a veritable shoestring, this faux-documentary purports to be the surviving footage left by a group of college kids who set off into the Maryland woods in search of a legendary witch who had been spooking the countryside for a century. Given the way it was made, *The Blair Witch Project* was a true cinematic phenomenon, making the covers of *Time* and *Newsweek* and throwing Hollywood into a turbulent period of self-examination and doubt.

The other 1999 independent we have in mind signals other, equally important kinds of changes in the industry. *Boys Don't Cry,* directed by Kimberly Peirce, garnered best actress honors for the virtual unknown Hillary Swank and a best supporting actress nomination for the bedroom-eyed wonder Chloe Sevigny. The film tells the story of Brandon Teena, a transgendered youth from Nebraska who finds love, friendship, betrayal, and ultimately death during a sojourn in the Nebraska countryside. Though shot independently by Peirce, the film, a surprise nationwide hit, was released, distributed, and backed by a major studio, suggesting

Director's Cut

"Being a young American filmmaker is worse than making films under Communism, because the commercial and ideological exigencies are so strict that they suppress creativity."

—Alexander Payne, independent filmmaker and director of *Election* a new awareness on the part of Hollywood moguls that politically daring films actually can do well at the box office and the Oscars.

While *Blair Witch* demonstrated that a couple of kids with a video camera or two can transform ingenuity into megabucks, *Boys Don't Cry* showed that major studios can and should take creative risks in what they choose to support. While the slick mainstream productions of Hollywood studios are seemingly "safer," more assured of making money, politically challenging movies may enhance the reputations of those who get behind them, paving the way for further innovation in the future.

The Postmodern Polyglot

With a few notable exceptions, American film directing was long a white guy's world. Read any mainstream history of cinema in the United States and you'll see very few African American, Asian American, Native American, or Chicano directors listed among the pantheon of American filmmakers. Yet mainstream histories tell only part of the story. Even as some popular independent directors—Jarmusch, Kubrick, and so on—have had the lucky distinction of actually getting their films seen on the nation's screens (no small accomplishment in an age of such fierce competition), an alternative independent cinema has arisen in recent years spearheaded by directors of color who have challenged more mainstream perspectives on issues of race and ethnicity in the contemporary United States. While these films will often be more difficult to find than your average Hollywood blockbuster, they're also more challenging and, we hope, more rewarding.

Some of the most innovative and exciting work in this direction comes from a new group of African American women directors. Zeinabu Irene Davis, whose work deals in depth with the depiction of women of the African diaspora, has made numerous documentaries, features, and shorts, including the experimental psychological drama *Cycles* (1989, included in the Whitney Biennial exhibition in 1991); a compelling story, made for children and adults, about a young slave girl, *Mother of the River* (broadcast on PBS in 1995); and the recent feature *Compensation* (1999), a love story that takes place in and around black deaf culture. And Julie Dash's first feature film, the hauntingly beautiful *Daughters of the Dust* (1992) won first prize for cinematography at the Sundance Film Festival.

A big hit in movie houses around the nation a few years ago was *Smoke Signals* (1998), directed by Chris Eyre. Based on a short story by Native American writer Sherman Alexie, *Smoke Signals* features two young men coming of age on the Coeur d'Alene Indian Reservation in Idaho and on a round trip they take together to Phoenix. Using flashbacks effectively to weave together past and present, the film sets its tale of friendship in an American West portrayed from a refreshingly un-Hollywood-like perspective.

Latino directors have also been making important contributions to American independent film. Some of their work is regularly featured in the Los Angeles Latino International Film Festival, which marked its fourth annual opening in 2000. Actor

Edward James Olmos (whose own 1992 directorial debut, *American Me,* was very well received) serves as a celebrity host of the festival, which regularly features a panoply of independent fiction and documentary directors.

Second Take

Kelly Loves Tony wouldn't have been seen by nearly as many viewers if it hadn't been for *P.O.V.* (Point of View), a showcase for independent nonfiction films, sponsored by public television, that has recently brought dozens of innovative works into the nation's living rooms.

Film's Hardest Nose: Documentary

In 1995, award-winning documentary filmmaker Spencer Nakasako gave a handheld camcorder to Kelly Saeteurn, 17, and Tony Saelio, 22, two Laotian immigrants living in East Oakland, California, and asked them to record their lives for a year and a half. They did, producing more than 120 hours of videotape; the edited result, *Kelly Loves Tony* (released in 1998), presents a surprisingly gripping and beautifully honest portrait of the pressures of love, family, law, and ethnicity along today's Pacific Rim. The executive producer of the film was the National Asian American Telecommunications Association (NAATA), which supports Asian American filmmakers and distributes their productions to a wide North American audience. (NAATA also executive-produced Nakasako's similar video diary, *A.K.A. Don Bonus,* in 1997.)

Short Cuts

One of the more popular documentaries of the '80s was Michael Moore's *Roger and Me* (1989), a hilarious, sad, and deeply moving look at the effects of General Motors factory closings and the resultant economic depression on the city of Flint, Michigan. Moore's juxtaposition near the end of the film of CEO Roger Smith's speech at the company Christmas party with the evictions of poor families from their Flint homes is just one of many devastating moments in the film.

NAATA and P.O.V. are just two of the many organizations at work today to bring alternative or marginalized perspectives to the viewing public through their support of documentary and other forms of nonfiction filmmaking. Documentary has a long history in American cinema, of course, beginning with Robert Flaherty's *Nanook of the North* (1922), a still absorbing portrait of Eskimo life that inspired a flurry of creative documentary-making that would continue through the later years of the silent era. World War II was perhaps the greatest documentary impetus of the twentieth century, with many of the era's most creative filmmakers (John Ford, Frank Capra, and others) pitching in to make propaganda movies to inspire the nation in its struggle against fascism. Our own era has witnessed a massive growth of the documentary industry, which now far exceeds in size its fiction film counterpart.

Michael Moore's effective use of humor and irony in *Roger and Me* contrasts with the dead seriousness of another acclaimed political documentary, *The Thin Blue Line* (1988). Made by Errol Morris, the film provided a terrifying examination of a murder case that put a defendant on death row for the murder of a Dallas police officer. As a direct result of the film's effectiveness, the case against the man was reopened, and he was soon cleared of the crime—a strong testament to the unapologetic social consciousness of much documentary filmmaking and the concrete, practical results that certain films can achieve.

Director's Cut

"Many filmgoers are reluctant to see documentaries, for reasons I've never understood; the good ones are frequently more absorbing and entertaining than fiction. *Hoop Dreams,* however, is not only a documentary. It is also poetry and prose, muckraking and expose, journalism and polemic. It is one of the great moviegoing experiences of my lifetime."

—From the review of *Hoop Dreams* by Roger Ebert in the *Chicago Sun-Times* (October 21, 1994)

Arthur Agee in Steve James's Hoop Dreams *(1994).*

Other well-received documentaries with a political edge in recent years have included Barbara Kopple's *American Dream* (1990), a disturbing portrait of corporate strike-busting and union despair; Jennie Livingston's dazzling *Paris Is Burning* (1990), which portrays with moving empathy the lives, aspirations, and rituals of an urban subculture of cross-dressers; *Hoop Dreams* (1994), an almost epic story of two Chicago kids who yearn for basketball stardom but must face their physical and familial limitations in the process; and *The Brandon Teena Story* (1998), released at the same time as *Boys Don't Cry* in order to document the "real" story behind the Nebraska tragedy.

The world of entertainment has also provided fare for the creativity of documentary filmmakers. Wim Wenders's *Buena Vista Social Club* (1999) traces the story of a Cuban garage band that took North America by storm and made these formerly obscure musicians top the Billboard charts.

Director's Cut

Ilisa Barbash and Lucien Taylor are anthropology professors and filmmakers who codirected the stirring ethnographic film *In and Out of Africa* (1992). They are also the coauthors of *Cross-Cultural Filmmaking* (University of California Press), a practical handbook for makers of ethnographic films. As Barbash and Taylor point out, "Ethnographic film, more than any other genre, explicitly addresses questions of cultural difference, and indeed often evokes, as much through its form as its content, an unfinished interplay between cultures—both at the level of a film's subjects, its maker(s), and also its spectators. In so doing, it interrogates a whole series of taken-for-granted oppositions: between record and discourse, documentary and fiction, the West and the Rest, and finally even that thorniest of all dualisms, Self and Other."

Cross-cultural filmmaking, including ethnographic documentary, has also taken off in recent years, spawning an entire academic subdiscipline known as "visual anthropology" and bringing cinema into play as an important part of conversations across the boundaries of nation, hemisphere, ethnicity, culture, and language.

Trinh Minh-ha, for example, one of the world's most acclaimed postcolonial theorists and filmmakers, has made numerous award-winning pictures while arguing in her writing for a self-consciousness among filmmakers about the political implications of the visual as such. After making *Naked Spaces—Living Is Round* in 1985, she turned to the experiences of women in her native country in *Surname Viet Given Name Nam*

(1989), which received awards at the Bombay International Film Festival and the American Film and Video Festival. *Shoot for the Contents* (1991) won a best cinematography award at Sundance and the best feature documentary award at the Athens International Film Festival.

New Technologies, New Cinemas

As you read these words, a quiet revolution is underway in the world of independent filmmaking, and especially in documentary. The revolution is taking place just a keystroke away from you on the World Wide Web, where you'll find a dazzling variety of uploaded, downloadable, instantly enjoyable, and—get this—*free* examples of experimental film that you won't want to miss.

We only have the space to talk about one of these sites, so we've chosen what we consider the very best. Picture Projects (www.pictureprojects.com) was founded several years ago by Alison Cornyn and Sue Johnson, who set out to adapt new and emergent forms of media technology to create innovative forms of oral history. As they announce on their Web site, "We combine photography, audio and the interactive dialogue capabilities of the Internet to tell stories and document the world in a way that has never been done before."

Their collaborations during the past five years have produced stunning results. One of the project's more moving recent efforts is Gilles Peress's *Farewell to Bosnia,* which started out as an attempt by Peress to collect numerous photographs of Bosnians affected by the war during the 1990s and post them on the Internet. Soon, however, the photo archive blossomed into a multimedia exploration of the tragic consequences of the war, a mind-numbing experience for the Web surfer in search of quality filmmaking.

The group's current project, titled *www.360Degrees.org—Perspectives on the American Criminal Justice System,* is an unprecedented attempt to provide a sweeping look at all aspects of the corrections systems. The site will ultimately include video clips from inmates, corrections officials, parole officers, lawyers, judges, and many others involved in the system; also planned are real-time cameras placed in holding cells and courtrooms and a variety of other creative ways of putting the vagaries and victims of the criminal justice system into moving and speaking images. As unique sites like Picture Projects attest, the Internet will undoubtedly be a crucial part of the future of documentary and independent film.

Declaration of Independents

Independent filmmakers have produced many manifestos during the years decrying the mainstream and lauding the efforts of the marginalized, the underfinanced, and the unbeholden. Here's our own "Declaration of Independents," a short list of reasons and ways to watch and make independent cinema part of your standard filmic fare.

- Simply put, there's a lot more independent film than mainstream film around these days. Though never as well financed as its Hollywood counterpart, independent film thrives all over the place.
- After a century of predictable if great Hollywood genre flicks, it's refreshing to watch an ever-growing film movement that thrives on unpredictability and innovation.
- By supporting independent film, you're supporting usually unknown artists and helping to give them a chance to emerge as major talents in world cinema.
- Some exposure to independent film will greatly enrich your understanding of mainstream film, showing you some of the creative and/or political sacrifices that had to be made in the name of money.
- In the often-challenging political stances it brings to cinema, independent film will inevitably force you to think harder and learn more about the community, the nation, and the world around you.

If you let yourself get into the spirit of this Declaration of Independents, you're sure to enjoy more and better films than you ever thought possible.

The Least You Need to Know

- Independent film has a long history in the United States, from the silent era "parallel cinema" of African Americans to the postmodern polyglot of the present.
- The 1960s and '70s saw the rise of the "New Hollywood" and the emergence of the independent auteur.
- During the '80s, independent filmmakers were often lured into the studios, though a number remained fiercely independent.
- Documentary filmmaking and new technologies such as the Internet have contributed greatly to the explosion of independent film during the past decade.
- Independent film thrives today, far outweighing its Hollywood counterpart in number of filmmaking companies, total films released, and directors.

Part 3

The Hundred Languages of Foreign Film

This is where you find out why everyone thinks Fellini, Bergman, and Kurosawa are such hot stuff. We will give you tips on why and how to watch foreign film, so that it's not all just Greek to you. Watching films from other countries can be magic carpet rides to other cultures, customs, and ways of seeing the world. Some filmmakers even consciously reflect the politics of their era in a manner really foreign to us. What were Nazi or fascist films like? How different (or similar) were they to films made in North America? Even if you've been on that whirlwind 10-cities-in-9-days trip to Europe, Fellini's films take you to the back streets (La Strada) *that the tour bus didn't go down. Fassbinder takes you through the latticed bedroom windows you can only glimpse from the German beer garden, and behind the lederhosen. So climb on our cinematic magic carpet, as we do world cinema wall to wall.*

Chapter 11

French Revolutions

In This Chapter

- How (and why) to watch and appreciate French film
- France's long history of cinematic splendor
- The first film avant-garde
- *La Nouvelle Vague:* the French "New Wave"
- Recent French film
- A list of our favorite French films

If you attended elementary school in the 1960s or '70s, chances are you'd already been exposed to French film by the time you were 12.

After winning prizes at the Cannes Film Festival and the Academy Awards, director Albert Lamorisse's short subject film *Le Ballon rouge* (*The Red Balloon,* 1956) made its way onto America's classroom projectors and into the hearts of a generation of school-children. Following the course of an elusive balloon through the alleys and streets of Paris and the balloon's charmed pursuit by a young boy who cries "Ballon! Ballon!" in its wake, *The Red Balloon* evokes the beautifully haunting poetry of French filmmaking beginning a decade after World War II, when the *Nouvelle Vague,* or "New Wave," of cinematic artistry swept across the nation's screens.

Beginning with the pioneering efforts of the Lumière brothers in the 1890s, France has produced a proud and often sublime century of film. The United States' only close rival in the history of cinema, the French nation has given the world some of the most captivating and unforgettable visual images there are. Rather than giving you a straight history of French film, then, what we offer here is a "taster menu," if you will, which, with any luck, will tempt you to sample further in this most delicious part of the medium of film.

It's Art, Stupid!

Perhaps the most important piece of information you'll need to remember about French as opposed to other film traditions is this: From the early silent years, many of France's filmmakers have been quite self-conscious of themselves as artistes and of the status of their work as "high art." Seems simple enough, but this one fact has enormous implications for the history of twentieth-century film.

As you learned in Part 2, "A Brief History of (Mostly American) Film," the history of American cinema is first and foremost a history of entertainment. Sure, directors like John Ford and Orson Welles should be considered artists (auteurs, to recall the term you'll read more about shortly); conversely, there are long stretches of French film history in which nothing artistically interesting was going on, and the studios were set on squeezing just as much money out of the nation's cinema-goers as even the most cynical American moguls.

Director's Cut

Antonin Artaud, the great French dramatist and theorist of theater, was also involved in avant-garde film culture in the '20s and '30s, acting in such pictures as *Le Juif errant* (1926) and *La Passion de Jeanne d'Arc* (1928), as well as writing the screenplays for *L'Etoile de Mer* (1926) and *Le Coquille et le Clergyman* (1927).

But the fact remains that in France, more than in any other country, the culture of the high arts and the culture of film have marched hand in hand since the turn of the last century. No other nation has produced such a massive library of theoretical writings on the aesthetics and philosophy of film, from the earliest treatises of the silent era avant-garde (Artaud, Canudo, and others) to the *Cahiers du cinéma* writers to contemporary theory of film by intellectuals like Gilles Deleuze.

Moreover, from the first decade of the twentieth century, numerous artists from other mediums—painting, drama, sculpture, music—have been involved in the art and culture of French film, establishing the country's motion picture industry as a leader in its wider artistic scene. And there has surely been more self-consciousness in France of film as artistic expression than in any other nation's cinematic tradition: more "mainstreaming of experimentalism," if you will.

After World War II, for example, while the tiny American avant-garde was largely living and filming abroad or "underground" and attracting small art-house audiences, Jean-Luc Godard helped finance Jacques Rivette's *Quadrille* (1950), an experimental 40-minute picture in which four people sit around a table just staring at each other silently. (Can you imagine an American audience paying to watch something like that at your local multiplex? Didn't think so.)

In short, to acquire a sophisticated appreciation of French film, you must learn to view a Godard the same way you'd take in a Manet at a museum. Look carefully, absorb, contemplate, and appreciate, bearing in mind that what you're viewing is often as carefully crafted a work of art as anything hanging on the walls of the Louvre.

Filmophile's Lexicon

The phrase **The Seventh Art** was coined by critic Ricciotto Canudo in the 1910s to connote film's status as a new and powerful rival to painting, music, sculpture, and the other fine arts. Though Italian by birth, Canudo established the "Club of the Friends of the Seventh Art" in Paris in 1920 in order to promote to the French intelligentsia the aesthetic possibilities and philosophical challenge of the emergent medium.

A Century of Cinematic Splendor

MGM was only a glint in Louis B. Mayer's eye when Léon Gaumont, a photographic merchandiser, began producing and marketing films at the turn of the century. Gaumont soon became one of the nation's leading studios. Charles Pathé created an even more massive corporation; by 1910, Pathé was marketing many more movies in America than all U.S. companies *combined*.

This French dominance of the international film industry had many practical effects, not the least of which was the huge influence of French filmmaking on American directors. Succeeding generations of Gallic geniuses would continue to exert unparalleled creative and artistic pressures upon world cinema.

The Movies' First Magician

Nearly a century before there was Industrial Light and Magic, there was Georges Méliès.

Among the enthralled attendees at the Lumière brothers' Grande Café showing on that fateful night in 1895 was a 34-year-old son of a rich shoemaker. A magician and illusionist by trade, Georges Méliès was taken by the new medium and vowed to transfer his considerable talents from the variety stage to celluloid.

With the family money he had inherited, Méliès constructed what would become the world's first real film studio in a huge structure in Montreuil-sous-Bois. His command over every aspect of his filmmaking was legendary, as he produced, directed, edited, and acted in practically every film he shot. During the next 20 years, he cranked out perhaps thousands of short films featuring some of the world's first trick photography—for example, scenes in which a figure would be standing on a street corner and magically disappear in the space of a single frame.

Director's Cut

One day, at the height of his career, Charlie Chaplin autographed a photo of himself for the French film comedian Max Linder. In the inscription, Chaplin identified Linder as "The Professor—to whom I owe everything." High praise indeed from the world's biggest movie star!

But Chaplin was serious about his debts to Linder, whose film career in the 1900s and 1910s soared to unprecedented heights and established him as the leading man of French film comedy. Playing the character of Max in dozens of silents with titles like *Max prend un bain* (1910), *Max victime de quinquina* (1911), *Max professeur de tango* (1912), *Max toréador* (1912), and later, in the United States, *Max in a Taxi* (1917), Linder created a debonair, sophisticated bungler whose deft antics provided a cool Parisian reply to America's Keystone Kops.

The personal and professional relationship between Linder and Chaplin wasn't all harmony and laughs, however. When Chaplin's films started pulling in the big bucks internationally, Linder faded into relative obscurity, an experience that left him embittered enough to take his own life.

Méliès's best-known and most beloved film remains *Le Voyage dans la Lune* (*A Trip to the Moon,* 1902), a charming and still quite enjoyable short that established his international reputation practically overnight. Though his star gradually faded as he ran out of cash and other filmmakers ascended into the public eye, he was "rediscovered" in the late 1920s and given a free place to live out his years.

Georges Méliès's illusionist moon from Le Voyage dans la Lune (A Trip to the Moon, *1902*).

Many film historians and theorists still credit the stylistic differences between the films of the Lumière brothers and those of Georges Méliès with giving rise to the split between the documentary film and the fiction film. This is probably something of an exaggeration, but it's undeniable that Méliès's tricky innovations inspired countless attempts at cinematic illusion-making during the past century.

Second Take

It's one of the greatest losses in the history of film. In 1923, penniless and virtually forgotten, Georges Méliès sold the negatives of practically all his films to a factory for the market price of the celluloid. Only a few dozen films survive out of the thousands he made.

Before the War

Like Hollywood, the French film industry churned out a massive number of films in the decade before the outbreak of World War II. Mainstream studios produced many great films, such as Jean Epstin's *L'Auberge rouge* and *Coeur fidèle* (both 1923). But the real story of French filmmaking in these years is the story of the avant-garde.

Avowing the Avant-Garde

Following the breakthroughs of the Lumière brothers and Méliès, the silent and early sound eras in France marked the emergence of the world's first bona fide cinematic avant-garde. Conscious of their public role as artists breaking new ground in a still unfamiliar medium, French filmmakers transformed film into a celluloid wonderland of aesthetic prowess. While some of these directors were truly independent, others, such as René Clair, maintained their ties with the major studios while taking film in often shocking new directions.

The most important figures from this era include directors like Spanish-born Luis Buñuel (*Un Chien andalou*, 1928), René Clair (*Paris qui dort* and *Entr'acte*, 1924; *Un chapeau de paille d'Italie*, 1927), Jean Cocteau (*Le Sang d'un Poete*, 1930), and Man Ray (*Le Retour à la Raison*, 1923). Abel Gance followed up his excellent anti-war *J'accuse* (1919) with the extraordinary 17-reel *Napoléon vu par Abel Gance: première époque: Bonaparte* (1927), an experimental epic featuring unprecedented innovations in editing, projection technology, and camera movement (one scene even involved strapping a camera onto a horse!).

Short Cuts

One of world cinema's first female directors, Germain Dulac (1882–1942) combined her public advocacy of female suffrage with a bold approach to impressionist filmmaking, producing visual feasts such as *La Souriante Madame Beudet* (1923) and the surrealist *La Coquille et le Clergyman* (1927).

The "Other Renoir"

Jean Renoir, one of history's greatest filmmakers, was born in 1894, barely a year before the Lumière brothers' first public showings of their films. Like Jean Cocteau's, Renoir's career provides an ideal example of the intimate relationship between film and other art forms in twentieth-century France. The son of the great impressionist painter Auguste Renoir, Jean began his cinematic life by financing several films with money he had inherited from his famous father. His directing debut, *La Fille de l'Eau* (1925), while not distinguished, captures something of the visual beauty and the poetry of nature with which the august Auguste had embellished his canvases.

Short Cuts

Adaptations of literary works appear frequently in French film of the pre–World War II era. Jean Renoir's *La Bête humaine* (1938) adapts Emile Zola's popular novel of the railroads into a haunting visual spectacle featuring the superb acting of Jean Gabin.

Renoir's career reached its peak during the 1930s, when he shot more than a dozen feature-length films that virtually redefined the art of French cinema. *Toni* (1934), *La Chienne* (1931), and *Le Crime de M. Lange* (1936) exhibit an unflinching willingness to confront deep-seated social tensions with wit and artistry. *La Grande Illusion* (1937) treats the complex human interactions arising from the adversity of a prisoner-of-war camp.

And the decade wraps up with *La Règle de Jeu* (*Rules of the Game*, 1939), universally regarded as Renoir's masterpiece, a film examining the self-destructive forces at work in French society; the film incited so much anger that it was successfully banned by the right wing the same year it was released.

Renoir came to the United States in 1941, the same year he released *Swamp Water* (1941), a mildly successful story shot on location in the dank fens of Georgia. Though he made some fine films during the next 30 years—*The Southerner* (1945), *The Woman on the Beach* (1947), *The River* (1951, shot in India), and his last film, *Le Petit Théâtre de Jean Renoir* (1971)—most agree that his best years were behind him. Nevertheless, Renoir left behind a legacy of cinematic beauty that would have made his pappy proud.

The Real *Poetic Realism*

1930s France is especially renowned for introducing the cinematic world to poetic realism, a style of filmmaking of which Renoir's *La Bête humaine* and Gance's *Paradis perdu* (1939) are prime examples. Other important directors in this style included Marcel Carné (*Quai des brummes,* 1938; *Le Jour se lève,* 1939), Pierre Chenal (*La Rue sans nom,* 1933; *Le Dernier Tournant,* 1939), and Jean Grémillon (*Gueule d'amour,* 1937). Jean Gabin was the leading actor of poetic realism; the future editor of the *Cahiers du cinéma,* André Bazin, would one day hail him as "the tragic hero of contemporary cinema."

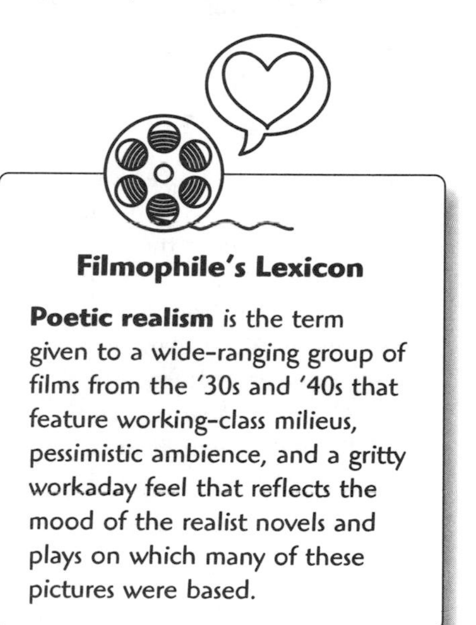

Filmophile's Lexicon

Poetic realism is the term given to a wide-ranging group of films from the '30s and '40s that feature working-class milieus, pessimistic ambience, and a gritty workaday feel that reflects the mood of the realist novels and plays on which many of these pictures were based.

An unheralded master of French *poetic realism* was Alexander Trauner, a painter by training who sought to apply his expertise in design to the construction of ever more realistic movie sets, primarily for the films of Carné. For Trauner, the mise-en-scène of a shot should reflect the psychology of a film's characters, giving the audience a real feel for what's going on inside the actors' heads.

Trauner's greatest films in the poetic realist tradition include *Quai des brumes* (1938), *Le Jour se lève* (1939), *Les Enfants du paradis* (1945), and *Les Portes de la Nuit* (1946). Above all poetic realism is a "look," and there was no one better at fashioning this look than Alexander Trauner.

Surfing the "New Wave"

The outbreak of World War II was a watershed for the thriving French film industry. During the Nazi occupation, many filmmakers (Jean Renoir among them) fled to Hollywood, where they launched highly successful American careers; others stayed on in Paris and made films that stayed safely away from the eyes of the censors while sometimes embedding hidden anti-German messages in their productions.

Ironically, as they would in Italy, the oppressive war years made possible the budding careers of a variety of directors, including Robert Bresson (*Les Anges du Péché,* 1943; *Les Dames du Bois de Boulogne,* 1945), Henri-Georges Clouzot (*L'Assassin habite au 21,* 1942; *Le Corbeau,* 1943), and Jacques Becker (*Goupi Mains rouges,* 1943; *Falbalas,* 1945).

The Changing of the 'Garde

For France, the 1950s was a period of rebuilding and rethinking. While the bombed and shelled edifices of Paris were being replastered and restored, the well-known directors from the prewar period returned to France and shot some of their most expensive (if in some cases less inspired) films. René Clément's *Jeux interdits* (1952) and *Plein soleil* (1959) shuttle between wartime melodrama and Hitchcockian suspense, while the German expatriate Max Ophüls kicks in with costume dramas like *Madame de...* (1953) and *Lola Montès* (1955).

Second Take

Though they were often castigated as reactionary and traditionalist by some of the *Nouvelle Vague* (New Wave) crowd, be sure not to miss Jean Renoir's post–World War II films, especially *Elène et les Hommes* (1956), *Le Déjeuner sur l'Herbe* (1959), and *Le Testament du Dr. Cordelier* (1961).

But things were changing in French filmdom. (For better or worse? We'll leave it up to you!) While the mainstream studios picked up production where they'd left off before the occupation, a cadre of young radical artists, writers, critics, and aspiring directors was emerging to challenge the dominance of the entrenched powers in the nation's industry.

Claude Chabrol's *Le Beau Serge* (1958) and Alain Resnais's great *Hiroshima Mon Amour* (1959) officially launched the *Nouvelle Vague,* or "New Wave" of French cinema, a movement dedicated to rejecting what were seen as the sappy pretensions of the older generations of filmmakers.

Cahiers du Cinéma

What united the main directors of the New Wave more than anything else was a new and immediately controversial journal called *Cahiers du cinéma.* The magazine was founded in 1951 by Jacques Doniol-Valcroze and, more important, André Bazin, a brilliant and iconoclastic writer on film who believed that cinema's greatest attribute was its ability to project "objective reality" to its audience without the interference of montage or other messy technical feats. His heroes were American directors like Ford, Welles, Howard Hawks, Otto Preminger, and Sam Fuller, as well as some true "B-movie" directors who never achieved much commercial or artistic success during their careers.

The *Cahiers* writers valued a director's individuality above all else; their most revered auteurs were not primarily independent directors, but rather those who had carved out a unique cinematic voice for themselves while financed and managed by the big studios. Indeed, it was here, in a famous 1954 essay, that François Truffaut launched what came to be called the "Auteur Theory," and the journal's pages were subsequently filled with essays and position papers arguing for the promotion of any number of obscure and previously unacclaimed directors to auteur status.

Second Take

Don't be a Franco-fool! *Cahiers* is not pronounced "*ku-HEERS,*" but "*ka-HYAY.*"

In addition to Truffaut and Godard, other writer/directors associated with *Cahiers du cinéma* whose films were deeply influenced by the journal's theoretical stances were Claude Chabrol (*Les Bonnes Femmes,* 1960), Jacques Rivette (*L'Amour fou,* 1968), and Eric Rohmer (*Chloe in the Afternoon,* 1972). The journal, still published today, remains at the forefront of world film criticism and opinion.

True Truffaut

Watching *The 400 Blows* (1959) is one of the most haunting, moving, and painful cinematic experiences you'll ever have. François Truffaut's first feature film was also his most autobiographical, tracing the experiences of an adolescent boy named Antoine Doinel (played brilliantly by Jean-Pierre Léaud) as he survives a sentence in a juvenile prison. Truffaut, too, had an extremely unhappy childhood that culminated in grueling work at a factory in his teenage years. After the war, Truffaut's passion for the movies was recognized by a prominent writer on the French cinema named André Bazin, who encouraged the cynical young moviegoer to join his growing staff at the offices of *Cahiers du cinéma.*

Jean-Pierre Léaud as the abused Antoine Doinel in Truffaut's Les Quatre Cents Coups (The 400 Blows, *1959*).

More than any other French filmmaker, Truffaut used his work to wed film theory and criticism with film production and artistry. Writing slavish encomiums to Hitchcock, the great British auteur, in the pages of his journal while imitating his style in humorous suspense films like *Tirez sur le pianist* (1960), Truffaut sought to provide filmmaking with a firm historical and intellectual grounding in the past of the art form. One of his greatest and most acclaimed films, *Jules et Jim* (1961), combines a passionate and technically brilliant meditation on the emotional violence of war (the title characters are, respectively, a German man and a Frenchman fighting it out over a woman they both love on the eve of World War I) with a lyrical sadness that makes the film one of the truly beautiful pictures to come out of the New Wave.

Other Truffaut films to watch include a few shorts, *Une Visite* (1954), *Les Mistons* (1958), and *Histoire d'Eau* (1959), which he codirected with Jean-Luc Godard; the other films featuring Antoine Doinel, such as *Baisers volés* (*Stolen Kisses,* 1968), *Domicile conjugal* (*Bed and Board,* 1970), and *L'Amour en fuite* (*Love on the Run,* 1979); and his great movie about the movies, *La Nuit américaine,* which won an Oscar in 1973.

Thank God(ard) for French Film

If Truffaut's contribution to the New Wave was a quiet pathos and a frank look at human emotions, Jean-Luc Godard's career was characterized by riveting portrayals of outsiders and the socially marginal: prostitutes, foreigners, political dissidents, criminals. His low-budget debut feature, *À Bout de Souffle* (*Breathless,* 1960), was a stunning break from convention. The story of a young Parisian car thief who befriends an American student who ultimately betrays him, *Breathless* features handheld camerawork, an original screenplay learned by the actors just before filming each scene, and even the use of a wheelchair for tracking. It remains one of the most technically influential films in history. (You know those wiggly, jumpy shots that open every scene of *NYPD Blue?* It's Godard, plain and simple.)

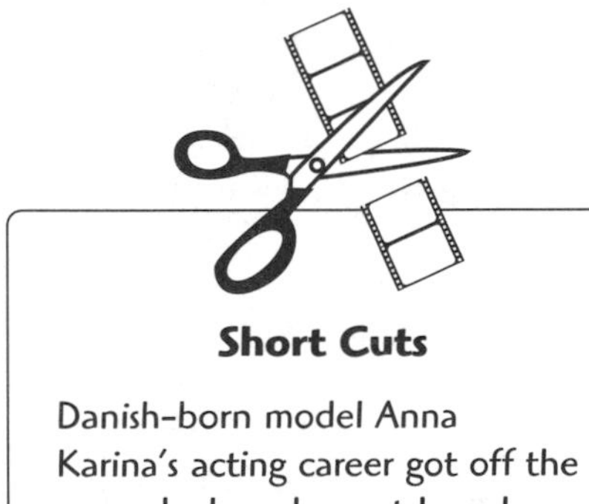

Short Cuts

Danish-born model Anna Karina's acting career got off the ground when she met Jean-Luc Godard in the early '60s. After their marriage in 1961, she starred in several of his films during the following years, including *Un Femme est une Femme* (1961) and *Vivre sa Vie* (1962).

Many of Godard's films inspired controversy as soon as they were released. *Le Petit Soldat,* planned for release in 1960, was banned by French censors for three full years because of its largely sympathetic portrayal of an Algerian terrorist. Other groundbreaking films from this period of his career include *Une Femme est une Femme* (1961), *Vivre sa Vie* (1962), *Les Carabiniers* (1963), and *La Chinoise* (1967).

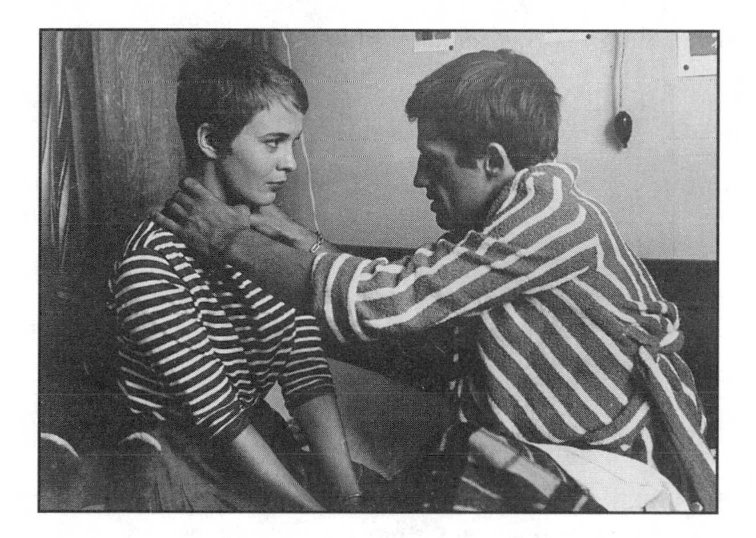

A typically grainy shot from Godard's À Bout de Souffle (Breathless, *1960*).

In 1971, after a close-call motorcycle accident, Godard took a break from narrative in favor of experimentation with explicitly political and ideological film essays. One of the best of these is *Tout va bien* (1972), which starred Yves Montand and Jane Fonda in a sweeping look at recent changes in French society.

He also went through a long video phase, experimenting with the possibilities of the new medium and producing a number of works that remain unwatched by all but the experts.

Many critics believe that Godard's politics were deeply naive, his turn away from the breathtaking innovations in narrative film that had won him an international following the act of a narcissistic chameleon who took on different political causes at the drop of a hat. But some of his films from the 1970s and '80s—we're thinking especially of gems like *Numéro Deux* (1975), *Passion* (1982), *Prénom: Carmen* (1983), and *Aria* (1987)—deserve much more acclaim than they've received from the purists. Godard gives you decades of filmmaking to enjoy; his career embraces an enormous artistic diversity and creativity that you'd be a complete idiot not to check out!

Second Take

Godard followed up *Tout va bien* the same year with a really nasty "conversation" film called *Letter to Jane,* in which he and his collaborator engage in a cruel critique of what they clearly regarded as Jane Fonda's politics of convenience.

The Eighties and Nineties

We could easily write another *Complete Idiot's Guide* focusing solely on the last 20 years of French film. You probably already know some of what we'd have to cover:

Luc Besson's *La femme Nikita* (1990), the acting talents (and majestic schnoz) of Gérard Depardieu. The tip of the new French film iceberg includes directors like Yannick Bellon, Leos Carax, Étienne Chatiliez, Nelly Kaplan, Jeanne Moreau, Coline Serreau, and many others.

The best we can do is ask you—*beg* you, more like it—to find out where you can either watch or get a hold of this fantastic stuff on video and DVD and devour as much as you can!

All in all, France's new crop of young directors has more than lived up to the legacy of their artistic forebears in the medium.

Filmophile's Lexicon

Cinéma du look is a catchword for the postmodern films of Jean-Jacques Beineix, Luc Besson, and other '80s directors who focused on the visual image per se as the overall "message" of film.

Ten Fabulous French Films

You can read about them till the moon turns blue, but until you actually sit down and watch them, you can't begin to appreciate the full menu of French films the twentieth century bequeathed to posterity. What we've given you here is a chronological list of our 10 favorite French films made during the sound era.

The key word in that last sentence is *our.* We're not aiming for historical coverage or stylistic range here. Some "real biggies" are on our list, as are a few more obscure masterpieces that we highly recommend. As with all of the film lists we've provided in this book, though, a few hours of visual pleasure a week will permanently transform you from head-scratching neophyte to discriminating connoisseur.

- *L'Age d'Or* (*The Golden Age,* 1930), directed by Luis Buñuel.
- *La Règle de Jeu* (*Rules of the Game,* 1939), directed by Jean Renoir.
- *Hiroshima Mon Amour* (1959), directed by Alain Resnais.
- *Les Quatre Cents Coups* (*The 400 Blows,* 1959), directed by François Truffaut.
- *À Bout de Souffle* (*Breathless,* 1960), directed by Jean-Luc Godard.
- *Jules et Jim* (*Jules and Jim,* 1961), directed by François Truffaut.

Filmophile's Lexicon

Cinéma beur refers to a new wave of naturalistic films directed by and featuring the lives of young North Africans in France; Rachid Bouchareb's *Cheb* (1990) and Mehdi Charef's *Le Thé au harem d'Archimède* (1986) are among the most influential examples of this recent genre.

- *Les Jeux Interdits* (*Forbidden Games,* 1952), directed by René Clément.
- *L'Amour l'après-midi* (*Chloe in the Afternoon,* 1972), directed by Eric Rohmer.
- *Diva* (1981), directed by Jean-Jacques Beineix.
- *Ma Vie en Rose* (1997), directed by Alain Berliner.

The Least You Need to Know

- France's film tradition has always been self-conscious about the cinema as an art form.
- Georges Méliès was film's first great illusionist.
- French film dominated the world industry in the early 1900s and exerted unparalleled influences on the subsequent century of filmmaking.
- The avant-garde movement known as poetic realism, spearheaded by Jean Renoir, came to prominence in the decade before World War II.
- A "New Wave" of French filmmakers—among them Jean-Luc Godard and François Truffaut—reacted strongly against the old guard in the postwar years.
- French film continues to thrive today in a wide variety of genres and styles.

Chapter 12

A Century of Italian Film

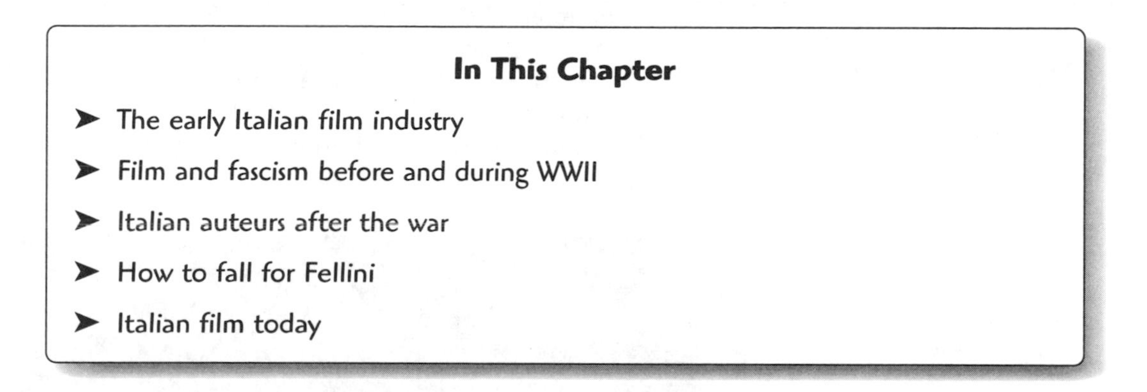

In This Chapter

- The early Italian film industry
- Film and fascism before and during WWII
- Italian auteurs after the war
- How to fall for Fellini
- Italian film today

Italy's first fiction film wasn't released until 1905. Filoteo Alberini's *La presa di Roma, 20 settembre 1870* (*The Capture of Rome, September 20, 1870*) represented the nation's relatively late appearance on the European cinematic scene. One of the problems was Italy's economic standing on the continent, which had never rivaled that of France or Germany. A bigger issue, though, was the dominance of French filmmakers and production companies over virtually every aspect of Italian cinema.

By 1910, however, the fledgling Italian film industry was establishing an identity of its own after the long French choke hold. Studios like Alberini & Santoni (eventually Cines), Milano Films, Ambrosio, Aquila, and Pasquali and Tempo gave strong impetus to the writers, directors, and other personnel who would go on to create a booming silent film industry in cities across the peninsula.

Turnin' to Turin

The Shroud of Turin, Jesus Christ's alleged burial cloth, isn't the only thing that established this small city as a famous name in Italy's long cultural history. While most of

Director's Cut

Despite the Italian name he adopted during his years in Turin, the great comedic actor Cretinetti was actually French by birth. Born André Chapuis in 1884, Andrá Deed, as he later came to be known, made numerous slapstick flicks for Ambrosia, including *Cretinetti alla Guerra* (1909) and *Cretinetti e le Donne* (1915).

us think of Rome, Florence, and Milan when asked to name Italy's artistic centers, Turin became one of the true capitals of European filmmaking by 1910, and remained so through the outbreak of World War I.

And indeed, for a while there it looked like the role would take. The peak of Italy's silent era, roughly 1910 to 1918, witnessed the rise of what would become the country's most dominant and recognized genre: the historical costume spectacle. Many of these films were truly innovative and outstanding. *Quo Vadis* (1912), directed by Enrico Guazzoni for Rome's Cines, featured huge crowds of extras and gigantic sets in its adaptation of the Nobel Prize–winning novel by the Polish writer Henryk Sienkiewicz. Giovanni Pastrone's monumental *Cabiria* (1914), made for the Turin company Itala, was the most grandiose film production to date, inspiring the great American director D. W. Griffith to expand his vision of what an epic film could be and featuring numerous innovations in camera movement and shot selection.

A shot from the 1919 Italian spectacle Theodora Empress of Byzantium.

Other directors, however, turned away from spectacle and sought to depict the workaday life of Italians. Febo Mari's *L'emigrante* (*The Emigrant*, 1915) and Emilio Ghione's *I topi grigi* (*The Grey Rats*, 1918) are excellent examples of this so-called "first wave" of Italian film realism that would culminate in "neorealism" after World War II.

Director's Cut

It was hoped by many that MGM's decision to film the massively expensive *Ben-Hur* (1922) in Italy would breathe some life into the nation's industry, which was suffering greatly after World War I. By following the American example of pumping the big bucks into film production, industry leaders thought, Italian companies might revive an art form that had flourished before the war.

It wasn't to be. After numerous staffing and financial problems (including the firing of both the original director, Rex Ingram, and the star, George Walsh), real disaster struck. During the filming of sea battle sequences off the coast of Livorno, several accidents led to the deaths of a number of crew members, and the film eventually moved production out of Italy and back to Hollywood.

The Wages of War

By the end of World War I, though, the Italian film business was hurting. Aside from the vast resources the economically bereft nation had to invest in the war (and thus drain from other sectors of life), competition from much more powerful American and European national industries put unprecedented pressure on Italian studios, and soon things simply dried up.

Although a few attempts were made at forging production and distribution monopolies or otherwise pumping money into the flagging industry, Italian film wouldn't see anything approaching a large-scale revival until several years after the Fascists came to power.

Filmophile's Lexicon

Divas, a term originally applied to opera heroines, were the sensuous, tragically beautiful, and passionate female leads of a subgenre of Italian film that dominated the screen during the 1920s. Women like Lyda Borelli, Rina De Liguoro, Pina Minichelli, Helena Makowska, and several others made dozens of stock melodramas that contributed greatly to the qualitative decline of Italian cinema during this period.

Ringing the White Telephone

Over the course of the 1930s, large sectors of the Italian film industry increasingly came to be dominated by the partisans of the Nazi's eventual Fascist ally in Italy, Benito Mussolini. A whole governmental department, called the Direzione Generale per le Cinematografia, was established to regulate content and oversee production. The Mussolini regime founded what would become one of Europe's most influential film schools, the Centro Sperimentale di Cinematografia, in 1935, and funded construction of the great Cinecittà studios two years later.

Filmophile's Lexicon

White telephone (*telefoni bianci*) films—glitzy, glossy dramas and comedies dripping with sentiment—were one of the predominant forms of motion picture during the Mussolini regime. The elegance of these films' glamorous settings was embodied in the image of the "white telephone," a symbol of their opulent refusal to comment on contemporary affairs.

And in perhaps the most direct sign of Fascist domination over Italian film, for a significant period of time between 1938 and 1945, the Duce's son, Vittorio Mussolini, became one of the leading "creative" forces in the peninsula's cinematic culture.

The numerous so-called *white telephone* films produced during this period—directed by now-forgotten filmmakers like Carlo Bragaglia, Guido Brignone, and Gennaro Righelli (who, interestingly enough, also made Italy's first sound film, *La canzone dell'amore* [*The Love Song,* 1930])—projected an image of serene glamour to the viewing public that was rarely sullied by the violent turmoil of the war. Other directors with promising careers—including even such future luminaries as Roberto Rossellini—were recruited by Mussolini's regime to make transparently propagandistic films.

Despite Mussolini's best efforts, though, there were literally hundreds of films only marginally affected by the regime's desires and demands. While most of these were (pardon our French) garbage, a few directors continued to make very good films. Alessandro Blasetti's superb historical drama, *1860* (1934), an important forerunner of neorealism, was followed at the height of World War II by the ominously titled *La Corona di Ferro* (*The Iron Crown,* 1941). Mario Camerini's comedies—especially *Il signor Max* (1937) and *Darò un milione* (*I'll Give a Million,* 1935)—rival the best German, French, or American films of the prewar era.

Short Cuts

"For us, cinema is the strongest weapon."

—Benito Mussolini

All in all, the Fascist era left a mixed legacy to film history, a strange blend of hateful propaganda, innovation, faux elegance, and unexpected charm that the succeeding generation of Italian filmmakers would voraciously reject.

A Few Good Films

The great cinema scholar Ephraim Katz, author of *The Film Encyclopedia,* calls the three decades after World War II a "vast wasteland" in Italian cinema, and for good reason. After 10 wonderfully successful and creative years of neorealism (keep reading!), the nation's movie moguls sought to create a "Hollywood on the Tiber" by pumping vast amounts of (largely American) money into the production of spectacular films that would reestablish Italy's greatness in the medium. It didn't happen.

Nevertheless, the period from 1950 through 1980 did produce a fair number of excellent films. Three directors in particular emerged from the ashes of World War II to become internationally acclaimed artists. And the postwar years gave birth to a small group of stars who lit up silver screens around the world with a dazzling and uniquely Italian combination of wit, irony, and sizzling gorgeousness.

The Other Michelangelo

It would be hard for an artist in any medium to live up to Michelangelo Antonioni's first name, though the great Italian director certainly did his best. After studying business at the University of Bologna, Antonioni took up a number of jobs in the film industry, collaborating on scripts, directing shorts and documentaries, and doing some producing before directing his first feature, *Cronaca di un Amore* (*Story of a Love Affair*), in 1950.

Like many of Italy's post–World War II directors, Antonioni had unmistakable ties to the Fascists during the early part of his career. He contributed to the journal *Cinema* during World War II, when it was being coedited by Mussolini's son Vittorio, and attended the Fascist-established film school, the Centro Sperimentale di Cinematografia, for a brief stint in the early '40s.

Second Take

If you're looking for riveting story lines, you won't find them in most of Antonioni's films, which tend to feature long but penetrating shots that go nowhere while revealing with often searing intensity the emotional depths of his characters.

Most importantly, perhaps, Antonioni's films are character-driven rather than plot-driven, a distinction that's crucial to bear in mind while watching his pictures. *Le Amiche* (*The Girlfriends,* 1955), for instance, is a highly complex meditation on the intricacies of human relationships, a theme treated with even greater success in *L'Eclisse* (*The Eclipse,* 1962).

Antonioni was particularly adept at using color to bring out psychological dimensions of his characters, though his first color feature, *Il Deserto Rosso* (*Desert Red,* 1964), failed miserably in this regard in its banal treatment of human alienation in modern society. His later American-produced films, such as *Blow-Up* (1967 for MGM) and *Zabriskie Point* (1970), while not critically acclaimed, created highly pessimistic views of contemporary materialism.

If you're planning an "Antonioni-othon," though, it'd be best to stick with the 1950s. Films like *I vinti* (1952), *La signora senza camelie* (1953), and *Il Grido* (*The Outcry,* 1957) clearly represent some of his best work, conveying with unrivaled depth and haunting drama the tortured inner world of human emotions. *Blow Up* is another film that you should make a real point of watching.

Filmophile's Lexicon

Neorealism was a cinematic movement, originating in Italy, that reached its peak in the late '40s and early '50s; in response to the feel-good pap of the "white telephone" era, neorealists demanded a turn to natural settings rather than artificially constructed sets, "real people" instead of actors, and authentic human stories rather than stale melodrama.

Getting Real(ist) with Roberto

Like Antonioni, Roberto Rossellini had Fascist ties during the early years of his career, collaborating on the script of *Luciana Serra Pilota* (1938), which was made under the watchful eye of the Duce's son, Vittorio. But the political commitment and consistency of his cinematic vision soon allowed him to triumph over the propagandistic wasting of his talents during World War II. The result was an illustrious and often notorious career that would change the face of filmmaking forever.

Above all, Rossellini gave crucial impetus to the aesthetic movement dubbed *neorealism,* a turn toward the hard reality of the human condition that many film historians would argue officially begins with his *Roma, città aperta* (*Open City*) of 1945.

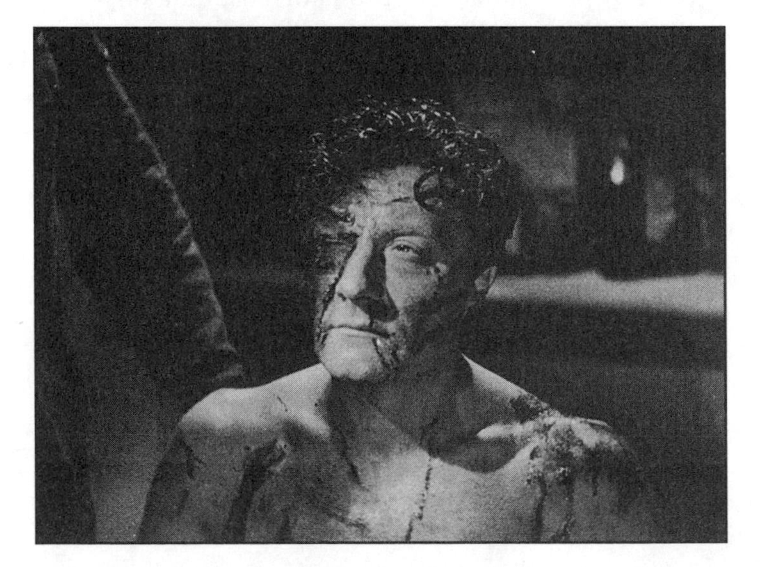

Marcello Pagliero as the resistance leader Manfredi in Roberto Rossellini's neorealist Roma, città aperta *(1945).*

Neorealism had important precedents in silent-era naturalism and films such as Luchino Visconti's *Ossessione* (*Obsession,* 1942). In fact, the term was coined by the critics Umberto Barbaro and Antonio Pietrangeli in a discussion of Visconti's thriller, which was adapted from the American novel *The Postman Always Rings Twice,* by James Cain. Rossellini was one of the undisputed masters of the new style, however, and many historians would agree that he exploited its possibilities with the greatest success.

Director's Cut

Some of the greatest film sequences of all time are contained in Rossellini's so-called "World War II Trilogy," which consists of three movies that should be on the very top of your foreign film must-see list:

Roma, città aperta (*Open City,* 1945), shot in the streets, alleyways, and apartments of Rome, was the hallmark film of neorealism and used the ancient ruined city as both setting and set.

Paisà (*Paisan,* 1946) is made up of six vignettes documenting the human side of the postwar liberation of the Italian peninsula.

Germania Anno Zero (*Germany Year Zero,* 1947) explores the Nazi-inflicted psychological turmoil of a young German boy who turns against his own family before committing suicide.

Aside from their enormous influence upon the succeeding decade of Italian and worldwide filmmaking, the three films in the trilogy are notable for the stark but moving performances of their mostly nonprofessional, untrained casts and the gritty realism of their camerawork. Make a bucket of popcorn and watch all three in one night!

Unfortunately for Rossellini's artistic legacy, his career is just as well known for his steamy and controversial marriage to Ingrid Bergman as for his filmic genius. Roberto and Ingrid hooked up, left their respective spouses, and got hitched in 1950. She starred in several of his films during the next few years—and, not coincidentally, gave birth to Isabella Rossellini of *Blue Velvet* fame. Isabella was their only truly successful collaboration, however; *Stromboli* (1949), *Europa '51* (1952), and *Viaggio in Italia* (*Voyage to Italy,* 1953) are considered some of Rossellini's weakest works.

Their marriage soon followed suit, ending in an annulment in 1958 after a decade of international scorn and condemnation and the virtual blacklisting of Bergman from American moviedom. Rossellini's later career was generally undistinguished, though he did win the Grand Prix at the Venice Film Festival for *Il Generale della Rovere* (1959), which is very much worth seeing.

Fellini the Fabulous

And then, of course, there's Fellini, perhaps Italy's most enduringly beloved director. Unlike both Antonioni and Rossellini (or, for that matter, Hitchcock and Welles!), Federico Fellini never had a real "low point" in his career. He made some clunkers, sure, but few would argue that his talents diminished with age. Instead, his early life as a cartoonist, a loafer, a draft-avoiding student, and a circus devotee would inspire 40 years of consistently fabulous filmmaking and 24 feature-length pictures that have few rivals on the European screen.

Fellini's career in film began with his collaborations on the script of the first picture in Rossellini's great World War II neorealist trilogy, *Roma, città aperta*. He also worked as an assistant director for prominent and emerging neorealist directors before collaborating with Alberto Lattuada in Fellini's directorial debut, *Luci del Varietà* (*Variety Lights*, 1951). His solo debut, though, had to wait one more year; *Lo Sceicco bianco* (*The White Sheik,* 1952), a commercial failure like *Variety Lights,* nevertheless foreshadows the farcical voice of his later films with wit and skill.

Fellini's big break came in the early 1950s with two films that immediately established his international reputation. *I Vitelloni* (*The Loafers*, 1953) is a quasi-autobiographical story about a group of urban loafers, while *La strada* (1954) tells a story of sexual domination that combines an almost claustrophobic personal intensity with a broad social drama on the costs and constraints of human freedom. While Fellini's career had been boosted by his early work with Rossellini, these two films marked a decisive break from neorealism in favor of an indomitable focus on the fantastical that is no less serious than neorealism's most jaundiced attempts at psychological portraiture.

Short Cuts

$8\frac{1}{2}$ was so named because Fellini had directed seven solo films and three collaborations previously; each collaboration counted for half of a film. (Get it? $7 + \frac{1}{2} + \frac{1}{2} + \frac{1}{2} = 8\frac{1}{2}$.)

Themes of sex and lapsed morals remained central to Fellini's subsequent films; *Le Notti di Cabiria* (*Nights of Cabiria,* 1957) features a disenchanted prostitute who can't get out of the world she yearns to escape, while *La Dolce Vita* (1960), which many consider Fellini's finest picture, starred Marcello Mastroianni as a gossip columnist uncovering dirty secrets about members of Rome's elite social circles.

It was in *$8\frac{1}{2}$* (*Otto e Mezzo,* 1963) that Fellini made his most complex and confessional autobiographical statement. A superb story of a film director who can't decide what to make his next film about, *8½* explores with visual audacity and psychological contortions the inner mental world of the artist. The film garnered Fellini his third Oscar for best foreign film.

Franco Interlenghi as Moraldo with his group of provincial ne'er-do-wells in Fellini's I Vitelloni (The Loafers, *1953*).

Fellini Satyricon (1969) was a less successful but quite controversial adaptation of Petronius's decadent Latin novel of the same name. The original *Satyricon,* which survives only in fragments, was written in the waning years of the Roman Empire (you know, when Nero was fiddling while Rome burned), and it features the appropriate amount of sexual and other forms of debauchery that Fellini clearly had a great time bringing to the screen. Opinion has always been divided about the merits of this film, but if you try reading the Petronius novel before watching it—which few of Fellini's critics seem to have bothered doing—we think you'll find that fewer literary adaptations have been so artfully true to the original.

Fellini won yet another Oscar for *Armacord* (1973), which turned back to his boyhood memories for inspiration, and delighted American audiences with a nostalgic homage to the nation's golden cinematic past with *Ginger and Fred* in 1985. Fellini's final film, *Voices of the Moon* (1990), was released four years before his death. A personal retrospective of his last 40 years, the film brought a moving and, in many ways, clarifying end to a career whose results continue to delight millions of filmophiles around the world.

Falling for Fellini

Here are four great reasons to start renting, watching, and absorbing the great Italian director's life's work today:

- Fellini made 24 films—a considerable number, but not insurmountable, meaning you can begin to master his entire *oeuvre* in two or three months of subtitle-packed weekends.
- Fellini's films are some the most frequently referenced foreign films by today's master directors (Woody Allen's work, for example, is loaded with clever allusions).
- When some snobby NYU grad at a cocktail party sneers "That guy's *so* eight-and-a-half" you'll know what he means.
- Fellini is so self-conscious about the history and artistry of the cinema that his work will continually whet your appetite for a broader range of Italian and European film.

Face Time

Other directors, if less distinguished and acclaimed than the three we've been discussing, also made important contributions to Italian cinema from the early '50s through the '70s. The eminently controversial Pier Paolo Pasolini clashed with the church and state establishments with sex-laden films like *The Canterbury Tales* (1972) and *The 120 Days of Sodom* (1975). Bernardo Bertolucci's cross-Atlantic career, which began with the notorious *Last Tango in Paris* (1972), would later culminate in nine Academy Awards for *The Last Emperor* (1987). Other important directorial names from this period are Pietro Germi, Francesco Maselli, Francesco Rosi, and Valerio Zurlini.

The period from 1950 through 1980 is equally well known for giving the world some of its most desired and admired faces. After Sophia Loren's discovery by producer Carlo Ponti in the late '40s, international audiences got to witness her incomparable beauty as she launched her film career with seductive roles in *La Tratta delle Bianche* (*The White Slave Trade,* 1952), *Aïda* (1953), and *Peccato che sia una Canaglia* (*Too Bad She's Bad,* 1955) before she took Hollywood by storm in 1958. Loren's greatest performance and the peak of her career came with her Oscar-winning role as the tragic maternal heroine of De Sica's *La Ciociara* (*Two Women,* 1961), a film that belongs near the top of your Italian list with Rossellini's trilogy.

Short Cuts

Marcello Mastroianni and Sophia Loren steamily starred together as romantic leads in several Italian films during the '60s. They were reunited as romantic retirees after a long hiatus in Robert Altman's *Ready to Wear* (1994).

Gina Lollabrigida was a close rival to Loren for sheer audience allure during the 1940s (see, for example, *Follie per l'opera* [*Mad About the Opera,* 1948] and *Campane a Martello* [*Children of Chance,* 1949]). But she lost much of her unique Continental sexiness at the hands of Hollywood's uniformity machine and ended her acting career by starring on—egad!—*Falcon Crest* in the 1980s. The great romantic lead, Marcello Mastroianni, came to international prominence with starring roles in films by Fellini, Antonioni, and Pietro Germi, becoming one of the world's most recognized male faces and the quintessential embodiment of raw masculine sexiness.

The Past 20 Years

During the 1980s, American movies virtually dominated the Italian film industry, constituting up to 75 percent of the motion pictures the nation's audiences watched. Even more than the '50s, '60s, and '70s, the '80s and early '90s were not boom years for Italian cinema, and few directors emerged to assume the auteur mantle worn proudly by Antonioni, Rossellini, and Fellini.

Director's Cut

There are two directors currently working in Italy who have, for better or worse, been dubbed "The Italian Woody Allen." Nanni Moretti disguises often biting social and political commentary beneath a seemingly innocuous comedic cover. Check out *Le Messa e finita* (*The Mass Is Ended,* 1986), in which Moretti himself stars as a priest.

Italy's other answer to Woody Allen (and the director who probably better fits the label) is Massimo Troisi, a director renowned for his lighthearted glimpses at Italian society in films like *Ricominci da tre* (*I'm Starting Again from Three,* 1980) and *Le vie del signore sono finite* (*The Lord's Ways Are Finished,* 1987).

New Blood

Things have started to change, though, due in large part to the considerable efforts of five or six filmmakers who have worked diligently during the past 20 years to establish once again Italy's reputation for cinematic innovation and brilliance. Foremost among these is Nanni Moretti, whose 1976 *Io sono un autoarchico* (*I Am an Anarchist*) marked a turning point in the nature of Italian film comedy. A committed Marxist and a brilliant humorist, Moretti laces his films with an ironic wit that receives its most bizarrely satisfying manifestation in *Palombella rossa* (*Red Lob,* 1989), a comment on the recent fortunes of Italian Communism through the allegorical veil of a water polo match. His recent film *Caro Diario* (*Dear Diary,* 1996) is a gently moving autobiographical meditation on motorbike riding, Rome, and the artist's own struggle with cancer.

Other important directors in recent years are Maurizio Nichetti (*Volere Volare* [*To Wish to Fly,* 1991]), Gabriele Salvatores (*Mediterraneo,* 1991), and especially Gianni Amelio, whose treatment of contemporary crime includes a spectacular terrorism film, *Colpire al cuore* (*To Strike at the Heart,* 1982), and *Il ladro di bambini* (*The Child Snatcher,* 1992), the story of a child abductor that marked a significant commercial success for mainstream Italian film.

Italy's "Little Devil"

Roberto Benigni became a household name in the United States only in the late '90s, when *Life Is Beautiful,* a film he directed and in which he starred as a father using humor to help his son survive a Nazi concentration camp, won an Oscar for best foreign picture (and was nominated for best picture).

But Italian and other European audiences have known Benigni for years as the "Little Devil," a humorous sprite who's popped up in any number of guises as a trickster, a rogue, and generally loud pesty little guy in numerous comedies beginning in the late '70s with *Letti Selvaggi* (*Tigers in Lipstick,* 1978). Benigni has also played supporting roles in several films of Jim Jarmusch, including *Down by Law* (1986), in which he's cast as Tom Waits's jail mate screaming through the bars for ice cream, and *Night on Earth* (1991), which features his brilliant performance as a taxi driver hurtling madly through the streets of Rome.

The Least You Need to Know

- Feature film came relatively late to the Italian peninsula, and the early studios struggled to catch up to their European counterparts.
- Costume drama and historical spectacle reigned during the early silent era, but World War I decimated the nation's film industry.
- The Fascist period produced hundreds of mediocre films while launching the careers of Rossellini, Antonioni, and others.
- Along with Rossellini and Antonioni, Federico Fellini became a dominant directorial voice in Italian cinema of the '50s, '60s, and '70s.
- The past 10 years have witnessed a wide-scale resurgence in Italian filmmaking.

Chapter 13

Cleaning Up Germany's History of Propaganda Film

In This Chapter

- Expressionism and German film before World War II
- Leni Riefenstahl and the aesthetics of propaganda
- The "Young German Cinema" movement
- Film in East Germany
- German film since reunification

One of the most important behind-the-scenes forces in the first 40 years of German film was the UFA, the Universum Film Aktien Gesellschaft, founded in 1917. This government-sponsored production behemoth exercised enormous power in the nation's industry through the end of World War II, during which it was firmly controlled by the Nazis.

Years earlier, though, and months before the Lumière brothers did their business at the Grande Café in Paris, Max and Emil Skladanowsky held a public showing of motion pictures projected from a device that Emil named the Bioscope. Though the Skladanowsky brothers were thus film pioneers of a sort, for the most part the early history of German cinema is not distinguished.

The country had to wait until the end of World War I for what would become the most influential and lauded German contribution to the history of world cinema. And, most would agree, it was worth the wait. Seemingly out of nowhere, a group of artists emerged to challenge the conventions of the emergent medium and change the face of film forever.

Germany's Greatest -Ism

In 1919, world cinema was changed forever with the release of director Robert Wiene's *The Cabinet of Dr. Caligari* (*Das Kabinett des Dr. Caligari*). The story of a hypnotist who uses a murderous somnambulist to abduct a desirous woman, *Cabinet* explores an underworld of madness, insanity, and institutional decadence that had generally been neglected by silent-era cinema in Germany and around the world.

Filmophile's Lexicon

Expressionism was a movement in early twentieth-century art—painting, music, film, and so on—that sought to make the inner psychological and emotional life of human beings its subject, rather than event-driven outer life (realism) or sensory impression (impressionism).

Second Take

Not everyone was enamored of *The Cabinet of Dr. Caligari,* or of Expressionism more generally. Robert Wolmuth's hard-to-find *Das Kabinett des Dr. Larifari,* released in 1930, is a brilliant parody of the movement's hallmark film—and, if you can get your hands on it, well worth viewing right after taking in the original.

Dr. Caligari and Beyond

The Cabinet of Dr. Caligari was the hallmark film of an aesthetic movement known as German *Expressionism.* The film's set design alone marked the beginning of a new era; Wiene's inventive directing created a dark world of fear and suspicion complemented by the fabulously dark acting of Werner Krauss (Caligari the hypnotist) and Conrad Veidt (Cesare the sleepwalker).

With its distorted perspectives, grotesque enlargements, skewed camera angles, and obliquely directed lighting throwing eerie and paranoia-inducing shadows every which way, the film created a climate of troubled inwardness that broke new ground in representing the repressions, fantasies, and unfulfilled desires structuring the human unconscious.

Wiene's subsequent films in the expressionist style include *Raskolnikoff* (1923) and the yucky *Orlacs Hände* (1925), the story of a pianist who loses his hands in a train accident and becomes convinced that his newly grafted-on hands once belonged to a murderer. This grotesque film is an almost over-the-top example of the German genre, though it's definitely worth a rent. (Maybe watch it one night as a warm-up to *Halloween 12.*)

The German Expressionist school is also famous for introducing the world to the "monster film," a subgenre that quickly captured the public imagination around the world. Paul Wegener's *Der Golem* (*The Golem,* 1920; not to be confused with the "presequel" of the same title that Wegener made in 1914) retells an ancient Jewish legend about a phoenix-like spirit created by a medieval rabbi. It was followed two years later by F. W. Murnau's *Nosferatu,* perhaps the most familiar Expressionist film to today's audiences.

Director's Cut

It's a little-known and rarely discussed fact that the full title of F. W. Murnau's 1922 vampire classic is actually *Nosferatu: Eine Symphonie des Grauens,* or *Nosferatu: A Symphony of Terror.* The musical term *symphony* is a curious metaphor given the film's status as a silent-era masterpiece. Perhaps the film's producers and director were attempting to enlist the power of orchestral music to convey the full range of terror embodied in world cinema's first vampire.

Nosferatu starred Max Schreck as the world's first film vampire in a massively influential performance that set the stage for literally hundreds of subsequent ghoulish and ghostly monster movies during the succeeding decades. Murnau's innovative use of negative film to create death-like effects, his employment of variable camera speeds to simulate fast-action motion, and his decision to shoot the film on location brought Expressionist filmmaking out of the confines of the studio and into the "real world," where an adoring public waited to feel the vampire's bite.

Short Cuts

If you want to spend an evening learning, dissecting, and theorizing the particular aesthetic and political elements that make *Nosferatu* such a superb and important film in all kinds of ways, skip ahead to Chapter 27, "From Theory to Practice: Putting It All Together," which is devoted entirely to Murnau's masterpiece.

Fantastic Fritz

Yet perhaps the most important director of Germany's Expressionist school—in fact, probably the most significant figure in the history of German silent *and* sound film—was Fritz Lang. Lang's variegated early career included stints as a scriptwriter, actor, and film editor. His directorial debut came with *Halbblut* (*The Half-Breed,* 1919), and the same year he began *Die Spinnen* (*The Spiders*). This two-part serial crime story was immensely popular among German audiences, and it immediately established Lang as something of a star in the nation's fledgling film industry.

Director's Cut

Robert Wiene wasn't originally slated to be the director of the Expressionist classic *The Cabinet of Dr. Caligari.* In fact, the producer Erich Pommer selected Fritz Lang for the job. But Lang's *Die Spinnen* was doing so well at the box office that he was pulled at the last minute in favor of Wiene so he could begin work on part two.

Lang's greatest silent film is *Metropolis* (1927), a tremendous, futuristic, *1984*-ish story of totalitarian subjugation and class solidarity that many regard as his greatest work. A four-and-a-half-hour tour-de-force directly inspired by the skyscrapers of Manhattan, *Metropolis* is an urban masterpiece of world cinema that was followed just four years later by another, *M* (1931), which starred Peter Lorre as a psycho child killer haunting a city with its own repressed fears.

The theme of a vengeful mob out of control carried through into Lang's first feature of his "American phase," which began when he came to Hollywood in 1935. *Fury* (1936) starred Spencer Tracy and Katharine Grant in an enduringly powerful and critical story about lynching and mob psychology. Other successful and well-worth-watching films from this phase of his career are *You Only Live Once* (1937), *Western Union* (1941), *Man Hunt* (1941), and *Hangmen Also Die* (1943), with a screenplay coauthored by Bertolt Brecht.

A typically weird shot from Fritz Lang's Expressionist masterpiece, Metropolis *(1926).*

Hitler's Hired Help

One of the most bizarre and fascinating documentaries you'll ever see is Ray Müller's *The Wonderful, Horrible Life of Leni Riefenstahl* (*Die Macht der Bilder: Leni Riefenstahl,* 1993), a three-hour epic look at the biography of one of filmdom's most perplexing figures. Ninety-nine years old and still kicking as of this writing, Leni Riefenstahl is truly one of the most remarkable and disturbing figures in the history of cinema. Her life and career testify to the inextricability of the cinema from the tragic history of Germany in the twentieth century.

Born into a wealthy Berlin family in 1902, Riefenstahl's first break into film was a role in *Der heilige Berg* (*Peaks of Destiny,* 1926), by director Arnold Fanck. In the following years she appeared in several other of Fanck's so-called *mountain films,* giving a recognizable, healthy, and properly Aryan face to a genre that would soon become associated with the racist aspirations of the emerging Nazi party.

Filmophile's Lexicon

Mountain films (*Bergfilme*) were a popular genre of Austrian, German, and Swiss motion pictures in the 1930s that featured dramatic, challenging mountain landscapes coupled with equally challenging human situations confronting the protagonists.

After becoming a well-known figure in mountain films, Riefenstahl wrote and directed her own contribution to the genre in 1932. In terms of its visual effects and cinematography, *Das blaue Licht* (*The Blue Light*) is one of a handful of remarkable pre–World War II German films. Combining a tale of mountain-climbing adventure with a story of passionate love, the film infuses its visual splendor with a deep-seated Germanic mysticism that celebrates the spirit and vitality of the Alpine landscape.

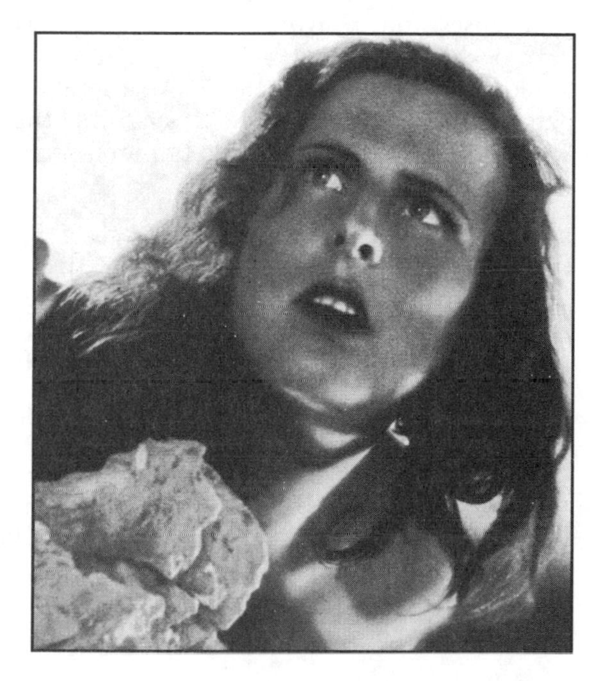

Leni Riefenstahl starring in her own directorial debut, The Blue Light *(1932).*

Second Take

You've probably seen clips from *Triumph of the Will* without knowing it: the mass of German troops marching in lock-step, the camera rising slowly from ground level to take in the rows and columns of Nazi military might, Hitler's triumphant arrogance as he surveys his loyal subjects. The film's haunting images have been permanently branded on the collective memory of Europe.

Short Cuts

"They kept asking me over and over again whether I was having a romance with Hitler. 'Are you Hitler's girlfriend?' I laughed and answered the same way each time: 'No, those are false rumours. I only made documentaries for him.'"

—Leni Riefenstahl

Unfortunately, however, *The Blue Light* and other German mountain films from this period also went to great lengths to celebrate the spirit and vitality of the Aryan *Volk* who were quickly becoming the Nazi regime's obsession. The whiteness of the driven snow and the robust Teutonic energy of Riefenstahl's heroines can and should be viewed as symbols of a growing sense of racial superiority that led to the greatest human tragedy of the twentieth century.

It's no accident that, in the early 1930s, Riefenstahl was hand-picked by Adolf Hitler to direct a series of documentary films in direct propagandistic support of the Nazi party. The first and most influential of these is *Triumph des Willens* (*Triumph of the Will*, 1935).

Shot as a commemoration of the 1934 rally in Nuremberg, *Triumph of the Will* will always be remembered and loathed as perhaps the most dazzling and successful propaganda film ever made.

Riefenstahl's other well-known Nazi-commissioned film is *Olympia* (1938). If less explicitly propagandistic, this two-part documentary treatment of the Olympic Games held in Berlin in 1936 is equally disturbing. Riefenstahl used novel camera positions, slow motion, long lenses, and creative editing to depict the athleticism of the human body in entirely new ways, all the while celebrating the specifically Aryan body at the expense of, for example, Jesse Owens and other non-white athletes who contributed importantly to the 1936 Olympics.

What makes Riefenstahl such a fascinating figure, though, is what's happened to her since the end of World War II. After a failed attempt at a "comeback" in the 1950s, she spent years living with and filming the Nuba tribe in Africa. Her latest project, which some refer to as "oceanographic cinematography," resonates disturbingly with the fetishization of the spectacular at work in *Triumph of the Will.*

Müller's superb documentary will give you an informative and appropriately grand entree into the life of German film's most confounding figure.

A Few Young Men

The most crucial moment in German film since World War II came at the Oberhausen Film Festival in 1962. There a group of two dozen-odd young screenwriters and directors demanded a revolutionary break with the studio-controlled film industry and a new way of thinking about and producing motion pictures.

The result was the Young German Cinema, a group of left-leaning, progressive, resolutely antibourgeois filmmakers who came into their own in the late 1960s and early '70s to challenge the staid conventions of postwar German film. United by a desire to use cinema as a vehicle of social critique (though always resistant to thinking of themselves as a "movement," the Young German Cinema artists made a host of films that won wide acclaim at film festivals worldwide. Several of the most prominent directors, such as Wim Wenders and Werner Herzog, remain leading figures in European film to this day, and it's impossible to understand the past 30 years of German cinema without at least some knowledge of their work.

Filmophile's Lexicon

The **Oberhausen Manifesto,** a petition-like declaration signed by more than two dozen young filmmakers at the Oberhausen Film Festival in 1962, was a collective vow to create a new German cinema that would resist the commercial demands of the nation's dominating film industry.

Here are the five most important directors in the Young German Cinema (and its cousin, the New German Cinema), as well as a list of some of the better (or more notorious!) pictures they've made since the 1960s:

- Volker Schlöndorff: *Young Torless* (*Der Junge Törless,* 1966), *The Rebel* (*Michael Kohlhaas—der Rebell,* 1969), *The Tin Drum* (*Die Blechtrommel,* 1979), *The Lost Honor of Katherina Blum* (*Die Verlorene Ehre der Katharina Blum,* 1975).
- Alexander Kluge: *Yesterday Girl* (*Abschied Von Gestern,* 1966), *Artists at the Top of the Big Top: Disoriented* (*Die Artisten in der Zirkuskuppel: Ratlos,* 1968), *Strongman Ferdinand* (*Der Starke Ferdinand,* 1976), *The Candidate* (*Der Kandidat,* 1980).
- Rainer Werner Fassbinder: *The American Soldiers* (*Der Amerikanische Soldat,* 1970), *The Merchant of Four Seasons* (*Der Händler der vier Jahreszeiten,* 1972), *Lola* (1981), *Veronika Voss* (*Die Sehnsucht der Veronika Voss,* 1982).
- Werner Herzog: *Signs of Life* (*Lebenszeichen,* 1968), *Aguirre, the Wrath of God* (*Aguirre, der Zorn Gottes,* 1972), *The Mystery of Kasper Hauser* (*Jeder für sich und Gott gegen,* 1975), *Fitzcarraldo* (1982), *Lessons in Darkness* (*Lektionen in Finsternis,* 1992).
- Wim Wenders: *Summer in the City* (1970), *The Anxiety of the Goalie at the Penalty Kick* (*Die Angst des Tormannes beim Elfmeter,* 1972), *The American Friend* (*Der Amerikanische Freund,* 1977), *Paris, Texas* (1984), *Wings of Desire* (*Der Himmel über Berlin,* 1987).

Take your time with the movies that have come out of Germany in the past 30 years. These films are all readily available, and given the rather heavy, often depressing themes many of them share, you'll want to swallow this stuff in small doses!

Nastassja Kinski as Jane in Wim Wenders's Paris, Texas *(1984).*

Roads Not Taken: Film in East Germany

The division of Germany into East and West during the Cold War led inexorably to the establishment of two entirely separate national film industries that had little more than celluloid in common. While West Germany made significant strides after the Young German Cinema movement got off the ground, East Germany remained for the most part a cinematic backwater until reunification. The Deutsche Film AG, East Germany's answer to UFA, became the only film-producing entity in the entire country (there were no independent studios to speak of), and it maintained a total monopoly on production for decades.

As with any rule, of course, there are a few exceptions to this one. If you can get your hands on some of the films made in East Berlin before the split in 1949, try to look at the work of Wolfgang Staudte, whose *The Murderers Are Among* Us (*Die Mürder sind unter uns,* 1946) is an anti-Nazi and neoexpressionist classic. (Staudte had starred six years earlier in *Jud Süss,* however, one of the most virulently anti-Semitic films ever made, so you might want to take the politics of *Murderers* with a healthy grain of salt.) Another important moment in East German cinema came between the building of the Berlin Wall in 1961 and the government's notorious crackdown in 1965 (see, for example, Frank Beyer's biting comedy *Carbide and Sorrel* [*Karbid und Sauerampfer,* 1963]). And East Germany's most famous director, Konrad Wolf, made some wonderful films, including *Stars* (*Sterne,* 1958), which won a jury prize at Cannes, and *I Was 19* (*Ich War 19,* 1968).

Unification and Beyond

Since the Reunification in 1990, German cinema has struggled to find its voice. Aside from the utter dominance of American movies (in 1993, the market share of German-made films was under 10 percent; by 1996, the figure was closer to 20 percent), the country remains torn between its divided past and its uncertain future, a cultural identity crisis that is clearly reflected in its films over the last decade. While Vadim Glowna's *Rising to the Bait* (*Der Brocken,* 1991) is the most familiar attempt to engage with the legacy of the Wall, there are many others. One of the most beautiful and moving treatments of the traumas of the Cold War is *The Promise* (*Das Versprechen,* 1994), directed by the brilliant Margarethe von Trotta. The film relates the heart-breaking story of two lovers separated by the Berlin Wall for more than 30 years, during which they meet only four times. The tearful reunion at the end resists sentimentalism and can be seen as a searching allegory of the sudden but tentative reunion of West and East during the past 10 years.

Director's Cut

"It was first after reunification that we started to feel the sense of wholeness that was necessary to start making films about regular people and regular situations. To look at ourselves and say, 'I'm okay.' Now we can make other films. Films that are more serious and have more substance."

—German director Rainer Kaufmann, 1997

Other directors have grown tired of explicit engagement with the nation's troubled history, opting instead for technical innovation and new modes of storytelling as a means of making German film competitive with foreign (especially U.S.) productions. One of the most entertaining German films made in recent years is *Run Lola Run* (*Lola Rennt,* 1998), a fast-paced thriller that combines spliced-in cartoon sequences with postmodern "flash-forwards," time-bending narrative montage, and a reckless pace (*Groundhog Day* meets *Sliding Doors* meets *Natural Born Killers,* perhaps?). Director Tom Tykwer's first film was *Deadly Maria* (*Die Tödliche Maria,* 1993), and his 1997 romantic thriller *Winter Sleepers* (*Winterschläfer*) was well received on the international festival circuit.

German directors today are among the best educated and most talented in the world. Don't miss an opportunity to take advantage of their work at local film festivals and art houses in your city.

The Least You Need to Know

- Expressionism was Germany's greatest artistic contribution to world cinema.
- Fritz Lang was Expressionism's foremost director and one of the leading directorial talents in the history of German film.
- During World War II Leni Riefenstahl was commissioned by Hitler to make propaganda films for the Nazi regime, of which the most famous was *Triumph of the Will.*
- The leftist Young German Cinema movement began in the 1960s with the Oberhausen Manifesto and, under the international appellation New German Cinema, continues to this day in the work of Wim Wenders and other contemporary directors.
- Reunification afforded new opportunities to German filmmakers while presenting unprecedented challenges as well.

Chapter 14

The Silver Screens of Scandinavia

In This Chapter

- The long history of Danish film
- The constraining networks of Norway
- Magnusson, Sjöström, and the early Swedish cinema
- Ingmar Bergman and the postwar years
- Tips for watching Bergman films

Tucked into the remote northern reaches of Europe, the nations that make up Scandinavia might not seem the most obvious places to look for cinematic splendor. Indeed, the region's films have often been rather quiet, understated, but consistently elegant contributions to the art form. In this chapter, we'll be giving you a thumbnail sketch of the Norwegian, Swedish, and Danish film industries—at the expense of their Icelandic and Finnish counterparts, we're afraid. The first feature-length film made by Icelandic directors was Gudmundur Kamban and Gunnar Robert Hansen's collaboration, *Hadda Padda* (1923), a thriller that concludes with a startling and beautifully shot cliff-hanger (literally!). Finland's film history also contains a few real gems (check out Aki Kaurismäki's *Shadows in Paradise* [1986] and *Drifting Clouds* [1996]).

Scandinavia has produced some of the most revered directors and films of all time. This necessarily brief tour of the region's silver screens won't teach you everything you need to know. What it will do, though, is introduce you to a treasure trove of motion pictures that you'd do very well to dig through more thoroughly on your own. From Olsen to Bergman and beyond, Scandinavian film is a visual feast that continues to appeal to audiences far beyond its modest borders.

Danish Directions

On September 17, 1904, the first movie hall opened in Copenhagen, signaling the beginning of what would be an illustrious century for Danish film. Though relatively small by American and French standards, the country's unique contributions to world cinema is often overlooked by all but the experts. The earliest Danish silent films—*Den hvide slavehandel* (*The White Slave Trade,* 1910) for example—were innovative on any number of levels; their frank treatments of sexuality launched what would soon become the international genre of the sensation film.

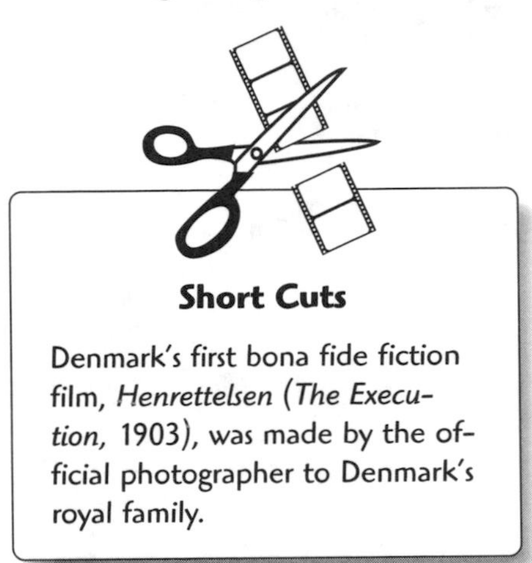

Short Cuts

Denmark's first bona fide fiction film, *Henrettelsen* (*The Execution,* 1903), was made by the official photographer to Denmark's royal family.

These wildly popular pictures involved unprecedented action shots and concordant experiments in numerous technical aspects of filmmaking. In some cases the actors themselves contributed to new effects in, say, lighting by holding a lantern while fleeing a bad guy. Others stood in front of mirrors or screens that heightened the paranoia-inducing effects of certain shots.

World's Oldest Surviving Production Company Shoots All

Denmark's most enduring contribution to world cinema, though, is undoubtedly Nordisk. Founded in 1906 by film pioneer Ole Olsen, within five years Nordisk rivaled France's Pathé for status as the largest production company on the planet. In Denmark itself, the studio's production values moved the nation's cinema away from a widespread preference for short films into the uncharted waters of full-length features. Olsen and Co.'s immediate success in worldwide distribution helped establish the full-length film as an international standard that was quickly imitated elsewhere.

Though not as familiar to most filmophiles as Gaumont, MGM, or the BBC, it's impossible to overestimate the lasting impact Nordisk has had on world cinema—to this day. Indeed, Nordisk is the oldest continually operating film production company in the world, strong testimony to its continuing role as a powerhouse of motion pictures.

Denmark's Fabulous Five

The filmic ferment created by Ole Olsen and other Danish pioneers of production launched the careers of numerous directors around the nation. There are five in particular we'd advise you to check out the next time you're feeling those Nordic notions tugging you to the video store.

- Benjamin Christensen starred in many of his own films, but he's most famous as an undisputed master of the early horror film. Pictures like *The Mysterious X* (*Det Hemmelighedsfulde X,* 1914) and *Häxan* (*Witchcraft Through the Ages,* 1921) exploited the visual possibilities of nighttime and gave the world a new mode of cinematic terror.
- Urban Gad achieved numerous successes with enduring masterpieces like *Den sorte drøm* (*The Black Dream,* 1911) and especially the world classic *Afgrunden* (*The Abyss,* 1910)—and by furthering the career of Asta Nielsen, among others.

Director's Cut

Asta Nielsen made her cinematic debut in Urban Gad's *Afgrunden* (*The Abyss*) in 1910, portraying a naive innocent caught up in a world of sexual bondage and moral decadence. (The film featured what may have been the first S and M scene ever caught on celluloid.)

Afgrunden established Nielsen as the first truly international movie star, breaking ground that would soon allow Charlie Chaplin, Sarah Bernhardt, and others to emerge as worldwide household names. During the following years (many of them spent in Germany) she starred in numerous films that allowed her to exploit her chameleon-like ability to cross class and gender roles, cross-dressing for the titular role in Sven Gade's *Hamlet* (1920) and even playing a ruthless killer alongside Garbo in *Die freudlose Gasse* (*Street of Sorrow,* 1925).

- August Blom's films featured audacious explorations of the passions of lovers in experimental horror and other grand genre films like *Dødens brud* (*The Bride of Death*) and *Den dødes halsbaand* (*The Necklace of the Dead*), as well as numerous adaptations of literary texts from *Hamlet* to *Dr. Jekyll and Mr. Hyde* (both 1910).
- Don't overlook the oeuvre of Forest Holger-Madsen, a master of visuality whose adept employment of new techniques in lighting, camerawork, and mise-en-scène won international acclaim for socially conscious films like *Down with Weapons!* (*Ned med vaapnene,* 1914) and his masterpiece, *The Skyship* (*Himmelskibet,* 1917), a bold science-fiction picture that uses a Martian landing on earth to explore issues of ethnic and cultural prejudice.

- One of Scandinavia's greatest directors before Bergman, the young Carl-Theodor Dreyer was already exploring with surprising sensitivity the depths of human psychology and the limits of rationality in early films such as *Leaves from Satan's Book* (*Blade af Satans bog,* 1920) and *Du skalaere din hustru* (*The Master of the House,* 1925).

Dreyer's silent career peaked with *The Passion of Joan of Arc* (*La Passion de Jeanne d'Arc,* 1928), which starred Renée Falconetti in the only role of her career as the French heroine. Dreyer's intimate delight in Falconetti's face, gesture, and movement established him as one of the era's great directors, though his transition to sound with *Vampyr* (1932) was not successful. But he returned with *Vredens dag* (*Day of Wrath*) in 1943, an acknowledged masterpiece that should top your "Nordic not-to-miss" list.

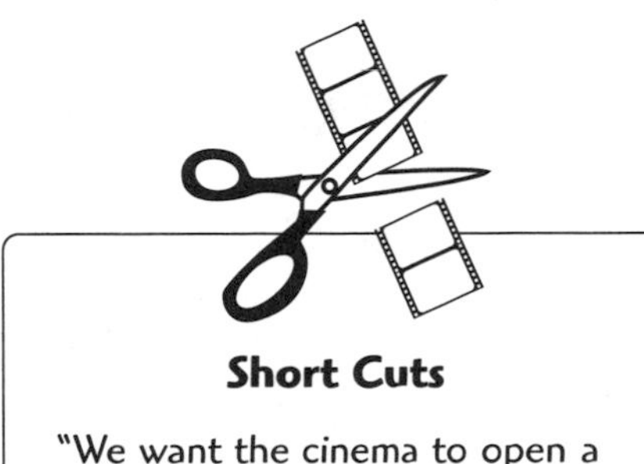

Short Cuts

"We want the cinema to open a door for us into the unexplainable. We want to undergo a tension that is the result less of an external action than of a struggle within the soul."

—Carl-Theodor Dreyer

From Olsen to Oscar Night

While Denmark's sound era has not achieved the recognition of its Swedish neighbor's, the country has produced some of the most lyrical and satisfying European films since World War II, particularly in the past 30 years. Indeed, the '70s, '80s, and '90s have been illustrious ones for Danish cinema.

Second Take

If you think the reputation of Danish film has remained largely confined to the Scandinavian region, think again: Bille August's *Pelle the Conqueror* (1987) and Gabriel Axel's *Babette's Feast* (*Babettes gaestebud,* 1987) won back-to-back best foreign film Academy Awards for the nation's always thriving industry.

While not an international name, Nils Malmros created a series of quietly elegant films dealing with themes of childhood and youth, such as *Boys* (*Drenge,* 1976), *The Tree of Knowledge* (*Kundskabens trae,* 1981), and *Arhus by Night* (1989). Bille August's first feature film, *In My Life* (*Honning måne,* 1978) signaled the beginning of an illustrious career that would include the dark and troubling tale of adolescent cruelty, *Zappa* (1983), and the Oscar- and Palme d'Or–winning *Pelle the Conqueror* (*Pelle erobreren,* 1987), with which his career reached its peak. (The great Swedish actor and Bergman protégé Max von Sydow also received a best actor nomination for his stellar performance in *Pelle.*)

Gabriel Axel made numerous films for many years in Norway, including *Golden Mountains* (*Guld og Grønne Skove,* 1957) and *The Red Mantle* (*Den Roede Kappe,* 1967), before achieving international recognition for the delicious drama *Babette's Feast* in 1988. And the decades-long career of the country's greatest woman director, Astrid Henning-Jensen, stretches from the 1947 *Denmark Grows Up* through *Unknown Man* (1953) and *Ballet Girl* (1954) in the '50s to *Early Spring* (1986) and *Winterborn* (1978) all the way to *The Birthday Trip (*1990*)* to kick off the '90s.

The Networks of Norway

It is typical of Norway's relatively small contribution to world cinema before the 1970s that the country's first movie, *The Dangers of a Fisherman's Life* (*Fiskerlivets farer,* 1907), was directed by a Swede, Julius Jaenzon. This situation might be very different indeed if the films of silent director and founder of the Christiania Film Compagni Peter Lykke-Seest had survived, but unfortunately almost all of them are lost.

Film historians agree that one of the major factors in Norway's less-than-impressive status on the world cinema stage was the lasting legacy of the Film Theaters Act of 1913, which gave local municipalities an astonishing amount of control over film licensing and distribution. The result was a unique but quite stifling network of local distribution arms that survives to this day and has often made it difficult for Norwegian directors to get their films seen by national audiences.

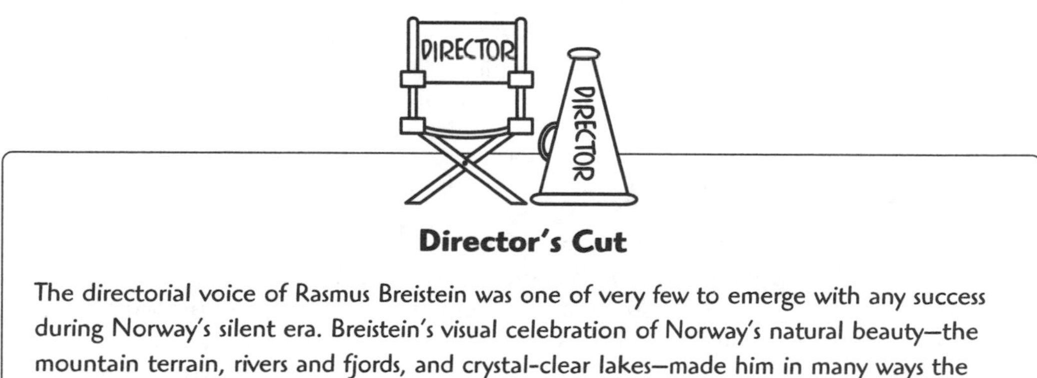

Director's Cut

The directorial voice of Rasmus Breistein was one of very few to emerge with any success during Norway's silent era. Breistein's visual celebration of Norway's natural beauty—the mountain terrain, rivers and fjords, and crystal-clear lakes—made him in many ways the John Ford of Norway, perhaps the country's only true auteur in the first half century of its cinematic history. (Breistein films to check out include *Anne the Gypsy Girl* [*Fante-Anne*] from 1920 and *Kristine, the Daughter of Valdres* [*Kristine Valdresdatter*], shot in 1930.)

Despite the FTA's choke-hold on distribution and exhibition, however, a few directors did emerge as national figures, in part due to family influence or name recognition. Tancred Ibsen, for example, was the grandson of the great Norwegian playwright Henrik Ibsen. His international career included a significant amount of time in the United States with Victor Sjöström and a range of early sound films that include *The Big Baptism* (1931), the popular thriller *Two Living and One Dead* (*To levende og en død,* 1937), and his masterpiece, *Gjest Baardsen* (1939).

With the end of World War II, Norwegian directors coped with the legacy of the Nazi occupation or "Quisling" in a variety of ways. The popular war drama *The Battle for Heavy Water* (1947) is a celebration of the industriousness of the Norwegian resistance that contains some fabulous battle scenes. Other films turned to everyday life and neglected social groups to shed light on the more practical aftermath of the war. Arne Skouen, the country's most notable director in the postwar decades, made his first big splash with *Gategutter* (*Street Urchins,* 1949), becoming a bona fide auteur with his obsessive attention to the details of production, including casting. Indeed, the Nazis portrayed in *Nødlanding* (*Forced Landing,* 1952) and *Omringet* (*Surrounded,* 1960) were played by actual Germans recruited especially for these roles. The capstone of Skouen's career was *Nine Lives* (*Ni Liv,* 1957), an impassioned World War II drama depicting one man's struggle against snow, desperation, and betrayal in a futile bid to survive in a forbidding Nordic landscape.

Norwegian directors who have been recognized for their work in the past 30 years include Anja Breien for *Rape* (*Voldtekt,* 1971) and *Wives* (*Hustruer,* 1974), which provide fascinating explorations of women's roles in Scandinavian society; Sølve Skagen's *Next of Kin* (1979) and *Hard Asphalt* (1986), Jim Jarmusch–like dips into an underworld of drugs, alcohol, and petty criminality; Ola Solum's political thriller *Orion's Belt* (*Orions Belte,* 1985), Norway's most lavish production to date that symbolized the country's breakthrough into Hollywood-style production; Erik Gustavson's "neonoir" pictures *Blackout* (1986) and *Herman* (1990); and Nils Gaupe's stunning *Pathfinder* (*Ofelas*), which was nominated for best foreign picture at the 1987 Oscars but lost out to another Scandinavian feature, Denmark's *Pelle the Conqueror.*

Swedish Sweetness

From the opening decade of the twentieth century, this relatively small and sparsely populated Scandinavian nation has made lasting and, in a few cases, even revolutionary contributions to the history of world cinema. It's hard to know why the country's film history has been so illustrious: perhaps its cultural isolation from the rest of Europe at times, perhaps an innate sense of performative artistry of the sort that gave Norway its great dramatists, such as Ibsen. Whatever the case, you're really missing something if you're missing Swedish film!

Magnusson the Magician

One of the truly towering figures from Sweden's silent era, Charles Magnusson was originally a news cameraman who joined forces with a number of businessmen to launch Svensk Biografteatern, a production and distribution company, in 1909 (the company became Svensk Filmindustri 10 years later). Magnusson's vital contribution to the history of Swedish cinema was his realization that film acting, directing, and mise-en-scène were still too bound up in the practice of the theater. Accordingly, he tried to find ways of divorcing cinematic practice from its theatrical roots, placing enormous confidence in the creative powers of the many directors he discovered and brought to prominence in the early part of the century.

Indeed, Magnusson was single-handedly responsible for launching the careers of many of the silent era's most notable directors, screen writers, and cameramen. A great example of his eye for talent is the career of George af Klercker, whose *The Victory of Love* (1916) is a true masterpiece of lighting and camerawork. *The Prisoner of Karlsten's Fortress* (*Fången på Karlstens fästning,* 1916), a melodramatic thriller, similarly exploits the possibilities of emergent film technology to create the dramatic mood swings that made it a popular exemplar of the genre.

Director's Cut

Scandinavia's first known woman director was Anna Hofman-Uddgren, whose feel for location has few parallels in early Scandinavian cinema. Her particular forte was the adaptation of Strindberg plays, including *Miss Julie* and *The Father* (*Fröken Julie* and *Fadren,* both 1912).

Victor's Victories

But the most important figure in Scandinavian film before Bergman was undoubtedly Victor Sjöström, one of a number of world-renowned silent era directors who deserve their own chapters. Already a successful actor when he came to Svensk Bio in 1912, Sjöström immediately became a national star with *Ingeborg Holm* (*Margaret Day,* 1913), an early masterpiece that many herald as one of the five or six greatest silent films ever made. The director's unparalleled and, for its time, remarkably unsentimental empathy for the poor comes to the surface in this story of an impoverished widow whose daughter is confiscated by the welfare office after her husband's death.

Short Cuts

"The thing that brought me to filmmaking was a youthful desire for adventure and a curiosity to try this new medium of which I then did not have the slightest knowledge."

—Victor Sjöström

Sjöström's international breakthrough was *Terje Vigen* (*Man There Was,* 1917), an adaptation of an Ibsen play that, like *Ingeborg Holm,* depicted familial agonies and the harsh demands of poverty upon its victims. *The Girl from the Marsh Croft* (*Tösen från Stormyrtorpet,* 1917) came on the heels of this instant classic, and soon Sjöström was being hailed as the world's greatest director, a distinction he would momentarily share with America's D. W. Griffith.

The widowed Mrs. Holm getting bad news in Victor Sjöström's Ingeborg Holm *(1913).*

Director's Cut

Victor Sjöström's dazzling national and international success still tends to obscure the career of Sweden's second-most important silent-era auteur, Mauritz Stiller—perhaps the world's first prominent gay male director. Stiller's *The Wings* (*Vingarne,* 1916) dealt covertly with themes of homoerotic passion, while many of his lighthearted but wonderful comedies—*Thomas Graal's First Child* (1918) and the popular innuendo-filled *Erotikon* (1920)—stayed safely focused on heterosexual love, jealousy, and courtship.

Perhaps most important, Stiller's *The Legend of Gösta Berling* (*Gösta Berlings Saga,* 1924) introduced the world to Greta Garbo, one of Stiller's greatest legacies to the history of world cinema. Garbo brought Stiller with her to Hollywood, but while her star rose ever higher, things went downhill for him in Tinseltown. Though some of his American films (*Hotel Imperial,* for example, from 1927) were successes, his health soon failed, and, at 45, he died too young in 1928.

Sjöström's greatest commercial success was *The Sons of Ingmar* (*Ingmarssönerna,* 1918), an allegorical and psychological tale of a young man who must climb a ladder to heaven to get advice from his ancestors. In a very different vein, *The Soul Shall Bear Witness* (*Körkarlen,* 1921), in which he also starred, was a ghost story that featured a series of flashbacks taking place in a gloomy (and masterfully lit) cemetery. Sjöström's Hollywood phase culminated with his English-language masterpiece *The Wind* (1928), which was actually a financial failure. Starring Lillian Gish in one of the great performances of her illustrious career, this haunting psychological exploration of geographical displacement and hysteria is strikingly modern, a must-see for all you soon-to-be Sjöström junkies out there.

Ingmar Bergman and the Triumph of Scandinavian Cinema

Though never one for exaggeration, Woody Allen once described Ingmar Bergman as "the greatest film artist ... since the invention of the motion picture camera." A bit over the top, Allen's superlative nevertheless reflects Bergman's massive influence upon world cinema—and, even more, upon the past 50 years of Swedish film.

Like Sjöström's for the silent era, Bergman's reputation and filmic vision tend to overshadow Sweden's many other great modern directors. Mai Zetterling's long and distinguished career has included features like *Loving Couples* (*Flskande Par,* 1964) and *Night Games* (*Nattlek,* 1966) in the '60s and *Of Seals and Man* (1980) and *Amarosa* (1986) in the '80s, not to mention an early and highly successful period as one of Sweden's border-crossing international actresses. Arne Mattson came to international prominence in 1951 with *One Summer of Happiness,* while Lasse Hallström's *My Life as a Dog* (*Mitt Liv Som Hund,* 1985) was a worldwide hit in the mid-'80s.

But Bergman has long been the name of the game in Swedish cinema, and the nation's directors have been dealing with his living legacy since the early '50s. And if you want to become at all knowledgeable about the breadth and character of world cinema, you'll have to begin dealing with it as well.

Short Cuts

As a young boy, Ingmar Bergman was locked in a dark and stifling closet for hours at a time by his dominating father. Many have speculated that these early childhood traumas lie behind Bergman's explorations of ominous paternal figures in early films he wrote and/or directed, such as *Frenzy* (1944).

A Cinema of Life, Death, and Everything in Between

In some ways the Mozart of twentieth-century filmmaking, Ingmar Bergman started making his own pictures while still a child. He began his artistic career proper as a theater director, however, and his first experience in the Swedish film industry was as the writer for Alf Sjöberg's *Frenzy* (*Hets,* 1944). Eleven years later, he gained his first international recognition for *Smiles of a Summer Night* (*Sommarnattens Leende,* 1955), a light comedy that's still very enjoyable, if much less complex than his subsequent pictures.

Second Take

They'll insist it's true till they're blue in the face, but don't let anyone tell you that Swedish-cum-American golden age superstar Ingrid Bergman is the daughter of Ingmar Bergman. Ingrid was an orphan from early on, and it was only in 1978 with Ingmar's *Autumn Sonata* that the two ever collaborated in a motion picture.

It was also in the mid-'50s that Bergman started getting medieval. *The Seventh Seal* (*Det Sjunde Inseglet,* 1957) is set in Europe during the Black Death, and it's a true allegory in the medieval sense, rife with hidden meanings and significances. The chess game staged between a knight returning from the Crusades and Death symbolizes wider human struggles to understand the nature of life and its limitations. And *Virgin Spring* (*Jungfrukällan,* 1960) is a medieval drama of murder, betrayal, and redemption.

Throughout his so-called *art films* Bergman tempered his enthusiasm for film as an art form with searching, sometimes parodic, often bitter exposés of the pretensions and limitations of the artist himself. *The Face* (*Ansiktet,* 1958), *Hour of the Wolf* (*Vargtimmen,* 1968), and *The Rite* (*Riten,* 1969) all center in very different ways around the figure of the existentially anguished artist searching for the meaning of it all. At the same time, in films like his powerful *Wild Strawberries* (*Smultronstället,* 1957) and a less successful early '60s trilogy that included *Through a Glass Darkly* (*Såsom i en spegel,* 1961), *Winter Light* (*Nattvardsgästerna,* 1963), and *The Silence* (*Tystnaden,* 1963), he dealt more broadly with questions of divine existence, human isolation, and metaphysical angst.

Filmophile's Lexicon

Art film (or *film d'art*) is a term generally used to distinguish more self-consciously artistic and "cerebral" films from their generally higher-budget counterparts, "commercial films." Though the term is still used by critics to separate art-house productions from mainstream Hollywood studio releases, it's often more of a convenience than an accurate reflection of a real division.

Bergman's last film was *Fanny and Alexander* (*Fanny och Alexander,* 1982), an uplifting family saga staged a century ago in Uppsala. The film won Bergman his third Academy Award for best foreign language film as well as worldwide acclaim for a long and illustrious career.

How to Watch a Bergman Film

Like most meat-eating Americans, you probably shy away from artsy Bergman films when it's time to rent. But there are a few simple insights that will help you get the most out of these often perplexing pictures and keep you from throwing your remote against the wall in frustration when things get slow. Here's a list of four:

- **Don't watch for the plot!** Very few of Bergman's films are driven by narrative sequence; when someone asks, "What's going on now?" the answer will more often be, "This guy's trying to figure out the meaning of life," than, "This guy's chasing a thief who just stole his wallet."
- **Watch for the overall psychological and philosophical questions** that Bergman is trying to ask (and get you to ask) in the film you're watching. When the old man in *Wild Strawberries* gazes at himself in the mirror, Bergman wants us to speculate on the inner turmoil that he experiences as he looks at his reflection and ruminates on the past and future of the life he's leading.

Victor Sjöström as Professor Isak Borg in Ingmar Bergman's Wild Strawberries *(1957).*

- These sorts of existential dilemmas are often refracted in Bergman's films through an overarching **allegorical structure** that determines the hidden meanings of the persons, dreams, symbols, and so on portrayed in the film. When Antonius Blok plays chess with Death or watches flagellants whipping themselves in *The Seventh Seal,* it's your job to determine what each individual event or gesture might mean within the overall framework of the allegory.
- One of Bergman's favorite allegorical figures is that of the **anguished artist,** who plays a central role in numerous films and whose inner struggles to define the place of art in society and in the ethical and psychological development of the individual can provide a powerful lens through which to view Bergman's oeuvre as a whole.

In short, don't give up on Ingmar! His films will take some getting used to, but once you've learned how to watch them with patience and intelligence you'll start to wonder what took you so long to discover them in the first place.

The Least You Need to Know

- Denmark is home to the world's oldest continually operating film production company, Nordisk.
- Carl Theodor Dreyer is one of a number of distinguished directors highlighting Norway's successful silent era.
- With some important exceptions, Norway's film industry has long been constrained by local municipal controls over distribution and exhibition.
- Charles Magnusson and Victor Sjöström helped make Sweden's silent era one of the most illustrious in the world.
- Ingmar Bergman's long career explored in film the depths of human psychology and the struggles of the artist seeking to define his role in society.

Chapter 15

In the Limey Light: England's Cinematic Century

In This Chapter

- Cecil Hepworth and foreign competition in the silent era
- British filmmaking during World War II
- The postwar years, Otto Rank, and "Free Cinema"
- The mini-renaissance of the '80s and '90s
- A look at recent Irish film

In Shakespeare's *Richard II,* the old duke John of Gaunt famously describes England as a "Fortress built by Nature for herself, / Against infection, and the hand of war." It's a nice description of the nation's geography, but it won't work as a comment on the history of British cinema.

In fact, from the very beginning English film has had to deal over and over again with the immense pressures of its cinematically more powerful allies, France and the United States. Though British film has flourished at certain moments and in the hands of certain directors, you can't write the history of English film without accounting for the long history of foreign influence upon every aspect of the industry.

The Beginnings

In the closing years of the nineteenth century and the earliest years of the twentieth, England's film industry got off to a bouncing start with showings by the Lumière brothers in London in 1896 and the efforts of the country's own pioneer, Robert Paul.

Short Cuts

Sir Alfred Hitchcock got his start during the silent era, getting his big directorial break as an assistant to Graham Cutt for *Woman to Woman* (1923), one of England's rare international successes in these years.

Paul was the first to present short films to a paying English audience, and he went on to become a highly successful director and distributor of some of the world's first newsreels and short comedies.

But the presound era wasn't all roses for Gaunt's "sceptered isle." In fact, by 1910 competition from the United States and France was driving the fledgling industry into the ground. The story of England's first 40 years of cinema is a story of native ambition coupled with foreign incursions that constantly threatened to overshadow whatever advances British filmmakers made. Of the few prominent figures to emerge from the United Kingdom's earliest malaise, the most important was the filmmaker whom many historians see as England's answer to the great American director D. W. Griffith.

England's Griffith: Cecil Hepworth

The towering figure of early British cinema is Cecil Hepworth, whose childhood had exposed him to the wonders of light-and-image apparatuses by virtue of his father, who traveled the country with a magic lantern show, son in tow. Cecil began his own slide and film show in 1896, a pursuit into which he channeled his considerable knowledge of projection and film technology.

Director's Cut

Cecil Hepworth wrote and published what most historians regard as the world's first bona fide textbook on the art and technology of motion pictures. *Animated Photography, or The ABC of the Cinematography* was published in 1898, just as Hepworth was becoming a household name among turn-of-the-century English movie audiences.

By 1899 Hepworth had set up his own film laboratory; at the turn of the century, he was producing more than 100 films a year, sponsoring many of the country's earliest and most important silent directors, and virtually launching the British film industry in its first incarnation. Hepworth's most famous work, *Rescued by Rover* (1905), starring his own family members, is an early comic masterpiece, featuring innovations in narrative continuity and especially in editing, of which he was the undisputed master before Griffith. Other comic shorts from this period included *How It Feels to Be Run Over* (1900), *The Glutton's Nightmare* (1901), *The Other Side of the Hedge* (1905), and *That Fatal Sneeze* (1907).

Hepworth's pre–World War I feature films as a director were generally successful, and it's undeniable that he was almost single-handedly responsible for making British film competitive in the international arena in the first two decades of the new century. These features include, among many others, *The Basilisk* (1915), *The Canker of Jealousy* (1915), *Sweet Lavender* (1915), *Comin' Thro' the Rye* (1916), and *Nearer My God to Thee* (1917).

Unlike Griffith, though, Hepworth wasn't able to keep up with continually advancing film techniques. By 1924 he was bankrupt, and he spent the remainder of his career directing commercials. Ouch!

Cecil B. Hepworth's family starring in his own Rescued by Rover *(1905).*

Those Bloody Americans

Hepworth's films were big hits in the 1900s and 1910s, and there were other directors who made some wonderful and even innovative pictures during the silent period: W. G. Barker (*Henry VIII,* 1911), George Pearson (*A Study in Scarlet,* 1914; *Love Life and Laughter,* 1923), Maurice Elvey (*Hindle Wakes,* 1918), Graham Cutts (*Woman to Woman,* 1923; *The Rat,* 1925), Herbert Wilcox (*Decameron Nights*, 1924; *Dawn*, 1928), and, of course, Alfred Hitchcock (*The Pleasure Garden,* 1925; *The Lodger,* 1926).

Second Take

Despite England's status as a world imperial power in the early part of the twentieth century and its victory in World War I, by 1925 only 5 percent of films shown on British screens were actually made on the island.

By the end of World War I, though, the situation was dire. Now even the government got involved in trying to come up with ways of protecting England's film industry from the flood of American products being shown on its screens, which represented a huge portion of what got distributed throughout the country.

Director's Cut

As film historian John Hawkridge has pointed out, one of the major factors contributing to the dominance of the American film industry over its British counterpart even in the silent era was the absence of a "star system" in the United Kingdom. While Hepworth made a few actors and actresses famous in his films, there was no Lillian Gish in England, no Florence Lawrence or Buster Keaton.

In an exasperated slam of the British film industry, the Russian-born American mogul Joseph M. Schenck, writing in 1925, said the following about England's lack of star figures:

> "You have no personalities to put on the screen. The stage actors and actresses are no good on the screen. Your effects are no good, and you do not spend nearly so much money."

In short, at least from the American perspective, early British cinema got very little respect.

The government's contribution was the Cinematograph Films Act, passed by parliament in 1927. The legislation established a firm quota system that demanded an increasingly large percentage of films released and shown in England to be English-made productions. While the immediate results were positive (the nation's film production shot up by 500 percent within a few years), the long-term effect was a steady decline in film quality as studios churned out low-quality productions just to meet the act's demands.

Filmophile's Lexicon

Quota quickies were low-budget, low-quality films that English studios shot, edited, and released in record time to satisfy the strict requirements of the Cinematograph Act of 1927.

The coming of sound might have helped matters some. With the rise of directors like Anthony Asquith (*The Battle of Gallipoli,* 1931), Walter Forde (*Condemned to Death,* 1932), and, of course, Alfred Hitchcock (the United Kingdom's first talkie was Hitchcock's early suspense film, *Blackmail,* 1929), it looked like the '30s would be something of a cinematic boom for England. While a number of very good films were made during this decade, the nation's film culture descended into a long period of mediocrity from which it only gradually recovered.

Alexander the Great

It took an immigrant to inject some momentary life into the flagging British industry after years of French and American domination. In the early 1930s, a Hungarian-born journeyman director and producer named Alexander Korda came to England after a wide-ranging career in his native country as well as Austria, Germany, and France. Cobbling together financing from a variety of sources, Korda built what was then the largest English studio and thereafter became the country's most prominent producer.

For the English public, Korda's most important accomplishment was his behind-the-scenes launching of numerous acting careers. Charles Laughton and Robert Donat, for example, were both made into international stars with their performances (Oscar-winning in Laughton's case) in *The Private Life of Henry VIII*. Korda's contributions to the culture of British film were recognized in 1942 when he was knighted and became *Sir* Alexander Korda (though there have always been rumors that it was spying for his adopted country during World War II that won him the sword tap).

Director's Cut

Though most famous and influential in England as a producer, Alexander Korda was also a virtuosic if flamboyant director. The dozens of films he made in his native Hungary have been lost; in Hollywood, his most notable success was the sexually suggestive *The Private Life of Helen of Troy* (1927).

In England, Korda's career soared into the stratosphere with *The Private Life of Henry VIII* (1933), an instant international sensation that helped finance his future directorial efforts. Among these, *Rembrandt* (1936) and An *Ideal Husband* (1948) are the best, combining Korda's legendary flair for spectacle with quite poignant examinations of the challenged faced by artists and the pressures of social constraints.

Shooting (in) the War

Not all movies made in England between 1940 and 1945 revolved around the momentous events of World War II. But most did, whether through their explicit engagement with the struggle itself or in their propagandistic vaunting of the nation's valiant fight against the forces of Fascism. There were essentially two ways of dealing with the war that was on the front of everyone's mind.

Short Cuts

Noël Coward, the great British playwright known for his wry, urbane treatments of upper-class life in plays like *Private Lives,* also contributed his considerable talents to England's cinematic culture during the war years, collaborating with David Lean on the propaganda film *In Which We Serve* (1942).

Second Take

American audiences know *Gaslight* as a classic 1944 MGM production directed by George Cukor and starring Ingrid Bergman. But MGM actually lifted the story wholesale from Thorold Dickinson's 1940 film of the same name. After making its own version, the American studio tried to prevent distribution of the British version by destroying the negative; luckily, though, several prints survived.

Of D-Day and Documentaries

For those on the home front, the massive effort required of England throughout World War II was most effectively reflected, celebrated, and projected through the medium of film documentary. Despite heavy demands on all sectors of the economy, the nation's documentary film industry truly came into its own during the war. Audiences yearning for escapism went to the cinema to watch and listen to news of England's battlefield setbacks and triumphs in newsreels projected at the front of every feature.

England's war documentaries during these years were commissioned and distributed by the so-called Crown Film Unit, a government agency that was responsible for such stirring successes as Humphrey Jennings and Harry Watt's *London Can Take It* (1940), Jack Holmses's *Coastal Command* (1942), and many other not-so-subtly-titled pictures. Though this book isn't nearly as concerned with documentary as it is with narrative film, these movies are well worth watching, testifying as they do to a crucial transitional moment in the relationship between filmmakers and the government in England.

True Lies

One of the immediate effects of the sudden explosion in documentary filmmaking was its influence upon feature narrative films. Practically all English story films made about World War II—Michael Powell's *49th Parallel* (1941), Leslie Howard's *Spitfire* (1942), Carol Reed's *The Way Ahead* (1944), and dozens of others—used documentary footage for battle scenes, cutting from a shot of, say, actual German warplanes flying low over Dover to the silhouette of a paid actor looking up in the sky in concern.

To point out the propaganda-saturated nature of British film during World War II is not to criticize the era's producers and directors for "towing the government line." England's leaders and its people—including its filmmakers—were trying to win a war; all other considerations were secondary, at least for the time being.

A battle scene from Noël Coward and David Lean's In Which We Serve *(1942).*

Nevertheless, some directors turned purposefully away from the war to make escapist flicks aimed at giving the British public a well-deserved mental break. Even some of these pictures, however, reflected an implicit concern with the psychological implications of modern warfare.

Consider, for example, Thorold Dickinson's *Gaslight* (1940), the story of a wealthy husband who drives his wife nearly insane by convincing her she's losing her mind. With all the English concern about German spies hiding under every bush, wartime audiences must have identified quite readily with the wife's slow realization that an evil force had infiltrated her home. The movie's "enemy within" theme was virtually guaranteed to strike a chord as England threw its collective might into the war effort, which permanently altered the nature of the nation's film industry.

The Lean Years

In the decades following World War II, the British film industry went through another period of American dominance, which in many ways continues to this day. The results are painfully obvious: Next time you're in England, go to any big multiplex in most any town, and what you'll be able to choose from will only occasionally include a UK-produced film. The government's solutions to this longstanding dilemma have included legislation and the institution of quota systems, as well as a number of if-you-can't-beat-'em-join-'em collaborations with American filmmakers (check out *The African Queen* [1951], for example).

Pulling Rank

It didn't have to be this way. The producer J. Arthur Rank came to cinematic prominence in England during World War II. By the end of the war, he was perhaps the most powerful man in the British film industry, the head of a vast empire of production companies, distribution facilities, and theaters controlled by the Rank Organisation.

One of Rank's major goals was to establish a solid market for English films in the United States. In the mid 1940s, he met with American movie moguls and began negotiating deals to sell distribution and exhibition rights to the enormous number of movies he controlled. For a while there, it looked like a pre-Beatles British invasion might very well change the nature of cultural relations between the two English-speaking world powers and put them on a more equal footing.

Suddenly, though, in 1947, the British Parliament passed a bill that imposed a huge tax on the importation of all foreign films. This understandably angered American industry leaders, who struck back by imposing a full-scale embargo on the distribution of Hollywood movies in the United Kingdom. Rank's dreams were shattered, and the brief hope for British economic parity in world cinema was finally put to rest.

Short Cuts

In a clear sign of his unparalleled power in the United Kingdom's film industry during and after World War II, England's favorite nickname for J. Arthur Rank was "King Arthur."

Second Take

It wasn't all bad news for the British film industry after World War II. Hammer Film Productions Limited opened in 1949 and dedicated itself to making good but low budget movies—including some of history's greatest horror flicks, many of which the company shot at Bray Studios outside of Windsor.

Freeing British Cinema

It's amazing how many important innovations in world cinema have come about through the exasperated efforts of various groups of angry young men. Britain's version of this phenomenon was a group of filmmakers who emerged in the mid-'50s to challenge what they perceived as the extreme commercialism of the nation's industry since the war.

What united the Free Cinema artists—Lindsay Anderson, Norman McLaren, Karel Reisz, Tony Richardson, the Swiss-born Alain Tanner, and others—was the recognition that commercialized cinema was not portraying the lived reality endured by the vast majority of England's population. Instead, they argued, the film industry was giving the public pap: melodrama, comedy, and escapism that bore little relationship to actual human conditions in the war-traumatized nation. In reaction, the Free Cinema artists developed a new form of documentary-style filmmaking that combined inventive camera work and cinematography with an unprecedented realistic approach to the nation's social ills and cultural conflicts.

Director's Cut

The actual program that launched Free Cinema in February 1956 consisted of three films that sought to reinject a social conscience into British film. The films were the following:

- *Momma Don't Allow* (1955), directed by Karel Reisz and Tony Richardson, provides a lively look at a jazz club in the north part of London. This hallmark of Free Cinema is distinguished by the brilliant camera work of Walter Lassally.
- *O Dreamland* (1953), directed by Lindsay Anderson, is a gritty but fabulous portrayal of a group of people living in an amusement park in the seaside town of Margate.
- *Together* (1955), directed by Lorenza Mazzetti, features two deaf-mutes portrayed by Eduardo Paolozzi and Michael Andrews whose dramatic relationship takes place against the backdrop of London's fabled East End.

There were other important Free Cinema films shown in subsequent programs, but these were the three that started it all.

In one of their several statements of purpose, the *Free Cinema* artists touted "the significance of the everyday" as the political motto of the movement as a whole, insisting that film could and should be employed as a vehicle of social commentary and reform. In hard-hitting pictures like Reisz's *We Are the Lambeth Boys* (1959) and *Saturday Night and Sunday Morning* (1960), Anderson's *Every Day Except Christmas* (1957) and *This Sporting Life* (1963), and Norman McLaren's Oscar-winning cartoon *Neighbors* (1952), these artists irrevocably changed the social fabric of British film.

Filmophile's Lexicon

Free Cinema was the term given to a six-part series of film showings screened at London's National Film Theatre from 1956 to 1959 that launched a socially conscious cinema movement of the same name.

The Atlantic Conduit Continues

As English and American film historians have noted with either nationalistic embarrassment or jingoistic pride, most British filmmaking in the '60s and '70s was in large part the result of American financing and American directing. In fact, during this period it's not an exaggeration to say that the English film industry was actually an *Anglo-American* film industry. Consider, for example, this quick list of 10 supposedly British films released during the course of these decades that were actually made by American directors living and shooting in England:

- *The Damned* (Joseph Losey, 1961).
- *The Victors* (Carl Foreman, 1963).
- *A Hard Day's Night* (Richard Lester, 1964).
- *The Masque of the Red Death* (Roger Corman, 1964).
- *The Spy Who Came In from the Cold* (Martin Ritt, 1965).
- *Two for the Road* (Stanley Donen, 1967).
- *The Deadly Affair* (Sidney Lumet, 1967).
- *Sleuth* (Joseph L. Mankiewicz, 1972).
- *Murder on the Orient Express* (Sidney Lumet, 1974).
- *The Man Who Would Be King* (John Huston, 1975).

This is not to say that native-born directors weren't contributing to the nation's struggling industry in these years. But the fact remains that England failed to establish and maintain its own national cinematic voice after the decline of the Free Cinema movement.

The Eighties and Nineties: Mixed Success

The Academy Awards in the first two years of the 1980s symbolized a small renaissance in British filmmaking. Hugh Hudson won a best picture Oscar for his moving portrayal of athleticism, grace, and friendship in *Chariots of Fire* (1981). The next year, Sir Richard Attenborough's *Gandhi* (1982) garnered another best picture Oscar for English cinema while making the journeyman actor Ben Kingsley into an international household name for his Oscar-winning performance as the Indian resistance leader.

Though American films continue to dominate the nation's industry, the past 20 years, and especially the past 10, have seen English film develop into a respected and respectable contributor to European cinema in general. Talented directors emerged to carve out an original space for themselves amongst all the pap being churned out by Hollywood: Peter Greenaway (*Drowning by Numbers,* 1988; *The Cook the Thief His Wife and Her Lover,* 1989), Mike Leigh (*High Hopes,* 1988; *Secrets and Lies,* 1996), and Anthony Minghella (*Truly Madly Deeply,* 1991; *The English Patient,* 1996) are just a few among the current generation of English filmmakers who have captured the minds and hearts of international audiences, promising many good things to come for the new century.

Director's Cut

The many collaborations during the past two decades between Ismail Merchant and James Ivory symbolize both the marvels and the ironies of the English film revival in the '80s and '90s. Producer Merchant and director Ivory, along with their talented screenwriter Ruth Prawer Jhabvala, have made numerous Oscar-nominated and Oscar-winning films, beginning as far back as 1965 with *Shakespeare Wallah.*

Among the most familiar and successful Merchant-Ivory productions are *The Europeans* (1979), *The Bostonians* (1984), *A Room with a View* (1986), *Howard's End* (1992), and *The Remains of the Day* (1993). Known for their opulent sets, understated scripts, and elegant direction, the many films made by this remarkable trio would seem to epitomize the new spirit of native cinematic ingenuity.

There's only one problem. Neither Merchant nor Ivory nor Jhabvala are actually English. Ismail Merchant is an Indian born in Bombay. James Ivory, born in Berkeley, California, is an American. And Ruth Prawer Jhabvala, though raised since the age of 12 in England, was born in Germany.

England's Left Foot: Irish Cinema

Like the larger relationship between England and its island neighbor to the west, the dynamic between English and Irish film has always been fraught with political and social turmoil. During particularly violent periods of conflict proindependence films were banned outright, often by force, and cinema played an important ideological role in struggles between separatists and loyalists throughout the first half of the twentieth century.

Despite the continuing conflict, Ireland has experienced something of a cinematic renaissance during the past 10 years. Dublin-born Jim Sheridan has made a number of consistently great yet highly contrasting films that provide intelligent meditations on the country's various political and cultural milieus. *My Left Foot* (1989) featured the Academy Award–winning performance of Daniel Day-Lewis as the paralyzed artist Christy Brown; though Sheridan's first film, it earned him an Oscar nomination for directing. *The Field* (1990) is the diametrical opposite of *My Left Foot:* an agonizingly slow but utterly gripping story of rural poverty and endurance that uses its pacing and camerawork to mimic an old man's laborious life clearing a field of rocks. *In the*

Name of the Father (1993) represented yet another change of pace, dealing head-on with "the Troubles" by telling the real-life story of an Irish man wrongly imprisoned for an IRA terrorist attack.

Forest Whitaker as an English soldier with a secret in Neil Jordan's The Crying Game *(1992).*

Neil Jordan is another prominent Irish director whose work has reached audiences across the Atlantic. *Mona Lisa* (1986) was a well-received tale of prostitution in the dark streets and back alleys of London, while *The Crying Game* (1992) garnered six Oscar nominations and became notorious for the famous "secret" revealed near the denouement.

The Least You Need to Know

- Cecil Hepworth was the most important creative force in early British cinema.
- Throughout the history of English film, competition from French and especially American cinema has been an enormous factor in the island's industry.
- British film during World War II consisted primarily of documentaries and war propaganda films.
- British "Free Cinema" emerged in the 1950s to challenge the studio-controlled and -financed conventions of English cinema.
- Irish filmmakers have recently come to prominence in the United Kingdom as creative forces to be reckoned with.

Chapter 16

Seeing Through the Red Filter: Eastern Europe

In This Chapter

- A history of Eastern-bloc cinema
- Soviet film theory in depth: montage
- Some recent filmmakers to look out for
- Eastern-bloc countries besides Russia
- Movies worth watching

It may or may not have been the Evil Empire, but the ex-Soviet Union (or Eastern bloc) has also been the origin and inspiration for diverse kinds of filmmaking. By turns creative and oppressive, it has had perhaps the most varied history of any of the national cinemas we have examined. It is really almost manic-depressive: Derivative of other national cinemas during the twilight of the czarist era, it became brilliantly avant-garde during the Leninist period and the 1920s, then oppressive and static from Stalin until the 1960s, and has since become in some arenas technically and ideologically progressive once again. As with so much of the arts, capitalism has been a sort of antidepressant, a kind of Prozac, providing a calming influence that has also meant fewer of the fireworks that have characterized the best moments of this strange, influential, and brilliant cinema.

Finally, the Eastern-bloc cinema has much to offer American filmgoers for several reasons. First, because communism is the ideology most opposed to ours in the twentieth century, it can give us a view of ourselves that it would be difficult for us to have. The images of Western capitalists in Soviet films are not as flattering as they are in even very critical, Frank Capraesque American movies like *Mr. Deeds Goes to Town* (1936). Second (though we won't be treating this aspect), our own filmic responses to the Soviet Union tell us much about ourselves. When actor/resident Ronald Reagan names a military umbrella defense system after a George Lucas film—*Star Wars* (1977)—and refers to the Soviet Union as that film's bad guy—the Evil Empire—you know something interesting is happening between politics and movies.

Short Cuts

Eastern-bloc cinema is also—and perhaps most importantly—incredibly diverse because we are talking about several national cinemas: Russian, Polish, Czech, and so on, each with a different history and, consequently, aesthetic.

Volga Displays: A Brief History of Russian Filmmaking

Not part of the train of inventions that led to the invention of film, existing most of the time in a condition of scarcity, generously supported at various moments by its government, the history of Russian filmmaking is in several important respects the exact opposite of American film history. Here are some specifics.

Czars and Stars: Pre-Soviet Moviemaking

Because Russia and other Eastern European countries were initially dependent on Western Europe and the United States for film technology (cameras, projectors, film stock), their films of the first two decades were not as technically or aesthetically innovative as the movies of their Western counterparts. Exhibitors relied heavily on well-made imports from other countries; 90 percent of the films shown before World War I were imported. The first native production company was not founded until 1907. One of the three production companies in Russia was foreign.

However, by the time of the October Revolution, there was a thriving if small national film industry, producing products made after the styles of other countries. For example, the first feature Russian film, *Stenka Razin* (1908) imitated the French style, *film d'art* (art film). The difference between foreign and domestic film was further confused by the fact that one of the major film companies in Russia was an offshoot of the French Pathé-Frères.

Though the industry was small, it managed to establish some film stars, especially director Yevgeny Bauer and actors Vladimir Maximov and Vera Kholodnaya. There were even fan magazines during this period and during the early Soviet period.

The Soviet Era: First Five-Year Plan

Well, really an eight-year plan. The high point in the history of Russian film comes during the early Soviet era. However, though Soviet film was born during the Russian Revolution, the form it would take was not clear until the 1920s. The few short years between about 1920 to about 1925 (in other words from the completion of the first phase of the film industry's nationalization to the release date of *Battleship Potemkin*) saw a breathtaking change in Russian—now Soviet—filmmaking. This rapid growth is all the more remarkable for the existence of stiff opposition to the new Marxist regime from the West.

Because of the success of the Bolshevik revolution, many figures in the Czarist film industry packed up their toys and left for other countries, leaving the new regime hard up for supplies and expertise. Further, Western countries imposed a blockade on Russia, so little new equipment could get into the country.

Still, the following events happened in rapid fashion: The film industry was nationalized; *agitki* were produced during and after the revolution, Nadezhda Krupskaia (Lenin's wife) cofounded the Cinema Committee; the Cinema Committee founded the very famous Moscow Film School; Lev Kuleshov founded the "Kuleshov Workshop" and discovered the "Kuleshov Effect"; Dziga Vertov established his "Kino-Eye" theory and style of filmmaking, blending a realist aesthetic with a propagandic goal; the Russian Soviet tried to coordinate film production with that of the other Eastern-bloc soviets; Russian montage theory began to be articulated.

Filmophile's Lexicon

Agitki are the propaganda films made by the Bolsheviks in support of their revolution. They represent the first organized instances by the Bolsheviks of an interest in using film as a propaganda device aimed at the masses. The trains used by the Bolsheviks to distribute, advertise, promote, and project the films were called **agitki-trains.** The word *agitki* is related to the English expression "agit-prop."

At the beginning of the Soviet era, and before the high moments of Eisenstein and Pudovkin, Soviet filmmakers and industry bureaucrats tried to fit the new Marxist ideology with the new art form in various ways. Among others, they denied that it was an art form, but not for the same reasons the Western intellectual elite dismissed film. The Soviet "constructivists," for example, did not think film was low-brow, but an essentially new way of presenting the world, without all the bourgeois apparatus of the "legitimate" stage, for example. Unlike aesthetic elitists, they liked the fact that movies appealed to the masses, seeing in film a powerful organ of enlightenment.

Director's Cut

The Russian Revolution was not equally attractive to all Russian film talent. An exodus of actors, directors, and technicians drained the new Soviet Union of some of its best minds. Actors who came to America included Ivan Mozukhin (the actor in the "Kuleshov Effect" demonstration), Mikhail Chekhov (nephew of Anton), Maria Ouspenskaya (Academy Award nominee, best-remembered as the gypsy in *The Wolf Man* [1941]), and Anna Sten (Goldwyn protégé, and star of *Nana* [1934]). Berlin and Paris were also centers of émigré filmmaking.

As we will discuss in Chapter 23, "Making the Cut: Film Editing," the establishment of the Moscow Film School (the first such school in the world) was a watershed moment for filmmaking. Because the Western blockade of Russia prevented much raw film stock from entering the country, and because such stock as existed was used to shoot propaganda films, student filmmakers cut and recut the same prints (of films by Abel Gance and D. W. Griffith) over and over again, emphasizing different narrative elements and emotional effects, and even telling different stories using the same film stock. Almost from the beginning, the Soviet filmmakers realized the importance of editing in the making of a film. Gradually, the idea of montage was born from such experimentation.

The Soviet Era: Second Five-Year Plan

Again, the period between 1925 and 1930 saw sweeping changes in Soviet film, but this time in the opposite direction: from experimentalism to totalitarianism. These are the high years of the great Russian formalist film experiment, the years during which the most famous Russian films are produced: Eisenstein's *Battleship Potemkin* (*Bronenosets Potyomkin,* 1925), *Strike* (*Stachka,* 1925), and *October* (*Oktyabr,* 1928, also known as *Ten Days that Shook the World*); Pudovkin's *Mother* (*Mat,* 1926), *The End of St. Petersburg* (*Konets Sankt-Peterburga,* 1927), and *Storm Over Asia* (*Potomok Chingis-Khana,* 1928); Alexander Dovzhenko's *Zvenigora* (1928) and *Arsenal* (1929).

However, these are also the years during which the Soviet industry began the move away from formal experimentation. Formally beginning in 1928, state policy increasingly dictated that films be made so that they could be immediately understood by the masses. In general, the state exerted an increasing control over the filmmaking industry.

Second Take

Before completely condemning the uniformity of Soviet filmmaking, keep in mind that the American genre system evolved at about the same time for pretty much the same reasons—a standardized and ideologically acceptable mass appeal—if in a different manner. In a sense the 1930s were all about uniformity; we can add to Stalinist tractor films Leni Riefenstahl's paen to social conformity, *Triumph of the Will* (1934), but also just about any Hollywood film directed by Busby Berkeley in which women dance in step in a chorus line.

The advent of sound in the late 1920s was, at least temporarily, a setback for formalist directors arguing over the best visual ways of getting meaning across to an audience. Dialogue and other soundtrack devices seemed to reduce the need for more subtle visual—especially editing—cues.

The Soviet Era: Totalitarianism

The Stalinist "Cultural Revolution" continued for several years the tendency to erase formal experimentation with simple films that would be accessible to the masses. Stalinists rerecognized that film was a powerful tool of propaganda; the 1930s saw the compulsory purchase of projectors by Soviets, and a consequent rise in film attendance all over the Soviet Union.

In the 1930s, the trend continued toward what would in 1934 ultimately and officially be called *socialist realism,* culminating during the Stalinist era in what are satirically referred to as "tractor films," monotonously unvaried movies about the exploitation of the virtuous worker by the bourgeoisie, and the ultimate triumph of the proletariat. These films were increasingly censored and more rigidly scripted.

Filmophile's Lexicon

Socialist realism included not only film but all the arts. Derived from the realist aesthetic in the novel of the nineteenth century, it was a blend of realistic setting and ideologically correct plot and message in which the proletarian hero wins against great odds over the enemy of the people.

By the 1930s and 1940s, the Soviet Union had finally become technologically self-sufficient, able to produce its own film and projection equipment. But it also made films less worth seeing, and it made fewer of them. The number of films produced in the 1930s was roughly one quarter of what it had been in the late 1920s.

The subjects of films in the 1930s and 1940s closely reflected the state message of the moment: anti-Nazi at one moment, antitraitor-to-the-revolution the next. Stalin and Stalinesque, paternalistic figures were invariably portrayed as heroic saviors of the people. Brilliant and established filmmakers like Dziga Vertov were no longer allowed to make films. Instead, Soviet films tended toward the entertaining, ironically taking as their model the "decadent" Hollywood flick.

A bureaucratic relaxing took place after Stalin's death in 1953 but, though more and better films were made, Russian film never regained the pride of place it had in the 1920s.

Late and Post-Soviet Filmmaking

However, the death of Stalin did create a "thaw" in bureaucratic control of the arts in the Soviet Union. The "generation of the '60s" would include the first set of world-famous Russian filmmakers to emerge since the 1920s: Andrei Tarkovsky and Andrei Konchalovsky, for example.

Soviet filmmaking opened up even more with the advent of *glasnost* and *perestroika* in the late 1980s and 1990s. Though entertainment films continued to be made, there were also films critical of the bad old Stalinist days. Some formal experimentalism even returned, after being banished for four or five decades by the state.

Other Eastern European Cinemas: Czechoslovakia, Hungary, Poland

Several Eastern European countries other than Russia were exposed to film almost immediately after its invention; the first showing in Belgrade and Poland occurred in 1896. Other regions had been exposed to Edison's Vitascope even earlier. Films were produced from at least 1910 in Poland, and 1912 in Hungary. Production companies sprang up in urban centers like Belgrade, Warsaw, and Prague.

Despite the fact that Eastern European film output was not nearly as prolific as in the West, some of the significant films of the period between 1920 and 1960 made it to the world stage: *Ecstasy* (*Extase,* Czech, 1933) made an international star of Hedy Lamar, in part because of a nude bathing scene. *Erotikon* (Czech, 1929) was even more risqué than American films tended to be.

Under Stalin, the regional, ethnic, and cultural differences that had tended to characterize various Soviet-bloc national cinemas were often effaced under Soviet centralization. (This tendency was, ironically, in direct opposition to Moscow's countertrend of financing and training—and so encouraging—satellite filmmaking.) The films to gain real attention were made, for the most part, at least a decade after Stalin's death. Sergo Paradzhanov's *Shadows of Forgotten Ancestors* (*Teni zabytykh predkov,* 1964), for example. As in Russia, several ex-Soviet "satellite" countries came into their own filmically; some countries produced directors and whole film communities of some note.

Short Cuts

All the satellite countries we are discussing have in common occupation by and/or collaboration with Germany and the Soviet Union—and a consequent fall in film production. The Czech experience can stand for all in this sense. *Ecstasy* and *The River* (*Reka,* 1934) catapulted Czech cinema into the international limelight by sharing the prize for best direction at the 1934 Venice Biennial. Then came the Nazis. Then, a short time after the occupation ended, the Venice Film Festival gave *The Strike* (*Siréna,* 1947) its Grand Prize. In the 1960s there was a brief "new wave." Then the Soviet tanks rolled in to crush the Czech uprising in Prague in 1968.

Czech and Counter-Czech

Czech cinema has had to survive five different political regimes in the past century: the Austro-Hungarian Empire, a brief stint with democracy after WWI, Nazi occupation, Soviet occupation, and now democracy again. Though some critics believe that this roller-coaster political climate prevented Czech film from reaching any kind of fulfillment or apotheosis, we believe that it often made Czech cinema a very odd combination of fun and responsibility. On the one hand, its early history is characterized by adaptations of great works of art: *Faust* (1912), *The Bartered Bride* (1913), *The Good Soldier Schweik* (1926), and so on. On the other hand, it could be rather titillating: *Ecstasy,* for example. On the third hand (this book is being transcribed by an octopus), Czechoslovakia also produced that surrealist maniac, Jan Svankmajer. (We won't discuss him much here because he has his own section in Chapter 20, "Director's Cut: Calling the Shots.")

Film production in Czechoslovakia began early—in 1898—with the amateur efforts of Jan Drizenecky, who used the Lumière apparatus. The first production company was founded in 1908. (It folded in 1912.) However, by the 1930s, the Barrandov filmmaking facilities (located just outside of Prague)—one of the best such facilities in Europe—were established, and Czech filmmaking had a brief flowering period before the country was occupied by Germany. As in so many other countries during the 1960s, cinema in Czechoslovakia had its own new wave, influenced by the French *cinéma verité* of the previous decade. The most famous of the new directors to emerge at this time is Milos Forman, whose most notable Czech films include *Loves of a Blonde* (*Lásky jedné plavovlásky,* 1965) and *The Fireman's Ball* (*Horí, má panenko,* 1967). Like the new waves of other countries, the Czech new wave was both aesthetically innovative and politically critical.

Short Cuts

Forman on the political anti-authoritarian satire of *Loves of a Blonde:* "You didn't try to express anything; you just wanted to have fun, and somewhere back in your head you knew that you are bugging these idiots ... and these totally corrupt people."

Director's Cut

Two prominent figures in the Hungarian film industry—Mihály Kertész and Sándor Korda—emigrated to the West, working under the names of Michael Curtiz and Alexander Korda. Curtiz went on to direct *The Adventures of Robin Hood* (1938), *Casablanca* (1942), and *White Christmas* (1954), among others. Korda produced *The Scarlet Pimpernel* (1934), *The Four Feathers* (1939), *The Thief of Baghdad* (1940), and *To Be or Not to Be* (1942).

The early 1990s saw some post-Soviet film revival, but was quickly squelched by the separation of Slovakia and the Czech Republic. The future of Czech filmmaking seems reduced and uncertain.

Hungary for Film

Hungary has had a remarkably influential run, despite its being small in comparison to other significant film-producing countries. Its first film showing (in 1896) occurred even before Czechoslovakia's. It has had its own significant industry, and it has exported major cinematic figures to the United States and elsewhere. In 1919 the fleeting Communist regime made Hungary the first country to nationalize its film industry, even before Russia. Mihály Kertész, later America's Michael Curtiz, directed the first film of note in 1912 (*Today and Tomorrow,* or *Ma es holnap*).

The Communists were toppled by a new repressive regime, which again privatized film, but forced figures prominent in the industry out to more hospitable countries. Among artists who left whose names we would know were Bela Lugosi and Peter Lorre.

Director's Cut

Bela Bálázs was another Hungarian who fled the country for more politically accommodating climes. He was an extremely famous and influential screenwriter and theorist of film who defended the young medium against the accusation that it was really too popular—and so too low-brow—to be a real art form. Extremely interested in the techniques that made film unique, Bálázs was especially interested in the close-up, which distinguished film especially from live theater. His most influential work was translated into English in 1972 in a book called *Theory of the Film.*

The 1930s and 1940s saw a relatively high output of films, but a relative dearth in quality; few films gained international exposure. These years saw Hungary's alliances with Axis Germany and then the Soviet Union.

A brief golden age in which young filmmakers began producing interesting films occurred in the years between the death of Stalin (1953) and the brutal Soviet repression of the Hungarian revolution of 1956. Some of these filmmakers remained active in the industry for decades. Films of note made at this time include *Merry-Go-Round* (*Körhinta,* 1955) and *Professor Hannibal* (*Hannibal, tanár úr,* 1956).

The major Hungarian figures of the post uprising era are Andrá Kovács and Miklós Jancsó. Like many filmmakers beginning in the 1960s, both are heavily influenced by the various new waves taking place in Western Europe, and especially by the French New Wave. One of Kovács's most famous films—*Difficult People* (*Nehéz emberek,* 1964)—sparked an enormous national controversy because of its frank portrayal of creativity stifled through official bureaucratic incompetence and stupidity. Jancsó's *The Round-Up* (*Szegénylegények,* 1965) brought international attention to its director when screened at Cannes. In a sense typical of Jancsó's later work in its emphasis on Hungary's past, it is a blood-curdling factual account of the torture and brutalization of a group of peasants by Hungarian authorities in the mid-nineteenth century.

Projecting Poland

As an ex-Soviet satellite country, Poland's film history parallels that of Hungary and Czechoslovakia (or the Czech Republic) in many ways: occupation, rebellion, resistance, and other kinds of political turmoil, which then become the stuff, directly or allegorically, of much film.

Short Cuts

Perhaps the most famous Polish filmmaker is another Eastern European exile: Roman Polanski. As a Jew, his childhood was spent living through the horrors of the Nazi occupation of Poland. Among other activities, the child was used for target practice by sadistic German soldiers. As a result of witnessing the atrocities of wartime Poland, his first feature film, *Knife in the Water* (*Noz w wodzie*, 1962) is about a sadomasochistic threesome consisting of a married couple and a hitchhiker. Even after leaving Poland, Polanski's films remained moody and murderous: *Repulsion* (1965), *Rosemary's Baby* (1968), *Macbeth* (1971), and so on.

Film in Poland got off to a slow start, remaining popular and/or literary rather than innovative through the silent era. World War II almost completely destroyed the Polish film industry, which suffered even further under the repression of Stalinism. Immediate postwar films were typically about the horrors of occupation. The best of these is probably Aleksander Ford's *Border Street* (*Ulica Graniczna,* 1948), a film about the Warsaw Ghetto revolt.

You can sample the history of postwar Polish film through the lens of one of its most famous directors: Adrzej Wajda. His most famous works of the romantic-realist Polish School era are probably *Generation* (*Pokolenie,* 1955) and *Ashes and Diamonds* (*Popiól i diament,* 1958), two films about Polish resistance fighters. After the government's crackdown on liberal filmmakers Wajda made his most introspective film, *Everything for Sale* (*Wszystko na sprzedaz,* 1969), ostensibly about the death of a friend, but also about the act and value of filmmaking itself. *Man of Iron* (*Czlowiek z zelaza,* 1981), was a pro-Solidarity movement film that won the Cannes Grand Prix. When Solidarity was temporarily crushed, Wajda lost his job as head of a film unit, and resigned as chair of the Polish Filmmakers Association.

After the death of Stalin, Polish film became more lively with the birth of the "Polish School," an influential group of filmmakers of the late 1950s and early 1960s. The government cracked down on these filmmakers because of their criticisms of the status quo. After some uncertain years, some filmmakers rallied around the 1980s Solidarity movement against the Communist regime. When Solidarity actually (and through election) took over the reins of government in 1989, it committed a significant amount of economic aid to the ailing film industry, whose output and quality improved through the 1990s. Some of the products of that decade have done extremely well internationally; the most famous contemporary Polish director is without doubt Krzysztof Kieslowski, whose films—*The Double Life of Veronique* (*La Double vie de Véronique,* 1991) and the trilogy *Three Colors: Blue* (*Trois couleurs: Bleu,* 1993), *Three Colors: White* (*Trzy kolory: Bialy,* 1994), and *Three Colors: Red* (*Trois couleurs: Rouge,* 1994) (all co-produced by France)—have been hugely successful.

Avant-Garde Directors and Theorists to Remember

Unlike most American directors, most of the following Soviet filmmakers are also famous as film theorists and critics. Most have had a profound effect on the way we think about filmmaking at every level: political, aesthetic, narrative, technical, and so on.

Lev Kuleshov

One of the earliest exponents of editing as the most important component of filmmaking, Lev Kuleshov discovered in the 1920s that meaning in film is determined more by the order of the shots than by what the shots contain. This realization is the precondition for montage effects. Kuleshov discovered the "Kuleshov Effect," or the manipulation of meaning through editing. His greatest example of this effect was the editing together of six shots:

- Shot 1: A bowl of soup.
- Shot 2: A still close-up of an actor's neutral expression.
- Shot 3: A dead woman in a coffin.
- Shot 4: The same still as in the second shot.
- Shot 5: A playing child.
- Shot 6: The same still as in the second shot.

Though shots 2, 4, and 6 of the actor's face are identical, audiences thought that they conveyed a subtle but wide range of emotional responses: hunger on seeing the soup, grief on seeing the dead woman, and joy on seeing the child. The audience was manipulated into believing in the greatness of the performance by the creativity of the editing.

Kuleshov also taught that editing could involve "creative geography" and "creative anatomy." In the former, a film cuts from two subjects walking on a Moscow street to their walking on the Capitol steps in Washington, making it appear as if the two locations are next to each other. Experiments in creative anatomy involved filming various body parts of various women. When the shots are spliced together, the whole conveys the impression that the various parts all belong to one person.

Filmophile's Lexicon

Kino-Eye is the name Vertov gave the camera eye, which is more perfect in recording impressions, and in moving through time and space, than our own eyes. For Vertov, the Kino-Eye is both a perfectly objective recorder and an ideal interpreter of reality.

Dziga Vertov (Denis the Red Menace)

Dziga Vertov was the pseudonym of Denis Kaufman. Poet, essayist, novelist, medical student, and musician, Vertov's interest in film coincides with the Russian Revolution itself, when, in 1917, he became a writer and editor for newsreels. At first working under Lev Kuleshov, Vertov ultimately started making his own documentaries about the war and the Revolution. During this period (between about 1919 and 1922), he also began publishing his ideas about realism in cinema, especially about the *Kino-Eye*.

Vsevolod I. Pudovkin

Another of Kuleshov's pupils, this brilliant physics and chemistry student became enamored of film after seeing Griffith's *Intolerance* (1916).

Another filmmaker interested in montage, Pudovkin saw shots as building blocks in which narrative and meaning were built bit by bit. It is probably easiest to think of Pudovkin as closer in style to Hollywood filmmaking than Eisenstein in these respects: While Eisenstein strived the most after an intellectual effect, Pudovkin was most interested in capturing an audience emotionally. Pudovkin's films had heroes, while the people were Eisenstein's main protagonist. Pudovkin's greatest film, *Mother,* contains characters who represent particular social positions: a son who favors the striking workers, a father on the opposite side. But the appeal of the film also resides in the very real and personal agonies of the title character.

Sergei Eisenstein

Part Jewish in an anti-Semitic culture, homosexual in a homophobic society, Sergei Eisenstein was probably the single most-influential thinker on the subject of film editing, and certainly the most famous Soviet director of the twentieth century.

In opposition to Pudovkin, Eisenstein did not think of individual shots as building blocks, but rather as related through antagonism and difference (despite his calling their relation one of "attractions"). He saw the editing process as dialectical, like the logic underlying Marxism itself. Like other Russian formalist directors, he referred to this special attention to editing as "montage" (defined in Chapter 23, "Making the Cut: Film Editing").

His best metaphor for this dialectical editing was the idea of the ideogram, a primitive mode of written communication in which you can take the symbol (really stick-drawing) of a man, overlay it with the symbol of a mouth, and you have a new symbol containing a new idea: hunger, or perhaps crying. Two nouns together form a verb, an action. Simple images juxtaposed can form complex ideas.

Several of the best examples of Eisensteinian montage at work occur in *Battleship Potemkin.* At a simple level a shot of a Cossack plunging his bayonet down is crosscut with a shot of a baby carriage, giving the horrific impression that a baby has just been skewered, when the closest infant was probably playing with kitchen knives somewhere down the street from the shooting location. Not only is infanticide suggested, but the brutality of the Cossacks in general and the callousness of their commander-in-chief, the Czar, is definitively asserted.

When sound came to film, Eisenstein theorized that the relationship between sound and image should also be dialectical. Sound was not simply a commentary on the images, like background music in American films, but brought its own set of meanings to the table.

Iconoclastic in other ways as well, Eisenstein favored nonactors in principle parts, and deemphasized the notion of individual heroes in favor of stories that, like *Potemkin,* featured the masses as the collective hero.

Andrei Tarkovsky

Andrei Tarkovsky is the first internationally recognized Russian director of real note after the death of Stalin. His 1966 *Andrei Rublev* was banned in Russia until 1971 because its vision of a cruel fifteenth-century Russian society seemed too much like contemporary Soviet society; this kind of critique did not conform to party standards of filmically cliché heroic Marxism. It did, however, win a prize at Cannes, and helped catapult Tarkovsky onto the international scene. (His other early festival winner, *My Name Is Ivan* [1962], did the same.) His next feature, *Solaris* (1972), is a quiet, thoughtful, uneventful science fiction film that probes the nature and origins of intelligence, memory, emotions, and selfhood.

It makes sense that Tarkovsky's father was a noted poet because his films are often referred to as lyrical. They were certainly personal enough to get him in trouble with Soviet authorities for making films too difficult for the masses (read: the authorities themselves) to understand. As one might expect, technology and uniformity are suspect in most of his films. His films generally condemn the materialism of both east and west, and seem to support the notion of personal and artistic integrity and autonomy.

Some Soviet Movies Worth Watching

Again, this field is impossibly large, so we are listing various categories (pre-Soviet, Czech, and so on) that may make choosing easier:

- *The Extraordinary Adventures of Mr. West in the Land of the Bolsheviks* (*Neobychainye Priklyucheniya Mistera Vesta v Strane Bolshevikov,* 1924). A broad, funny, playful satire of capitalism's fear of communism.
- *Aelita* (1924). Brilliant constructivist sets make this early fantasy/sci-fi flick a terrific spectacle.
- *Battleship Potemkin* (*Bronenosets Potyomkin,* 1925). The most-often cited and acclaimed film of acclaimed director Sergei Eisenstein. The brilliant photographic (including montage) bits includes, first and foremost, the "Odessa Steps Sequence."
- *Mother* (*Mat,* 1926). Most acclaimed film by Eisenstein's chief rival, Vsevolod I. Pudovkin, in many ways this film is technically indistinguishable from the contemporary Hollywood product.
- *Moscow Does Not Believe in Tears* (*Moskva Slezam ne Verit,* 1979). The Oscar for best foreign film went to this psychological/social drama about three contemporary Russian women urbanites.
- *Solaris* (*Solyaris,* 1972). A beautiful film, very unlike the average American sci-fi entry. A psychologist is sent to examine the disintegration of the denizens of a space station hovering over a planet with an odd intelligence that seems able to make his wife, dead for several years, appear.
- *Repentance* (*Pokayaniye,* 1987). Hysterically, but bitterly, comic allegory about the vestiges of Stalinism in the newly opened Soviet society. The body of the town's mayor/dictator simply will not stay buried.

Other Eastern Bloc-Busters

The following films are some of the best and most representative works of Eastern Europe's film industry:

- *Erotikon* (1929). An early and terrific example of Czech cinema and of erotic film.
- *The Round-Up* (*Szegénylegéyek,* 1965). Miklóncsó's Hungarian period piece about the nineteenth-century torture and coercion of peasants is also visually haunting.
- *The Fireman's Ball* (*Horí, má panenko,* 1967). This early Milos Forman Czech film is a thinly disguised allegory of the absurdity of authoritarianism. It's also hilariously funny, even slapstick at times.
- *The Man of Iron* (*Czlowiek z zelaza,* 1981). Andrzej Wajda's film homage to the Polish Solidarity movement that mixes footage of actual striking workers a decade earlier to provide a sort of prehistory of Solidarity.

The Least You Need to Know

- The pre-Soviet Czarist filmmaking community was small, and the dissemination of film surprisingly weak.
- The Soviet Union very quickly realized the propaganda power of film and disseminated it all over Russia via agitki-trains.
- Russia in the 1920s saw the rise of one of the most brilliant periods in world filmmaking history, both in theoretical writing and in actual filmmaking.
- The two most important names to remember in Soviet film theory are Sergei Eisenstein and V.I. Pudovkin.
- Filmmaking in Stalinist Russia became extremely repressive, recovering only in the 1960s with a new generation of directors uninfluenced by the Stalinist "tractor" film.
- Several Soviet satellite states have had equally interesting film histories, formed in part by patterns of occupation by Germany and the Soviet Union.

Chapter 17

Asian Angles: Filming in the Far East

In This Chapter

- Chinese cinema from the silent era to the Fifth Generation
- The Taiwanese "New Cinema" of the 1980s and '90s
- Hong Kong's Cantonese and martial arts traditions (and the New Wave)
- Classic and modern cinema in Japan
- Akira Kurosawa and the triumph of Asian film

With more than a fifth of the world's population, it's not surprising that the nations of the Far East have developed some of the most important cinematic traditions in the history of film. But our American readers are probably much less familiar with the histories of Chinese, Japanese, and Taiwanese film than they are with their European counterparts. This chapter gives you a quick, flash-in-the-pan overview of some of the crucial moments and personages in the development of Asian film.

Don't take what we have to say as a definitive treatment of this vast and virtually limitless repertory. Rather, read this chapter as a rough sketch of one little stretch of a shoreline bordering a vast continent of film that you'll have the rest of your life to explore!

Two Chinas, Two Cinemas

The People's Republic of China and Taiwan have been at military and cultural loggerheads since 1949, when the Kuomintang Nationalist party split with the Communist Party leadership and fled to the island with thousands of supporters. As a result, the

Second Take

The two oldest surviving Chinese narrative films, *Romance of a Fruit Peddler* and the three-reel melodrama *Love's Labours,* were both made in 1922, making it difficult to know very much about all but the last eight or so years of the nation's silent cinema.

history of Chinese cinema looks very different when viewed through the contrasting lenses of mainland and insular politics. The two Chinas have produced two cinemas, entirely distinct in their ideological orientation, style, and international success.

Before 1949, of course, there was only one China and only one Chinese cinema (though its history is written very differently by mainland and insular partisans).

Historians agree that the era's films were almost exclusively sentimental, feel-good comedies and dramas that made few significant contributions to world cinema. A notable exception is *The Peach Girl* (1931), a classic tale of a peasant girl and the son of a rich landowner that starred Ruan Lingyu in one of her most acclaimed performances. (This is one of those "must-rent" classics of world cinema.)

It isn't until the '30s that Chinese film gets interesting with a series of left-leaning, populist motion pictures that combine tales of familial drama with in-your-face critiques of the large-scale economic and social forces affecting the lives of Chinese families. If you want to get a taste for this genre, check out Tsai Chu-sheng's well-known *The Song of the Fishermen* (1934), an intensive look at the daily strains of labor upon the Chinese citizenry.

Director's Cut

The great Chinese silent star Ruan Lingyu was sometimes referred to as the Greta Garbo of China. Perhaps the most idolized movie star in pre–World War II Asia, she was featured in almost 30 films before 1935. Tragically, Ruan Lingyu succumbed to the pressures of fame and committed suicide in 1935—at the tender age of 25.

Movies on the Mainland

The Communist regime that stayed put on the mainland under Mao Tse-tung has only occasionally allowed artistically innovative or politically challenging films to be released. There is probably no government on the planet that's invested more time, energy, and bureaucracy into the regulation of film content. The results of this profound and longstanding propagandism will be immediately obvious if you take a look at some of the so-called *revolutionary realist* films from the late '40s and early '50s, such as *The Bridge* (1949), one of the first feature-length examples of the genre.

At certain very brief moments in its history, China has adopted a more liberal approach to the arts, allowing more politically subversive films to be released and discussed in the nation's media. During the Hundred Flowers Campaign in the '50s, Mao even allowed filmmakers to criticize those working in his regime (though never himself). Lu Ban's comedies, for example (*Before the New Director Arrives,* 1956; *The Unfinished Comedy,* 1957) took sharp jabs at the inefficiencies of the Communist bureaucracy. For the most part, though, film content remained tightly regulated and constrained by governmental censors. Only recently has there been a significant new direction in Chinese cinema.

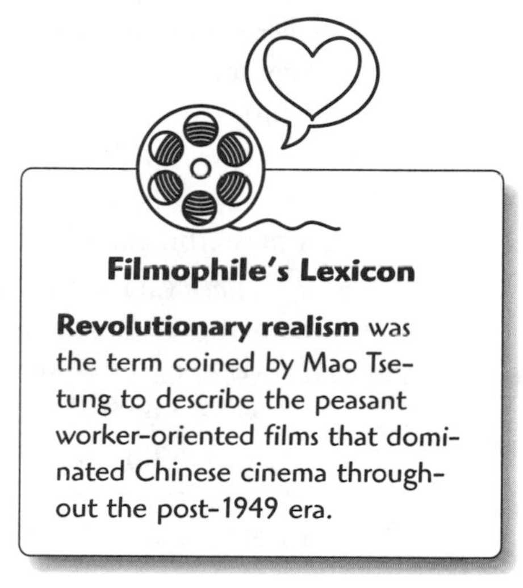

Filmophile's Lexicon

Revolutionary realism was the term coined by Mao Tse-tung to describe the peasant worker-oriented films that dominated Chinese cinema throughout the post-1949 era.

Top of the Fifth

Beginning in the mid-'80s, a coalition of young Chinese filmmakers emerged who immediately began to reshape the language of the cinema to create a new way of representing the nation's troubled past and envisioning its alternative futures. With their uncompromising willingness to introduce new filming techniques and innovative cinematography as well as often opaque dialogue and obscure story lines, these artists produced a series of pictures over the next 15 years that their critics pejoratively dubbed "exploratory films."

The filmmakers themselves, though, brashly referred to their own loose group of Beijing Film Academy graduates as the "Fifth Generation," a label that distinguished them respectfully from the less experimental and more humanist style of older but still active directors like Huang Jianzhong and Hu Binliu. The 20-odd well-known directors of the Fifth Generation have brought the first wide-scale international recognition to Chinese film during the past 15 years (though their work has often failed commercially at home). There are five pictures in particular that stand out as powerful legacies of the Fifth Generation. Here they are:

- *One and Eight* (1984). Directed by Zhang Junzhao. The hallmark film of the Fifth Generation, this story of a Communist-imprisoned chain-gang was immediately controversial when it was released. Though heavily reworked by government censors, the film's bold innovations in the use of camera angles and space can still be appreciated; these and other techniques marked a decisive break with the humanist realism of the previous decade.

- *Yellow Earth* (1984). Directed by Chen Kaige. One of the greatest Chinese films ever made, *Yellow Earth* combines an austere visual style with deceptively simple symbolism reflecting on the political and ideological constraints of 1980s China.
- *The Last Day of Winter* (1986). Directed by Wu Ziniu. This bleak but hopeful drama, set in a prison labor camp in the far northwestern reaches of China, is a masterful example of Fifth Generation filmmaking techniques.
- *The Black Cannon Incident* (1985). Directed by Huang Jianxin. One of the few comedies to emerge from the Fifth Generation directors, *The Black Cannon Incident* crafts a sardonically humorous look at the Chinese bureaucracy and its tedious inefficiency.
- *Ju Dou* (1990). Directed by Zhang Yimou. Made in the immediate wake of the Tiananmen Square massacre, this moving story of a young woman (the incomparable actress Gong Li) who rebels against a traditional agrarian patriarchy won awards at the Cannes Film Festival, scored a nomination for best foreign film at the Academy Awards, and was shown widely in Europe and America.

Director's Cut

Taiwanese New Cinema is characterized by a determined focus on Taiwan as an aspiring nation in its own right; at the same time, the nationalism of the New Cinema directors is tempered by the training many of them received at American film schools such as USC and NYU, which has allowed them to incorporate foreign techniques and perspectives into their celluloid meditations on Taiwan's fate since the split with the mainland in 1949.

Hou's Who in Recent Taiwanese Film

Like Communist China, which has carefully regulated the content of practically all motion pictures produced and released on the mainland, the Taiwanese government has kept a censorious eye on its filmmakers and their productions, and the government has its own agency responsible for overseeing its cinema. During the past 20 years, though, the island's heavily Westernized film industry has given rise to a thriving culture of directors, screenwriters, actors, and other film artists generally referred to under the rubric "New Cinema."

The most prominent among the New Cinema directors is Hou Hsiao-hsien, the undisputed master of Taiwanese film. In a series of films released in the mid-'80s—*A Time to Live and a Time to Die* (1985), *Daughter of the Nile* (1987), and others—Hou became the first Taiwanese director to achieve international recognition. *A City of Sadness* (1989), a historical epic that treats the emergence of Taiwan after World War II through the eyes of a single family, is a modern classic of Asian cinema that won the Golden Lion at the Venice Film Festival.

Tony Leung starring in Hou Hsiao-Hsien's New Cinema masterpiece A City of Sadness *(1989).*

Though harder to find than Hou's films at your local video store, the work of other Taiwanese New Cinema directors offers rare treats for those of you scanning the Pacific Rim for films worth seeing. Three films to keep in mind are Edward Yang's *On the Beach* (1983) and *Brighter Summer Day* (1991) as well as Ch'en K'un-Hou's *Growing Up* (1983).

Hong Kong: Cantonese, Kung-Fu, and a New Wave

Despite its small size, Hong Kong has produced one of the most vibrant, lucrative, and internationally successful Asian cinema traditions during the past 40 years. While films from the mainland in the Mandarin dialect were dominant in the years following World War II, by the mid-'50s a solid majority of films produced in Hong Kong were made or at least subtitled in Cantonese, reflecting the more southern, working-class origins of the large emigrant population from the mainland.

Initially, Cantonese cinema focused primarily on social ills and problems faced by Hong Kong's urban laborers, and production quality was not high on the priority list. With the founding of the Zhonglian studio in 1952, however, directors such as Wu Hui (*Family,* 1953), Qin Jian (*How to Get a Wife,* 1961), and Li Chenfeng (*Broken Spring*

Dreams, 1955; based on Tolstoy's *Anna Karenina*) worked to bring a modicum of artistic respectability to Cantonese cinema. Though most of this period's films were melodramas, derivative comedies, and opera adaptations, Hong Kong Cantonese flourished for more than a decade before giving way to a new, butt-kicking (literally) genre of Mandarin film that took Asian cinema by storm beginning in the late '60s.

Bodies in Motion: The Violent Art of Kung-Fu Films

The most familiar Hong Kong films to Western audiences are kung-fu and other martial arts movies. These violent visual vehicles burst onto the scene in the late '60s with Chang Cheh's *One-Armed Swordsman* (1967), which broke all previous box-office records for Hong Kong film. Combining quick-cut action sequences with an almost mystical reverence for eastern martial arts traditions, these films lit a fire under the city's somewhat moribund film industry and brought the first international recognition to Hong Kong cinema. In a sign of the genre's growing prestige, King Hu's *A Touch of Zen* won the Grand Prix at Cannes in 1975.

Director's Cut

One of the major factors in the success of the Hong Kong kung-fu film was the considerable martial arts talent of Bruce Lee. Born in San Francisco and long employed in Hollywood playing bit parts since the early '50s, Lee spent many years in Hong Kong and came to international prominence with *The Big Boss* (1971), directed by Luo Wei.

Unlike many stars of the martial arts genre, Lee was an actual expert in kung fu and karate, inspiring millions of fans to take up these arts themselves and launching a "karate craze" in the United States in the early '70s. After subsequent films like *Fists of Fury* (1971) and *Way of the Dragon* (1973), Lee became a household name in many parts of the world. His legend only grew after his early death in 1973 from a brain hemorrhage.

Indeed, perhaps the most significant aspect of the new genre's popularity was its effect upon Hong Kong cinema's relations with its international competitors. Unlike all of the European nations, as well as Japan, South Korea, and Taiwan, Hong Kong has the unique distinction among westernized nations of having established an indigenous cinema tradition that actually outsells Hollywood.

As you should know very well by now, this is no minor accomplishment in the world of feature film, which is so often dominated by American product.

Rolling with the Punches: Hong Kong's "New Wave"

Hong Kong's martial arts genre continued to attract some of the principality's best directing talents into the '80s and even '90s, decades that witnessed a "New Wave" of directors, writers, and actors emerge onto the world stage. John Woo's career was launched with *The Young Dragons* (1973) and *The Dragon Tamers* (1974) before he went on to make his even more violent action thrillers *Hard Boiled* (1992) and, in the United States, the artful *Hard Target* (1993), *Broken Arrow* (1996), and *Face/Off* (1996).

Some of Hong Kong's most popular actors during the past 10 years also got their start in martial arts films: Chow Yun-fat starred in several Woo pictures before breaking into the Hollywood mainstream. Jackie Chan became one of the most important and influential actor-directors to emerge from the Far East in the past 30 years with his unique blend of slapstick comedy and traditional martial arts wizardry (*Half a Loaf of Kung-Fu*, 1978).

Short Cuts

Throughout the '90s, Hong Kong–produced films maintained a market share above 50 percent—a considerable accomplishment considering the worldwide dominance of American film during the past 20 years.

Jackie Chan kicking his career into high gear in Snake in the Eagle's Shadow *(1978).*

Benching the *Benshi:* Japan's Illustrious Century

Japanese film before Akira Kurosawa is one of the great but generally neglected treasures of world cinema. Though the country's directors followed theatrical conventions up through the early 1920s (including the use of the *benshi,* or narrator, the dominance of the costume drama, and the employment of male cross-dressers to play female roles), there are numerous masterpieces from the silent and early sound eras that are well worth seeing. Major studios opened in Japan from the century's first decade onward, including Nikkatsu in Kyoto and Schochiku in Tokyo, and minor, independent production companies flourished, often under the leadership of a single inspired director (Shozo Makino's Makino Films is the most familiar example). With more and more of the nation's cinematic legacy being remastered and released on video and DVD, there's a virtual undiscovered country of early Japanese film out there for you to explore.

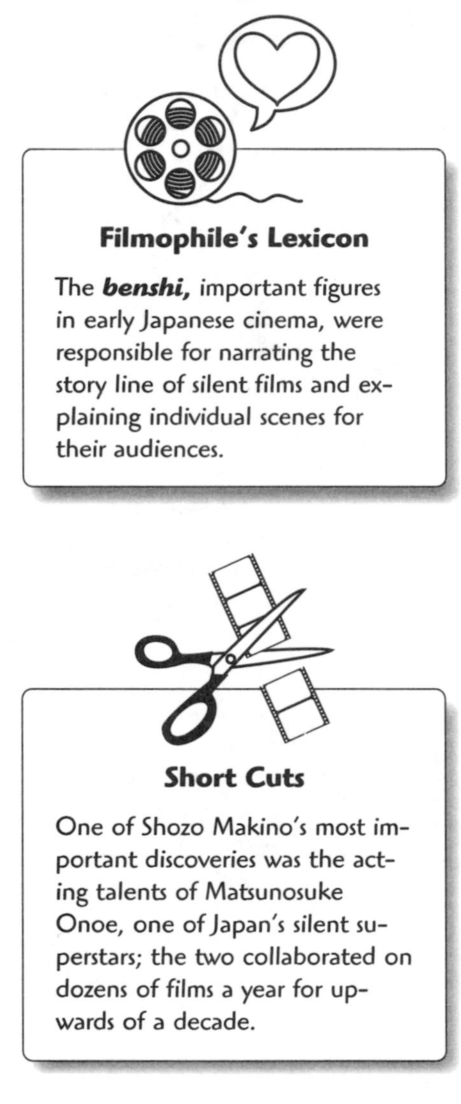

Filmophile's Lexicon

The ***benshi,*** important figures in early Japanese cinema, were responsible for narrating the story line of silent films and explaining individual scenes for their audiences.

Short Cuts

One of Shozo Makino's most important discoveries was the acting talents of Matsunosuke Onoe, one of Japan's silent superstars; the two collaborated on dozens of films a year for upwards of a decade.

The producer-director Shozo Makino is sometimes dubbed the "father of Japanese film"; he was responsible for creating the "period film" genre almost single-handedly.

The 1928 *True Record of the 47 Ronin* remains a true world classic, influencing the historical epics of Akira Kurosawa and many others, and *Raiden* (also 1928) still dazzles with its camerawork and inventive editing.

The first wave of cinematic realism in Japanese film was largely the responsibility of Yasujiro Ozu, whose focus on everyday life and middle-class folks made the phrase "Ozu Art" synonymous with an artistic appreciation of the mundane human dramas that could make great pictures. In acclaimed films such as *Dreams of Youth* (1928), *I Was Born, But …* (1932), *Until the Day We Meet Again* (1932), and *A Story of Floating Weeds* (1934), Ozu established a strain of realism for Japanese cinema that rivals France's poetic realism in its humanity. A later film, *Tokyo Story* (1953), garnered international awards and recognition for the elder filmmaker, who continued working until shortly before his death in 1963.

Other important figures in the silent and early sound eras include the reformer Norimasa Kaeriyama, who sought (with little success) to eliminate the traditional role of the *benshi* and made important innovations in location selection and camera work; Daisuke Ito, whose original approach to the *jidaigeki* film brought an avant-garde sensibility to this most tradition-bound of Japanese genres (see, for example, *A Diary of Chuji's Travels,* 1927); Kiyohiko Ushihara, whose spectacular epic *Shingun* (*Marching*

On, 1930, recently made available on video) combined a rich historical sensibility with a flair for the mundane comedy of everyday human situations; Kenji Mizoguchi, whose extraordinarily diverse career began with Western-influenced "New School" comedies, melodramas, thrillers, detective stories, and so-called "tendency films" in the 1920s (for example, *In the Ruins* [*Haikyo no naka,* 1923], *Nihonbashi* [1929], and *Tokyo March* [*Tokyo koshinkyoku,* 1929]) but also included historical dramas in the '50s like *New Tales of the Taira Clan* (1955) and the acknowledged masterpiece *The Life of Oharu* (1952); and Teinosuke Kinugasa, whose 1928 *Crossroads* (*Jujiro*) was one of the first Japanese films to achieve any distribution in Europe.

Filmophile's Lexicon

Gendaigeki were modern drama films set in Japan's larger cities, especially Tokyo and Kyoto, in the present.

Jidaigeki is the term for period drama set in the Japanese past but always very much concerned with the present.

Perhaps the most important thing to remember about pre–World War II Japanese cinema as opposed to that of other nations is its relative narrative simplicity. While most European national cinemas were led (often unwillingly, it's true) by an experimental avant-garde during the '20s and '30s, Japan's directors drew on the artistic resources inherent in basic, everyday human dramas to create an enduring cinematic legacy of unparalleled humanity and lyricism.

Second Take

Though superstar Matsunosuke Onoe may have made more than 1,000 movies in his career, only three survive: *Loyal 47 Ronin* (1910), *Goketsujiraiya* (1921), and *Bangoro Shibukawa* (1922).

Japan's Modern Masters

The great towering figure in Japanese cinema during the past five decades has been Akira Kurosawa, whom you'll read about in more detail in the next section. Like Bergman for Scandinavian film, Kurosawa's long career and deep-seated influence on his nation's film history threatens to obscure other directors who have often worked in his shadow.

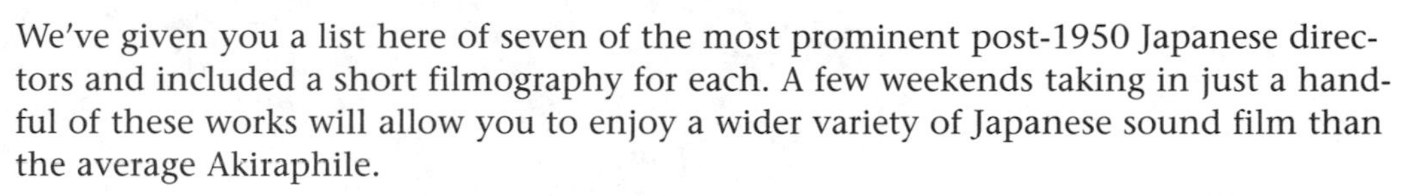

We've given you a list here of seven of the most prominent post-1950 Japanese directors and included a short filmography for each. A few weekends taking in just a handful of these works will allow you to enjoy a wider variety of Japanese sound film than the average Akiraphile.

- Tadashi Imai: *And Yet We Live* (1951); *Bushido: Samurai Saga* (1963); *Takiji Kobayashi* (1975); *War and Youth* (1991).
- Kon Ichikawa: *The Burmese Harp* (1956); *Fires on the Plain* (1959); *My Enemy the Sea* (1963); *The Wanderers* (1973); *47 Ronin* (1994).

- Nagisa Oshima: *A Town of Love and Hope* (1959); *A Cruel Story of Youth* (1960); *Death By Hanging* (1968); *In the Realm of the Senses* (1976); *Merry Christmas, Mr. Lawrence* (1982); *Max, Mon Amour* (1987).

Second Take

Don't let American Kurosawa-philia blind you to the work of Nagisa Oshima, whom many film buffs regard as a vastly superior artist to Akira Kurosawa!

- Masaki Kobayashi: *The Human Condition* (trilogy, 1959–61); *Harakiri* (1962); *Kwaidan* (1964); *Glowing Autumn* (1979); *The Empty Table* (1985).
- Shiro Toyoda: *Whisper of Spring* (1952); *Marital Relations* (1955); *Evening Calm* (1957); *Madame Aki* (1963); *Illusion of Blood* (1965); *Portrait of Hell* (1969).
- Mikio Naruse: *Sound of the Mountain* (1954); *Floating Clouds* (1955); *Untamed* (1957); *When a Woman Ascends the Stairs* (1960); *The Wiser Age* (1962); *Moment of Terror* (1966).
- Juzo Itami: *The Funeral* (1984); *Tampopo* (1986); *The Gangster's Moll* (1992).

The Master: The Art of Akira Kurosawa

In 1951, a virtually unknown director from Japan stunned the cinematic world when his *Rashomon,* the heavily allegorical story of a nobleman caught in a psychological struggle over the nature of truth itself, garnered top awards at the Venice Film Festival and won an Oscar for best foreign film. Since that illustrious moment, Akira Kurosawa has ranked in the forefront among world directors.

The tragically beautiful Takashi Shimura in Akira Kurosawa's Drunken Angel *(1948).*

For more than 50 years, from his first feature *Judo Saga* (1943) to 1993's *Madadayo* and beyond, Kurosawa crafted an utterly unique style that combines elements of traditional Japanese theater (*Noh* drama and *kabuki,* for example) with an unparalleled sensitivity to the global reach of human dramas. His seemingly fearless willingness to tackle any theme, genre, or setting distinguishes him as one of the most inventive directors of the twentieth century.

Among Kurosawa's many must-see films, three that he made after *Rashomon* truly stand out. *Seven Samurai* (1954) starred Toshiro Mifune in his most enduring role as the leader of a band of traditional Japanese warriors defending a village against marauders. *Ran* (1985) is an award-winning adaptation of Shakespeare's *King Lear* that brings out some surprising and generally unacknowledged themes in the Bard of Avon's story of a flawed father and his three daughters. And *Dersu Uzala* (1975), most of which he shot in the Soviet Union, won the Oscar for best foreign picture and other prestigious international awards.

Short Cuts

Hollywood's classic Western *The Magnificent Seven* (1960), directed by John Sturges, was a direct adaptation of Kurosawa's *Seven Samurai* (1954), which was itself alternatively titled *The Magnificent Seven.*

Kurosawa's most enduring legacy may be the opening of Asian cinema as a whole to Western audiences. While some of his best pictures remain relatively unknown to all but film specialists and junkies, his cultural ambassadorship gave world cinema one of its most vital modes of artistic exchange between east and west.

How to Watch a Kurosawa Film

Though visually arresting, Kurosawa's films can sometimes feel a bit slow, laden as they are with often heavy symbolism and long gaps between significant points in the narrative. But these are precisely the qualities that make his pictures so unique, and it would be a mistake to fast forward to get to the next sword fight. Here are four simple attributes of many Kurosawa films that you'll need to remember if you want to learn how to appreciate these modern filmic masterpieces. If you watch for them carefully, you'll get much more out of these pictures than you would otherwise.

- **The art of repetition.** Kurosawa will often repeat discrete narrative elements in his films in order to highlight the dynamic nature of specific events or the cyclical nature of life. In *Seven Samurai,* a village is repeatedly attacked by bandits and valiantly defended by noble warriors; *Rashomon* narrates an attack upon a nobleman by a bandit four different times from four contrasting perspectives.
- **The significant pause.** Though deceptively simple in terms of technique, long narrative pauses are a staple of Kurosawa films, encouraging viewers to reflect on what has come before in order to better understand what will follow. When you

come to such a pause (say, the long gaps between attacks in *Seven Samurai,* or the lingering shots of landscapes in *Akira Kurosawa's Dreams* [1990]), consider its impact upon the sequential progression of the film. How would the texture of the story change if he had moved straight on to the next narrative event?

- **Occidental motifs.** Though long revered for giving native Japanese film unprecedented international recognition, Kurosawa was virtually obsessed by American and European film, drama, and literature. Before watching *Throne of Blood* (1957), be sure to reread Shakespeare's *Macbeth,* of which *Throne* is a brilliant adaptation; in a similar vein, brush up on your *King Lear* before renting *Ran.* The films of John Ford were a particular inspiration for Kurosawa, who may have based *The Hidden Fortress* (1959) upon some of the American director's greatest Westerns.
- **Humanism.** Kurosawa's film oeuvre is unified by the director's deep-seated belief in the fundamental goodness and dignity of the human being. Though his protagonists are often caught in seemingly impossible situations struggling against seemingly insurmountable odds (as in *Seven Samurai* and *Dersu Uzala*), the old-fashioned notion of the "human spirit" generally triumphs in Kurosawa's films, providing a narrative goal that informs a surprising number of his works.

The films of Akira Kurosawa join a deep sense of tradition with a commitment to artistic innovation—a combination that characterizes much of the best filmmaking in the Far East during the past 20 years.

The Least You Need to Know

- China's cinema developed along two separate trajectories, reflecting the political cultures of the Communist mainland and Taiwan.
- In Hong Kong, post–World War II Cantonese cinema gave way in the '70s to mainstream and internationally successful Mandarin features, especially kung-fu and other martial arts pictures.
- Japan's tradition-bound silent cinema took a while to break from the theatrical conventions that deeply influenced the film medium.
- Japan's modern directors have made innovative and enduring contributions to Asian film.
- Akira Kurosawa, one of the twentieth century's greatest directors, combines a complex approach to film aesthetics with an abiding humanism and self-consciously Occidental artistry.

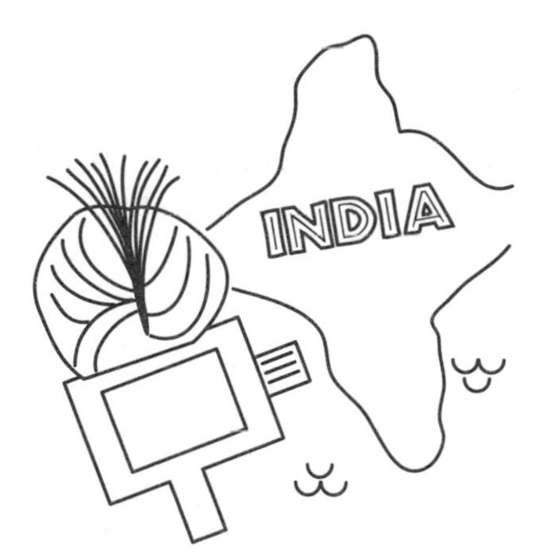

Chapter 18

Third (World) Cinema

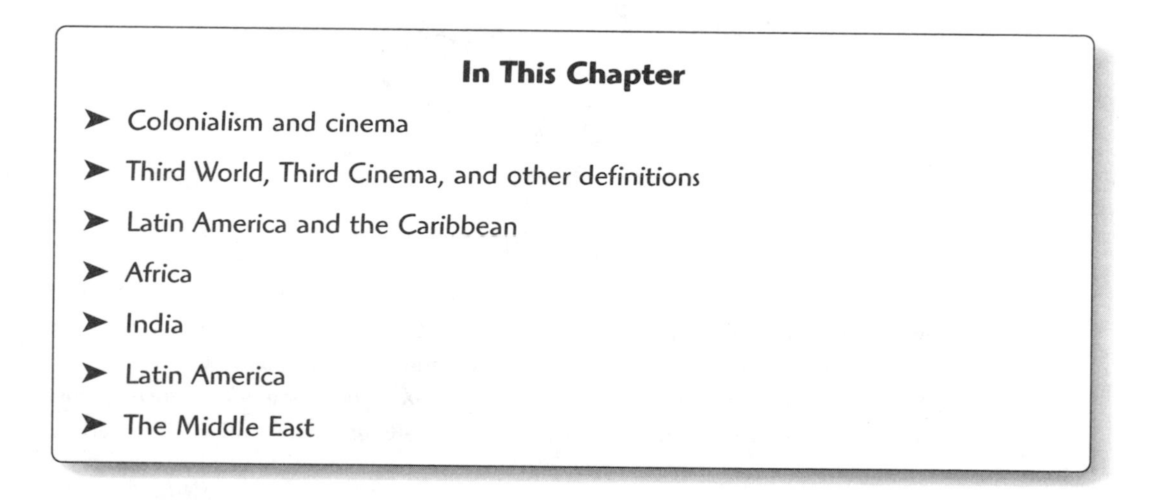

In This Chapter

- Colonialism and cinema
- Third World, Third Cinema, and other definitions
- Latin America and the Caribbean
- Africa
- India
- Latin America
- The Middle East

What about the cinemas of those "other" countries, the ones whose industrial revolution happened later than ours, or not at all? The countries colonized by the "developed" countries with developed film industries. Is there a cinema in Korea? South Africa? India? Egypt? Israel? These are the countries for which most histories of film give no account until the post–World War II era. But would you be surprised to discover that India's film output is larger than that of the United States?

In this chapter, you'll learn a bit about the cinema of countries that did not start World War II or inflict Christianity on the rest of the world, countries that might not have the atomic bomb, and countries without a Coca Cola bottling plant, a Mercedes dealership, or an outlet mall. We will examine their vision of the world.

Because the subject of Third-World cinema is huge, we've narrowed our discussion down to a handful of those countries with a thriving cinema. Some regions—Latin America, for example—are more completely covered because they are more prolific.

Conversely, China, though declaring itself a Third-World country (China itself originated the notion of the three worlds, aligning itself with the third), is not really a Third-World country in the sense we mean. In fact, it is a major world power. So we've placed it (and other Pacific Rim nations) in the chapter on Asian cinema (see Chapter 17, "Asian Angles: Filming in the Far East").

Colonialism, Neocolonialism, Postcolonialism

Though of course the countries we are discussing are radically different, most share the fact that they have had to negotiate colonialism and its aftermath in one or another ways. Sometimes—as in the case of China—colonization by the West was somewhat less dramatic. Sometimes—as in the case of India—it was devastating and complete. Among other things, we shall be tracking filmic responses to colonialism.

Filmophile's Lexicon

Colonialism: The historical relationship since at least the eighteenth century between Third-World regions and European nations, in which the latter assumed the power to administrate the governments of African, Asian, and Latin American countries, under the triple banner of liberation, modernization, and Christianization. Sometimes sincere, this political relationship was for the most part one of cruelty and exploitation, enforced by a strong military presence.

Postcolonialism: The historical moment in which ex-colonies have to deal with the repercussions of colonialism.

Neocolonialism: The economic and cultural—rather than explicitly political or military—control of Third-World countries.

Politics and Filmmaking

Though most countries produce their own commercial, entertainment-oriented films, we have tended, since the 1960s, to think of Third-World cinema as more political than our own. (Many critics see a chronological development from dependent Hollywood entertainment models to a greater degree of criticism, experimentation, and originality in the various Third-World histories of postcolonial filmmaking.) We tend to think of our own society as fat and happy, while the socially conscious African filmmaker has to think about famine, border conflict, dictatorships, colonial and neocolonial oppression.

And, though the Third World produces its own entertainment films, many Third-World filmmakers think of their own movies as critiques of the First World (Western Europe and the United States), and of First World cinema. In fact, these filmmakers have invented a phrase to describe this "countercinema": *Third Cinema*. We shall be using this phrase in preference to "Third-World cinema" from now on.

Filmophile's Lexicon

Third Cinema: This term derives from an Argentine political manifesto titled "Towards a Third Cinema: Notes and Experiences on the Development of a Cinema of Liberation in the Third World." Third Cinema has gradually become the preferred expression for critics in the know for national cinemas not a part of the ex-Soviet Union or of the Western, industrially developed countries. It is preferred because it derives from the Third World itself (and so is not a name given these regions by the West), and because it has come to mean a kind of filmmaking different from the Western concentration on entertainment and empty formalism. Third Cinema suggests to its exponents, not a lesser movie industry, but a cinema that provides a third way, avoiding the ideological power struggles of Eastern Europe on the one hand, and Western industrialized nations on the other.

Filmmaking Collectives

Third Cinema often connotes more than simply anticolonial Third-World filmmaking. It implies, for example, an awareness of and solidarity with the political concerns of other countries. It is a fact that during the 1960s, almost every major Third-World film-producing nation saw the emergence of some politically conscious group of filmmakers: from Brazil's Cinema Novo to India's parallel cinema.

The term *Third Cinema* also implies a different way of making films: more collective. In conservative *Star Trek* mythology the Borg "collective" is bad. In Third Cinema, it often represents an alternative to the Hollywood-style corporate studio system. The theory is that a different economy for filmmaking will result in a different kind of film. Some film cooperatives—most conspicuously Argentina's Cine Liberacion and

Brazil's Cinema Novo—seem to bear this out. Both products of the radicalism of the 1960s, the first produced one of the most influential documentaries to come out of Third-World filmmaking—*The Hour of the Furnaces* directed by Fernando E. Solanas and Octavio Getino (1968). The second produced extremely famous feature films: *Antonio das Mortes* directed by Glauber Rocha (1968).

Local Color

It would be a little naive to assert that all Third Cinema is about colonialism and other international concerns. This would be like saying that artists can only paint vases. We shall also be examining the "local color" in Third Cinema, the manner in which the regional cultures, customs, manners, and psyches are portrayed. The best films tend to recognize that politics and culture are not easily distinguishable. Carlos Diegues's *Xica* (1976) is about both the relationship between a mistress-slave and her owner, and slavery in eighteenth-century Brazil.

Filmophile's Lexicon

Cultural hegemony: Cultural theorists use this phrase to describe the invasion of a country by economic and cultural rather than military means. The greatest fear of custodians of much of rest of the world is not that the United States will use bombs to take over a country, but that the whole world will eventually be one long strip mall dotted with Gaps and Burger Kings.

U.S. and Them

The United States and European film industry has had a long, neocolonialist history of exploiting Third-World markets in several ways. First, we tend to discourage indigenous filmmaking communities. We use the power of our film economy to produce expensive films that are difficult to resist.

While not a military invasion, our films sometimes have the effect of a cultural and economic takeover. American films tend to be *culturally hegemonic,* making over the cultures of other countries in which they are exhibited. We have forced Third-World exhibitors to take several of our films at once, in a kind of block-booking endeavor. We don't import many Third-World films for our own consumption, so that not much money goes back to the their film industries from here. Finally, and perhaps most insidiously, we appropriate films and stars from other countries.

Africa

First, we have to acknowledge the utter futility of trying to summarize in a few paragraphs the filmmaking practices of an entire continent whose nations' politics and histories vary widely. (Egypt, for example, is so different from South Africa that we are discussing it in a different region.) But we're going to do it anyway. Wish us luck.

Tarzan films notwithstanding, there was not much indigenous filmmaking in sub-Saharan Africa before World War II. The first work by a sub-Saharan filmmaker was *Mourani* (Guinea, 1953).

The most important earlier filmmaker is Ousmane Sembene. Painter, poet, novelist, French soldier in World War II, union leader, and Communist Party member, this Senegalese citizen became internationally famous with his first feature film. Winning several awards, *Black Girl* (1966) is an examination of neocolonialism through the story of a black servant girl transplanted to France. (Many among the French audiences were not crazy about the movie. Amazing.) Other of Sembene's films examining colonialism and/or neocolonialism include *Mandaba* (1968, also called *The Money Order*), *Emitai* (1972, also called *God of Thunder*), *Ceddo* (1978), and *Xala* (1974, also called *Curse of Impotence*). While *Ceddo* is probably the most typically anticolonial as it follows an illiterate dock worker who tries to cash a money order and is cheated by a succession of townspeople, *Xala* is probably Sembene's most famous meditation on neocolonialism. Perhaps this is so in part because this story of a corrupt bureaucrat who exploits his people, and whose hellish marriage to a woman young enough to be his daughter becomes a sort of poetically just comeuppance, has a strong if oddly erotic component.

Thierno Leye and Younouss Seye in a scene from Ousmane Sembene's Xala *(Senegal).*

However, only after most African nations achieved their independence from their colonizers (around 1960) was a wider indigenous filmmaking practice able to grow on the continent. Even after colonialism officially ended, filmmaking resources and expertise remained (and remains) scarce on the continent. Many of the most famous filmmakers (like Sembene, Haile Gerima, and Souleymane Cisse) were educated in Europe or the United States.

Today, African movies more truly represent Third Cinema than almost any other national cinema. Though entertainment films are produced there (remember South

Africa's *The God Must Be Crazy* [1981]?), African filmmaking is highly committed to political issues and aesthetics, perhaps because the poverty and economic inequities of the continent are themselves so dramatic. Many African filmmakers care how their filmmaking is financed, taking into account the strings that might be attached by funding from former colonizing countries like France and Belgium.

Director's Cut

However, it is still the case that, because of funding by the French and Belgian governments, the most significant filmmaking in sub-Saharan Africa comes from the former French-speaking colonies.

Of the dozens of significant African filmmakers, the most famous outside the continent are probably Haile Gerima, Souleymane Cissé, and Med Hondo.

Though a major figure in African filmmaking, Gerima is often not considered regional because he has been an expatriate for many years, having partially learned his craft at UCLA. Still, his two major films—*Harvest: 3000 Years* (1975), and *Sankofa* (1993)—are justly considered powerful and moving.

Mali's Souleymane Cissé was trained in Moscow. His most significant films include *The Porter* (1978), *The Wind* (1982), and *Brightness* (1987). Perhaps the most famous of his films, *The Porter* is about a laborer who is given a job by a leftist engineer who is himself murdered by his boss for trying to unionize a factory.

Short Cuts

As *O Sun* indicates, one major postcolonial impulse of African filmmakers has been to counter the Tarzan/Jungle Jim/Trader Horn/Stanley-and-Livingston vision of Africa and Africans as a colorful background for the melodramas of white Euro-Americans with their own anthropology.

Overtly Marxist Med Hondo, of Mauretania, named his *O Sun* (*Soleil O,* 1967) after a song intoned by transported African slaves, as if asserting that the film is an attempt at finding an indigenous African voice. Other of his films include *The Negroes, Your Neighbors* (1973) and *Sarrounia* (1986), both of which are about colonialism/neocolonialism.

The major festival for the region—the Pan-African Film and Television Festival—is hosted in Upper Volta by the Pan-African Federation of Filmmakers.

India

Unlike Africa, India has had an indigenous movie industry from very early on; the first Indian feature film—*Rajah Harishandra*—was released in 1913. During the silent era the region was producing 100 movies per year.

Director's Cut

At 900 feature films, shorts, and documentaries per year, India, not the United States, produces the most films on earth. It accounts for one fourth of the global output. About a quarter of this output comes out of Bombay industry, known popularly as "Bollywood." This is attributable in part to the fact that the population—at 900 million—is more than three times the American population. Further, television was not accessible to the Indian public until relatively recently.

As with American cinema, Indian cinema's bread and butter has been the entertainment film produced within a studio system and dependent in some measure on a star system and conventional genres. (There has been a significant independent movement in the post–World War II era, also producing mainly entertainment.)

The musicals are especially interesting because they are at the same time so like and so unlike our own. As in America, the first all-talking film in India was a musical—*Beauty of the World* (*Alam Ara,* 1931). Its popularity assured the continuation of the formula. The degree of adoration that singers (often providing their voice to lip-synching actors) is reminiscent of American audience's affection for Mario Lanza, Jeanette MacDonald, Frank Sinatra, and Judy Garland. But the moments at which actors burst into song seems unmotivated by the plot. It is difficult for Western audiences not to squirm at these moments because they seem like almost surreal interruptions of the narrative.

We have included the most famous Indian director—Satyajit Ray—in the chapter on directors (see Chapter 20, "Director's Cut: Calling the Shots"). After Ray, probably the most famous classical-era Indian film star—Raj Kapoor—was also a respected director/producer, whose films, though popular, often contained significant social commentary. These films include *The Vagabond* (1951) and *Boot Polish* (1954).

However, the late 1960s saw the rise of a more truly alternative Third Cinema. "Parallel cinema" was independent and took on social issues. Generally acknowledged to be the first such film,

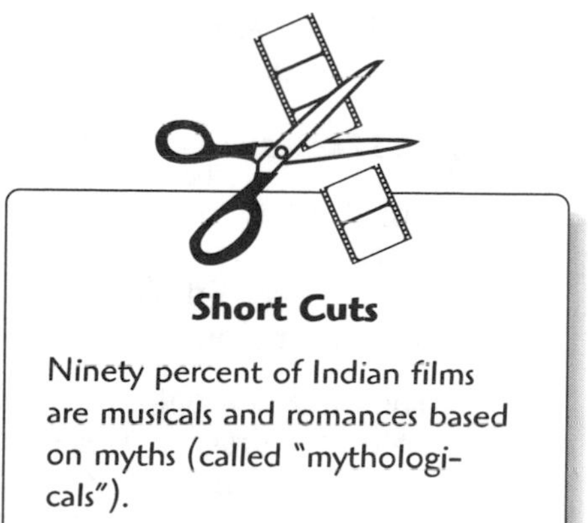

Short Cuts

Ninety percent of Indian films are musicals and romances based on myths (called "mythologicals").

Director's Cut

Himself the son of a film director, Torre Nilsson gained international fame—after making several films and often in collaboration with his wife—with *The House of the Angel* (1957). His most significant subsequent films include *The Fall* (1959), *Martin Fierro* (1968), and *Painted Lips* (1974).

Mrinal Sen's *Mr. Shome* (1969) is about a small-minded, conventional government official whose life is shaken up by an unconventional village girl. Its success opened up government funding for other such films through the 1970s. The most polished and successful of the parallel cinema directors is probably Shyam Benegal, whose most significant films include *The Seedling* (1974), *The Obsession* (1978), and *The Essence* (1987).

Latin America

American films have gone over big time in Latin America since about 1916, making the indigenous films more difficult to produce. Even the sound era did not reduce Latin American dependence on American film; Hollywood just made Spanish-language versions of its biggest productions, or, easier still, simply dubbed their films into Spanish. Among other neocolonialist dynamics mentioned above, we also remake foreign films for greater distribution in the United States, so that *Dona Flor and Her Two Husbands* (Brazil, 1977) gets remade as a miserable James Caan vehicle called *Kiss Me Goodbye* (1982). (Haven't heard of it? Big surprise.) And we import major Latin American stars, including Carmen Miranda (the cult figure with the enormous fruit hats) and even directors like Hector Babenco (*Kiss of the Spider Woman,* 1985). Still, three or four countries have had significant film industries over a period of several decades. The most significant Latin American cinemas—the ones that consistently turn out intriguing movies that get international play—come out of Argentina, Brazil, Mexico, and Cuba. This occurs in part because these countries have—or have had—protectionist policies that encourage local production and limit the presence of foreign entertainment.

Argentina

Argentina has traditionally had a higher film output than most other Latin American cinemas, reaching a peak of 50 films per year under Juan Peron. But except for the appearance of director Leopoldo Torre Nilsson in the 1950s, its international fame rests mostly on films made from the 1960s onward.

The international reputation of Argentine filmmaking rests mainly on its interest in politics. Perhaps this is because, as a result of Juan Peron (you know, Madonna's husband in *Evita*), post–World War II Argentine politics has swung wildly back and forth from populist to fascist to democratic. In the early 1960s the "1960 Generation" produced *The Candidate* (1959) and *The Odd Number* (1961).

Photo still from The Hour of the Furnaces *(Argentina).*

The coup that left a military junta in charge of Argentina through the late 1970s and early 1980s put a dead stop to interesting filmmaking. Then the Falklands War put a dead stop to the military junta. Throughout the mid- and late 1980s, the best Argentine movies tended to explore the meaning and repercussions of that military coup. Most famous among these films are Hector Olivera's *Funny, Dirty Little War* (1983) and Luis Puenzo's *The Official Story* (*La Historia Oficial,* 1985, Oscar winner). The first film is a scathing comedy in which a small-town elite recapitulates the macho military stupidity of the nation as a whole. The second is a domestic drama about a couple whose adopted child may be the daughter of one of the *desaparecidos* (disappeared), the people secretly tortured and killed by government death squads.

Most recently, Argentina has exported some major talent to the United States. Though born in Argentina, director Hector Babenco is most noted for his Brazilian and American work. After making the much-honored *Pixote* (1981) Babenco directed *Kiss of the Spider Woman* (1985), *Ironweed* (1987), and *At Play in the Fields of the Lord* (1991). Sonia Braga, who crashed the American market in the Brazilian *Dona Flor and Her Two Husbands* (1977), gained some recognition in American cinema, appearing in *Kiss of the Spider Woman, The Milagro Beanfield War* (1988), *Moon Over Parador* (1988), and so on.

Director's Cut

The most famous leftist/Peronist political movie to come out of Argentina is a product of the worldwide turmoil of the late 1960s: *The Hour of the Furnaces* (1968). Banned in Argentina, this product of the Liberation Cinema Group gained worldwide recognition. The directors of this film (Fernando Solanas and Octavio Getino) were the ones who coined the term *Third Cinema.* Its combination of newsreel footage of regional underdevelopment and reenactments of acts of exploitation are meant explicitly as propaganda rather than as entertainment.

Brazil

Film begins early in Brazil. The first documentary was released in 1903; the first feature film in 1906. After a moderately successful silent era, the Brazilian film industry was devastated by the cost of mounting sound productions. The major figure of the pre–World War II era was Humbert Mauro, whose films, like *Ganga Bruta* (1933), were somewhat more serious than the average entertainment film.

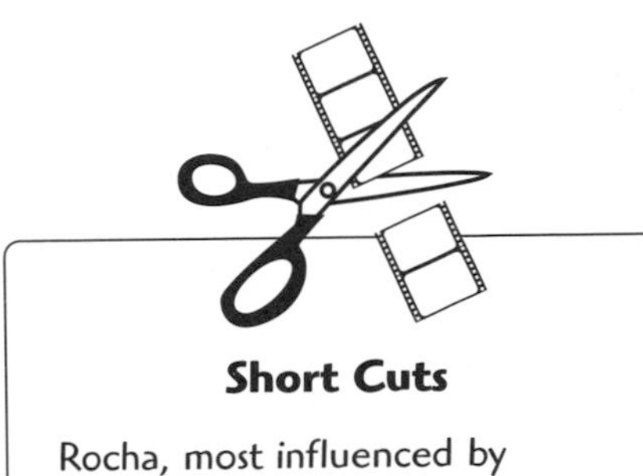

Short Cuts

Rocha, most influenced by Italian neorealism and French New Wave cinema, gained recognition with his early film *Black God, White Devil* (1964), and international fame with *Antonio das Mortes* (1969). Awarded at Cannes and banned in its own country, this film extolling the virtues of revolution in the person of a bounty hunter/bandit was heavily criticized by the Brazilian right wing.

As with much of the Third World, Brazilian cinema came of age with government support in the 1960s. Along with the establishment of the Instituto Nacional do Cinema as a federal funding agency, and a national filmmaking prize (the "INC Prize"), the most significant development in this decade was the establishment of Cinema Novo, a loose organization of young filmmakers intensely interested in politics and aesthetics over simple entertainment. Many of the films produced in this era are highly recognizable to American audiences, perhaps in part because they often display not only a high degree of technical sophistication, but a delightful urbanity and cosmopolitanism as well.

The most significant names in post-1960 Brazilian cinema are Nelson Pereira dos Santos, Carlos Diegues, Joaquim Pedro de Andrade, and, most significantly, Glauber Rocha.

Mexico

Mexico is today the most significant producer of films in Latin America. Though not quite as innovative as the other Latin American cinemas covered here because it tried most to follow the Hollywood model, Mexican cinema had a real golden age of entertainment films (the 1940s), a sort of silver age of counterculture filmmaking (the 1970s), its own films school (the Centro Universitario de Estudios Cinematográficos [CUEC], established in 1963), and Luis Buñuel, a Spanish surrealist filmmaker, some of whose most famous films were made in Mexico between 1946 and 1960. (We discuss Buñuel more in our chapter on directors: see Chapter 20.)

Until the 1970s, Mexican cinema, funded in large measure by the government-supported Banco Cinematográfico, created Hollywood-style studio, star, and genre systems. The most significant films of the period were *María Candelaria* (1943), which won a prize at Cannes, and *Río Escondido* (1947). Both were made by director/cinematographer team of Emilio Fernández (known as El Indio) and Gabriel Figueroa. Figueroa photographed for Buñuel as well, and worked on such American films as *Two Mules for Sister Sarah* and *Kelly's Heroes* (both 1970).

As a result of a leftist government's encouragement of critical filmmaking, the 1970s saw an explosion of independent-style films, the most famous example of which is probably Alexandro Jodorowsky's *El Topo* (1970). (It stands up marvelously today as a rather hallucinogenic experience.)

The Middle East

Because the Middle East was another colonial outpost at the time film was invented, significant indigenous filmmaking began long after it appeared in Europe, and was often initiated by foreigners—Europeans. Though most Middle Eastern nations produce some films, only about three have a significant filmmaking community that has attained a significant international reputation: Egypt, Iran, and Israel. (Lebanon, Syria, and, until the Gulf War, Iraq would come next.)

Short Cuts

The two significant Mexican genres of Mexico's golden era were the ranch comedies (popular throughout Latin America) and the cabaret melodrama. Like American genre films, these films tended to reflect conservative, prosocial, middle-class values.

Egypt

Egypt is cinematically prolific. With a huge regional viewing population in the surrounding Arab states, it is behind only India and the United States in output. Egyptian cinema prevails throughout most of the Arab world even over the films of other Arab countries. Most films are produced at the Cairo "Cinema Town" facilities. Egypt also has its own national film school. In recent years, Egypt has produced as many as 80 features per year. Most often it produces entertainment films. However, when government funding is available, it has produced more films of social relevance.

The most internationally recognizable Egyptian director is probably Youssef Chahine. Like so many other significant Third-World directors, his career begins in the 1950s, in the postwar era of decolonization. He is most famous for films that, though popular, are also social/psychological "message" dramas: *Cairo Station* (1958) and *Saladin* (1963), for

Director's Cut

The Egyptian-born film icon probably most recognizable to American moviegoers is Omar Sharif, of *Dr. Zhivago* and *Lawrence of Arabia* fame. Born with the much less exotic name Michael Shalhoub, Sharif has since become one of the world's most renowned bridge players.

example. Later in his career (after Egypt loses the Six-Day War against Israel), such films as *Alexandria ... Why?* (1978) become more overtly politicized.

Israel

Though strictly speaking there could not have been an Israeli cinema before the creation of the State of Israel in 1948, there was still some significant filmmaking in Palestine from at least the 1910s. For example, Yakov Ben Dov made feature films in Palestine since 1917 on various Jewish themes: *Judea Liberated* (1917), *The Land of Israel Liberated* (1920), and *Return to Zion* (1921). Filmmaking in the 1920s consisted mainly of newsreels and Zionist propaganda. The first fiction feature film was not produced until 1933 (*Oded the Wanderer*).

The era of Israeli statehood saw a fitful burst of activities from the 1950s onward. First, two studios were established: Herzliya and Geva. At first their function was simply to provide the fledgling government with documentaries. But the *Encouragement of Israel Film Law* (1954) enabled the rise of feature filmmaking. Not only were indigenous films like *Hill 24 Doesn't Answer* (1955, directed by British filmmaker Thorold Dickinson), *Pillar of Fire* (1959), and *Rebels Against the Light* (1964) made, but American directors came to Israel to make films like *Exodus* (1960).

The last four decades have produced mixed results in Israeli filmmaking. Many films tackle the evolving face of Israeli cultural life. Several films were made about the conflict between European and Eastern Jews (*Sallah* [1964] and *Fortuna* [1966], for example). Other films simply try to show authentic versions of Sephardic or Ashkenazi culture (*I Love You Rosa,* 1972). Still others take on the task of discussing various national issues and traumas. *The Vulture* (1981) examines Israeli disillusionment following the 1973 war.

Films Worth Remembering

The following films reflect both the political sensibilities and the regional color of the countries they represent. Some have a sharp, satirical bite, while others are difficult to watch because they are less interested in entertaining us and more interested in conveying a painful truth:

- *María Candelaria* (Mexico, 1944). Emilio Fernández's touching and Technicolor vehicle for Dolores del Rio about the star-crossed love of two Mexican peasants.
- *Xala* (Senegal, 1974). Ousmane Sembene's most famous work about neocolonialism, it is both a satirical and oddly erotic story about a corrupt bureaucrat whose comeuppance is his hellish marriage to a young girl.
- *Jai Santoshi Maa* (India, 1975). Vijay Sharma's tremendously popular Hindi "mythological" musical.

- *The Vulture* (*Ayit, Ha-*, Israel, 1981). A morbid tale of a returning soldier who makes a memorial album for a friend he saw die in action. The soldier begins making a business out of such memorials, making him the vulture of the piece.
- *The Official Story* (*La Historia Oficial*, Argentina, 1985). Luis Puenzo's Oscar-winning story of a high school history teacher's gradual discovery that her adopted child is probably the daughter of one of the *desaparecidos* tortured and murdered by the military junta with which her husband collaborates.
- *Sankofa* (Ghana, 1993). Haile Gerima's Complex narrative about a model who mysteriously travels back in time to the slave era of the Ghana coast on which she is doing a "shoot."

The Least You Need to Know

- Third-World cinema has had to negotiate in one way or another the effects of colonialism, postcolonialism, and neocolonialism.
- The more socially conscious and politically active version of Third-World cinema is referred to as Third Cinema.
- Unlike the United States, Third-World cinema is frequently enabled by government support. As a result, this cinema is not driven by a profit motive and can often afford to be more serious than Hollywood entertainment.
- In response to problems ranging from a dearth of skilled labor to Western hegemony, Third-World countries try to respond by limiting the number of foreign films that can be distributed.

Part 4

The Aesthetics, Technologies, and Artistry of Film

This is the anatomy lesson in which we triage films, putting them on the table to prod, poke, and maybe even dissect them, and take tissue samples to put under the microscope. We discuss the finer points of mise-en-scène (including its pronunciation). We determine whether films test positive for framing, camera movement, color, editing, sound, and acting, and we discuss a bit how to encourage good direction while amputating bad directors. So if all these hospital metaphors haven't made you start hemorrhaging yet, get busy learning something about the heart of film aesthetics and technology.

Chapter 19

Frame and *Mise-en-Scène:* Film and Its Space

In This Chapter

- Mise-en-scène: initial definitions
- Framing: what's outside and what's inside the screen
- Space, lighting, character placement, and decor
- Films worth remembering

In this chapter we will talk about film space and the stuff that fills it. Not *Star Trek* space, but the area photographed, and the objects in that area. After a director has decided where to shoot a scene, he or she then has to figure out *how* to shoot. What do you leave in the picture? What do you leave out? Do you want the audience to pay attention to just one element on the screen, or to several at once? How do you divide the screen so that the eye will be attracted to more than one element? These are concerns about mise-en-scène.

This chapter will really separate the film viewer from the casual moviegoer because framing is an issue that no one ever thinks is important enough to consider. But it is: what goes into the picture, how it fits in, and why it does. We will examine why what is on the edge of the picture is often as important as the star's face in the center. Who ever thinks about what's *outside* the frame? Well, here we will.

You will also be able to find some more information about framing in Chapter 21, "The Fine Art of Camera Movement."

The Mise-en-Scène Really Means Everything, Almost

In a certain sense, the *mise-en-scène* includes almost everything pertaining to the picture that isn't actually movement.

Filmophile's Lexicon

Mise-en-scène (pronounced *meez-on-SEN*), literally means "placement in the scene" in French. This phrase refers to

- Every visible element in the frame: lighting, costume, decor, and so on.
- How these elements are related to each other.
- How you see them (how they are photographed).

A Little History

Borrowed from the theater, this phrase—and the idea of deriving meaning from film by examining its space—was popularized in the 1950s by filmmaker/critic Jacques Rivette and the French New Wave directors, who admired the effect in the films of Eric von Stroheim, Roberto Rossellini, F. W. Murnau, and Fritz Lang. The assumption is that the greatest directors—the auteurs—are not simply interested in including visual elements that further the story, but rather elements that create thematic richness. Directors actively create meaning, not just story. Examining the mise-en-scène in film became the equivalent of doing a "close reading" in literary criticism.

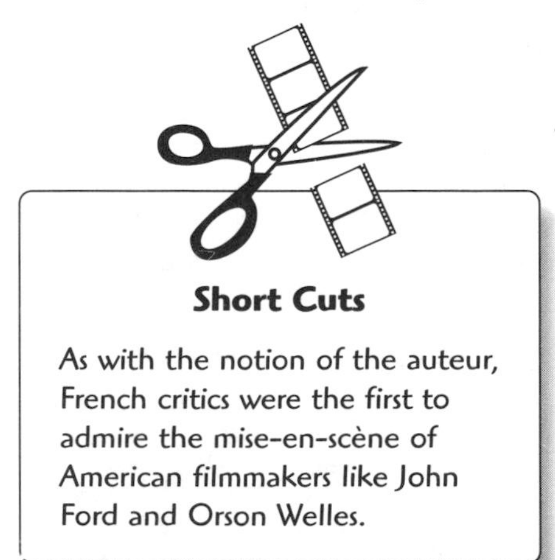

Short Cuts

As with the notion of the auteur, French critics were the first to admire the mise-en-scène of American filmmakers like John Ford and Orson Welles.

The word is a little fuzzy to define, first because it seems to refer a little too broadly to everything in a film, and second because some critics exclude sound, actors, and/or other elements from the mise-en-scène, while other critics really do mean everything. While some critics really think of the mise-en-scène as a still picture—a crosscut of a moment from a film—others take movement into account.

Control Freaks vs. the Look of Reality

Have you ever wondered why documentaries tend to *look* so different from feature films? Let's take nature documentaries as an example. Mr. Naturalist is near a river, trying to catch a shot of salmon as they swim upstream. Once he's established his setup, he's pretty committed to it. He can't travel by canoe over the boulders in the stream, even if he does have a Steadicam. He only has one camera, so he can't do a shot-reverse shot combination from the other bank. (In this instance, shot-reverse shot is an edit in which the camera moves from the looker to the thing looked at.) In short, and in comparison to the feature filmmaker, he's up the creek without a paddle as far as control over his environment is concerned.

Second Take

Actually, television nature series are famous for doctoring and artificially setting up their "back-to-nature" photography. Some finagling has been going on from *Nanook of the North* (1922) to the latest National Geographic special.

This powerlessness means that things go in and out of the picture without the director's control. That deer coming into frame and blocking the view of the river just can't be helped. The two fishermen walking up the path, onto the screen from the left, and then off to the right on the opposite bank, draw away our attention, and don't make the director's job any easier. The salmon emerge to the left of the camera's frame, so the cameraman has to swivel awkwardly to get to them, leaving us with a blurry pan to look at. An airplane flies overhead, the sound ruining the feeling of wilderness solitude. Seems hardly worth the trouble, right?

Hardly. For the very reason that the documentarist seems powerless to control the mise-en-scène, his films seem that much more *real,* less a product of special effects, studio executive decisions, and big budgets. Gullible or not, we believe in the truth of his world more than we do that of the feature filmmaker.

On the other hand, the feature filmmaker can (relatively speaking) control every aspect of the mise-en-scène, especially if she is shooting under studio conditions. She can keep everything extraneous out of the shot. She determines how quickly the camera is going to move so that the picture is not blurry. If any plane noise is heard on the soundtrack, the microphone boom operator is fired and replaced with someone who doesn't snore while working. Nice, huh?

Well, there is the downside that we *don't* believe in the absolute reality of this director's world as much as we do that of the documentarist, no matter how captivated we are while watching her film. *Star Wars* (1977) is a film, but *Wild Kingdom* is real life. Sort of.

In brief, because conventions vary from one kind of film to another, part of our sense of the reality of the film depends on our sense of how much control the filmmakers exert over what gets on screen and what stays off.

Elements of the Mise-en-Scène

Despite the confusion about what exactly constitutes it, we understand the essential elements of the mise-en-scène as follows:

- The degree and quality of artifice.
- The frame.
- The space in the frame.
- Composition.
- Lighting.
- Character placement.
- Decor.

We will discuss all these elements in the following sections except for lighting, which is treated in Chapter 22, "Color My World."

Aleatory vs. Artificial Cinema

The Hollywood studio director knows precisely what she wants in the frame through every second of shooting.

The documentarist relies to some extent on an *aleatory* camera, hoping those fish will come up in the right spot, and that a bear will come along to catch them and feed them to her cubs. If this doesn't happen, maybe something else will.

Filmophile's Lexicon

Aleatory: "Dependent on chance, luck, or an uncertain outcome." (*American Heritage Dictionary,* 3rd ed.) Originally used for the other arts, in film this means setting up the camera in such a way that you allow the possibility of interesting things happening without artificially preparing their occurrence.

Experimental and avant-garde filmmakers often rely on an aleatory camera to catch something interesting, or to prove that nothing interesting is happening. Andy Warhol's *Empire* (1964) is an eight-hour shot of the Empire State Building. The drama is in the changing lighting and, then, in the realization that the film has been about iconography, fame, urbanness, and a host of other issues. Much of Rossellini's *Open City* (*Roma, città aperta,* Italy, 1946) is shot on the streets of Rome just as the Nazis are evacuating, and it all feels much more breathlessly real than the studio John Wayne films, in part because you sense that Rossellini can't really keep Roman street life from bubbling all around him. Nor does he hide the terrible vision of buildings damaged by Allied bombing. *Open City* is a little different from, for example, the relatively artificial Audrey Hepburn–Gregory Peck studio production *Roman Holiday* (1953). Also shot outdoors in Rome (it was in part influenced by the Italian neorealism of directors like Rossellini), it is incredibly romantic, and incredibly contrived.

Framing: Mr. Inside-Outside

In our example of the nature documentarist versus feature filmmaker, we postulated that the documentarist has less control over what is actually in the scene, and what enters and exits the shot. The feature filmmaker makes certain actors enter and exit according to their proper cues.

Filmophile's Lexicon

Frame: This word really has two related meanings. The first is roughly equivalent to "screen," and alludes to the border separating the picture from the theater auditorium. Everything thrown on-screen by the projector is in the frame. Everything in the dark is outside the screen: the theater stage, the walls, the popcorn, your lover's legs, and so on. The second meaning is simply one picture on the film strip. In this chapter we will be interested in the first meaning.

What gets in and out of the *frame* can be either artificially controlled or aleatory. Films like Truffaut's *The 400 Blows* (*Les Quatre cents coups,* France, 1959) contains exterior scenes in which traffic, pedestrians, and even characters, flow in and out of frame in a haphazard manner. The prostitutes in Lizzie Borden's *Working Girls* (1986) enter and exit the brothel's anteroom in a casual manner that suggests something about the spirit of the sexuality of the place. On the other hand, Buster Keaton's films are models of careful framing: Rarely does something enter the screen without a reason; rarely are the main characters (and machines) not carefully centered when the shot begins. In another example of careful framing, this time in Marx Brothers films, Harpo walks into the frame from the left carrying the front end of a board, exiting right. But when the end of the board appears at the left, it is still being carried by Harpo. The joke depends on your seeing Harpo enter and exit each side of the frame at precisely the right moment.

Open frame: Still from The 400 Blows.

Director's Cut

Perhaps the most famous example of framing has to do with what is left *out* of the shot. In Eisenstein's *Battleship Potemkin* (*Bronenosets Potyomkin,* Russia, 1926), the cruel Cossacks move down the Odessa Steps in lockstep fashion. You can see the guns, the jackboots, the military precision. But you can't see their faces; their heads are cut off at the shoulders. They move, but they do not think.

As a rule, when the frame is aleatory, the audience has a sense of space opening out beyond the frame because we actually experience things going on and offscreen, so we have a sense that there *is* an offscreen, a great big world beyond what we can actually see. When the frame is artificially cut off from everything outside itself, we may have sense (even if not consciously) that the space in the frame is limited, even claustrophobic.

Spatially Speaking

That last point brings us to the notion of space within the frame. Space is not equal everywhere at all times. Think about sci-fi film space. Sure, it's incredibly expansive in *Star Wars,* with all that hyperspacing, space battling, and all those planets that, like Luke's home, are big, empty, and roomy, a little like the most benign vision of American suburbia. But what about outer space in *Apollo 13* (1995), where you spend most of your time, not in the eternal ether, but in small, crowded spaces, especially the command module of the rocket itself? *Apollo 13*'s space suggests, not the suburbs, but the irritatingly crowded and inefficient spaces of American urban centers at their worst. Have you looked at a college dorm room recently?

Space means depth as well as width. How far back into the picture is your eye supposed to dig? In most American films it isn't very far because most of the time you're supposed to keep your attention focused on the actions of the lead players, who are typically the most expensive item of decor on the screen. Some directors make more interesting use of space. In *Citizen Kane,* you can see little Charlie Kane playing in the snow at a remote distance through the windows of the old Kane Boarding House, innocent and heartbreakingly unaware that his parents—who are in the foreground—are about to destroy his edenic existence by sending him back East with a heartless lawyer. You are torn between laughing gently at Charlie's awkward play and feeling terrible about his changed circumstances.

Serious depth: Still from Citizen Kane.

Composition

Another term borrowed from art criticism, composition refers to the way in which objects relate to each other in the frame. Classical composition refers to the high Renaissance tendency (itself influenced by the classical world) to keep all elements in balance. A little simplistically put, your eye is drawn to a *dominant* object at the center of the frame, and other objects are arranged around them to give a sense of evenness and fluidity.

Filmophile's Lexicon

Dominant: Also known as the dominant contrast, it is the place on the screen where your eye first rests. The subsidiary contrast is the next place your eye goes to.

In silent films, directors and editors often created the dominant by means of an iris shot or other *masking* device to zero in on a face, or kittens playing, or a hand holding a gun.

Though directors don't now—for the most part, they use masking devices—some directors evoke this effect within the frame. For example, in one shot during Ingmar Bergman's *The Seventh Seal* (*Det Sjunde inseglet,* Sweden, 1957), the figure of Death (who looks a lot like the Death in *Bill and Ted's Bogus Journey,* 1991) walks away from us, his cape raised, and toward his victim, a knight back from the Crusades. The black cape acts like a masking shot, and starts to envelop the figure of the knight, giving us the impression that he is about to expire. (He doesn't, at least not then.)

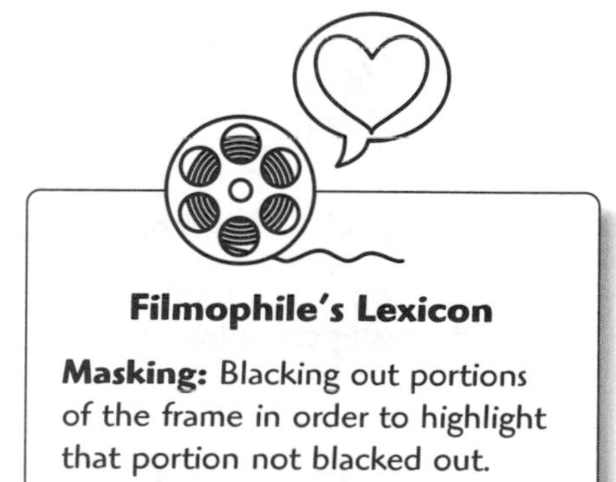

Filmophile's Lexicon

Masking: Blacking out portions of the frame in order to highlight that portion not blacked out.

The dominant is further determined by two other effects: lighting and movement.

We tend to be drawn to the place on-screen where the greatest contrast between light and dark occurs. (Hence the alternative name: "dominant contrast.") In *Lawrence of Arabia* (Great Britain, 1962), our eyes are drawn to the line of the desert horizon, where the contrast between the setting sun and the bright sand is stark. In the last moments of *The Seventh Seal* our eyes go to the silhouettes of the dancing dead people on the mountain ridge.

The last example suggests as well that we attend to the most kinetic element in the frame. No matter what the lighting effects might be, our eyes are drawn to the galloping horse, the formula racing car, the Millennium Falcon, and the long-distance runner.

Sometimes the dominant is determined not by any formal element like movement or contrast. Rather, it can be intrinsically interesting. The boat on which Fredo and his bodyguard are fishing near the end of *The Godfather Part II* (1974) is small, motionless, and far away from the camera. But we are riveted to that tiny object because we know that Fredo is about to die.

Finally, another way of describing composition refers to two different but related formal dynamics:

- The form of and relationship between colors and shapes.
- The relationship between objects.

Are the objects and space in a sequence, imagined as abstract shapes, square and hard, soft and rounded, or otherwise related in an interesting manner?

Director's Cut

To some degree the dominant is not biologically but culturally determined. In determining where the dominant is, it is also important to remember that, in our culture, we tend to scan the screen left to right, and top to bottom, after the way we read. Israeli film directors might make different assumptions about the way the eye scans the screen because Hebrew is read right to left.

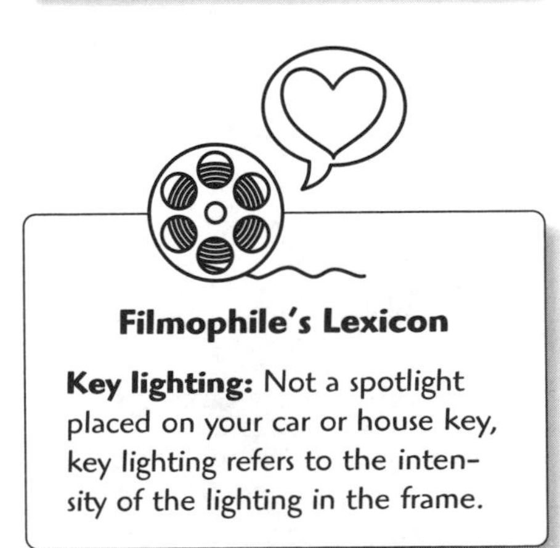

Filmophile's Lexicon

Key lighting: Not a spotlight placed on your car or house key, key lighting refers to the intensity of the lighting in the frame.

Lighting Up the Room

Like the camera, this element of the mise-en-scène deserves a chapter by itself because the technology of lighting has evolved in ways that has had important repercussions for movies. In the same way that the increased sensitivity of film stock allowed for more subtle makeup and acting styles, so the improved quality of lighting also allowed actors to begin moving away from flat makeup, allowed cameramen to begin using deeper focal ranges and more subtle in-camera effects, and allowed directors and decorators to employ more subtle decors.

The most important dimension of lighting is its key. There are two kinds of key lighting:

- High-key lighting is bright, intense light. American comedies tend to be shot in high key.
- Low-key lighting is more diffuse and shadowy. Film noir and *The X-Files* tend to be shot in low key.

Filmophile's Lexicon

Contrast: The amount of difference between lighting in one part of the frame and an adjacent part.

Next in importance is contrast, or the amount of difference in lighting from one part of the mise-en-scène to another. High-contrast lighting tends to be more dramatic; low contrast less so.

Other kinds of lighting also produce distinct effects: back lighting, spot lighting, and so on.

Closed frame: Still from Barry Lyndon.

Character Placement

The way that characters relate to each other and to the audience—referred to as blocking or proxemics—says something about how we are supposed to think of them. There are the obvious cues: Characters close to each other may be romantically inclined, even if they are not touching each other, while physical distance between characters perhaps suggests alienation between them.

There is of course a relationship between the characters and the audience. Is the character facing the audience fully? Is the character partially in shadow, making him or her somehow ambiguous?

Decor

What kinds of choices does the director make about where to shoot? Mainly interior or exterior? If interior, what kind of rooms will the action take place in? What kind of furniture goes into those rooms? What does the decor say about character, mood, and theme?

Director's Cut

Directors sometimes try to shoot without use of artificial lighting at all. One of the most famous films to try to use as much ambient lighting as possible, for example, is *Barry Lyndon* (Great Britain, 1975). Stanley Kubrick tries to make the interior scenes as realistic as possible by filming the eighteenth-century novel's interiors in ambient lighting, sometimes with nothing more than candles.

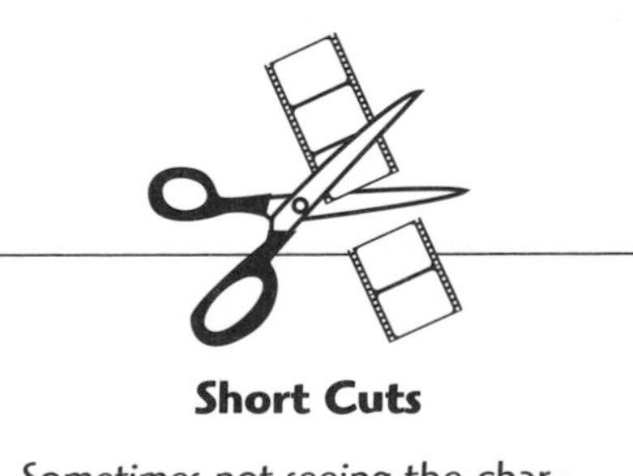

Short Cuts

Sometimes not seeing the character's face at all makes us curious, as in the opening sequences of *Raiders of the Lost Ark* (1981), when Indiana's back is to us for a significant amount of time.

Films Worth Remembering

The following films or moments from films are striking for the care and attention to mise-en-scène in one or more of the ways we have discussed.

- *The World According to Garp* (1982). The opening credit sequence is striking for its play with the frame. Watch the baby.
- *The Blair Witch Project* (1999). The scariness of this movie is *completely* dependent on the fact that the shooting style is documentary. Faces and figures wander in and out of frame, and the woodland mise-en-scène seems completely out of the control of the filmmaker.
- *12 Angry Men* (1957). Almost the entire film takes place in a small sequestered jury room. No special effects, no special decor. The blocking of the actors—their location in space in relation to each other and the camera—says as much about their attitudes toward the murder trial and toward their own lives as anything they say.
- *The Women* (1937). Incredibly interesting decor, costuming, and character proxemics in this all-woman cast that takes place almost exclusively in the 1930s version of the haunts of feminine idle rich: perfume counters, fashion shows, Reno divorce ranches, very tony beauty parlors, and so on.
- *Alien* (1979). How do you make *all* interior spaces look womblike?
- *Berlin: Symphony of a City* (Germany, 1927). Brilliantly odd combination of found urban objects and formal placement in the film.

The Least You Need to Know

- The totality of location, objects, decor, lighting, and character placement in the frame is called mise-en-scène.
- Greater and lesser degrees of reality are produced according to the amount of control (seemingly) exercised over the mise-en-scène.
- The frame and its space are important in determining meaning: how and when people and things enter the frame, and how they are spaced in relation to each other.
- Lighting, composition (including the dominant), character placement, and decor are also important considerations in determining the meaning of the mise-en-scène.

Chapter 20

Director's Cut: Calling the Shots

In This Chapter

- Criteria for judging directors
- The auteur
- Other theories about directors
- Diversified notions of directorship
- Who are the great directors

Okay, everybody knows his or her favorite actors. But how many people know who the directors of their favorite films are? Sure, James Cameron directed *Titanic* (1997). But who directed *The Wizard of Oz* (1939)? *Sleepless in Seattle* (1993)? *Casablanca* (1942)? We all know what constitutes a Julia Roberts film: It will be winsome and a little wry. Her character will be threatened if the film is a thriller. She will weigh one or two pounds less than in her last film. But who can say what a John Ford or Peter Greenaway film feels like? In short, how many directors' names do you know? It's a little like naming all eight of your great-grandparents. Almost everyone can name one or two; no one can name all eight. (Or is it four? Or sixteen?)

In this chapter we explore the meaning of great direction through the examples of some of the best directors the world knows. We have tried to fulfill three criteria in making the whole list: The names are representative of a wide variety of world directors; we have tried to represent a range of styles and genre interests; and we have tried to stay away from filmmakers who, like D. W. Griffith, have been extensively treated elsewhere in this book.

Rating the Directors

Here are some of the dimensions along which we will be discussing the directors in this chapter:

- Those who work in the system: auteurs
- Those who work outside the system: independents
- Those who specialize in meaning
- Those who specialize in technology

How to Recognize a Great Director

Great is pretty vague and subjective. That's why *greatest* lists generally say much more about the people who make them up than about the list items themselves. Still, and for what it's worth, here are some criteria for judging greatness in filmmaking. The one criterion we are leaving out is box-office receipts. You can get those on *The People's Choice Awards* or *Entertainment Tonight.* By this criterion, *Porky's* (1981) was a better film in its first week than *Citizen Kane* (1941). The following criteria are not exhaustive; you may think of more on your own. And we don't want this list to seem like a series of merit badges on the way to Eagle Scout. But a really terrific director should have accomplished one or more of the following:

- Made a contribution to the technology, aesthetic, politics, or industry of filmmaking.
- Had a social impact.
- Had an impact on her/his contemporaries.
- Had a continuing influence on later filmmakers.
- Achieved lasting recognition.

Several of these criteria overlap; it's hard to imagine how one could have a social impact without achieving some kind of recognition. Still, the following paragraphs are meant to more carefully define and distinguish between these criteria.

Technical, Aesthetic, and Political Innovation

Perhaps most important, any artist worthy of recognition should have *done* something meriting recognition. That innovation may be technical: George Méliès coinvented the genre of fantasy film by inventing trick photography. Or it may be aesthetic: D. W. Griffith did not invent the close-up, but he gave it emotional impact. Sergei Eisenstein is a great filmmaker because he consciously wedded an ideology (Marxism) with a particular film technique (editing) to create a new kind of filmic continuity: montage.

Social Impact

For many critics, movies always reflect the society in which they were made. *Always.* (Even *Pretty Woman,* 1990; a Cinderella story that works as a 1990s feminist backlash film.) Even the various Muppet movies (infantilization of culture), or a Bugs Bunny cartoon (homoerotic/homophobic when Bugs kisses Elmer). Appropriate questions are about how conscious a film is in being about its society, and how big an impact it makes—or seeks to make—on that society. Such Andy Warhol films as *Trash* (1970) and *Heat* (1972) show a side of American society—seedy, gritty, run-down, mercenary, valueless—that Americans in the 1960s did not like to think of as part of their culture. Kenneth Anger's *Scorpio Rising* (1964) discusses homosexuality in symbolic but often very graphic terms well before the Stonewall era, making the contemporary Hollywood product (films like *Philadelphia,* 1993) seem very timid in comparison.

Second Take

Sometimes a strong influence may not be completely terrific. The resurrection of the blockbuster American film in the 1970s of the *Star Wars* variety is sometimes seen as having helped discourage the production serious smaller films in favor of big-budget entertainment.

Contemporary Impact

Does a filmmaker influence other filmmakers in his own time? George Lucas's *Star Wars* (1977) revived interest in space operas, and *American Graffiti* (1973) promoted a fondness (God help us) for the 1950s. The Italian neorealists (Rossellini, de Sica) got filmmakers around the world to get out of the studio.

Continuing Influence

A director may have influenced other filmmakers at later historical moments. Orson Welles's *Citizen Kane* did mediocre business at the box office when it first appeared in 1941, but a host of "noir" films in the late 1940s and early 1950s show the influence of this film's dark lighting, depth-of-field photography, and somber subject matter. The film is a cultural landmark, continually cited in popular culture. Everybody has heard the word *Rosebud,* even if he doesn't know what it refers to. The film is even cited on *The Simpsons* all the time. (Mr. Burns is more or less Charles Foster Kane.) Pinky's voice, of the duo Pinky and the Brain, is a fair approximation of Welles's. In the 1990s, *Kane* was cited by the American Film Institute as the best American film of all time.

Orson Welles.

Lasting Recognition

This is the "test-of-time" criterion, and it's a bit tricky because it's a little circular: We recognize a filmmaker is great because everyone else has always recognized that he or she is great. An example of this problem is the Shakespeare paradigm. There were actually lots of innovative and brilliant Renaissance playwrights. But who has heard of John Webster, Ben Jonson, Thomas Dekker, or John Lyly? Who has actually seen a play by Christopher Marlowe? Most people only know, or know of, the plays of William Shakespeare. Some critics theorize that this occurs because Shakespeare was a much more conservative writer than many others, more easily canonized because not as explicitly critical of English culture. George Méliès and D. W. Griffith were almost forgotten figures near the end of their lives, until resurrected by critics interested in film history.

Still, some directors are perhaps deservedly forgotten, and we do seem to get around to recognizing some artists of distinction. And this criterion can temper the tendency to automatically designate contemporary directors we really like now—say John Cameron or Jerry Bruckheimer—as "great" when they may simply have been really good at getting Hollywood to fork over multimillion-dollar budgets to make high-profile films.

Theories of Directing

This section covers various theories of directing.

Auteur Theory

Until 20 or so years ago, the United States had rather little intellectual regard for its own popular culture. As a result, the French in the 1940s and 1950s were the first to notice that there were some pretty terrific American movies out there, directed by people who were supposed to be little more than studio hacks, just cranking out popular and inferior products. Not Siskel and Ebert terrific ("Sparky the wonder dog says two paws up"), but thematically serious works of art deserving the same consideration as *Hamlet, War and Peace,* the *Mona Lisa,* and the Sistine Chapel. These themes tend to come up consistently over a large body of work by the same director.

For example, though they are "merely" slapstick comedies, Charlie Chaplin's "little tramp" films tend to be about the disparity between rich and poor, and about the harsh repression exercised by American society on its less fortunate members.

Filmophile's Lexicon

Auteur: French term. With the accent on the second syllable, this word is pronounced *oh-TUR.* This term is generally synonymous with "great director."

In a way, these French critics are responsible for the fact that film is taught at American universities, and is now a discipline in which students can major. (You can thank them later.) Their largest point was that even a very repressive and oppressive (mostly Hollywood) studio assembly-line production system that insisted on movies conforming to genre, budget, audience expectations, profit considerations, and studio style, could not prevent really great directors from expressing a complex "personal vision" that was also often political.

So, though you will often hear *auteur* used to mean any flavor-of-the-month director, the term does not simply mean someone who makes films that make money. It specifically refers to directors working in a regularized production system who yet manage some thematic seriousness. Luis Buñuel is a truly great director. But he remains fairly independent, so he is not truly an auteur.

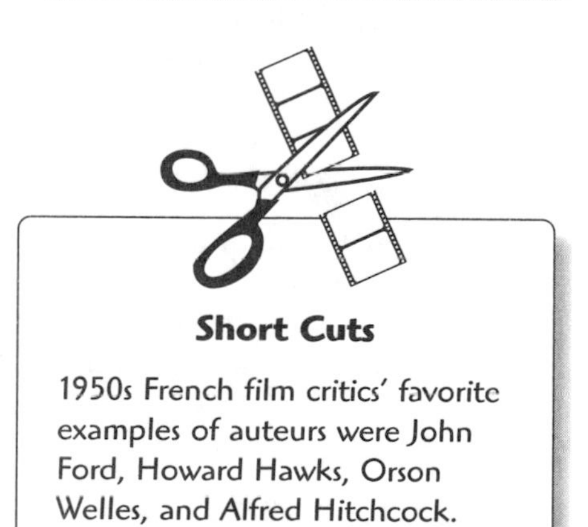

Short Cuts

1950s French film critics' favorite examples of auteurs were John Ford, Howard Hawks, Orson Welles, and Alfred Hitchcock.

Though auteurism is the notion most discussed in relation to directors, other ideas about how directors function include the following:

- Filmmaker as traditional artist.
- Filmmaker as social conduit.

Filmmaker as Traditional Artist

Like an author or artist, the director is completely responsible for the meaning of a movie. She is the individual who is in the end far outside of anyone else's sphere of influence. She is like the artist or writer in a garret, creating in solitude. The camera, scenery, and even actors are mere tools. Alfred Hitchcock is a good example of this vision, because to him actors were simply cattle or furniture, their positions and movements simply subordinate parts of the scene as a whole. Because the emphasis is on the individual, this kind of theory tends toward the psychological. Again, Hitchcock is a terrific example. *Psycho* doesn't seem so unusual after the dozens of slasher films released in the past 25 years, but how many people, before 1960, thought about psycho killers?

Filmmaker as Social Conduit

The director is a conduit for social influences. Any film the director makes can't help but say something about the society in which the director lives, no matter what spin he puts on the movie. Genre films can be metaphors or allegories for larger social issues. John Ford films like *She Wore a Yellow Ribbon* (1949) and *The Quiet Man* (1952) tend to promote traditional and conservative American values like competition, the superiority of the individual, and the inevitability of social Darwinism.

Related to this notion is the idea that the director is a conduit for his or her own unconscious, which reflects the underside of society: its fears, ambivalences, and anxieties. Ideas burble up through our internal censors to make themselves felt on screen. Frank Capra films like *It's a Wonderful Life* (1946) both affirm American family values and display a real anxiety at the fragility of the society in which those values occur. (The absence of one person—George Bailey—spells doom for that society.)

The Directors

Now to the directors themselves. We've tried to be inclusive by creating categories that ensure we won't pick the same Hollywood films plus Fellini and Bergman that everyone else does. We've also stayed away from contemporary American directors, who get their own chapter (Chapter 9, "Staying Afloat in the Hollywood Mainstream").

Western and Central European Directors

This list is too tough because it is the pool from which most of the great canonical directors come. So we are going to discuss two directors with very different palettes.

Fritz Lang is on this list both because his films are technically innovative and because they cover a huge range of styles and subjects. He worked in both Germany and (after Hitler gained power) the United States. Even if you haven't seen them, you have probably heard of his most famous films: *Metropolis* (Germany, 1926), *M* (Germany, 1930), *Fury* (1936), and *Rancho Notorious* (1952). His works are incredibly influential. The impossibly tall skyscrapers and airborne urban transports of the futuristic science-fiction film *Metropolis* have helped determine the look of such films as *Blade Runner* (1982) and *The Fifth Element* (France, 1997). As a psycho-killer film, *M* predates *Psycho* by 30 years. In subject matter it's actually more edgy than most contemporary slasher films because, though it isn't as graphic, its central character is a child molester/killer.

Lina Wertmuller is on this list in part because she is a woman who has managed to make it in a distinctly male profession. Lina Wertmuller is probably one of the best political satirists of the post–World War II era. Probably her best and most famous film, *Swept Away* (Italy, 1974) equates political affiliations with particular class roles, which keep switching back and forth in this dark comedy about a love affair between two incredibly obnoxious castaways on an otherwise incredibly idyllic desert island. *The Seduction of Mimi* (Italy, 1972) similarly satirizes every political stance from the point of view of a poor underdog who is taken advantage of by all of them.

Eastern European Director

We've discussed the Soviet formalists of the 1920s. After them, the Czech surrealist school of filmmakers is probably the most interesting aesthetic to come out of what used to be called the "Eastern bloc." Surrealism as an aesthetic within which to make interesting texts died in the West just before World War II. But no one told the Czechs. The most interesting of the Czech surrealists is Jan Svankmajer.

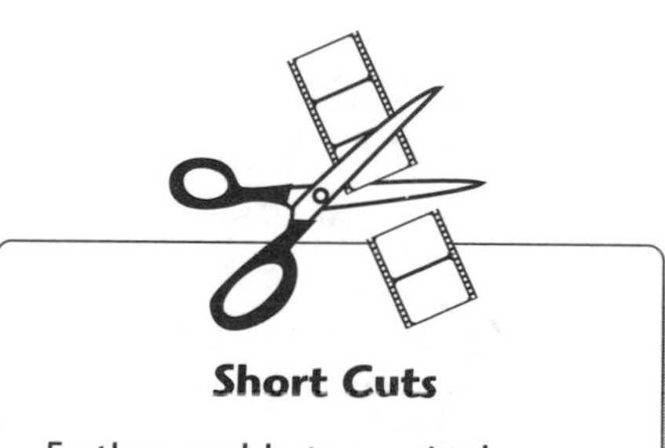

Short Cuts

Further, and lest we mistake surrealism for a cute but empty aesthetic, Svankmajer is making films with a political bite, even when it is still dangerous to do so in the Soviet Union. For example, the short film *The Death of Stalinism in Bohemia* (1990) is ironically titled. The film really asserts the continuing influence of repressive totalitarianism despite official anti-Stalinism.

Svankmajer is the only one on our list who works primarily in animation, specifically stop-motion animation and a version of "Claymation." But, unlike Gumby, Mickey Mouse, and Bugs Bunny, his images and stories are not made for children. They are dark and haunting. His *Alice* (Czech, 1988), a marvelously creepy interpretation of *Alice in Wonderland*, is the anti-Disney film. Though she never does, you get the feeling that the little girl could really get hurt. The White Rabbit has very sharp teeth, which he gnashes from time to time. Wonderland is filled with sharp and nonchildproof objects—scissors, knitting needles, pins, and so on—that hurt. The Wonderland denizens are almost all incredibly if unaccountably hostile. Unlike the Disney version, this film represents the dark side of childhood: the feeling of helplessness, the need to understand the uncanny, the burgeoning sense of unaccountable cruelty in the world, the dim emergence of a sense of sexuality. Though this film is about childhood, you might want to think twice before showing it to your kids.

Svankmajer has been doing animation for 36 years, and the Czech surrealists have been making films for 40 years, so he was producing well before Americans made *The Simpsons, Cool World* (1992), *Fritz the Cat* (1972), and *Nightmare Before Christmas* (1993). It is unclear how much he overtly influenced these texts, but if Tim Burton did not see any Svankmajer films before dreaming up *Nightmare Before Christmas,* we would be extremely surprised.

Third-World Director

Though there are several contenders, including such major international figures as Trinh Min-ha (Vietnam), Ousmane Sembene (Senegal), and Carlos Diegues (Brazil), certainly one of the most famous and enduring non-European filmmakers would have to be Satyajit Ray of India. Trained in childhood as an artist, and working in advertising early in his life, Ray had a disparate range of influences. Perhaps most heavily influenced by Italian neorealism, his films are alternately called "realist," "psychologically realist," "regionally realist," and so on. Ray was extremely interested in representing the current political/ideological/social Indian scene through minute examinations of a few characters per film. His Apu trilogy brought Indian film and culture onto the world stage.

Director's Cut

Chaplin is a renaissance filmmaker who produced, directed, wrote, and starred in most of his own work. He wrote the music for sound films like *Modern Times* (1936) and *City Lights* (1931). He cofounded a major studio: United Artists. He made films from the 1910s to the 1960s, spanning the Keystone Kops to Marlon Brando (whom he directed in *Countess from Hong Kong* [1967]).

Hollywood Director

As with Western Europe, there are just too many auteurs to choose from, so we are going to discuss two. Along with D. W. Griffith and Orson Welles, one of the most innovative and influential directors would have to be Charles Chaplin.

We know with absolute certainty that Charles Chaplin has "stood the test of time" because, in our film classes, students of the twenty-first century still love the films made by a man whose movie career began with the "flickers" in 1914.

Though his films are not technically innovative (like most silent comics who wanted the emphasis to remain on the movement of his body and face, he favored a static camera), Chaplin magnificently exploits the technologies he does use in extremely sophisticated ways.

Chaplin on location shooting The Gold Rush *while in tramp regalia.*

For example, Chaplin's "little tramp" is heard for the first time in *Modern Times,* a film made 10 years after sound had been introduced to movies. Chaplin waited this long because, like many early critics, he thought that sound detracted from the art of making movies. So the first time we hear the little tramp, he is singing a song in a completely nonsensical nonlanguage. To understand the song's meaning you have to watch his simultaneous pantomime performance, in which the story of a hooker and her john are laid out in a way that must have sneaked right by many audience members—and certainly the censors—completely. The moment asserts that sound makes movies too easy, that dialogue in movies is often mindless, and that there is a delight in simply reading images. These are difficult points for today's movie audiences to get, until we remember how simplistic and boring about 90 percent of contemporary Hollywood dialogue is.

Avant-Garde Director

Avant-garde directors are independent directors seeking either to create images, sequences, and films that warp or ignore the rules of Hollywood narrative movies, or to fly in the face of film audience expectations. Most often, avant-gardists seek to do both. Again, this category is a tough call, especially since so much of the avant-garde deplores the kind of canon-making we are doing here. Some amazing filmmakers in this camp include Chris Marker, Maya Deren, Stan Brakhage, and Kenneth Anger. But Luis Buñuel is probably hands-down the most notable avant-gardist. As an early surrealist, he is perhaps the aesthetic grandfather of all the artists just named.

Buñuel was not the first avant-gardist. But he did codirect the earliest avant-garde film that people recognize: *An Andalusian Dog* (France, 1928). The other director was Salvador Dalí, a fact which should immediately and correctly suggest that Buñuel was a surrealist. The surrealists did not make art to please audiences (at least not initially). Like the other "-isms" of the first three decades of the last century—cubism, Expressionism, futurism, and so on—surrealism confronted its middle-class audience, forcing them to see the world in a less safe, repressive, and conformist way. Until everyone got used to Dalí's melting watches, the surrealists often achieved this goal.

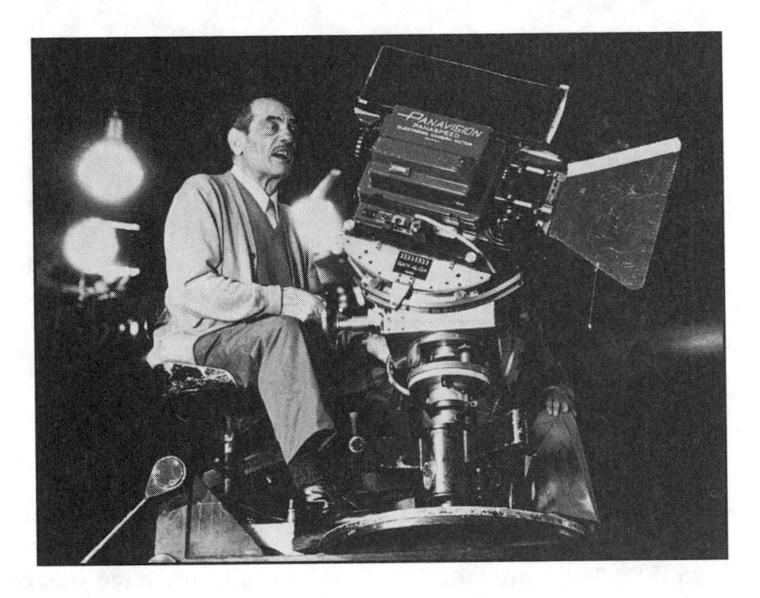

Luis Buñuel.

An Andalusian Dog retains its bite in contemporary film classes. Students still wince and groan at the initial sequence of this silent, black-and-white film: a woman having her eyeball cut out with a straight razor. The movie opens this way to let us know that, as we are watching, our own eyes will be assaulted as well, if not quite so viscerally. In this and other films, Buñuel uses standard photographic techniques to create rather startling images and sequences. He uses slow motion, not for a cliché romantic glow, but for an eerily comic and dreamlike feeling. The narrative cuts are really anti-narrative: nonsensical, or at least not dictated by Hollywood-style "cutting to continuity." A woman walks through the front door of her urban home and finds herself on a beach. Two lovers seem happily engaged when we cut, for no reason at all, to a shot of them buried up to their necks in sand and left for dead. At this point the film ends.

Buñuel's next film, *The Golden Age* (1930), so aggravated the far right wing that some ur-Nazis went into the theater and shot it up while the film was playing. Of course, authorities responded by banning the film.

Later Buñuel films become more traditionally story-oriented, though all retain surrealist touches. *Los Olvidados* (*The Young and the Damned,* Mexico, 1950), shows the poverty-ridden, amoral, senseless lives of urban Mexican street urchins. *The Discreet Charm of the Bourgeoisie* (1972) is about a group of affluent friends who try to eat dinner. They never succeed. The movie demonstrates the idleness, uselessness, and futility of the petit bourgeois.

Some Films on Directing

Here is a list of films that treat the reality and the fantasy of directing:

- *8½* (1963). Federico Fellini creates a film about a director who can't seem to get started on his ninth film.
- *Living in Oblivion* (1995). Everything goes wrong for the director, played by Steve Buscemi.
- *The Stunt Man* (1980). This film stars Peter O'Toole as a positively Mestiphophelean director.
- *Day for Night* (1973). Noted French film director François Truffaut directs this noted French film about a noted French film director (played by François Truffaut).
- *Alex in Wonderland* (1970). *8½*, American style.

Director's Cut

After Buñuel, the most interesting director is probably American Maya Deren. Her most famous film is *Meshes of the Afternoon* (1943), which is perhaps the most dreamlike film made, not because it has any outstanding special dream effects—no alien landscapes or sea serpents—but because its visual multiplication of the central character, played by Deren herself, gives a real sense of the various roles we play in our own dreams.

The Least You Need to Know

- Great directors can be found in and out of the Hollywood system.
- The dominant theory of directorship remains auteurism.
- Determinants of great direction include technological/aesthetic innovation, social impact, impact on contemporary filmmakers, and lasting influence.
- The idea that the work of directors can be studied for thematic unity, though not invented by the French, is most carefully theorized by French critics.
- Gauging the greatness of non-American filmmakers will depend in part on the social climate of the filmmaker's country of origin.

Chapter 21

The Fine Art of Camera Movement

In This Chapter

- Camera movement evolves
- Five basic kinds of camera motion
- The moving camera and the things it photographs
- Some ways of interpreting camera movement
- Some films whose movement is worth watching

The word *cinema* comes from "kinematoscope" and is derived from the Greek word *kinēmatos,* meaning the science of pure motion. Think of some of the most exciting and kinetic filmic moments in your movie-going experience and in movie history: the chariot race in *Ben-Hur* (1959); the police chase in *The Blues Brothers* (1980); a young adolescent escaping the reformatory in *The 400 Blows* (France, 1959); and hundreds of space and cyborg battles in films whose very names are about movement and action—*Star Wars* (1977), *Star Trek* (1979), *War of the Worlds* (1979), *Blade Runner* (1982), *The Running Man* (1963), *Logan's Run* (1976), and all their sequels and television spin-offs.

We realize that people and things move in the frame, but most of the time we don't realize that the camera is in motion as well, either following the movement of people and their machines, or creating movement themselves around static objects. In this chapter, we will talk about the history of camera motion, the way the camera moves, and what it means when we see things in motion on the screen. We will also suggest some films that might be useful in beginning to read camera movement.

Tracking the History of Camera Movement

The camera has not always moved the same way in all film eras. Conventions, technologies, and audience expectations change from decade to decade, and sometimes from year to year.

The Primitive Era

In one sense the camera moved very early in the history of cinematography even while seeming very still. It could be made to move to catch the light of the sun. This was the idea behind the Black Maria, the moveable shooting stage Edison used to keep daylight as long as possible.

For the most part, however, the earliest filmmakers made film with a largely stationary camera. Despite the fact that some of the most important photographic moments leading up to the invention of moving pictures—the Eadward Muybridge motion experiments and the Edward Marey camera "gun"—were all about the movement of birds, horses, the human body, the early moving picture cameras were stationary because it was thought by early moviemakers that a moving camera would only confuse spectators (much the same way that the early filmmakers thought that editing would be confusing to audiences.)

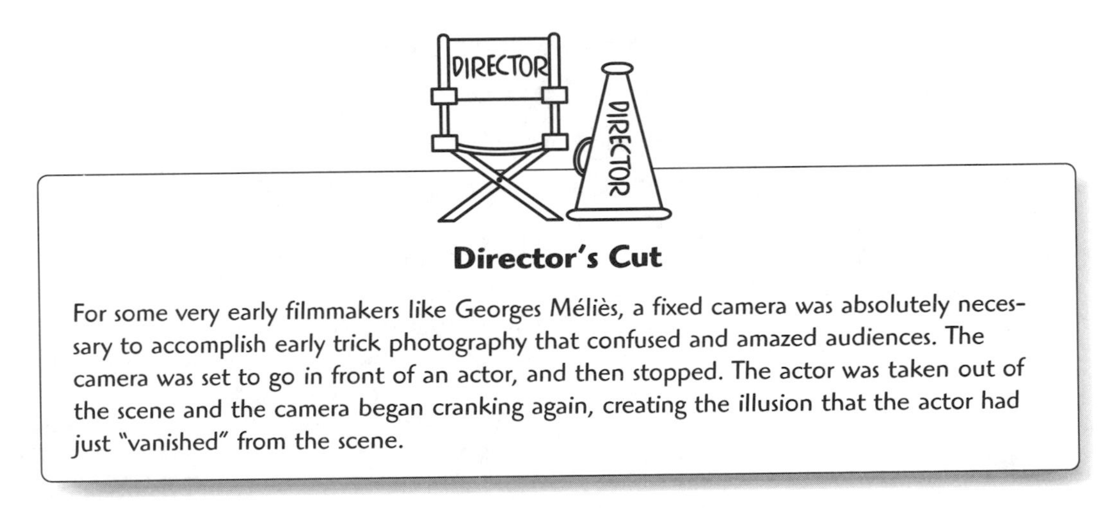

Director's Cut

For some very early filmmakers like Georges Méliès, a fixed camera was absolutely necessary to accomplish early trick photography that confused and amazed audiences. The camera was set to go in front of an actor, and then stopped. The actor was taken out of the scene and the camera began cranking again, creating the illusion that the actor had just "vanished" from the scene.

As well as being concerned about confusing the audience, early cinematographers wanted to keep the camera fixed in a particular place to make the audience feel privileged. The camera was stationed several feet away from the action, in a perpetual medium shot, in order to give all members of the audience the illusion that they had a front-row center seat at the theater. Though containing some interesting examples of editing, the silent Sarah Bernhardt vehicle—*Queen Elizabeth* (*Les Amours de la reine Élisabeth,* France, 1912)—is quite without camera movement, putting the spectator front-row center.

Further, the technology was so tricky that moving the camera could be rather cumbersome. (Because Edison was wedded to the idea of a motorized camera, his equipment was not as mobile as the hand-cranked cameras of the silent era.) It is also generally more expensive to move the camera both because it takes more time to plan moving shots, and because movement often requires its own technology: Steadicam equipment, tracks, helicopters, airplanes, trucks, and so on.

However, cameramen eventually became more adventurous. Cranes and dollies were widely used by the 1920s, and the steadicam became a standard item by the 1960s (enabling, for example, the Vietnam War photography that brought the sounds and movements of the war into the living rooms of middle America for the first time). The camera became progressively more mobile as each decade passed, so that even standard Hollywood light urban comedy could easily contain exterior shots. (A slight hiccup interrupted this mobility when early sound equipment made the camera stationary once more in the late 1920s.)

Director's Cut

A high point in camera movement occurred late in the golden era of Hollywood filmmaking when, in the late 1940s and early 1950s, the camera was so mobile that it actually danced with the musical stars of that era. Look for example at *Singin' in the Rain's* (1952) two musical numbers "You are My Lucky Star" and "Would You." In the first, the camera performs a sort of pas de trois with Debbie Reynolds and Gene Kelly, while in the second it waltzes lyrically in time with the music. With the introduction of the Steadicam and its location-shooting aesthetic, such lyricism would rarely appear again for several decades.

The continued evolution of film technologies offers at present digital and special effects that enable illusions of camera movements not previously possible: being able, for example, to fall to one's death from atop a skyscraper in *The Hudsucker Proxy* (1994) or, with 3-D modeling, to navigate in virtual spaces like the computer CPU in *Tron* (1982).

Shot of camera, crane, and boom microphone in exterior location for Sweet November *(1968).*

The Five Basic Techniques of Camera Movement

Camera movement can itself be broken down into seven different kinds: tilt, pan, track (or dolly), crane, zoom, handheld, and aerial shots. Of course, the camera can do more than one of these at one time. And, in animation and digital effects, you don't even need a camera to accomplish these shots. Here are most of the movements possible to the moving picture camera, in order of least to greatest camera mobility:

- To **zoom,** the only part of the camera that moves is the lens, whose focus changes in order to bring us into or pull us back from the scene it is photographing.
- On a tripod, or in an otherwise stationary mount, the camera **pans,** when it swivels on its horizontal axis, moving from side to side, for example back and forth between tennis players.
- Again from a fixed mount, a camera **tilts** up and down on its vertical axis, for example up the side of the Empire State Building to emphasize the skyscraper's height. (See the photography of the Hudsucker Building in *The Hudsucker Proxy*.)
- No longer fixed on its mount, the camera moves mostly along the horizontal in a **tracking** (or **dolly**) **shot**. In *Day for Night* (France, 1973) we cut from a shot in which one of the characters is tracked, to another shot of the track, the camera, and the actor trying to walk on the irregular tracks as if walking on a smooth pavement. A dolly can be a complex, motorized bit of equipment, or the back of a flatbed truck.

- The **crane shot** is so-called because the cinematographer/director and her camera are perched on a crane to allow the camera vertical (and some horizontal) movement.
- The **bird's-eye** (or **aerial**) **shot** takes us up even further from the action than the crane shot, in a helicopter or atop a mountain or skyscraper.
- The **handheld** (or **steadicam**) **shot** was largely enabled by the invention of the Steadicam, which allowed the camera to be shouldered by a cameraman with a minimal amount of visual jogging. Because the cameraman can keep the camera steady, the camera can go anywhere he can. An entire film aesthetic—*cinéma verité*—is based in part on the possibilities of this technology.

Filmophile's Lexicon

Cinéma verité: Loosely translated as "cinema of truth." In the United States, "direct cinema." All these phrases refer to the tendency in the late 1950s and early 1960s to try to film the world without the artificial intervention of a director's style, but rather simply recording and reproducing the visible world.

The Camera Moves in Relation to Something

Another way to think about movement than the purely technological means is the kinetic relationships between the camera and the elements it photographs.

Movement in relation to the camera traditionally takes five forms:

- The camera moves in relation to people.
- The camera moves in relation to the objects.
- People move in relation to the camera.
- People move in relation to each other and other objects in the frame.
- Framing elements move in relation to themselves or each other.

The most important elements for this chapter, and the ones we will treat at greatest length, are the first two, because they are most purely about the camera, and because the other dynamics are treated more fully in the chapter on mise-en-scène (see Chapter 19, "Frame and *Mise-en-Scène:* Film and Its Space").

But to generalize about all, the significance of each kind of movement is dependent both on the shot itself, and on its context. For example, the aerial shot is probably most often associated with "epic" actions or vistas: the view of earth from a space shuttle, for example.

Second Take

Though associated with the epic, the aerial shot can suggest that epic quality ironically, undercutting the grandeur suggested by the shot. *One Day in the Life of Ivan Denisovitch* (Great Britain, 1971) begins with a nighttime aerial shot of what looks like stars in the sky. As the camera approaches the scene, however, we see that the stars are actually the floodlights of a gulag, or prison camp. The "reaching-for-the-stars" utopian sense of Soviet Russia is undercut by a cruel social reality. *The Birth of a Nation* (1915) pans from a medium shot of onlookers on a bluff viewing a battle with fear and sadness to an aerial shot of the battle itself, and back again. The battle looks epic, but our sense of its glory is utterly deflated by the knowledge that the family at home will suffer no matter who wins.

The Camera Moves in Relation to People

As the last example suggests, camera movement in relation to people can be thematically meaningful beyond simply following them around to let us in on the significant actions of significant characters. In *His Girl Friday* (1940), the camera tracks ace reporter Hildy Johnson (Rosalind Russell) and her editor and ex-husband Walter Burns (Cary Grant) as they move through a fast-paced city paper newsroom buzzing with activity. We understand that the relationship between these two characters will be equally fast and furious. In Eric von Stroheim's *Foolish Wives* (1922), the camera tracks in on a character's face as she goes from grief at her abandonment to the very obvious emotions of rage and vengefulness.

For an utterly opposed meaning, the camera dollies in a full circle around Julie Andrews onstage in drag in *Victor Victoria* (Great Britain, 1982), first showing her in isolation, but gradually revealing her onstage to an appreciative on-screen audience. Or again: The camera swoops from an aerial shot of a mountain top to the twirling figure of Julie Andrews (the woman just begs dramatic representation) at the beginning of *The Sound of Music* (1965) in order to give us a sense of the expansiveness of her soul and emotions.

Julie Andrews in The Sound of Music.

Cameras move not only *with* characters, but from their point of view. In most horror films of the past 25 years, some of the camera movement is photographed from the point of view of the monster/slasher; we are in the eyes—and so minds—of Michael Myers in the *Halloween* movies, Freddy Kreuger in the *Nightmare on Elm Street* series, and Jason (or his mom) in the *Friday the Thirteenth* series, as they track their prey around their various neighborhoods, bedroom communities, and summer camps. The filmmakers want to give us the odd feeling of identifying with the slashers while at the same time feeling horror at their actions.

Director's Cut

In a more high-minded but famous sequence in *The Graduate* (1967), Benjamin Braddock (Dustin Hoffman, in the role that made him a star) wanders slowly and aimlessly around the bottom of a sterile, blue swimming pool in new diving equipment he doesn't want. We see his sense of the sterility of suburbia from his eyes, behind the scuba mask. He becomes for us the perfect icon of 1960s late adolescent alienation from a barren suburban culture.

The Camera Can Move in Relation to Things

Citizen Kane's camera seems always to be tracking in through windows and over fences to voyeuristically let us in on the private and secret life of its principal character. (This shot is satirized in contemporary moments like *Saturday Night Live*'s "Wayne's World," where the camera sneaks up on and gets literally in the face of the show's guests. Mel Brooks loves using this device; in *High Anxiety* [1977], for example, the camera crashes right through the window.) One of Spike Lee's signature shots is a camera seeming to vertiginously circle over something in order to make his audience feel a discombobulating sense of vertigo.

One early master of the pan and tilt, Jean Renoir, can make his camera's trip across a room tell you everything you need to know about a character before you even meet him, as when the camera pans the bedroom/office of Rauffenstein in *Grand Illusion* (1937). Before we see him, we see the cross on a wall, a picture of the Kaiser, a copy of *The Memoirs of Casanova,* a framed picture of a pretty woman, traditional military accouterment like saber, and equestrian equipment like spurs, a military aid cleaning a pair of white gloves, and so on. We understand that Rauffenstein is part of World War I's German military elite, fancies himself a ladies' man, is intensely patriotic, and excessively neat. In short, a perfect representative of his class and time. (In a similar manner, opening credits to television's *Murder She Wrote* tells us everything we need to know about Angela Lansbury's character.)

Zooming and Steadicam shots feel more contemporary and realistic because they are more recent technologies than panning and tracking. Steadicam shots can feel especially realistic. Again, because they are associated with location shooting, nature documentaries, and crime-scene, prime-time journalism, they feel more aleatory. The camera work in prime time's *NYPD Blue* is jumpy to really give you a feeling of anxiety-ridden cops on the mean streets of New York. The littered alleys and weathered apartment-building facades emit grit all over the place, but that jumpy camera gives a strong sense of something real happening.

Director's Cut

Sometimes the easier movement choice is not the right one. The cinematographer for *The Godfather* (1972), Gordon Willis, discusses camera options: "Period movies are a tableau form of filmmaking. They are like paintings. If you're going to move, don't move with a zoom lens. It instantly lifts you right out of the movie because it's such a contemporary, mechanical item. It's not right for the turn of the century. Tracking can work. You lay it in at the right level and you're not really aware of it." (In Vincent LoBrutto, ed., *Principal Photography* [Westport, Conn.: Praeger, 1999], p. 22.)

This Steadicam sense of realism can give a sense of freedom, as when it follows a character running through an open field, because it allows the cinematographer to leave the sound stage. Or this realism can be depressing because we associate it with the crimes and disasters portrayed on evening the six-o'clock news.

People Move in Relation to the Camera

Sometimes the camera is fixed while the characters in the frame change their relation to it. In *Annie Hall* (1977), Alvy Singer (Woody Allen) and his friend Max (Tony Roberts) walk toward the camera on a New York street from some distance. We can barely distinguish them at first, but they get clearer as they approach. In the meantime, we have been able to hear their conversation at precisely the same level. The photography establishes them and their interests as both idiosyncratic and typically urban: They blend into this street scene at the same time they are individuals. (The same type of shot is used on a Paris street in *The 400 Blows*.)

Characters Move in Relation to Each Other

Though we have discussed proxemic patterns—the distance between characters and the camera and each other in Chapter 19—it is worth noting that the *movement* between characters and things is also significant. And not just to tell us something about the plot of the film: two characters approaching each other and kissing passionately. When we watch the scenery go by from the point of view of the weekend warriors in *Deliverance* (1972) we are struck with the beauty of the disappearing Southern landscape. But when we are seeing the canoes move from the point of view of the forest itself, their position seems fragile, the forest sinister. The boats move so slowly they barely seem buoyed by the water, and we are not terribly surprised at the accidents toward which they are slowly drifting downstream. In one sequence of the otherwise black-and-white *Schindler's List* (1993), a very young child is colorized so that her movements in the drab ghetto surroundings become even more significant than they might otherwise seem.

The Framing of a Picture Can Move

The most straightforward examples of the changing frame are the iris in and iris out. The black frame ("mask") around the picture gets larger or smaller, making us concentrate on the single element within the frame the director wants us to notice: the melodramatic sight of a mother's hands wringing over the fate of her son. But various editing transitions are movements as well: the "wipe," in which one picture lays over another from one side of the screen to another, as if being imprinted on the screen by a windshield wiper. The "push," in which one picture pushes another picture off screen in one direction. Or, when there are multiple images within the frame, one can enlarge while the other reduces.

A few films play with the idea of multiple frames on one screen. These include films as otherwise different as the Rock Hudson–Doris Day apple-pie vehicle *Pillow Talk* (1959), and Peter Greenaway's intensely erotic *The Pillow Book* (1996), for example. Rock Hudson and Doris Day speak in different apartments but to each other on split screen, while the gorgeous manuscripts of *The Pillow Book* "speak" to and about the action of the principle characters. Elements of different frames move in relation to each other as well as in relation to elements in their own frames.

No Motion Is Good Motion

Sometimes the camera is perfectly immobile to make a point. Jim Jarmusch (whose minimalism we will visit in our chapter on editing, Chapter 23, "Making the Cut: Film Editing") sometimes keeps his camera and actors perfectly immobile as a way of emphasizing thoughtfulness, indecision, drunken indecision, mindlessness, or whatever other state of mind—most often comic—seems to suggest contemporary deracination and inertia.

Films Whose Movement Is Worth Watching

The following films are chosen with an eye toward variety of camera techniques and the content of their applications:

- *The Wind* (1928): A great example of silent camera movement.
- *All Quiet on the Western Front* (1930): A good example of how early sound film begins to get over the static quality of sound.

- *Breathless* (*À Bout de Souffle,* France, 1959): A French New Wave experiment with a very mobile camera.
- *Singin' in the Rain* (1952): Especially in the musical numbers "Would You" and "You Were Meant for Me," the camera dances.
- *Mystery Train* (1989): Minimal camera movement can be very effective in its own right.
- *Lumière and Company* (1995): See how 39 world-famous contemporary directors (like Spike Lee and David Lynch) use the camera that the turn-of-the-century Lumière brothers used to make their films.

The Least You Need to Know

- The history of moving pictures is in part the history of a greater variety of motions possible to the camera.
- Most of the possible moving shots can be summarized as zoom, tilt, pan, track, crane, and Steadicam.
- These techniques become thematically significant when you think about what they are used to photograph, and why.
- The camera always moves in relation to someone or something.
- Sometimes the most effective movement is none at all.

Chapter 22

Color My World

In This Chapter

- A brief history of black-and-white and color film
- Classical uses for black and white
- The uses of color
- Black and white and color mix it up
- Some political dimensions of color
- Contemporary uses of color
- Some films that will tickle you pink

Color. In our culture it has been an aesthetic concern almost forever, from a Tintoretto to the tint on your bedroom wall. In our society color has been an issue of some political concern. But it is not one of the dimensions we notice in watching film. In fact, in Hollywood, when it is most expertly used, we don't notice it at all, except for a general sense that the mood of the film was somehow romantic, melancholy, or exciting.

In the following pages we shall try to make that sense of color a little more conscious. We'll talk about the history of color film technology, and then get right into a discussion of how and why what colors get chosen for which films. Next we'll discuss the political as well as the aesthetic dimension of the color spectrum. Finally, we will suggest some films whose use of color you might find interesting. So here is the story of color, concisely presented in black and white.

Blitz-Klieg: A Brief History of Black-and-White Film

Even if we don't know the history of color in film, we can feel that it has one. Black and white are the tones of old films; color is the color of today. This section will give a bit of depth to that intuition.

Filmophile's Lexicon

Orthochromatic film stock was used in the production of silent film from its earliest days to about the mid-1920s. Its main limitation was that it was not sensitive to yellows and reds, which then did not show up as any appreciable shade of gray at all on this black-and-white film.

Panchromatic film stock, or **panchro,** is the name given now-standard black-and-white film stock. It is so called because it is sensitive to the whole range of color in the spectrum.

Black-and-White Film Stock

Early *orthochromatic film stock* profited from the history of nineteenth-century photographic photography, which had invented film able to photograph at fairly rapid shutter speed, so that even the quick movements of racing cars, moving trains, and galloping horses could be photographed without blur. Orthochromatic film stock, the earliest widely used film, was initially much faster than the presumably superior *panchromatic film stock* (superior because it could register more colors). In fact, there was an overlap in the 1920s when both were used. Panchromatic ultimately won out, however, because, without filter adaptation, the older orthochromatic stock had a difficult time registering such things as clouds in the sky. Also, panchromatic stock registered images quickly, so it could be used for indoor, more moody lighting effects, instead of simply outdoors, where the natural lighting was brightest.

Second Take

Until recently, orthochromatic stock was thought to be inferior because it rendered its images flatter, with less a sense of depth, than panchromatic stock. However, some more recent critics of silent film believe that this flatness is due more to the way such films have been transferred and preserved than to the film stock itself. So, ironically, the problem with the older stock is not its own technology, but ours.

Early Lighting for Early Film

Because early film stock did not pick up detail very well and, though we have talked about lighting in more detail in Chapter 19, "Frame and *Mise-en-Scène:* Film and Its Space," it is worth remembering that early arc lamps and floodlights, like the *Klieg light,* had to improve rapidly to make up the deficit in film stock sensitivity.

Filmophile's Lexicon

The **Klieg light** spotlight was produced by the Kliegl brothers around 1914 for use on the live stage. It was imported into film by the early Lasky film company, and was the most famous arc lamp in use during the silent era.

Second Take

The need to consider lighting even for daylight exterior scenes is still a basic consideration for contemporary filmmakers. Action sequences like those in *Steel Dawn* (1987) necessitate artificial lighting even during the day.

Contemporary lighting for exterior location shooting of Steel Dawn.

A Condensed History of Color

Probably the most important fact to remember is that, though early on, most movies were shot on black-and-white film stock, it was always possible to manipulate that celluloid to create color; color film has been around almost as long as moving pictures. Photographers in the nineteenth century had been retouching their black-and-white portraits and landscapes to make them look more realistic. (Though the effect could actually be rather surreal.) So within a very short time after the invention of cinema, filmmakers started retouching their own film stock.

The various schemes for injecting pigment into the picture before the introduction of Technicolor include

- Hand-coloring each frame.
- Stenciling.
- Tinting.
- Toning.

Coloring in the Lines: Hand-Coloring

Hand-coloring was the earliest kind of film shading. Unbelievably, it was done precisely as the name implies. Painters colored each part of each frame of each copy of the reel by hand. This labor-intensive technology was only possible because the earliest films were very short, only several hundred feet in celluloid length. Very high quality early films, like the fantasy productions of Georges Méliès, might have this extra attention lavished on them.

Coloring in the Lines: Stenciling

Used in such landmark films as *The Birth of a Nation* (1915) and *Intolerance* (1916), stenciling was markedly easier than hand-coloring, though still very labor-intensive. Primarily used by the French Pathé company and marketed as PathéColor, it involved etching glass plates with the outline of the main photographic shapes, and then using these plates as master stencils, that covered portions of the film so that colored dye could be applied to appropriate sectors of each frame.

Totally Tinted

Perhaps the most common coloring technique was tinting. This relatively inexpensive way of producing color in the film stock involved dying the entire frame of a shot or sequence to match the shot's mood or activity: a yellowish-sepia for a lantern-lit cabin, a lurid red for the flames of battle or hell, dark blue for night, and so on. This technique was used from very early on—in films like *The Great Train Robbery* (1903)—until relatively late, in productions like *Portrait of Jennie* (1948).

Killer Color: The Technicolor Solution

By 1929 there were more than 20 companies holding color patents. Most of these methods, however, were very expensive because they tended to be extremely labor-intensive, requiring many workers in what amounted to an assembly line factory, painting each frame of each film—or portion of film—that was colored. And the results were not as natural as audiences and the industry desired.

Technicolor had been invented and reinvented since 1916, when Herbert Kalmus co-founded the Technicolor Corporation. It was an unusual company in the Hollywood scene because, though a major player in the film industry, it was not (except very early in its career) a studio but an engineering firm. Except for some very early experiments it did not make films but hired out its technology and technicians.

Director's Cut

Becky Sharp (1935) was the first full-length feature Technicolor film.

The Technicolor Corporation went through a two-strip *additive* process (mixing two colors on the screen for an approximation of the spectrum), and finally, in the 1930s, a three-strip *subtractive* process that required a very expensive and temperamental camera through which three strips of film ran simultaneously, each emphasizing a different color of the spectrum.

Filmophile's Lexicon

The **additive** color process mixes colors on the screen's surface itself, rather than dying the dying the film strip.

The **subtractive** color process involves dying the film itself, subtracting some color from each of two or three strips of film that, when projected simultaneously, mix to give a wider and more naturalistic experience of color. This was the final form classic Technicolor took.

Technicolor is the technology behind the classic color films like *Gone With the Wind* (1939), *The Wizard of Oz* (1939), and *An American in Paris* (1951). But though representing the spectrum, Technicolor was not often used to represent "natural" colors. It was a world of heightened colors: the fantasy world of Oz, the romance world of *Gone With the Wind,* the cartoon world of Disney.

Director's Cut

There's a very odd political/aesthetic pairing between subject and technique in the early history of film color because early Technicolor experiments often involved "peoples of color" in films like *La Cucaracha* (1934). Almost all the landmark Technicolor features (or features With Technicolor sequences) are connected to race and/or ethnicity: *Ben-Hur* (1959), *Gone with the Wind, The Godfather Part II* (1974, the last film to use Technicolor for several years), *The Three Caballeros* (animation, 1945), *Song of the South* (1946), *Showboat* (1951), and *Black Narcissus* (1947). Possibly racist, all of these films certainly "Orientalized" the people they photographed.

Post-Technicolor Technologies

Short Cuts

We are making it sound as if color film stock was strictly an American affair. But other countries were originating color technology as well. Germany had Agfacolor, while Britain and Belgium had Gasparcolor, for example.

Though the results of Technicolor were spectacular, and added considerably to the production value of a film, it was a cumbersome and expensive technology. Further, the Technicolor Corporation insisted that a Technicolor expert be present in the filmmaking process, determining color schemes and so heavily affecting the look of a film. The co-inventor's wife, Natalie Kalmus, was often used as this expert, and was sometimes seen as an unwanted kibitzer.

So, after Technicolor's supremacy in the 1930s and the 1940s, other companies came forward with easier technologies. By the 1950s, Eastman Color's "monopack" color film contained all color on one strip of celluloid, a much less cumbersome technology than Technicolor's three-strip process. In part because of Eastman Color technology, and in part because of some government trust-busting of Eastman and Technicolor in the 1940s, a host of other color companies emerged, beginning in the 1950s: DeLuxe, TruColor, and Warner Color, for example. In fact, Technicolor went unused for several years in the 1960s, until resurrected in a spectacular manner by Francis Ford Coppola for *The Godfather* (1972).

The Aesthetics of Black and White and Color

So now you know about how we got to the color you see in today's films. But how do filmmakers choose what kinds of colors to use? And how are we supposed to respond to those colors as intelligent filmgoers? In this section we will talk a little about the aesthetics of color from both sides of the spectrum.

Black and White and Technicolor in Hollywood's Golden Era

In the 1930s and 1940s cost was not the only factor determining which film stock a film project would employ. Hollywood Technicolor tended to be used to make everything pretty, so that the most serious dramas often tended to be black and white: *Citizen Kane* (1941), *The Little Foxes* (1941), the entire genre of film noir, and so on.

Black and White

It's extremely important to remember that black and white can be just as subtle as color because you can do so many things to it. First, black and white is never just that: It is also all the gradations of gray in between. And silver. And beiges. And so on. When you walk into a paint store and ask for black the clerk (after laughing at your naïveté) will hand you 50 color chips: jet black, deep-space black, Frederick's of Hollywood black, midnight blue, and so on. White has, if anything, even more variations, and gray is practically infinite.

Black and white is the color of glamour cinematography. The most glamorous icons of the screen, those actors who only require last names—Garbo, Bogart, Bacall, Gable, Dietrich—are most famously photographed in black and white.

And, as its name suggests, at least one whole film genre is defined in large part by the fact that it was shot in black and white: *film noir.*

Director's Cut

Silver nitrate stock, on which much silent film was shot, produced a shimmering, otherworldly quality, seeming to set the screen on fire. Unfortunately, because it was rather unstable, it could also set the projector, the booth, and the theater on fire, so that its projection is now illegal in all but a handful of theaters in the country specially equipped to contain a blaze.

Shimmering black and white: still with Marlene Dietrich from The Devil Is a Woman.

Filmophile's Lexicon

Film noir was named by the French who, finding themselves culturally and nationally humbled (for a moment) after World War II, discovered a love of all things American, including American movies. The French loved the existential angst of the antihero (Humphrey Bogart, Robert Mitchum, Kirk Douglas, Glenn Ford), and the dark, gloomy atmosphere created by moody lighting. Typically, Americans only started appreciating **noir** films as anything other than low-budget, low-brow entertainment for 14-year-old boys *after* the French did.

Black and White Today

Directors still sometimes opt for black and white to make a political and/or aesthetic point. *Street Scene* (1989)—a film by an African American director—restages Charlie Chaplin's *The Kid* (1921) in the contemporary inner city, suggesting both that inner-city denizens have at least the humanity we grant to the little tramp, and that nostalgizing poverty is cruelly absurd.

Some films are shot in black and white as a kind of homage to earlier cinema genres. Steve Martin's *Dead Men Don't Wear Plaid* (1982) pays tribute to film noir, while *Movie Movie* (1978) and *Young Frankenstein* (1974) fondly recall the 1930s backstage musical and the 1940s horror film.

Contemporary filmmakers often decide that black and white is an appropriate medium to evoke a sense of the past, as in Mel Brooks's comic homage to an earlier horror era, Young Frankenstein.

The Golden Era: Color Classic

Especially for the Technicolor technicians, the principal job was to figure out how to make color film acceptable to an audience and an industry that was at first hesitant about the technology. Some actors, for example, did not think they photographed as glamorously in Technicolor as in black and white. Still, after the box office successes of films like 1939's *Gone With the Wind* and *The Wizard of Oz* (we wonder whether Shirley Temple is still kicking herself for not taking on the role of Dorothy), studio execs came to realize that adding color to a film would measurably increase its box-office appeal. So this expensive technology was used for high-profile prestige pictures, like the Errol Flynn vehicle, *The Adventures of Robin Hood* (1938), which cost $2 million, an amazing price tag for the Great Depression years.

Second Take

Colorization—the digital coloring of classic black-and-white films—has been criticized by contemporary filmmakers and critics because it ruins the lighting and color values of those films. The somberness of *Citizen Kane* would disappear if Ted Turner decided to recolor it (as he wanted to do) in the irritatingly synthetic colors offered by this technology.

Black and Blue: Using All the Crayons in the Box

Some directors have been thinking outside the Crayola box, mixing panchromatic and color stock in the same film. Early on the decision was in part economic: Technicolor was incredibly expensive. But even early on the decision to mix it up could be motivated by plot and theme as much as by economics. The most famous example is of course *The Wizard of Oz* (1939). Monotonous Kansas is also monochromatic. But when, after her tornado-driven house landed in Kansas, Dorothy opened the front door and found herself in a Technicolor Oz, the 1939 audience shared her sense of wonder at their introduction to a prismatically colorful new world.

Self-Reflexivity and Other Kinds of Color

Though we shall visit the notion of self-reflexivity in some detail in Chapter 26, "An Idiot's Guide to Film Theory," it is worth noting that sometimes black-and-white clips appear in color films in order to suggest that these films have a connection to the history of film. Old horror films play on television in the background while the new horror takes place in *Halloween*'s foreground (1978). *Gilda* (1946) plays on the monitor of a video store while a disturbing love relationship takes place in the foreground of *The Fisher King* (1991). Steve Martin and Bernadette Peters desperately dance during the Great Depression against the very ironic backdrop of Fred Astaire and Ginger Rogers dancing on film, in *Pennies from Heaven* (1981).

Short Cuts

Contemporary films remain interested in eccentric uses of color. *Pleasantville* (1998) is a tour de force of black and white and color, also (if much more gently) making some of Downey's points about racism in America. In a traditional town where both the color scheme and the attitudes are black and white, those characters who begin developing flesh tones are treated like "colored people."

Sometimes black and white is used in a color film as a way of establishing a biographical past for a principal character. This technique is used in *Mishima* (1985) and *Zelig* (1983). Sometimes it establishes a point of view, as for a gay man looking down desiringly on a group of schoolboys in *If …* (1969). Other older experiments with black and white and color include *Portrait of Jennie* (1948) and Eisenstein's great experiment with ideologically mixing it up in *Ivan the Terrible* (*Ivan Grozny*, Russia, 1944).

The Politics of Color: The Contemporary Scene

Almost as if taking their cue from those oddly Orientalizing tendencies of early Technicolor experiments, more contemporary directors have played with mixing panchromatic and color film for different kinds of effects, simultaneously aesthetic and political. They have produced terrific films in which technique is used for something more than simply enhancing audience sensory pleasure. Robert Downey Sr.'s wildly savage satire *Putney Swope* (1969), about an advertising firm that accidentally hires its first African American CEO, is shot in black in white, as if to suggest the absolute division between races. But the advertisements Swope makes while head of the company are startlingly shot in color, making them seem almost surreal by contrast. Woody Allen's *Zelig* (1983), a mock-documentary switching back and forth between a black-and-white 1920s and a color present comically documents Jewish assimilation in America.

Finally, director Maurizio Nichetti's comedy *The Icicle Thief* (*Ladri di Saponette,* Italy, 1989) gently satirizes nostalgia for the past. The film contains lengthy portions of a modern black-and-white homage to Italian neorealism (especially to Vittorio De Sica's *The Bicycle Thief* [*Ladri di Biciclette,* 1948]). The poverty-ridden characters of the film, however, break out of the black-and-white movie, much preferring the colorful present in something like the same way Dorothy is at first delighted with the land of Oz.

Draining Away and Saturating with Color

In fact, it's almost impossible to say what "natural" color looks like. That bottle of Cabernet that looked blood-red in the kitchen pantry the night before is gloriously rosy outdoors on the picnic cloth the next day.

After the Hollywood studio love affair with *saturated* color, cinematographers experimented with taking away the richness of color for special effects or ironically exaggerating it even more. As an example of the latter, *Dick Tracy* (1990) is a live-action movie with the bold coloring-book or Sunday-comics primary colors to match the grotesque makeup of its comic-book villains. The colors are rich and supersaturated.

Filmophile's Lexicon

Saturated color refers to those color films in which the color is rich and bright.

Desaturated color refers to the tendency—most pronounced since the 1960s—to remove the richness from the usual Technicolor-style shot.

Desaturated color can be found in Michelangelo Antonioni's *Red Desert* (*Deserto Rosso,* Italy, 1964), whose very title suggests that the film is about thematizing color-draining as the absence of values. The title's desert is also the desert of contemporary society.

In contrast, the "Ascot Opening Day" sequence of *My Fair Lady* (1964), though shot in color, photographs mainly black, white, and gray objects for a paradoxically hard-edged nostalgic effect. Suits, dresses, hats, furniture: All are black and white.

Many thrillers since the 1980s have been filmed in color, but very darkly, in a style called "color noir." Films as disparate as the murder mystery *Body Heat* (1981), the science fiction thriller *Blade Runner* (1982), and the Tim Burton fantasy *Batman* (1989) share this style. Some critics believe that it reflects the same cultural anxiety that the original 1940s film noir style denoted: an anxiety about cultural values in the middle of an affluent but spiritually empty society.

Famous Instances of Black and White and Color

The following list of films presents a fairly wide spectrum of film stock choices; we've tried to pick the best of color, black and white, and combinations of the two:

- *The Wizard of Oz* (1939) is the classic example of Technicolor. You might also want to view *An American in Paris* (1951).
- *Fantasia* (1940). Academy-Award–winning Disney classic in part famous for fantasy and abstract use of color.
- *Citizen Kane* (1941). Contains the classic film noir use of black and white.
- *The Icicle Thief* (1989) is perhaps the funniest mix of color and black and white ever.
- *The Cook the Thief His Wife and Her Lover* (1990) is a marvelously "postmodern" color text, if you can stomach the strong content.
- *Schindler's List* (1993) is one of the best contemporary black-and-white film texts.

The Least You Need to Know

- Black and white is as complex an aesthetic choice as color, and is often interestingly used even at present.
- Color is also an intriguing political choice.
- Color has been part of film since the beginning.
- Technicolor is not "real" color.
- Cinematographers are constantly choosing how to use color, sometimes even opting to use both black and white and color in one movie.
- You can change the quality of the color you are using, saturating or desaturating it for effect.

Chapter 23

Making the Cut: Film Editing

In This Chapter

- A brief history of editing
- About the various functions of editing
- The major thinkers in editing
- Editing today
- Some editing worth cutting to

For many filmmakers the real art of making films is not in the photography but in the splicing together of film clips, in the editing. You can almost chart the progression of film from an early invention to its primitive stage to its "golden era" to the present moment by changes and advances in editing.

In this chapter, you will be exposed to the history of film editing, the major players, some of the most important editing techniques, and different ways of gauging the significance of editing in a film. We will also suggest a few films whose editing makes our final cut.

Fade In: A Brief History of Editing

As with most other film techniques, editing has evolved over time as the technology and audience expectations change. The following is a brief history of this technique.

Before Editing

Like almost every basic idea about movies, the idea of editing has its precursors. Flashbacks had existed in novels; scene changes were already part of live theater; even narrated sequences had been a part of visual culture from medieval altar triptychs to late nineteenth-century comic strips.

Even the middle ages had its version of editing, as this church altarpiece by Hugo van der Goes, The Portinari Altarpiece (ca. 1476), shows. The piece gets you from one scene to the next via simple cuts.

But the very earliest filmmakers were afraid to edit film shots together because they assumed that splicing together different shots of different things from different positions would simply confuse audiences.

Filmophile's Lexicon

Shot: The basic temporal unit of film photography and editing. A shot consists of the celluloid used from the moment a camera begins rolling on a scene to the moment it stops.

Sequence: A number of shots edited together and unified, either through the plot, the character(s), the time and/or space, or the theme.

"Primitive" Editing

However, filmmakers quickly discovered that editing shots into a sequence not only contributed to the audience's sense of tale, but also enabled them to tell more complex stories as a result. You can see primitive instances of editing in films like *Rescued by Rover* (Great Britain, 1904) and *The Great Train Robbery* (1903).

Early on the cuts were made in the camera, so that the cameraman would simply stop cranking at the exact end of a shot, and begin cranking again when it was moved somewhere else, or when something else was put in front of it. This kind of editing could allow for some early special effects. In movies he is making at the turn of the century, Georges Méliès stops the camera after detonating a magic puff of smoke in front of his actor, then begins the camera again after the actor has left the stage, making it seem as if the actor has magically vanished.

Griffith and Beyond

In Chapter 5, "The Earliest History of the Movies," we will read in greater detail about D. W. Griffith's contribution to editing. Here we can just note that, though he did not invent any of the editing techniques he used, he made them emotionally and thematically significant. So much so that he influenced the art of editing worldwide. The Moscow Film School of the 1920s, for example, played his *Intolerance* (1916) over and over again in order to use Griffith's techniques for the films of its students. One of the most notable of the Soviet directors of this era was Sergei Eisenstein, who transformed the principles of classical editing into something more consciously intellectualized he called montage.

Though the idea of putting together shots to forward theme as well as action—one way of seeing montage—had occurred to other filmmakers before Griffith and the early Soviets, Griffith made it a regular practice and the Russian filmmakers theorized its meaning.

The first rigorous use of the term is by Soviet filmmakers like V.I. Pudovkin and Sergei Eisenstein, who saw montage principally as a useful propaganda film tool. Montage was a way to put together a number of shots, more or less quickly, in a manner that pointed out a moral or an idea. In Charlie Chaplin's *Modern Times* (1936), a shot of a faceless, crowded group of men emerging from a subway on their way to work is followed by a shot of a herd of sheep being led to slaughter. There is one black ram in the middle of the herd. We immediately cut back to Charlie emerging in the midst of the crowd: the one black sheep in the fold.

Director's Cut

Did you know that the first real film school in the world—the Moscow Film School—was founded as a propaganda device? Lenin knew early on that the cinema was going to be an important ideological tool for communicating ways of seeing the world. Lenin's way—Marxism—was so controversial in the early part of the century that the United States and Western Europe blockaded Russia after that country's communist revolution.

In Editing, Sometimes Less Is More

Some filmmakers chose to minimize editing, seeing it as the "death of 1,000 cuts" for realism. For example, though some documentarists saw editing as a way to make their anthropological visions appear more interesting, others saw minimal intrusion as the more authentic way to go. Other documentary styles emerged in which editorial intervention was minimal, if never entirely absent.

Filmophile's Lexicon

Montage is a confusing term because, like *love,* it means different things to different people. In Hollywood it most often simply means a number of shots edited quickly together in order to form a brief impression of a character, place, or time. The Madonna musical number "Back in Business" in *Dick Tracy* (1990) underscores a visual montage of several quick shots of gangsters engaged in various illegal rackets: gambling, robbery, and so on. This montage simply conveys the idea that a lot of illegal activities are going on in a compressed time.

But even in feature filmmaking some directors chose to avoid the manipulation of reality that montage and heavy editing seemed to imply. In the silent era, some American comics such as Buster Keaton and Charlie Chaplin often relied on long takes in order to demonstrate that no special effects had been used and the acrobatics of the comedian were not camera tricks but dangerously real events.

Second Take

The laws of gravity and insurance prevent most contemporary he-man stars from performing a tenth of the feats the very small Keaton performed, which is one reason that action sequences tend to be so heavily edited. Harrison Ford and Arnold Schwarzenegger could not—even if they had the skill—have a house fall on them, leap around on top of a moving train, or actually tumble head-over-heels down a hill. The feats that the he-men seem to do in their films are, most of the time, special effects. While also a master of editing effects, Keaton was very careful to make sure the camera continued cranking and focusing on him when he took real chances.

In the 1930s, Jean Renoir's films were filled with shots of long duration. The best examples are probably *Grand Illusion* (*La Grande Illusion,* France, 1937) and *Boudu Saved from Drowning* (*Boudu Sauvé Des Eaux,* France, 1932). The subsequent movements most associated with less emphasis of montage are Italian neorealism and the French *Nouvelle Vague* (New Wave) and cinéma verité.

Editing Today

Even in an era of incredibly advanced special effects, some filmmakers are still enamored of the photographic realism in sustained shots. Perhaps the most conspicuous is Jim Jarmusch, who will hold his camera on his subjects for an agonizingly hilarious amount of time.

But the past 20 or so years has also seen the rise of "digital editing" (also called nonlinear editing), which makes any kind of editing easier. The notion of editing film on video originated when films were transferred to video for television viewing. Then filmmakers used video to edit their work more quickly and less expensively than they could on film. The task of cleanly splicing together video clips was then taken over by computers using advanced graphics programs that could then also perform various special effects functions. Finally, computers convert digital images back into film or video. These digital cuts are a very far cry from Méliè's editing in the camera.

Director's Cut

The unkindest cut of all: editing and censorship. Films can and have traditionally been censored even after release simply by cutting out anything deemed unsavory. In the first three decades of film, even individual American cities routinely cut out parts of films with overt sexual content or controversial subject matter.

The Purposes of Editing

At the most significant level, editing form determines meaning in a film in the same way that the sonnet form helps determine meaning in poetry. In most Hollywood films, editing helps determine at least four dimensions of film narrative: in what order you receive information about the plot, how much information you are supposed to receive about the narrative, how you are supposed to feel about events and characters at any given time, and how you are supposed to experience the pace of the narrative. In addition, as the idea of montage suggests, editing can serve an intellectual function, often making aesthetic, political, or ideological assertions about the activities you are seeing, as well as emotional appeals. This latter activity tends to belong more to the world of avant-garde and experimental films.

Determine the Speed at Which Events Move Along

At the simplest level, editing determines the pace, and so the mood, of a film in three different ways:

1. The editor determines the duration of a shot. Generally, the longer the shot duration, the slower the pace.
2. The editor can decide what goes in or out of a sequence. In *Lawrence of Arabia* (Great Britain, 1962), in one of the most famous cuts in British filmmaking, instead of showing T. E. Lawrence travel from his safe office in Cairo to the desert, we see him extinguish a match in that office, cutting immediately from a close-up of the match light in a cramped office to the gloriously epic establishing shot of the desert and the desert sun.
3. The kind of edit between shots determines speed. The slow dissolve can leave us lingering on a disappearing image for several seconds (for example, the last shot of *Psycho* [1960], when Norman Bates's face slowly becomes superimposed on the skull of his mother). Or the cuts between shots can be very quick: Gunfights at the O.K. Corral tend to cut very quickly between the various participants so that you won't lose a bit of the bloodbath.

Filmophile's Lexicon

Insert shot: A shot of an object that generally informs or reminds the audience of something it needs to know: the missing gun lying in a gutter on the outskirts of the city.

Detail shot: A close-up of a graphic element of the previous shot.

Shot-reverse shot: A series of two shots, the second of whose angle is approximately 180° opposed from the first. Generally used to show two characters speaking, or to show the relationship between a character and the object of his gaze.

Give or Withhold Information

Sometimes editing gives you access to bits of information that will be important to subsequent events. We see a long shot of a man in the street. He looks harmless enough. But then we cut to an insert or detail shot of a hand holding a gun behind its owner's back. We realize that the man is waiting for someone he is going to shoot. Sometimes information is withheld in order to surprise us. Only at the very end of *The Usual Suspects* (1995) do we get detail shots of the various elements of the police chief's office out of which Verbal Kint has fabricated the elements of the tale of the phantom Keyser Soze: a coffee mug with the name of a made-up company, a bulletin board with the names of places and characters, and so on.

Determine Your Feeling for Events and Characters

How do you know when you are supposed to like a character? How characters are supposed to feel about each other? Music and casting of course help. Tom Hanks and Julia Roberts don't usually play the heavies. But the way characters are edited also says something about who they are. For example, when a man and a woman talk to each other they can be shot either in a two-shot or in a *shot-reverse shot*. The two-shot can imply (though certainly not always) a level of intimacy between them that cross-cutting may not, because the characters in a shot-reverse shot sequence can seem emotionally further apart when they are not physically close.

The Illusion of Unity

Editors cut together material from disparate sources to give the illusion of unity and continuity. This editing constitutes the practical Hollywood use of the "creative geography" the Soviet filmmakers theorized about. (See Chapter 16, "Seeing Through the Red Filter: Eastern Europe.")

Short Cuts

One editor describes her best editing moment in terms of "creative geography": "In *Aces High* I made battle scenes out of nothing. I made them out of footage from *The Blue Max, Darling Lili,* stock material, our own full-size flying planes, 20-foot miniatures that were electronically controlled, little baby miniatures that were flown, and real live people on the ground firing guns in machines that rocked about and had clouds rush past them."

Cutting for Content

Especially for Hollywood, editing is all about conveying as much information about the plot, characters, and mood as an audience can stand. Various cutting techniques were initially created in order to get an audience efficiently from one chunk of information to another in a way that looks like cause and effect. Some of the most-often used methods for creating order through editing are determined by the content of where you begin and where you end. They include (but are not limited to) the following:

- Cutting to continuity.
- Parallel editing or crosscutting.
- Match on action.
- Eyeline match.
- Flashback and flash forward.

Cutting to Continuity

Cutting to continuity involves taking out all the inessential moments in a conventional action. Editing takes out the dead, boring moments in a film. Imagine having to watch all 31 miles of celluloid shot for *Lawrence of Arabia!* When James Bond travels from London to The Bahamas, do you really want to watch the whole trip: snoring for eight hours on the plane, brushing his teeth in the airport bathroom, renting an Aston Martin at Avis, and so on? Cutting to continuity just includes Bond's leaving M's office, boarding a plane, leaving the Jamaica airport, and driving his car down an ocean-side road. All this activity takes just a few seconds. Wouldn't it be great if we could cut all the boring bits out of our own lives?

Parallel Editing

Parallel editing, or crosscutting, is of two kinds: parallels in space and parallels in time. Parallel spatial editing includes those crosscuts between the bandits and the posse: We go back and forth between two temporally simultaneous events happening in different spaces. Parallel temporal editing includes for example flashbacks and flash forwards, when someone begins narrating the story of her childhood, as when Ninny Threadgoode (Jessica Tandy) tells the story of her younger alter ego Idgie Threadgoode (Mary Stuart Masterson) in *Fried Green Tomatoes* (1991).

Match on Action

Match on action occurs when an action that begins in one shot is continued or completed in the next. In an exterior shot Julia Roberts opens the front door to a house. In the next shot the camera, now indoors, photographs her entering the foyer and closing the door.

Eyeline Match

An eyeline match occurs when a character looks in a particular direction and the film cuts to the object at which he is looking. The scientist looks into a microscope. We cut to a super close-up of a virus expanding on a slide at an exponential rate. The logical opposite of this sequence is the reaction shot sequence, in which we see an action, and then cut to the reaction—say, a comic double take on David Spade's face as we cut away from something very clumsy or stupid that Chris Farley has just done.

Flashback

A flashback occurs when the film cuts from the film's present (most often our own present as well) to a moment before that present. The structure of *Citizen Kane* (1941) is a series of flashbacks from a journalist in 1941 interviewing various people who knew Kane in his youth, to sequences in which we see recollections of that youth in the minds of his friends and lovers. Flash forward of course works in the opposite way: We cut from the prehistoric opening of *2001: A Space Odyssey* (1968) to a future of interplanetary travel.

In this flash forward from 2001: A Space Odyssey, *Kubrick seems to be saying that the object and the technology have changed, but that the aggressive fascination with flight has not.*

Cutting for Chaos

With some notable exceptions, Hollywood tends to use editing to create order for its audiences because order is more entertaining. But sometimes filmmakers create a meaningful and interesting chaos, purposely confusing their audiences, sometimes in order to make intellectual connections, sometimes in order to assault the viewer's emotions with an unexpected, sometimes offensive image. We have briefly discussed (Chapter 20, "Director's Cut: Calling the Shots") the opening sequence of *An Andalusian Dog,* which contains a cut from a cloud passing over the moon to a man cutting open a woman's eyeball, and this silent (with music track) 1929 black-and-white French/Spanish production still has the ability to make audiences blanch. The film's apparently arbitrary connection between shots suggests absolutely meaningless connections between various places and between different times.

The Manner of Cutting

Cuts are also defined by the manner in which you get from one shot to another, as well as by the content. Here are some of the most frequently used and discussed edits:

- A **cut** is the simplest kind of edit. The shot just ends, with no editing effect added.
- At the next level, **fade-in** and **fade-out** simply mean, respectively, going from black to an image, and vice versa.
- A **dissolve** is an edit in which, while one picture fades out, another fades in to replace it.
- A **jump cut** occurs when an edit is not smooth, when, for example, five seconds of a character's movement is removed from a film every 10 seconds so that his movements look jerky and unreal. The photography sequence near the beginning of *Blow-Up* (Great Britain, 1966), when Thomas, a photographer, becomes aroused while photographing a model is a marvelously kinky example of this effect.

From Shooting to the Final Product

Excluding the additional steps necessitated by modern nonlinear editing, traditional editing goes through most of the following stages.

Before the Cutting: Storyboarding and Shooting

Surprisingly, editing can begin in the mind of the scriptwriter and/or director before the first shot has been fired. This stage is called storyboarding, and consists of actually drawing the various shots that will be included in the movie. Some directors storyboard a film so carefully as to minimize the input of both the photographer and the editor.

Even while shooting, filmmakers must keep the editor in mind by, for example, making certain that a great enough variety of shots has been taken so that the editor can crosscut, match-on-action, cut to continuity, and so on. Editors are dependent on directors and cinematographers to provide the appropriate amount of coverage of an actor's performance. Too much may give a choppy sense of the actor's performance, as the editor has to choose between a number of "takes." Too little coverage ("undercovering"), or trying to shoot simply the shots the director believes will be needed ("cutting the picture in the camera") results in perhaps choppy editing, or not enough options for assembling a sequence.

The Editing Process

Typically, after the day's shooting, the developed but unedited bits of film—the dailies—are projected so that decisions can be made about which takes are to be used in which order and for what duration. A rough cut is assembled: the film shots in the right order but with little or no attention paid to the kind of edits used, and only a rough sense of the timing of each shot. Either now or later sound is also mixed in with the visuals. (See Chapter 24, "BOOM! The Sonic Side of Film.") After going through a fine cut, when the edits are further refined, the editor (and director) decide on the final cut, which is the form the film will take on release to the public.

Some Films Whose Editing Is Worth Visiting

Here is a list of films worth examining for their editing excellence:

- *Intolerance* (1916). Griffith's monumental film about intolerance through the ages edits together stories from four different eras, so that the stories unfold simultaneously rather than sequentially. No one would try this trick again until the end of Hollywood's golden era.
- *Battleship Potemkin* (*Bronenosets Potyomkin,* 1925). No discussion of editing is complete without referring to Eisenstein's masterpiece of montage. Watch especially the very famous "Odessa Steps Sequence" for a terrific example of "intellectual montage."
- *Rope* (1948). Alfred Hitchcock gives the illusion that the entire film was shot in one long take, with no editing at all. See if you can spot the editing seams.
- *Dead Men Don't Wear Plaid* (1982). Watch Steve Martin insert himself into the narrative of various famous film noirs via simple crosscutting.
- *Groundhog Day* (1993). Very few special effects; instead, the fantasy of this imaginative piece resides in how the central character relives the same day over and over. The editing that gets you from one day to the next is smart and hysterical. Check out the suicide montage.

The Least You Need to Know

- Despite the fact that putting pictures together to tell a story had long been part of visual culture, earliest filmmakers were afraid to edit shots together for fear of confusing audiences.
- After a primitive era of filmmaking, Griffith and others established the rules of continuity editing, which are operative to the present time.
- Alternative theories of editing like montage and cinéma verité offered alternatives to the straight narration of story favored by Hollywood.
- Editing structures the experience of a film, determining its spatial and temporal relations.
- Film is edited by content and by technique. Content editing includes such dynamics as cutting to continuity, parallel editing, match-on-action, and flashback. Techniques include fade-in and fade-out, dissolving, and jump-cutting.

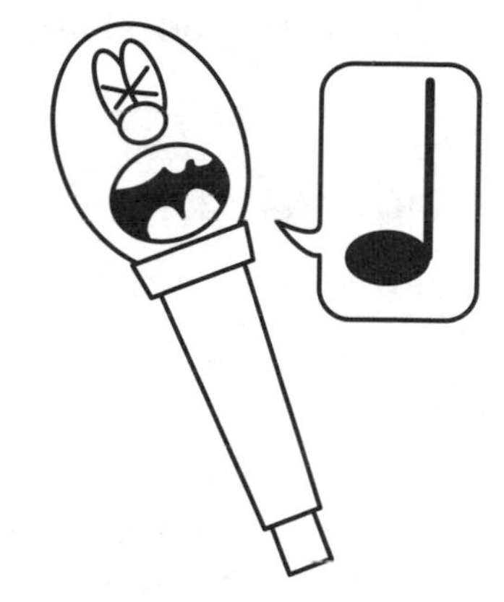

Chapter 24

BOOM! The Sonic Side of Film

In This Chapter

- The history of sound in movies
- Synchronous and nonsynchronous sound
- Sound effects and their functions
- A musical interlude
- Some films worth lending an ear to

Sound is the input we take most for granted when watching a flick. We take the explosions, kisses, gunshots, and thunderstorms as simple recordings when there is a whole set of technicians and technologies put in play to give you a sense of what a Jedi light saber sounds like in action.

In this chapter, you'll learn about both the history that leads up to the effects you hear in present movies, and something about the technology of the effects themselves. You'll learn about the different effects experts use, and even some of the theories that inform those uses. Finally, we'll suggest some films for which you should crank up the volume. So put on your earphones and make sure the bass is ready to rumble.

A Brief History of Sound in Movies

We all know that first there was silent film and then there was sound. But that's not the whole story. Before films talked they still made themselves heard through intertitles and musical accompaniment. And after the introduction of the microphone, there were still questions about how to use the technology. Here is a brief breakdown of the evolution of sound.

You Ain't Heard Nothing Yet: Before Sound

Though Edison did not invent film, he always conceived that this visual medium and his phonograph would mesh to make sound film, and was busy trying to invent sound film almost from the birth of cinema—from about 1885—more than a third of a century before sound film became commercially feasible.

Inventors and entrepreneurs needed to overcome several problems before sound could be accepted. First, silent film audiences seemed perfectly happy with silent movies, perhaps because the movies were never completely silent, almost always accompanied by music of some kind: from a multipieced pit orchestra for big openings, to a single piano, or even a guitar if no one in a small town could play the larger instrument.

Early on, when film prints traveled from small town to small town in the American heartland, they were often narrated by a live raconteur, who would explain the action on-screen to audiences. "Intertitles"—those cards between moments of action—contained explanations of action, or important moments of dialogue, or even bits of poetry to set the mood.

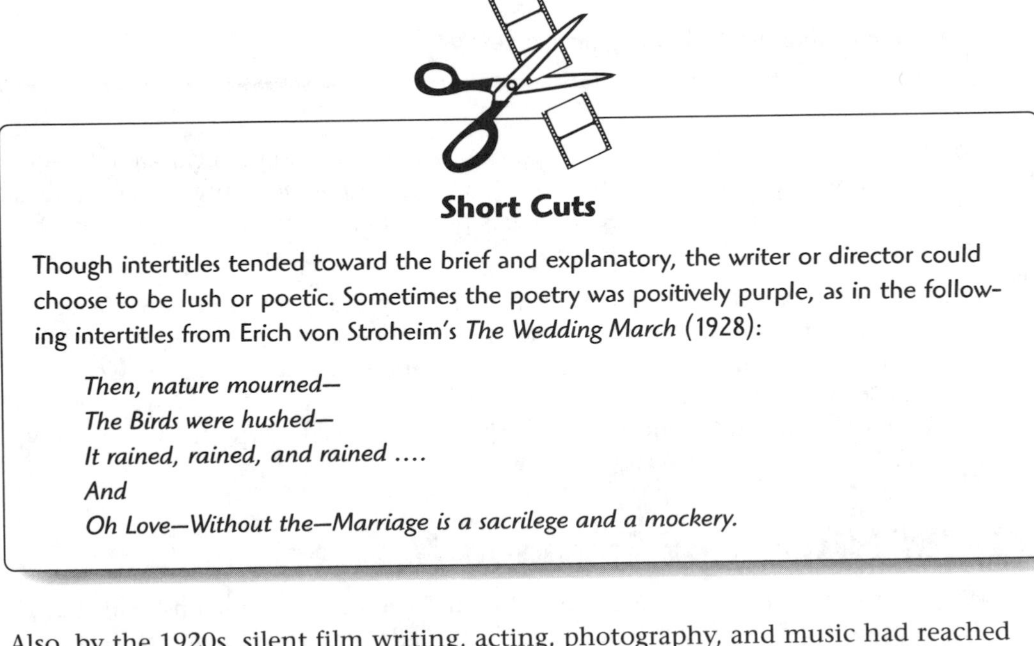

Short Cuts

Though intertitles tended toward the brief and explanatory, the writer or director could choose to be lush or poetic. Sometimes the poetry was positively purple, as in the following intertitles from Erich von Stroheim's *The Wedding March* (1928):

> *Then, nature mourned—*
> *The Birds were hushed—*
> *It rained, rained, and rained ….*
> *And*
> *Oh Love—Without the—Marriage is a sacrilege and a mockery.*

Also, by the 1920s, silent film writing, acting, photography, and music had reached an aesthetic pinnacle: very subtle emotional and plot nuances could be conveyed without the use of any accompanying dialogue. In fact, as the era of sound film drew to a close, filmmakers were able to convey their stories with a bare minimum of intertitles.

Inventing Sound

More important than audience satisfaction with silence, however, was the technological difficulty of matching sound and visuals in such a way that everyone in the audience could hear. In other words, the problems were synchronization and amplification.

Unlike the invention of film, the solutions to these problems were largely American, the result of the work of several American corporations: RCA, Western Electric, AT&T, and Warner Brothers. Two of those corporations formed a third, Vitaphone, which produced the first commercially viable sound system, essentially a very large phonograph platter hooked up to a film projector with large leather belts, like straps or harnesses. Soon this clumsy apparatus was replaced by the now-standard strip of celluloid prepped for sound that runs down the side of the film strip, so that the two modes remain in synch.

Second Take

The Jazz Singer (1927) was *not* the first commercially released sound film. Warner Brothers and Vitaphone had earlier been releasing "shorts" in which people sang and told jokes, and released a feature-length film called *Don Juan,* which contained a musical score, in 1926, the year before Al Jolson sang "Mammy" on film. In fact, Jolson's talking was in large measure an accident: The filmmakers simply couldn't shut the irrepressible entertainer up before his musical numbers.

Al Jolson belts out "Mammy," and Warner Brothers becomes a major film studio.

Second Take

The cliché assertion that silent film stars with funny voices could not take to the new microphones and so sank into oblivion is, for the most part, untrue. In fact, lots of very famous sound actors had perfectly successful silent careers: Joan Crawford, William Powell, Myrna Loy, Ronald Colman, and Gary Cooper, to name just a few. When silent actors did not succeed, it was not so much because of their voices as because they did not adapt well to the new kinds of roles demanded by sound film.

Even after its invention, sound presented a host of problems. The early sound cameras and equipment were big and noisy, and had to be kept in their own soundproof room, called a "blimp." And it took a while for someone to figure out that you could move the microphone around by placing it at the end of a stick—called a "boom"—just above the range of the camera. So very early sound films tended to be very static because actors had to speak to a static mike, and cameras movement no longer had that graceful and supple fluidity it had been developing for 30 years. (Some of the problems with early sound film are hilariously portrayed in the MGM musical *Singin' in the Rain* [1952]).

Other nontechnological problems had to be resolved at the advent of sound: Some actors did not sound the way they looked on the silent screen.

It was difficult for silent scene writers to find the right balance in sound scripts between action and dialogue. Studios justifiably feared losing the international audience that silent film could automatically rely on. And so on. However, after these and other early problems with sound were solved, this technology became another element that filmmakers could play with to make filmgoing even more pleasurable than it had been.

Director's Cut

It is rumored that the person to solve the problem of speaking into a static microphone was a woman—director Dorothy Arzner—who is supposed to have invented the "boom microphone" to get those actors moving, and to get the motion back into motion pictures.

Director's Cut

In the early sound era, the same film would be shot in two or three languages, so that they could still appeal to an international audience before subtitling and dubbing had been widely used. For example, after the shooting of the English version of *Dracula* (1931) and everyone went home, the night crew came in to shoot the Spanish version, with a different director and Spanish actors, which many horror film aficionados believe to be the superior version. Unfortunately, this solution proved cumbersome, and was not used very frequently. As a consequence, movies are no longer as international as they were, at least in the sense that American audiences are now less likely to watch foreign films because dubbing and subtitles just seem to most people like inefficient substitutes for plain speaking.

Look Who's Talking: Sound Changes the Industry

The addition of sound did not simply mean that actors could now talk; it meant big changes in the way that films were produced. Scenarists now had also to be dialogue writers. Literary types from the other arts were imported to Hollywood to help write the new talkies: Dorothy Parker, Robert Benchley, William Faulkner, and Ernest Hemingway, for example.

Actors now had to be paragons of articulateness and fluency as well as pantomime artists. Certain exotic roles became far less fashionable, in part because foreign accents were harder to understand with primitive microphone and amplification technologies, in part because the fantasy of the Asian vamp or the Italian villain seemed more kitschy with the added reality of sound, and in part because some foreign types began to seem rather stereotypical and xenophobic. With the exception of Chico Marx, dumb immigrant Italians started disappearing from the screen, along with Jewish shyster lawyers. Native American stereotypes—monosyllabic grunts and all—persisted much longer, but finally began being scrutinized in the 1950s, and even satirized in such films as *Blazing Saddles* (1974) by the 1970s.

Some verbal kinds of comedy—most conspicuously typified by the Marx Brothers—was simply not possible until sound. A host of comedians came from vaudeville and the stage to help round off the new cast of talking characters: Jack Benny, Bob Hope, George Burns and Gracie Allen, and so on. At least one new comedy genre sprang up at this time: screwball comedy, a combination of romantic comedy and some very silly behavior, that relied on sophisticated banter of the leading couple. The traces of screwball remain in our culture to the present day in films like *Pretty Woman* (1990) or *When Harry Met Sally* (1989), and in many prime-time sitcoms.

And, of course, at least one whole genre would not have been possible without sound: the musical. With a volatile history, going in and out of popularity very often, this genre persists in some form to the present day, from the "backstage musical" of the late 1920s, to the Fred Astaire–Ginger Rogers films of the Great Depression, to the big color MGM productions of the 1950s, to the MTV video, to the rockumentary, to the musical interludes of *The Simpsons.*

Bring on Da Noise: Synchronous and Nonsynchronous Sound

There are two large categories of sound: *synchronous* and *nonsynchronous*. These two categories define all possible film sounds.

Filmophile's Lexicon

Synchronous sound: Synchronous sound includes all noises whose origins can be seen on-screen: in a "two-shot" conversation between two lovers you simultaneously see their lips flapping and hear the words they speak. In a barroom brawl you see and hear the chair crash over the cowboy's head.

Nonsynchronous sound: Nonsynchronous sound is any noise whose origin you can't see: that gunshot in the dark that almost hits the hero; the train whistle offscreen signifying that the two lovers must break their embrace as one leaves; the anvil whose rush of air we hear just before we see it hit the Coyote; and the love song that swells as the lovers kiss. (This last is often lampooned, as in *Last Tango in Paris* [1973], when the romantic background music is suddenly extinguished, and we realize that it has come from a tape player; or in *Bananas* [1971], when Woody Allen opens a closet door to find the orchestral accompaniment hiding within.)

Synchronous sound can be either ambient (sound recorded during the filming of a sequence and retained in the final cut) or a sound effect, the product of a Foley or *ADR* (*Automated Dialog Replacement*) technicians. In other words, that dialogue you hear could have been live, or it could have been dubbed if the filmmakers were not satisfied with the sound on-screen. For example, in one sequence of *Spartacus* (1960), Los Angeles traffic noise could be heard in the background. Filmmakers had the dialogue dubbed over the ambient soundtrack so that audiences would not wonder what the purr of a '57 Chevy was doing in ancient Rome.

Nonsynchronous sound can also be ambient: While we watch children at play, a mother calls them home just offscreen. While the camera captures the exterior of Fort Anxiety, we hear the pony-soldier captain ask for a parlay as we see the white truce flag go up. More frequently, however, nonsynchronous sound is the product of postproduction technicians determining the emotional and intellectual impact of a certain scene through sound. At the simplest level, music is used to determine how the audience's response to a particular moment. The violins swell as the two leads pucker up for the climactic kiss.

Filmophile's Lexicon

This matching of music to mood is called **mickeymousing.** The term probably derives from Walt Disney's early sound cartoons, whose soundtracks were almost completely indexed to the characters' and the audiences' emotional states from sequence to sequence. The term is a little contemptuous because it describes a rather easy sound technique, and because it manipulates the audience too visibly.

Sound Effects and Their Functions

As sound editor Marvin M. Kerner says in *The Art of the Sound Effects Editor,* "the function of sound effects is three-fold":

- To simulate reality.
- To add or create something off scene that is not really there.
- To help the director create a mood.

Simulating Reality

The simulation of reality can be something as small but distinctive as the sound of a door opening and closing on the Starship *Enterprise,* to the extremely complex creation of a language for the *Star Wars* series' Ewoks.

Sometimes the reality that sound creates is so compelling that even though it contradicts what we know to be scientifically true, we believe it anyway. Though we know, for example, that because space is a vacuum sound cannot travel in it, we are still utterly compelled by the sounds of intergalactic battle or just spaceships traveling at warp speed in nearly every space opera produced since the creation of Buck Rogers in the 1930s. And gunshots never sound as satisfyingly long or loud in real life as they do in Dolby with the bass cranked way up. Finally, in many of those great Hollywood musicals, the best songs are not actually performed by Audrey Hepburn or Debbie Reynolds, but by unsung singers like Marnie Nixon, whose faces and figures don't look as appealing on-screen as those of the major stars.

Adding or Creating Something That Is Not Really There

You are the director of *Victor/Victoria* (Great Britain, 1982), and you want more emphatic applause for Julie Andrews's big number than the actual audience of extras was able to provide. This is the kind of sound effect provided by the *Foley artist,* who creates sound tracks that amplify or add sounds not easily available as ambient noise. Sometimes sounds can be added to a film from a "library" of sound effects. But for more particular and idiosyncratic sounds, the Foley artist creates effects on a *Foley stage,* which is simply a production room in which everything is a sound prop, including the floor, which can provide different kinds of footfalls. The film rolls on-screen, and the Foley artist matches the kind of sound the filmmaker wants to the image projected: submarines submerging, horses clopping into the distance, echo effects, crowds roaring, and so on.

Filmophile's Lexicon

A **Foley artist** invents the sound effects that are dubbed onto the visuals.

A **Foley stage** is the workshop in which the props used to make sound effects are used.

ADR stands for **Automated Dialogue Replacement,** or a computerized method for looping, which is itself a method for redubbing dialogue.

Creating a Mood

Test your ability to create a mood. Here is the shot: A woman gets into a bath or shower. Match the movie to the background music we hear.

Music:

A. Driving, shrill string music leading up to discordant screeches.

B. Slow, stately full-orchestra music, filled with pomp.

C. Five-piece jazz combo playing something with a slow, bluesy beat.

Movies:

1. *Cleopatra.*
2. *Psycho.*
3. *The Happy Hooker.*

Obviously, the erotic Cinemax soundtrack is meant to titillate, while the *Cleopatra* (1963) music is supposed to impress you with the royal pomp of the queen's most elementary activities, and *Psycho* (1960) sound effects are supposed to set you on edge from the very beginning of the famous shower scene. Of course the photography in these films is very different, but the mood of each is still dependent on the musical accompaniment. The same music, depending on context, can actually mean different things. The terrifyingly screechy violins in *Psycho* have a more comic effect when used as background music when a character stabs Mel Brooks with a newspaper while he is showering in *High Anxiety* (1977).

Besides setting the mood, sound can introduce important elements of the plot, or even intentionally confuse or mislead audiences. Because nothing about the voice of the transvestite Dil in *The Crying Game* (1992) is masculine, and because she sings the title song in a feminine manner, we assume the character is female until a full frontal shot informs us otherwise.

Because he describes himself as a nebbishy, nerdy character while narrating the story of *The Usual Suspects* (1995), we don't know that the small-time hood Verbal is actually the arch-criminal Keyser Soze. *Sunset Boulevard* (1950) is narrated by the film's hero. However, we don't learn until the end of the film that he is telling the story from beyond the grave. Narration can reflect a film's meaning in other ways. For example, documentaries have traditionally been narrated by male voices, suggesting that history is essentially a masculine domain.

Director's Cut

One of the most significant theorists on the use of sound is a director we've encountered already in our chapter on editing: Sergei Eisenstein. Already a proponent of clashing visual effects, he saw sound effects as wasted if they simply helped explain the plot of a film. Rather, as with editing, he hoped that sound could be used "contrapuntally" with the visuals to make a thematic, political, or ideological assertion about a particular sequence. In brief, his theory of editing was precisely the opposite of mickeymousing.

Another theory—cinéma verité—suggests that ambient sound is most appealing because it is the most authentic and realistic. If, like the French New Wave filmmakers, you are trying to create a "slice-of-life" film school, you allow the imperfections that the Foley artist deletes to remain on the soundtrack because they contribute to the believability of the movie. The New Wave filmmakers were famous, for example, for allowing street noises to remain in the final cut, despite the fact that they could make it difficult to hear the dialogue. See François Truffaut's *The 400 Blows* (*Les Quatre cents coups*, France, 1959) or Jean-Luc Godard's *Masculine Feminine* (*Masculin/Feminin*, France, 1966) for terrific examples of such use of ambient sound.

A Musical Interlude

Music is one of those filmic elements that we tend to take for granted. But it is a major determinant of how we feel about characters and narrative from moment to moment.

Music: In or Out of the Plot

Most of the time, music can be part of a film in one of two ways. It can be used as the background music for a film—the theme song that plays at the opening and, perhaps, recurs over the course of the film, as with "Tara's Theme" in *Gone With the Wind* (1939). Or it can be an integral part of the film's plot, as in the tinny piano music played by Charles Aznavour in *Shoot the Piano Player* (1960). Sometimes the musical score may seem to be one, but is actually the other, as in the previously mentioned examples from *Bananas* and *Last Tango in Paris*. Sometimes, as in George Lucas's brilliantly funny and poignant *American Graffiti* (1973), music (in this case the very nostalgic rock-and-roll of the early 1960s) serves both functions at once.

Music sets the mood for the sequence, as described earlier, but it can also describe the mood of the character. You can tell the moments that Blanche Dubois is going mad in *A Streetcar Named Desire* (1951) because the soundtrack begins very softly playing a waltz associated with her youth very softly, almost as an echo. When Dr. Zhivago looks out over the Russian countryside and we hear "Lara's Theme" (not to be confused with "Tara's Theme") we know he is thinking of his main squeeze even though she is not present.

Musicals

Classic musicals—*Golddiggers of 1933* (1933), *Singin' in the Rain, Fame* (1980), *Yellow Submarine* (Great Britain, 1968)—most of the time have in common the ability to make us think that the world is a musical place, that music springs naturally from the human psyche and soul. Though this kind of message sometimes seems corny in a Fred Astaire movie, it is equally present (if a bit ironically portrayed) in *Amadeus* (1984), *James and the Giant Peach* (1996)—feature-length Disney animation—and much MTV. Sometimes, however, the musical becomes a vehicle for overt irony and satire: *Pink Floyd: The Wall* (Great Britain, 1982) satirizes, among other things, war and the self-centeredness of artists. *All That Jazz* (1979) examines the self-destructive nature of artistic creation. However, most of the time people in musicals tend to burst into song, and this bursting is a reflection of an innately human joie de vivre, spontaneity, community, and cultural values such as friendship, monogamy, and decency. Even famously mediocre singers have made names for themselves growling their way through musicals: Yul Brynner in *The King and I* (1956), Rex Harrison in *My Fair Lady* (1964), and even Clint Eastwood in *Paint Your Wagon* (1969).

To summarize, from now on, when you exit the theater, you should not simply sing the theme song and promptly forget the rest of the sounds in the film. Rather, you should be asking what kind of theme music was used, what other use of music within the narrative, what sound effects were created for which situations, whether certain effects were synchronous or asynchronous, and why. So get out to the local multiplex and start listening with both ears!

Some Sound Worth Hearing

The following films provide a cacophony of sound options, from the critique of film noise provided by the kind of silent *Modern Times* to the incredible synthesis of music and camera work in *Singin' in the Rain:*

- *The Jazz Singer* (1927). Well, if not the first sound film, at least the most famous, and a real product of its time.
- *Modern Times* (1936). The most famous silent comedian of them all, Charlie Chaplin "sends up" sound films in this silent/sound hybrid.
- *Citizen Kane* (1941). Orson Welles had just come from radio, so he was very aware of the possibilities of sound.
- *Sunset Boulevard* (1950). Director Billy Wilder has star William Holden narrate the story from beyond the grave.
- *Singin' in the Rain* (1952). Oh the woes of transitioning from silent to sound! A great musical.
- *American Graffiti* (1973). George Lucas in 1970s helps invent 1950s retro. Keen music.
- *Silent Movie* (1976). Totally silent Mel Brooks film, except one line, by French mime Marcel Marceau!
- *The Hunt for Red October* (1990). How much tension can you build in submarine chase movie with just silence and those little sonar pings?

The Least You Need to Know

- Matching sound to picture was the dream of filmmakers almost from the invention of film.
- The difficult technologies to perfect were synching and amplification.
- Sound can be synchronous or nonsynchronous.
- Much of what you hear in a film has been enhanced by additional sound effects done by Foley artists and ADR technicians.
- Music has had a long and interesting career in film, from the piano accompaniment for silent films to the rock video.

Chapter 25

Artists or Stars? The Aesthetics of Acting

In This Chapter

- Acting as an ancient and controversial art form
- The origins and nature of the "star system"
- The major schools of film acting
- Film directors and their various approaches to actors
- The 14 greatest American actors and actresses

When actors and actresses, whether on stage, television, or screen, speak their lines, move their bodies, or change their facial expressions, they are participating in a tradition of imitation that goes back to the ancient Greeks and the tragedies of Sophocles and the comedies of Aristophanes. Actors have long been most despised of all artists, principally because their craft requires them to become someone they're not, with all the fakery, disguising, and chicanery such imitation requires. Yet despite its deliberate artifice, acting is one of the most demanding and all-absorbing of the arts, requiring extreme coordination of voice, body, gesture, and movement.

Playing the Human Instrument

In one of his many treatises on the art of oratory, the Roman writer and politician Cicero compares the body of the orator to that of the actor, which is "tuned" just like the strings on an instrument: "For nature has assigned to every emotion a particular look and tone of voice and bearing of its own; and the whole of a person's body and every look on his face and utterance of his voice are like the strings of a harp, and

Short Cuts

At the risk of shameless authorial self-promotion, if you want to read more about the long and often gruesome tradition of figuring the human body as a musical instrument, check out Bruce Holsinger's *Music, Body, and Desire in Medieval Culture: Hildegard of Bingen to Chaucer* (Stanford University Press, 2000).

sound according as they are struck by each successive emotion. For the tones of the voice are keyed up like the strings of an instrument, so as to answer to every touch."

Compare Cicero's vision of the actor's body with this one, which was written in the last century: "To exercise daily is of utmost importance. The body is an instrument which must be finely tuned and played as often as possible. The actor should be able to control it from the tip of his head to his little toe."

The writer of these lines? The classically trained actor Sir Laurence Olivier, by any measure one of the twentieth century's greatest and most versatile performers. Despite the centuries separating these two visions of the craft of acting from one another, perhaps things haven't changed all that much: Acting is an art of the body, a "tuning" of the self that enables the actor to portray the variety of emotions, neuroses, and personalities he or she is called upon to perform.

Film Acting vs. Theater Acting

With the advent of film in the early twentieth century, and in particular with the introduction of sound in the late '20s, there was a need for a new kind of acting style from that which had dominated the stage and the theater for centuries. Thus was born the art of film acting, a demanding and innovative discipline that has now been around for almost a century. Here are four of the main differences between stage and film acting:

- Unlike the theater actor, who gets to develop a character during the course of a two- or three-hour performance, the film actor lacks continuity, forcing him or her to come to all the scenes (often shot in reverse order in which they'll ultimately appear) with a character already fully developed.
- Since film captures even the smallest gesture and magnifies it 20 or 30 times, cinema demands a less flamboyant and stylized bodily performance from the actor than does the theater.
- The stage is more friendly to the unattractive, the overweight, and the flawed, while film—despite the advantages of makeup, lighting, soft focus, etc.—is relentlessly cruel to any sign of imperfection in the actor or actress.
- The performance of emotion is the most difficult aspect of film acting to master: While the theater actor can use exaggerated gestures and exclamations to express emotion, the film actor must rely on subtle facial ticks, quivers, and tiny lifts of the eyebrow to create a believable character.

Toshiro Mifune possessed one of the most expressive faces in world cinema; here he appears as one of Akira Kurosawa's Seven Samurai *(1954).*

Director's Cut

Film historians agree that it was D. W. Griffith who first experimented on a large scale with a mode of acting that would suit the cinema rather than the theater. Recognizing that theatrical acting—with its exaggerated gestures, its over-the-top facial expressions, and its stilted body movements—often looked ridiculous on film, Griffith put his company of actors and actresses through weeks of meticulous drills and exercises to show them how to alter their skills and adapt them to the new medium.

In short, film demands a fundamentally different kind of performance work from its actors than does the stage; as D. W. Griffith himself put it, the stage actor projects an emotion or a character to an audience, whereas a film actor must in some way embody and perform these emotions in as true and believable a way as possible. Though some have made the theater-to-cinema transition quite successfully (Olivier, Glenn Close, and Julie Andrews, for instance), others have not, and there are many examples of silent stars who fell off the movie planet after sound was introduced. They just weren't able to compete with the bell-voiced theater actors who instantly flooded the studios.

The Star System

One of the most important, familiar, and controversial contributions of film to the long cultural history of acting is the *star system.* It is true that opera, theater, and other performing arts created international stars well before the advent of cinema. The Italian singers known as *castrati* dazzled the seventeenth- and eighteenth-century operatic world with their unparalleled vocal virtuosity, becoming heroes to the flocks of adoring fans who showed up at every performance to worship them.

Filmophile's Lexicon

The **star system** is the cinematic practice that fashions a select number of actresses and actors into box-office sensations by constantly giving them leading roles, which in turn inspires a massive fan base that perpetuates the system.

Second Take

One person can only travel so much. Once the faces and bodies of actors and actresses could be transferred to celluloid, packed into a crate, and shipped around the seven seas for projection to worldwide audiences, the nature and identity of the star were forever transformed.

The world's first bona fide movie star was Mary Pickford, who won the heart of D. W. Griffith in the early 1900s and, by the mid-1910s, was known the world over for her sweet disposition and the aura of innocence she projected onto the screen. Like all American film actors in the early years, Pickford wasn't known by name until years after her cinematic debut. By the time she started her own production company, The Mary Pickford Company, she was pulling in more than half a million a year in dozens of pictures that made her an international sensation.

The American star system is one of the most dominant shaping forces in contemporary moviedom. While studio heads still control the purse strings, individual stars can make or break a blockbuster deal with a single phone call. An ideal example of how the star system works can be found in the career of Harrison Ford, who got his big break (there's an understatement!) playing Han Solo in George Lucas's *Star Wars* (1977). Ford's swashbuckling space cowboy propelled him through the two sequels and directly into the *Raiders of the Lost Ark* series, by the end of which he was America's most popular and highly paid male lead whose presence in the credits continues, with a few scattered exceptions (for example, *The Devil's Own,* 1997), to guarantee a film's smashing success.

What makes the star system so fascinating, though, is that no matter what kinds of roles Ford plays—a Philadelphia cop (*Witness,* 1985), an American businessman abroad (*Frantic,* 1988), a CIA bureaucrat (*Clear and Present Danger,* 1994), a fugitive from the law (*The Fugitive,* 1993)—we'll always view his films through the original lens of his performances in *Star Wars* and the Indiana Jones series. This explains why the blockbuster Ford vehicle *Air Force One* (1997) worked so well: Even as the president of the United States, Harrison Ford will machine-gun and karate and commando his way out of any situation and save a planeload of loyal followers in the process.

Another crucial point to remember: The successful entry of any given actor or actress into the pantheon of American superstars often has nothing to do with his or her actual talent. Sometimes ambition, luck, looks, and persona can carry the day, and there are plenty of box-office sensations out there (we won't name names because we don't want to get sued!) who have displayed less skill in their entire careers than Laurence Olivier did in a single scene of *Henry V* (1944). Nevertheless, the star system is a bizarre, often disturbing, but probably permanent part of American and world cinema.

Director's Cut

The first American movie star to be known to the public by name was Florence Lawrence, who began her film career at Griffith's Biograph company, where she was known simply as "The Biograph Girl." In one of film history's greatest publicity stunts, Carl Laemmle, the head of a competing studio, circulated a fake story that was widely published in newspapers reporting the death of the actress known to the public as "The Biograph Girl." Once the "news" was out, Laemmle publicly denounced the lie that alleged enemies of his studio had been spreading around. As he proudly announced, Florence Lawrence, Biograph's former box office sensation, was alive and well, and working for him!

The Schools of Film Acting

There's a famous Hollywood story about an exchange on the set of *Marathon Man* (John Schlesinger, 1976). Hoffman plays a student who gets caught up in a nasty black-market diamond-smuggling scheme involving a Nazi war criminal (Olivier). In an attempt to make sure the diamonds are safe, Olivier's character straps Hoffman's to a chair, pulls out some dental implements, and leans over his victim. Thus begins one of the more notorious torture scenes in modern filmdom.

In preparing for the scene, legend has it, Hoffman stayed up for three nights straight, refusing to sleep or eat, so that he'd look properly haggard, bedraggled, and exhausted for the shooting of the torture scene. When Hoffman showed up on the set the third day, Olivier couldn't believe the young American had sacrificed himself to such an extraordinary degree in creating the role. The great English actor rolled his eyes, turned to the director, and asked a simple question: "Why doesn't the boy just act?"

The now-legendary exchange typifies the contrast between the two most prevalent acting styles in English-language film. Understanding the differences between these styles will go a long way toward helping you appreciate some of the finer aspects of the actor's performance as an artist.

The Repertory System

Like practically all well-known actors from the United Kingdom, Olivier was trained in the repertory theaters of England, where he received rigorous training as a Shakespearean actor. Repertory actors learn all kinds of skills in the course of their "classical" training: gesture, accents, body movement, dancing, the use of makeup, and so on. What this variegated training allows the "rep actor" to do is create his or her character by moving from the external accouterments of the trade to the "inner reality" that is the character: In other words, the repertory actor studies the various aspects of the character and decides what particular attributes of his or her craft—a certain dialect overheard at a Norfolk pub, a facial expression copied from an old silent film, the idiosyncratic strut of a pompous aristocrat on the evening news, or perhaps a particular way of applying eyeliner to make her gaze more sinister—will render the most effective performance possible.

Filmophile's Lexicon

The **repertory system** is an English network of local and national theater companies that has turned out most of the country's foremost acting talents.

To see repertory work in action, consider the filmography of Daniel Day-Lewis. Day-Lewis began his acting career with a few bit parts in some British films (including *Sunday, Bloody Sunday* in 1971) before beginning formal repertory training at the Old Vic theater in Bristol. He first came to international attention for his performance in London's theater circles for his performance in *Another Country.*

Watching the following four film performances by Daniel Day-Lewis will give you a taste of the range and skill that a classically trained actor such as this brilliant star can bring to cinema.

- *A Room with a View* (1985). Playing a prim, wimpy aristocrat with a nasty cruel streak, Day-Lewis performed this role with a cold precision that made audiences just *hate* him. His flawless diction and precise body language is a direct product of the repertory system.
- *The Unbearable Lightness of Being* (1988). In this adaptation of Milan Kundera's international bestseller, Day-Lewis plays a serious yet unbelievably sensuous and

attractive doctor whose secure masculinity and effortless charisma could not contrast more vividly with his character in *Room with a View.*

- *My Left Foot* (1989). This film features Day-Lewis's depiction of an artist afflicted with cerebral palsy, which won him an Academy Award as best actor. Though Lewis's performance is earthy and heartwarming, it's also highly cerebral, and it's obvious how much intellectual preparation went into it.
- *In the Name of the Father* (1993). Playing a young Irish man wrongly imprisoned for years for a terrorist bombing he didn't commit, Day-Lewis successfully combines a flair of youthful irresponsibility with a deeply moving familial loyalty to his dying father. So convincing was his Northern Irish accent and persona, though, that many American reviewers wrongly identified him as "Ireland's most promising star."

Filmophile's Lexicon

Method acting (often called simply **the method**) refers to the system of acting developed by Constantin Stanislavsky that emphasized the emotional and psychological bond between actor and character, the goal of which was to discover the "inner spirit" of the latter.

Despite its extraordinary influence upon American film acting during the past 50 years, the classical, "external" training provided by the English repertory system has had to face a powerful challenge from another direction during the past five decades.

"The Method" to Their Madness

Shortly after the end of World War II, a Russian theater director named Constantin Stanislavsky started experimenting with new ways of making his actors and actresses identify more closely with the characters they were performing. For Stanislavsky, the actor must "live the part" he is playing, identifying on a deep emotional level with the "inner spirit" of the character by figuratively joining the character's sense of self to his own.

While Stanislavsky rejected the privileging of raw technical elements of acting as the most important, it is wrong to see the two systems, method and repertory, as diametrically opposed; indeed, most method actors, whatever psychological intensity they bring to their roles, are masterful at exploiting the "external" details that make up the technical side of any performance. Dustin Hoffman, for

Short Cuts

"If the ability to receive the creative mood in its full measure is given to the genius by nature, then perhaps ordinary people may reach a like state after a great deal of hard work with themselves—not in its full measure, but at least in part."

—Constantin Stanislavsky

example, was fanatical about getting the makeup right for his role in *Tootsie* (1982), while Paul Newman made a long study of pool shooting before playing opposite Jackie Gleason in *The Hustler* (1961). And no method actor will ever portray a brilliant serial killer more effectively than the rep-trained Anthony Hopkins was able to in *The Silence of the Lambs* (1991).

But it can't be denied that method acting created an entirely new way of bringing characters to life on the silver screen. While repertory-trained actors might spend months thinking about the specific techniques to bring to bear on a given performance, method actors searched their own personal experiences and emotional lives in order to immerse themselves profoundly (and often obsessively, at times even unhealthily) in the lives of their characters.

One of the generally unacknowledged dangers of the method, you may be thinking, is the possibility that the method actor will actually assume on more than a temporary basis the personality of the character being portrayed. In the case of, say, Mother Theresa, this might be fine. But if an actor is portraying a serial killer or a deranged rapist—well, enough said!

Filmophile's Lexicon

Emotional memory, a term from nineteenth-century European psychology, refers to the method-based idea that an actor has had certain life experiences that will allow him or her to forge a deep-seated psychological connection with the character being portrayed.

"You talkin' to me?": Improvisation and Amateurs

One final mode of film acting you should keep in mind is improvisation, the spontaneous performance of dialogue and action that hasn't been written or rehearsed (at least in detail) beforehand. Not surprisingly, silent cinema is full of improvisation; Charlie Chaplin rarely knew what exact facial expressions he would use at specific moments in a scene. Some sound film directors—Jean-Luc Godard of the French New Wave is the most famous example—hired untrained people virtually off the street to portray their characters, thinking (usually correctly) that nonprofessionals would deliver convincingly raw performances without the baggage of their training.

Filmophile's Lexicon

Typage was the term given by Russian director Vsevolod Pudovkin to the practice of casting nonprofessional actors in motion pictures to create a heightened sense of realism.

In recent times improvisation has been used most effectively by less Hollywood-constrained directors, such as John Cassavetes, who built entire films around it, and Martin Scorsese, who integrated it skillfully into otherwise scripted films.

Robert Altman is also a big improv partisan. That amazing nine-minute opening tracking shot around the movie studio lot in *The Player* (1992) featured entirely ad-libbed dialogue. As Altman explained it, he didn't want to tell folks playing themselves how to act like themselves. Makes sense to us!

"The Actor's Director": Priming the Prima Donnas

Before setting you loose on your tour of acting and its artistry, we want to make sure you're aware of the obvious but crucial role of the director in shaping the nature of performances in any given film. The greatest directors have held widely varying views on the role of actors in cinema, some of them holding great reverence for the ancient imitative art, others thinking of them as nothing more than props.

A quick comparison of two of the golden era's greatest directorial talents reveals the possible extent of such contrasts. Alfred Hitchcock, by any measure one of the world's top-five film directors of all time, frequently angered members of his casts by allowing them virtually no artistic voice in the blocking, filming, or dialogue of his movies. He thought of them in essence as nothing more than stage props, like a table or a bed. Think of Jimmy Stewart in *Rear Window* (1954), for example: With his leg broken, confined to a bed, Stewart's immobility and concordant ability to see out his window from a fixed point of view provides the perfect metaphor for Hitchcock's more general treatment of actors-as-props. It's a tribute to many of the leading actresses and actors in Hitchcock's films that they've crafted memorable performances while working in such constraining circumstances.

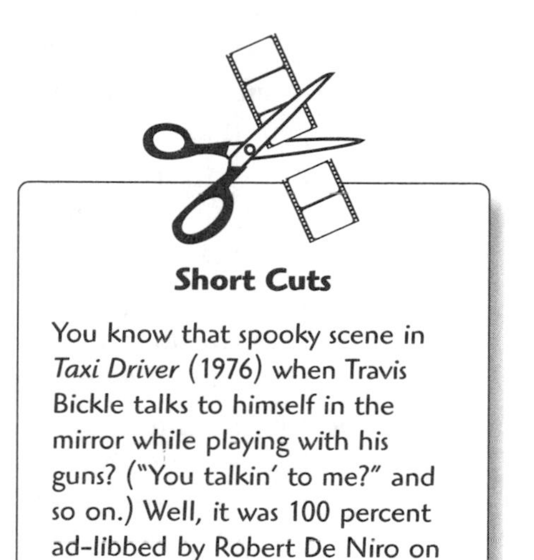

Short Cuts

You know that spooky scene in *Taxi Driver* (1976) when Travis Bickle talks to himself in the mirror while playing with his guns? ("You talkin' to me?" and so on.) Well, it was 100 percent ad-libbed by Robert De Niro on the spot.

On the opposite end of the spectrum from Sir Alfred is Elia Kazan. The most accurate measure of Kazan's privileging of acting in his films is his central role in bringing method acting to the American screen. In 1947, he cofounded the Actors Studio in New York, which became the American headquarters of the method and slowly began to transform acting styles on the silver screen.

Every director has his or her own unique and idiosyncratic approach to the role of the actor. It's up to you to determine how these individual approaches are discernible (if in fact they are) in each director's work.

The 14 Most Influential American Film Actors and Actresses

You can quibble, but here is a list of the stars we regard as the most influential and important in the history of American filmdom. We haven't necessarily included the most talented stars, but rather those who have exerted the clearest and most lasting impact on the art of acting.

- **Mary Pickford.** Perhaps the first truly international American film acting phenomenon, Pickford was one of the most powerful figures in silent film and the figurative "mother" of all U.S. movie stars.
- **Lillian Gish.** The "First Lady of the Silent Screen," she surpassed Pickford in sheer acting talent and glorified even the most mundane films in which she appeared.
- **Charlie Chaplin.** Chaplin crafted the ideal silent acting mode, pantomime, into its greatest incarnation in his hundreds of comedic, parodic, and always moving performances.
- **Buster Keaton.** The closest thing to an "actor-auteur," Keaton was the duke of Deadpan, using the most expressive face in the history of film to express his genius as an actor.
- **Douglas Fairbanks Sr.** The prototype of the swashbuckling American leading man (without him there'd be no Errol Flynn!), Fairbanks was an immensely popular figure on the screen throughout the silent era.
- **Clark Gable.** From the early '30s through the end of World War II, Gable virtually redefined American movie masculinity into the virile sexiness that made women across the country swoon.
- **John Wayne.** The Duke once famously remarked that the only acting he ever did was to act like John Wayne—which was enough to ensure him a lasting and defining role in American cinema.
- **Edward Everett Horton.** Though you may not have heard of him, we put Horton on the list as our plug for great character actors—and he was the greatest!
- **Marilyn Monroe.** The icon of feminine sensuality, Monroe created a look and a persona that will never be forgotten in the annals of film history.
- **Marlon Brando.** Perhaps the most gifted pure actor in the history of American film, Brando brought method acting into the cinematic mainstream.
- **Sidney Poitier.** A great acting talent by any measure, Poitier was also a huge barrier-breaking force in the integration of American film.
- **Jack Nicholson.** A dazzlingly talented artist, Nicholson is one of the most dynamic, exciting, chameleon-like actors to grace the American silver screen.

- **Meryl Streep.** With a strong claim to the title of Greatest Living Film Actress, Streep has been nominated for and won so many Oscars that most of us stopped counting years ago.
- **Dustin Hoffman.** Hoffman saved method acting for the contemporary era with his combination of dour melancholy and utter absorption in his roles.

The incomparable Lillian Gish, shown here in Orphans of the Storm *(1922).*

Meryl Streep, in one of countless Oscar-nominated roles, starring in Sophie's Choice *(1982).*

From the open-air theaters of ancient Athens to the twenty-first–century projecting booth, acting has embraced a dizzying variety of technique, talent, and titillation. If you learn how to watch and listen for the craft's distinguishing features, your appreciation of film will be all the more enriched in the long run.

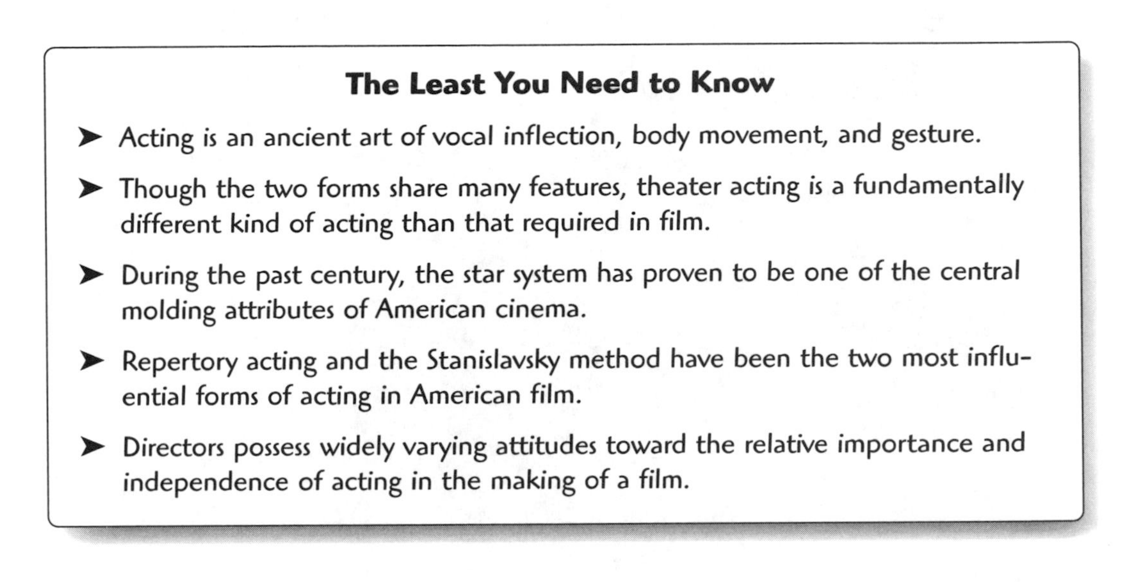

The Least You Need to Know

- Acting is an ancient art of vocal inflection, body movement, and gesture.
- Though the two forms share many features, theater acting is a fundamentally different kind of acting than that required in film.
- During the past century, the star system has proven to be one of the central molding attributes of American cinema.
- Repertory acting and the Stanislavsky method have been the two most influential forms of acting in American film.
- Directors possess widely varying attitudes toward the relative importance and independence of acting in the making of a film.

Part 5

Becoming a Filmophile—For Life!

You made it through the rest of this book in one piece. (Or you skipped to the end to see what happens. I'll bet you also tell people how movies turn out.) You're now at the really challenging but fun stuff: putting together all the disparate information you've learned into a coherent conversation, and assembling a great good place where you can luxuriate in the comfort of your home with this newfound knowledge. In Chapter 26 we provide discussions of the largest theoretical paradigms and ways to connect them to particular films. Then, in Chapter 27, we actually go through and do a thorough reading of one film, talking about camera work, editing, and other filmic dimensions, and relate these to the film's historical context and its largest themes. And that's it. Congratulations. You are now officially a film maven.

Chapter 26

An Idiot's Guide to Film Theory

In This Chapter

- Film theory versus film reviewing and criticism
- A brief history of film theory
- Descriptions of theoretical models
- Some books worth reading

What do people mean when they talk about semiotic, deconstructive, psychoanalytic feminist, and neo-Marxist "readings" of film? We'll give the broadest outlines of the various arguments, offer some examples of particular theorists and theories, and even try to discuss why these ideas are sometimes difficult to encompass.

Remember, this is a very down-and-dirty theory primer. If you remain interested in the subject, it's probably a good idea to do some additional reading on your own. To that end, we will provide a brief bibliography of readings at the end of this chapter instead of our usual list of films.

What Do We Mean by Theory?

Just as there tends to be a great if unnecessary divide in America between people who create and people who talk about creation—in other words between artists and critics/theorists—so there is a wide gap between different kinds of discussions about art, or in our case film.

Filmophile's Lexicon

Discourse: Refers to the particular rhetoric used to discuss a subject, and the ideology, politics, and institutions that rhetoric implicitly represents. A Marxist discourse will tend to emphasize capital, labor, and the "means of production" of its object. Feminist discourse may emphasize gender questions that a text raises.

The people who talk about creation—and their actual discussions (or, for the academically inclined, *discourses*)—can be usefully categorized in the following way:

- Movie reviewing.
- Film criticism.
- Cinema (or film) theory.

It might be easier to remember that, the more pretentious the language (movie → film → cinema) the more abstract the conversation becomes. Of course, these discourses often overlap. Probably the best film criticism slides over into theory. Pauline Kael, the former film reviewer for the *New Yorker,* received her Ph.D. in philosophy, so her reviews were almost always consciously informed by larger social and aesthetic issues.

We will spend most of this chapter reviewing major film theories, but it is worthwhile establishing the distinction between these discourses a little further, so that you have a better idea of what film theory is *not.*

Second Take

A few people manage to bridge both worlds as both artists and theorist-critics: Martin Scorsese, Peter Bogdonavich, Trinh Min-ha, and the French New Wave directors.

Movie Reviews

The movie reviewer answers one large question about one film at a time: Is the movie entertaining for the reviewer's audience? This is what Roger Ebert does for a living. The reviewer asks a limited number of smaller questions over and over about different, generally popular films: Is the film appropriate for the kids? Is it exciting? Will audiences identify with the main characters? Is the plot coherent? In other words, the reviewer helps you figure out whether the film is worth eight bucks on a Friday night. Or $16 if you're on a date. Or $25 if you're taking the spouse and kids.

Film Criticism

This is the intermediate discourse between reviewing and theorizing, and is often difficult to distinguish from theory. While most of the time movie reviewers discuss one film at a time, film critics tend to discuss larger numbers of texts: perhaps the works of one filmmaker, or the history of a genre, or the aesthetic of a particular studio. History is more important for the critic than for the reviewer, since the former should be able to discuss how the current monster movie harks back to *King Kong* (1933), while the movie reviewer only has to compare that film to other films produced in the recent past: to films the audience will have seen. (Again, the best reviewers will also be able to refer to *King Kong*.) Critics ask larger questions than reviewers: How does a film, a genre, or an industry reflect the culture from which it sprang? What do the works of a particular filmmaker say about that artist's psychological makeup? Critics are less interested with whether a film is entertaining, and more concerned with the film's *meaning*.

Theory of Cinema

Theorists question the assumptions that reviewers and critics make. For example, what does "entertainment" mean, exactly? Who is entertained? Are all people entertained the same way at all times? If not, how do notions of entertainment work? How does entertainment correspond to other notions of pleasure? Is entertainment always a bit erotic, or voyeuristic?

Film theory tends to be the most difficult discourse of the three in part because it asks questions that prevent our easy enjoyment of film. In fact, as the last set of questions should indicate, theory often works against our immediate ability to enjoy a film by questioning the very grounds that make enjoyment possible.

Some theory is difficult because it goes against some of our basic cultural assumptions, against official ideology. For example, Marxism is, among other things, a critique of the corporate capitalism that is the basis of our economy, and which we take for granted. Feminist theory in a postfeminist era strikes some (granted rather limited) thinkers as unnecessary or even "strident."

In fact, because film theory tends to ask the largest questions, it is often impossible to distinguish it from the largest questions asked by philosophy. As we shall discuss, much theory derives from certain strands of Western philosophy.

Second Take

Theory is also often difficult to read because it invents its own vocabulary and syntax: *discourse* instead of *discussion, text* instead of *movie, deconstruction* rather than *critique,* and so on. The first use of these words is almost always necessary and legitimate, but their subsequent use is often unnecessarily pretentious. When possible, we will refer back to the original meanings of words whose usage has become debased.

A History of Film Theory: Plato to Pluralism

We can look at the history of theory from either the long or the short perspective. In either case, we have to begin before the invention of film itself. In the former case, theory actually begins with the beginnings of aesthetic theory, from for example Plato's sense that we should not be overmuch given to representation (specifically poetry) because it diverts and subverts us from consideration of how to lead a good life as a citizen. This theory of representation is oddly similar to, for example, Marxist theorists for whom the classical Hollywood style is largely about creating an insidious standardization and uniformity among its citizenry. Other important moments in this long view would include Renaissance theories of optics, which assert that the world is seen in a particular (three-dimensional) fashion. It would also involve the development of the novel from the seventeenth to the nineteenth centuries. Film borrows heavily from the narrative style of the novel: flashbacks, omniscient and first-person narration, genre conventions, and so on.

The more immediate view of film theory is that, like most theoretical discourses, it derives from several relatively recent philosophical trends. These would include

- Kantian humanist, traditional aesthetic theory.
- Marxism.
- Historicism.
- Psychoanalysis.
- Nietzsche and the subsequent German philosophical tradition.
- Structuralism/semiotics.
- Feminism and gender theory.
- Ethnic theory.

The earliest of these discourses—Kantian humanism—constitutes an eighteenth-century enlightenment and post-enlightenment paradigm. Marxism is mid–nineteenth century, while psychoanalysis and German philosophy are turn-of-the-twentieth-century models. Though feminism has been around for a long time, feminist theory takes its inspiration from contemporary feminist discourse, from the 1970s to the present moment.

It is important to remember that these categories are explanatory rather than definitive; there is a lot of overlap in an increasingly eclectic theoretical universe. There are for example structuralist psychoanalytic critics and Marxist feminist theorists.

Theory to Go

We will present a précis of several of these theoretical models. Though each section will be brief, we shall try to present the most important assumptions, arguments, examples, and figures for each. We will not discuss at least one important humanist theory—auteurism—here, because we have already discussed it in Chapter 20, "Director's Cut: Calling the Shots."

Traditional Aesthetics: It's Art, for Pete's Sake

"Art for art's sake," "Truth is beauty, beauty truth." These are some of the rallying cries of traditional aesthetics. Aestheticians tend to be interested in the rules that govern the creation of the beautiful, or "aesthetically desirable." Such theories tend to be prescriptive, creating the rules they pretend simply to discover.

The earliest and most important figure here is probably Rudolph Arnheim, a German aesthetician who transferred his interest in the more traditional visual arts like oil painting for long enough to begin establishing some rules for film in his 1932 *Film As Art.* Like many aestheticians, he found the art of film in its limitations: principally in the facts that film is silent and black and white. Telling a story within these limitations is a little like writing a sonnet; part of the talent of sonneteering is staying within 14 lines and writing in iambic pentameter. When sound and color became viable technologies, Arnheim argued for the rest of his life against their use because they too easily seduced audiences away from the more important formal elements of film and made people too aware of story.

As the last assertion suggests, the upside of aesthetic theory is that it makes one more aware of film values other than just the plot and characters. The downside is that it tends to be ahistorical, uninterested in examining the industry of film, or audiences except insofar as they are little receivers of form. Also, the values formalists tend to look for in films are values they tend to invent themselves. For theorists who come after Arnheim, truth and beauty tend to be relative rather than absolute terms that say more about the theorist than about the text under examination.

Marx at the Movies

As you might guess, Marxist theory is interested in an opposite set of concerns from much traditional humanism. Where humanist criticism tends to be interested in "art for art's sake," Marxists are by definition interested in the relationship between the work of art and its social context. Art always has an effect or is effected by society.

In a sense, we have already visited one Marxist theorist: Sergei Eisenstein. His theory of montage is *dialectical* in the same manner that Marxism itself is: His theory that shot elements should conflict reflects the Marxian notion that history is about class conflict.

Sooner or later, most Marxist criticism will be interested in the "means of production" of a movie, or the industry that produces films. This includes an interest in audiences as well as filmmakers, and (as one might expect) an interest in where the money comes from to make film, and where that money goes. Marxists are interested in the history of film, and especially in the dialectical movement of film, and in the relationship between film technology and sociology.

Director's Cut

The most famous "neo-Marxist" (that is, Marxism after Marx and Lenin) approach to culture is probably the Frankfurt School, the most famous exponents of which are Theodor Adorno and Max Horkheimer. These German cultural critics continued writing in Germany until the 1930s, when they came to the United States to escape the Nazis. Once here, they saw that in some important respects twentieth-century democratic capitalism rather resembled European fascism. Especially important was the fact that uniformity was emphasized in both cases through the organ of mass culture. They referred to the production of mass culture in the United States as the "culture industry." The culture industry included radio, the as-yet-to-be-born television, and, especially, the movies. The fact that Adorno and Horkheimer were not particularly interested in movies made them rather distanced critics who could afford to be very harsh about its cultural effect.

For Frankfurt School critics, American film represented the most subtly repressive cultural organ, essentially creating a generation of conformity-minded Americans not too unlike the Hitler youth. Hollywood produces the same films in the same half a dozen genres featuring the same half dozen overvalued stars from the same half dozen studios, producing the same half dozen stories reflecting the same half dozen ideologically conservative values.

The most important inheritor of the Frankfurt School is probably Frederick Jameson, who returns to the notion of the production of culture 40 years later in an essay called "Postmodernism." He expands the argument of the Frankfurt School by saying that the culture industry now shuts down all oppositional representation by "appropriating"—buying or silencing—it. Essentially, we live in a culture in which there is little or no real political opposition. He observes for example that it is now virtually impossible to shock our culture the way the surrealists, whose early films were shot at by right-wing extremists—were able to do. In politics it is almost trivial to observe that there is little difference these days between the Republican and Democratic parties.

On film this appropriation translates, for example, into stories that turn revolutionary historical moments into entertainment. Student unrest of the 1960s and the Vietnam War become atmosphere in *Forrest Gump* (1994). The Holocaust becomes the subject of comedy in *Life Is Beautiful* (1997).

The up-side of Frankfurt School criticism and its inheritors is that it presents a hard-headed critique of the worst aspects of Hollywood, a cogent explanation of the "dumbing-down" of America as the desire to create an acquiescent, satisfied, non-critical public. The point of all Marxist critics is to change such dynamics, rather than simply to observe how they work.

The downside of Marxist criticism is that it wants to change such dynamics rather than simply observe them. A lot of people don't really desire the Hollywood film to change. Another downside is that many Marxists have to oversimplify the meanings of films in order for their arguments to work. As later theorists will point out, all texts, even in the same industry, do not propagate the same message at all times.

Second Take

Remember, while the Frankfurt School critique of American culture may sound a bit extreme, it is also rather prescient. These theorists writing in the 1930s and 1940s are looking forward to the very conformity-minded McCarthy-Eisenhower 1950s, the era of the man in the gray flannel suit and of anticommunist witch hunts.

Historicism

This is a rather broad term that includes any method interested in interpreting film through its historical context. Traditional historicism is not very theoretical; it does not tend to examine basic cultural assumptions about its subject. Rather, it simply recounts the most important events and figures in film history. Biographies of stars and directors are an example of traditional historicism.

More contemporary histories try to question this traditional method, finding other objects to examine.

One such way of reading history arises with a French theorist named Michel Foucault, whose work, though not especially about film, is groundbreaking for all humanities scholarship. Foucault is not interested in the great men of history, but in the establishment of institutions, which he sees as the real foci of power. For our purposes his two most important observations are about how institutions function (as "panopticons") and about how institutions allow us to speak ("discourse"). The panopticon is the institution as prison: All institutions—hospitals, insane asylums, corporations, universities—create the illusion that we are being watched at all times. As a result, we begin watching—or "policing"—our own behavior.

Partially as a result of this self-policing, we tend to speak only in the language of modern institutions, only in sanctioned "discourses." Since language determines thought, we can only think down paths that institutions allow us.

Foucaultian critics and theorists will study the institution of film and the way it imposes a manner of speaking and thinking on us. This concern is in some respects like

Short Cuts

The upside of Foucaultian historicism is that it tries to see history in a more interesting light than you might have learned in high school. The downside is that it paints all relations and discourses as power relations between institutions, from your place in the institution you live in (school, family, job) to the way you talk to your significant other.

Marxist concerns, but without, as Marxists lament, the same overtly revolutionary impetus. But Foucaultian critics would be somewhat less interested in the industry of film—in the history of each film studio as its own institution—and more interested in the film-as-a-whole as an institution.

Foucaultian critics ask: How does film exercise authority? How does it make us behave? How does it make us talk? What does it allow us to think about? They might notice (though they would not be the only ones), for example, that social problems tend to be resolved through the discourse of the romantic couple in the screwball comedy. From *It Happened One Night* (1934) to *Pretty Woman* (1990), movies encourage us to think that the uniting of the couple at the end will solve society's problems. The couple in *It Happened One Night* resolves the Great Depression, while Julia Roberts and Richard Gere solve the problems of prostitution *and* heartless corporate raiding. Political discourse takes place as romantic discourse.

Cinema and Psychoanalysis

Psychoanalysis was invented at about the same time as film (the 1890s). Both involve explorations of fantasy. While not referring to movies, Sigmund Freud talks about a "dream screen"—a background against which our fantasy life is projected—that sounds an awful lot like going to the movies in your head. So it is no surprise that psychoanalysis has become an important method for determining meaning in movies.

At the simplest level, one can psychoanalyze characters, a little like the famous interpretation of Hamlet as indecisive and mother-fixated. However, though sometimes interesting, there's something a little ridiculous about psychoanalyzing fictional characters. They are, after all, fictional; a character can't properly be said to have an unconscious that we can examine.

The next most likely candidate for psychoanalysis is the director or auteur, or principal artist. Probably the most noted examination of the mind of the abutter is William Rothman's *Hitchcock: The Murderous Gaze* (1982), a critical biography of Alfred Hitchcock, in which the various birds, psychos, necktie stranglers, and falling bodies are connected to the somewhat disturbed psyche of the "master of suspense."

At a more general level, the next candidate for psychoanalysis is the particular society that produces a particular film, genre, or even technology. This society can be seen as the actual audience for movies, the culture that produces them, the industry that makes them, or all three. In *From Caligari to Hitler* (1947), Siegfried Kracauer suggests that you can see the German predisposition for authoritarian rule that will lead to Nazism in the 1930s already in the Weimar Republic films of the 1920s. Writing several decades later, Roger Dadoun, in "Metropolis: Mother-City"—"Mittler—Hitler," (in *Close Encounters: Film, Feminism, and Science Fiction*), sees Hitler himself as oddly fulfilling a sort of maternal role for Germany that is again preceded by similar characters in 1920s films, especially Fritz Lang's *Metropolis* (1926).

Finally, in "The Apparatus" (in *Film Theory and Criticism*)," Jean-Louis Baudry psychoanalyzes Western culture by examining the "apparatus"—the technology—of film. He notices, for example, that film creates the same "dream screen" that Freud discusses, even serendipitously using some of the same vocabulary that psychoanalysis does ("screening" and "projection," for example).

Today the revisionary psychoanalytic theorist used as much as Freud is Jacque Lacan. Lacan's notion of the "mirror stage"—that, in other words, the crucial moment that personality is born in the infant is the moment that he recognizes himself in the mirror for the first time—has obvious affinities to the film-going experience. As with the mirror stage, film going is primarily visual. As with the mirror stage, we identify with images we see on the screen. As infants derive a sense of power from the mirror experience, so the 12-year-old boy's identification with Arnold Schwarzenegger makes him feel powerful as long as the identification lasts. As infants mistakenly believe that the mirror image is a real image, so we "believe" in the fiction on-screen, at least for 90 minutes.

Short Cuts

The advantage of psychoanalytic criticism is that it can tell us a lot about the character, auteur, and culture that produces film. The downside is that the psychoanalytic paradigm feels "counterintuitive" to most people who can't sense an unconscious in themselves, the whole notion of which seems to take power away from the individual and invest it in a part of himself over which he has no control.

Gender

The great example of gender repression actually derives from Foucault's work (see the previous section). Though almost always criminal in some respect, homosexuality was not seen as a medical problem until, in the nineteenth century, it was defined as such by the medical establishment, which categorized it as a medical pathology, a sort of disease that, depending on which doctor you read, was or was not curable. As a result you could be locked up or fired as a degenerate, unfit to cohabit with other people.

Gender theorizing in film really begins (and continues) as feminist theory. In the 1970s feminists were initially interested in the history of feminine representation, and the stereotyping of women into sinister femmes fatales, silly screwball comediennes, and Madonna figures, but almost never as strong, active, capable characters. Probably the most important early books here are Marjorie Rosen's *Popcorn Venus* (1973) and Molly Haskell's *From Reverence to Rape* (1974).

At almost the same time, however, feminists started looking at the film industry and at the process of filmmaking itself to understand the "deep structure" of filmic sexism.

Some feminists like Claire Johnston and Judith Mayne began claiming a woman-centered film heritage, for example rediscovering the works of the few pioneering women filmmakers in Hollywood and elsewhere: Ida Lupino, Dorothy Arzner, Alice Guy, and so on.

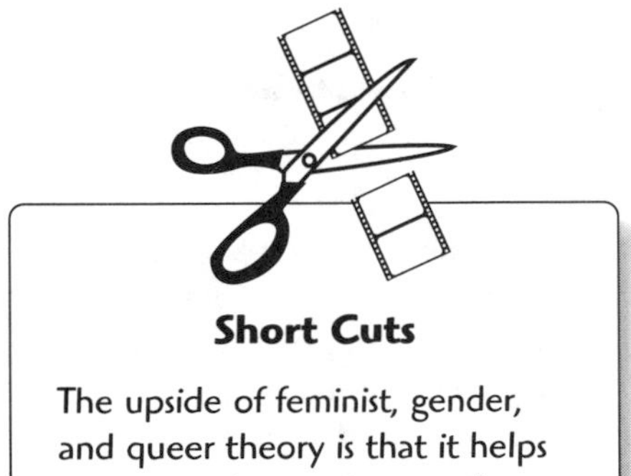

Short Cuts

The upside of feminist, gender, and queer theory is that it helps negotiate changes in a gender-inequitable system. Frankly—and as with the next section's subject—ethnic theory—it's is hard to see a downside here.

Because feminism defines a goal rather than a method, feminist theorists have been ingeniously eclectic in their approaches, employing just about all the other models we are discussing in this chapter. Some have made use of multiple approaches at the same time.

Some time in the late 1980s feminist theory evolved into gender theory in order to take account of the fact that women are not the only oppressed gender: gays, lesbians, transvestites, transsexuals, and people of other gender persuasions have been equally oppressed. The past 10 years especially has seen the rise of "queer theory" to examine the representations of these alternative sexualities. The goal in queer theory is rather the same as in feminist theory: to chart representation and oppression, to explode standard cultural gender definitions and categories, and to provide a critical space for a more enlightened structure of gender representation.

Race, Multicultural, and Ethnic Theory

While feminist activism takes some of its inspiration from the Civil Rights movement of the 1950 and 1960s, race theory in popular culture and film studies is in part modeled after feminist theory of the 1970s. Like feminist theory, it is deeply invested in canon-busting, questioning the stereotypes that come out of the film industry, and positing actual and theoretical "countercinemas" that offer narrative models different from the dominant classical Hollywood style. In addition, race theorizing is connected to colonial and postcolonial, and anticolonial theorizing, and is interested in the question of Third-World cinema. Aesthetic concerns tend to be subordinate to the political goal of "multiculturalism," or the desire to allow alternative filmmakers representing alternative cultures to be seen and heard as actively as Hollywood directors.

Like feminist critics and theorists, scholars of race are interested in aspects of film history that canon-bound scholars tend to forget.

Director's Cut

Until the 1980s, film scholars almost completely ignored the fact that there was a thriving African American film community from the 1910s to the 1930s that was fairly obliterated, first by Hollywood and then by critical neglect. The principal voice in this industry was a director named Oscar Micheaux, whose many films in many genres on and off race-specific topics have since taken their place in the American film canon, though they have yet to make their way to regular AMC- or TCM-cable-channel screenings.

Structuralism and Semiotics

Semiotics is the "science" of textual interpretation. Its models are the classificatory sciences—biology, chemistry—though it tends toward the psychoanalytic and Marxist in practice. It seeks to find the basic units in a text and then decide how these units determine meaning.

The most famous exponent of semiotics in film is probably Christian Metz, whose language for interpreting film derives in part from linguistics. Like most semioticians, he is interested in "signs," "signifiers," and "signifieds." He invents a word for the primary unit of signification in film: various kinds of "syntagma."

Further Reading

Some *Idiot's Guide* readers will want a little more depth than we are able to give here, so we suggest these books as the logical next step a) because they are standards on the subject, b) because they tend to be pretty comprehensive, and c) they try to make the subject as accessible as possible.

- J. Dudley Andrew, *The Major Film Theories* (London: Oxford University Press, 1976). This older text is still a brilliant bit of history, and is especially strong on classical theory up to the mid-1970s.
- Leo Braudy, Marshall Cohen, Gerald Mast, eds., *Film Theory and Criticism: Introductory Readings,* Fifth ed. (New York: Oxford University Press, 1999). A collection of some of the most important theory articles.
- Louis Giannetti, *Understanding Movies,* Seventh ed. (Englewood Cliffs, N.J.: Prentice Hall, 1996). This book is really more generally an introduction to film studies, but it contains one chapter on film theory that is short and sweet, and clear.

- Contance Penley, ed., *Feminism and Film Theory* (New York: Routledge, 1988). The classic feminist anthology. A slimmer volume than the rest on this list, but it contains a good range of approaches, including Mulvey's "Visual Pleasure."
- Philip Rosen, ed., *Narrative, Apparatus, Ideology: A Film Theory Reader* (New York: Columbia University Press, 1986.) A good supplement to either the Stam or the Mast anthologies, this volume leans toward French and Marxist theory.
- Robert Stam, *Film Theory: An Introduction* (Malden, Mass.: Blackwell Publishers, 2000). While including a more synoptic version of the classical theory in Andrew's book, it picks up theory history where Andrew left off and brings it to the present day. Clear if not always easy to read.
- Robert Stam and Toby Miller, eds., *Film and Theory: An Anthology* (Malden, Mass.: Blackwell Publishers, 2000).

We recommend beginning with the Giannetti chapter, moving on to Dudley Andrew's book and Robert Stam's introductory text, and then approaching the other eclectically.

The Least You Need to Know

- Film theory is different from both film criticism and film reviewing because it asks larger, more philosophical questions.
- Film theory derives from a number of intellectual traditions: especially Western humanism, psychoanalysis, and twentieth century German philosophy.
- The major theoretical paradigms and subjects remain humanism, psychoanalysis, Marxism, historicism, feminism, race theory, and semiotics.
- Most of these paradigms have undergone significant revisions in the past 20 years so that they seem less reductive or simplistic.

Chapter 27

From Theory to Practice: Putting It All Together

In This Chapter

- Why *Nosferatu* works so well as the subject of this chapter
- A brief plot summary and overview of the film
- The aesthetics of *Nosferatu:* camera work, lighting, acting, and everything else
- *Nosferatu* through the lens of film theory
- Tying it all together and learning from this experience
- Films to compare once you're finished

If you ever *were* a complete idiot where movies, flicks, and film are concerned, you certainly aren't anymore. By now you've learned all about the industry and economy of film, and how a movie gets put together from start to finish. You've read a minihistory of American movies from Edison to Spielberg as well as a dozen overviews of various national cinematic traditions. And you've started to learn the ropes of directing, cinematography, editing, and all the other technical and aesthetic aspects of filmmaking. You've even begun to understand how film theory works—no small task for the uninitiated! So pat yourself on the back.

But only once. You've still got work to do, after all. This chapter will get you started on the years of educated film appreciation ahead of you by assimilating all that you've learned into a much more in-depth analysis of a single film: F. W. Murnau's classic

1922 German Expressionist *Nosferatu* (*Nosferatu—eine Symphonie des Grauens*). Your first task is simple: Go out to your local video store, find the foreign or silent film section, and rent *Nosferatu.* Be careful, though. There are a number of remakes and rip-offs out there, and our expert analysis won't necessarily apply to any of them. So be sure to ask for F. W. Murnau's 1922 version.

Watch the film one time all the way through (it's only about 90 minutes long). Sleep on it, then read this chapter. Read it again (it's only about 10 pages long). The next evening, after you've absorbed everything we have to say about *Nosferatu,* view the film a second time, watching for the technical and aesthetic specifics we've identified below and asking yourself whether you agree with our theoretical interpretations later in the chapter (you don't have to—in fact, we hope you'll *disagree* and come up with your own!).

Why *Nosferatu?*

Among the thousands of films we could have chosen for this "close reading" chapter, why did we choose this one?

- First, *Nosferatu* is one of the important films to come out of German Expressionism, the first real wide-scale artistic movement in the history of world cinema.
- Though there are better, more artistically satisfying examples of German Expressionism out there, *Nosferatu* is the first bona fide "monster flick," the movie that spawned one of film's most influential genres and has distant ancestors in *Friday the 13th* (1980), *Creature from the Black Lagoon* (1954), *Predator* (1987), and so on.
- The special effects and idiosyncratic camerawork make *Nosferatu* a visually arresting film ripe for analysis.
- The film was culturally important in its own historical moment, and thus important to read as a cultural artifact of the early 1920s.
- Finally, a major American movie about the making of this classic film, called *Shadow of the Vampire* (2000), has been recently released at the beginning of the twenty-first century. At least someone in Hollywood believes that this film about eternal evil, life, and love speaks to the zeitgeist of the new millennium.

Unpacking *Nosferatu:* Plot, Aesthetics, and Technique

Here's a quick plot summary of *Nosferatu* that might have been the totality of your conversation about the film before reading this book:

Real estate agent Hutter is sent by his oddly behaved boss, Knock, to the Carpathian mountains to arrange for the sale of a house in their native city of Bremen to the mysterious Graf (Count) Orlock. After an evening in an inn near the castle of the mysterious count, during which he is warned against vampires and finds a book on the subject by his bed, Hutter continues the next day to the castle.

After a furious ride he arrives, to find the count, a strange-looking fellow with a penchant for blood, waiting up for him. Held prisoner while Orlock leaves for Bremen, Hutter finally escapes, and we follow their parallel journey—Hutter by land and Orlock, in a coffin on a boat, by sea. Hutter's experience leaves him a ruined wreck of a man. Orlock's ship mysteriously docks itself, all of its crew having died en route. Orlock debarks, seeming to bring rats and the plague to his new home.

Second Take

When you go to the video store to rent Nosferatu for this chapter, be sure you get F. W. Murnau's 1922 version (ask the clerk to double-check). There are a number of remakes that are ripoffs out there, and our expert analysis won't necessarily apply to any of them.

Director's Cut

Here are some of the basic facts you need to know about *Nosferatu* before settling in for a night of thrills and chills:

The cast:

Orlock/Nosferatu: Max Schreck
Hutter: Gustav von Wangenheim
Ellen Hutter: Greta Schroeder
Knock: Alexander Granach
Professor Bulwer: John Gottowt

Year released: 1922
Director: F. W. Murnau
Producer: Prana Film
Director of photography: Fritz Arno Wagner
Screenwriter: Henrik Galeen
Running time: 94 minutes

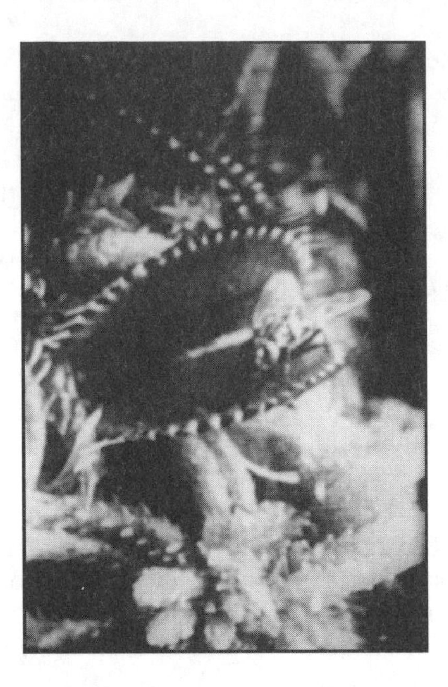

Professor Bulwer explains the vampiric workings of the Venus's flytrap.

After some side trips in which we discover a scientist explaining the actions of a Venus's flytrap (the "vampire" of the vegetable world), and a subplot involving Knock, discovered to be an insane devotee of Orlock, in which he is killed by a mob, we return to Orlock. The count, taken by the charms of Hutter's wife, Ellen, spends the evening with her. She sacrifices herself (in an implicitly erotic fashion) so that her husband might recover. Keeping Orlock with her until dawn, she succeeds, and the vampire's vulnerability to light destroys him.

Mise-en-Scène

Nosferatu's mise-en-scène is identifiably German Expressionist, if not so extremely as *The Cabinet of Dr. Caligari* (1919). Murnau initially learned much of his craft—lighting, decor, acting, and staging—by working with Max Reinhardt, a famous Expressionist theater director. As a result, though silent and black and white, the film is one of the creepiest-looking Dracula entries ever made.

Ellen's home and the opening exterior scenes of Bremen seem visually balanced and relatively real. So do the exterior scenes, most of which were shot on location rather than in a studio, like the more typically expressionist *The Cabinet of Dr. Caligari.* But most of the other venues (sets by designer/producer Albin Grau) throughout most of the film are dark and off-kilter: the office of real estate agent Knock, the inn at which Hutter stays before going to Orlock's castle, and the various rooms in the castle itself. It is as if all the venues in Orlock's sphere are contaminated by his inhuman status, while Ellen's sphere remains both visually and emotionally centered and secure.

An interior scene in Orlock's castle.

Rats are everywhere in this film: in the town of Bremen after the arrival of Orlock, in the castle, and most conspicuously on the ship that carries Orlock to his new home. Not until Herzog's version of the film does the story become vermin-infested again. (While other effects may seem dated, the rats are still a little hard for beginning film students to take. They tend to have the originally desired effect of creeping one out something awful.)

Rats galore!

At another level, the mise-en-scène is nineteenth century, a significant change from Bram Stoker's novel that set its story at the moment that Stoker was writing. The story of *Nosferatu* is set about 70 or 80 years before 1922, making the film a period piece. It is possible that making the film a period piece makes its theme about evil authorities an allegory that could not be easily related to the present moment and so could not, like *The Cabinet of Dr. Caligari,* be censored.

Camera Work

Though there is not a great deal of camera movement, the camera placement is sometimes breathtaking. The single most famous still is probably the low-angle shot of Orlock before the mast on the ship. He looms powerful and menacing, not just over the crew, but over the audience.

Nosferatu shot from a low and creepy angle on board his ship.

The shot setups can be creepy, such as the super close-up of the count in his coffin, or uncomfortably close-up shots of rats.

Editing Counts

Nosferatu is famous for containing relatively early instances of thematic montage, most significantly the crosscutting between Count Orlock advancing menacingly on Hutter in the count's castle, and Ellen waking and crying out hundreds of miles away in Bremen, which seems to make Orlock retreat. This editing suggests a spiritual connection between Ellen and Hutter, as Ellen worries about and protects Hutter from afar. But more significantly, it is Orlock on whom she acts, as if the real connection is somehow between the good and evil, and with Hutter as an almost superfluous onlooker.

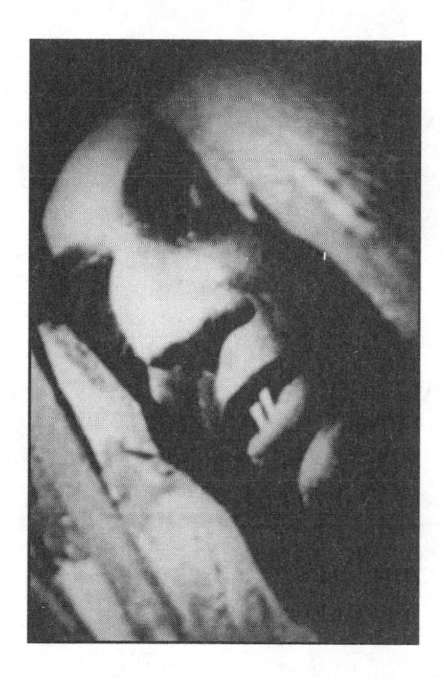

A close-up of Nosferatu in his comfy bed.

Special Effects

The most striking effect in this film is Orlock's makeup. It presents us with a vampire utterly unlike the suave villains with whom we have been acquainted since Bela Lugosi in the 1931 American version of *Dracula*. Orlock is repulsive: taloned hands, tremendously exaggerated nose, raised bald cranium reminding one of the rats his presence constantly evokes, and a hunched figure.

The vampire's shadow cast upon a wall in the castle.

Short Cuts

A scene from Jean-Luc Godard's *Alphaville* (1965) directly references the famous effect from *Nosferatu* in which Hutter's coach crosses the bridge and the film changes to negative.

The only significant exceptions to the suavely villainous portrayals of the dead count are both influenced by *Nosferatu*. The first, a 1979 vampire film, is also called *Nosferatu* (German). Klaus Kinski dons almost precisely the same makeup Schreck did. The second is Francis Coppola's *Bram Stoker's Dracula* (1992), in which Gary Oldman's makeup, though not identical to Schreck's, is, in its grotesque enlargement of the cranium and fingers, and in its pallor, reminiscent of Schreck's (though through half the film Oldman is presented as the suave count, in the tradition of Lugosi, Christopher Lee, and Frank Langella).

Some of the film's other special effects include:

- A fast stop-motion carriage ride, giving the im pression of demonic speed. This effect was digitally reproduced in the Francis Coppola version of the story, to show the world from the point of view of the vampire.
- Printing a positive of the negative of a forest scene on the way to Orlock's castle gives the impression of an eerie, lurid, and terrifying woodland nightmare.
- Superimposition as Orlock slowly fades away and disappears at the break of day at the end of the film.

Negative film used to capture forest sequence to emphasize occult quality of Orlock's domain

Here primitive superimposition is used to show the death of Orlock at sunrise.

Acting Up a Storm

The acting is to some degree the exaggerated acting style of Expressionism, to some degree the melodramatic acting style in film as adapted from the nineteenth-century stage (and before the advent of the method), and the somewhat broader acting style used by actors in film during the early middle silent era, as well as in the era of improving but imperfectly recording film stock.

However, before condemning the performances as "overacting" and "primitive," try to notice some of the subtle but real differences in acting styles between the characters. For example, the lead character—Count Orlock—is actually rather understated when compared to Hutter. Orlock's body and facial movements tend to be small: the rubbing together of hands à la Uriah Heep, or the faint leer. Max Schreck, the actor playing Orlock, often simply allows the makeup or special effects to work for him. The most chilling moment in the film—Nosferatu's rising from the coffin—involves no voluntary movement on Schreck's part at all. Rather, a winch or some other device raises him from the horizontal to the vertical, giving a sense of occult movement. Perhaps Schreck's modulated expressionism is the result of working, like Murnau, with the Max Reinhardt theater troupe earlier in his career.

By contrast, Hutter, played by Gustav von Wangenheim, acts much more broadly, even hysterically. He faints at moments of real terror, and is by turns exaggeratedly elated and depressed. An interesting performance style for the putative hero of the piece, no?

Low-Key but Not Laid-Back Lighting

Most of the film is very low key, with the notable exception of the outdoor sequences, in which the German countryside through which Hutter rides on his way to the count's castle is seen as bright and beautiful. (Some sequences in which the vampire appears to be abroad in daylight were actually tinted blue to give the appearance of moonlight, but monochrome film stock loses this effect.)

High-key naturalistic lighting surrounds Hutter as he travels out of Bremen.

Low-key interior shot of Castle Orlock.

Otherwise, the lighting is typically expressionistic: dark, with some high contrasts. For example, while Hutter is in bed, the menacing shadow of Count Orlack hovers over him. This shadow is alluded to in the Coppola version, when the count's shadow seems to have a life of its own. The Coppola version is itself referenced in an episode of *The Simpsons*.

More seriously, this kind of expressionist lighting is partly responsible for the American film noir style, which is itself in part invented by German expatriates in America, including Fritz Lang.

Specters of *Nosferatu:* Theorizing the Film

Now it's time to play around with some of that film theory you learned in Chapter 26, "An Idiot's Guide to Film Theory." Don't be intimidated: Film theory can seem a bit arcane and obtuse when you first start out. At this point, though, you've mastered the "primary text"—*Nosferatu* itself—to which we're now going to apply the theory. While not all of these interpretive angles on the film are complementary to one another, they do provide a somewhat more sophisticated intellectual angle on the film's cultural work in its own moment.

Second Take

The producers of *Nosferatu* apparently never asked permission for the use of Bram Stoker's novel *Dracula,* which they adapted pretty transparently into the film. They didn't pay any royalties for the use of the novel either. This angered Stoker's widow, Florence, who promptly sued Prana for its unauthorized appropriation of the novel—yet another way economics enters into the strange history of this film.

Negotiating Nosferatu: *A Marxist Approach*

Nosferatu has gone down in history as one of the most innovative films in German Expressionism. As you've just read in the sections above, the camera placement, acting, mise-en-scène, and so on make this movie a brilliant example of the aesthetic that begins with *The Cabinet of Dr. Caligari,* of which *Nosferatu* is a direct and immediate descendant. Why not just appreciate its status as a work of art and leave it at that?

The problem is, the aesthetics of German Expressionism were influenced from the very beginning by contemporary economic conditions. The original director of *Dr. Caligari* was not Robert Wiene, who now gets credit for this hallmark film, but Fritz Lang, who would go on to make *Metropolis* (1927) and *M* (1931) in the succeeding years. Once production got under way, however, Lang was pulled from the project in favor of Wiene.

The reason? Profit, pure and simple. Seems that *Dr. Caligari* producer Erich Pommer had just released the first part of *Die Spinnen* (*The Spiders,* 1919), a criminal melodrama that was doing a smashing success at the box office. Rather than allow Lang to continue making the weirdo vampire flick, Decla's Pommer calculated that a second part of *Die Spinnen* might equal the success of the first and thus fill the company's coffers all the more.

What this means in practical terms is that the directorial vision that produced the hallmark film of German Expressionism—and thus the style that would lead in three short years to *Nosferatu* itself—was fundamentally determined by the desire on the part of a production company for more capital. The realities of the economic base and the nature of mass culture in post–World War I Germany determined the most intimate details of the film that initiated the genre in which *Nosferatu* would quickly assume pride of place.

On a more internal narrative level, consider the main plot of *Nosferatu.* What brings Hutter to the Carpathians in the first place? Do you remember?

A real estate transaction—in fact, a real estate transaction in which the middle-class Hutter is hoping to sell a house to a member of the aristocracy, the evil count. Thus, not only is the film's artistry determined in large part by economic conditions, but the film's very story line originates in a commercial transaction that serves as a catalyst for everything that follows.

What Lies Beneath: A Psychoanalytic Approach

By the time *Nosferatu* appeared in 1922, Freudian psychoanalysis was quickly becoming part of the fabric of postwar German culture. Freud's ideas circulated widely in numerous social and intellectual spheres, and it's very difficult to look at any cultural artifact from the period—let alone an Expressionist masterpiece like *Nosferatu*—apart from its relation to contemporaneous psychoanalytic culture. In fact, Expressionism is the film aesthetic that lends itself most easily to psychoanalysis because the whole movement was precisely an attempt to make visible in the arts humanity's internal psychological world. To put it another way, Expressionism was all about exploring the inner world of psychosis, madness, repression, and the unconscious that Freud had only recently brought into wide-scale public discussion.

To give you just one example of Expressionism's deep-seated concern with the relationship between the conscious and the unconscious, take the visual techniques deployed in *Nosferatu.* As you read in the "Special Effects" section earlier in this chapter, one of the most frequently cited technical innovations Murnau incorporated into Nosferatu was the use of negative film to convey the eerie quality of Hutter's journey through the Carpathian countryside. Trees appear white against the black sky, a harrowing effect that conveys the strange reversals of nature that will occur whenever a living human being ventures into the realm of the monstrous and the undead.

Director's Cut

"Nosferatu is an evil name suggesting the red letters of hell—the sinister pieces of it like -fer- and -eratu and nos- have a red and heinous quality like the picture itself (which throbs with gloom), a masterpiece of nightmare horror photographed fantastically well in the old grainy tones of brown-and-black-and-white."

—Jack Kerouac, in *New Yorker Film Society Notes* (January 1960)

In psychoanalytic terms, we might say that Murnau's use of negative film in this way constructs the occult as the unconscious itself: a negative image of the conscious, knowing self that we inhabit in our daily lives that is always threatened by the chaos that lies just beneath. Orlock and Hutter themselves play out the ongoing struggle between the unconscious and the conscious; perhaps the final lesson of the film is that the ego can achieve victory over the id only at the expense of its own security. *Nosferatu* is ultimately a tale of alternately repressed and sublimated unconscious desires that, in good Freudian fashion, never achieves secure narrative closure.

In more explicitly political terms (and here we're thinking of the Freud of *Civilization and Its Discontents*), Orlock represents the unconscious of the European people in general in the years following the Great War. The continent's collective guilt over the unprecedented bloodshed on its soil assumes the form of a creature disfigured and even animalized by the evil that produced him.

Vamping with the Vampire: Gender and Sexuality

It's no mistake that *vamp*—a term coined in the 1910s to refer to a woman who uses her sex appeal to seduce and exploit men—is derived directly from *vampire*. The image of a wily woman "sucking the blood"—money, sexual energy, virility, children, whatever—out of her unknowing, naive victim is an enduring misogynist trope of twentieth-century popular culture.

But what's so interesting about this image in terms of gender and sexuality, of course, is the fact that *men* are the original "vamps." The figure of the vampire, who first comes to world cinema in the person of Orlock in *Nosferatu*, is the ultimate symbol of sexual omnivorousness. The vampire will eat, suck, and seduce anybody anywhere and anytime.

In this respect, Murnau's brilliant representation of Orlock constantly works against the film's overriding Victorian values. Near the end of the film, when Hutter's wife, Ellen, realizes that her status as a good and virtuous woman demands that she sacrifice herself to the vampire in order to save the population of Bremen, the film clearly leads us to believe (or at least momentarily suspect) that Ellen may not be as unwilling a victim as she appears to be. Orlock's night with Ellen is a night of adultery just below the surface: an encounter with a vampire, the quintessential monstrous bachelor, is inherently erotic, and in *Nosferatu* constitutes the only loosely "romantic" moment in the entire film. After Orlock has died, of course, Victorian family values are reaffirmed—but at the price of the sacrificial lamb, the wife who gave herself, body and soul, to another man.

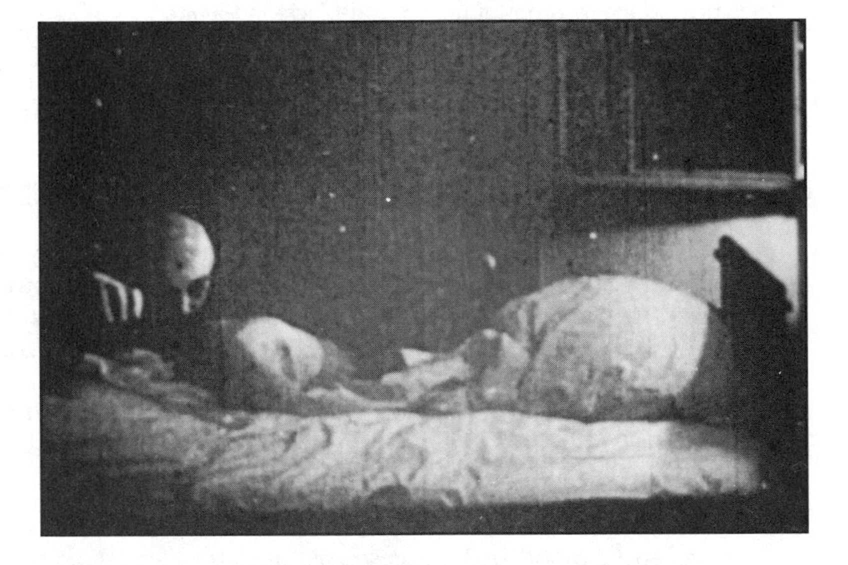

Ellen Hutter "seducing" Nosferatu during the vampire's last night on earth.

On another level, *Nosferatu* clearly embeds a homoerotic dimension to Orlock's desires. When Hutter cuts himself while eating in the castle, the Count sniffs the blood appreciatively and expresses the full range of his carnal desires without regard to Hutter's gender.

The blood he sucks from Ellen later in the film could just as easily be Hutter's—and thus the implicitly adulterous night he spends with her could just as easily have been spent with the movie's male hero. The vampire, and in particular *Nosferatu*'s vampire, is the paradigmatic cinematic example of the psychoanalytic category of the "polymorphous perverse."

Nosferatu, *the Nazis, and the Jews*

In a famous and much-disputed book written just after the end of World War II, the film critic and sociologist Siegfried Kracauer argued that German Expressionism contributed significantly to the rise of Hitler and the Nazi party by distracting the German people from the social and political realities of the time with what he called the "empty artistic *formalism*" of films like *The Cabinet of Dr. Caligari, Orlac's Hands (Orlacs Hände,* 1924), and *Nosferatu.* Kracauer's book, *From Caligari to Hitler: A Psychological History of the German Film,* originally published in 1947, also argued that Expressionism contained premonitions or foreshadowings of the form of totalitarianism that would arise in Germany during the next decade.

Filmophile's Lexicon

Formalism is any artistic or critical practice that privileges the outer form or structure of a work over its political, social, and ideological content; in fact, formalists will often deny such content when producing or analyzing a work of art.

While Kracauer's thesis has been argued over for decades by film historians, it's undeniable that Nosferatu resonates disturbingly with the rising tide of German anti-Semitism in the 1920s and '30s.

Consider the physical representation of Orlock himself. The count/vampire possesses a sharp, hooked nose, pointy, devilish ears, and clawlike hands constantly clutching one another in a Uriah Heep–like gesture that renders his gentle caress of Ellen all the more ghoulish. As a number of critics have pointed out, Nosferatu's physical characteristics seem to be drawn rather directly from prevalent anti-Semitic stereotypes common in Germany before and after World War I. During this period, many German representations of Jewish bodies depicted them as satanic and almost animal-like with exaggerated features; it's not hard to see how the same ethnic stereotypes would have appealed to a German filmmaker seeking to render the monster he had created in the most contemptible way possible.

Short Cuts

The homoerotic dimensions of the relationship between Hutter and the Count may relate to elements of Murnau's own sexuality. As a gay man in a repressive society, he may have been expressing in the guise of a monster-human relationship a dynamic that only film allowed him to explore in its full complexity.

If Nosferatu does indeed stand in for the Jews in the unconscious of the film, Murnau's larger adaptation of Stoker's plot takes on more insidious implications. While Hutter returns by carriage from the Carpathians, Nosferatu travels by sea, landing at Bremen with his hideous cargo of coffins, rodents, and dirt. He then becomes the "evil within," the monstrous foreign presence that has invaded the city, threatened its citizens with death—and created the justification for his own violent elimination.

Kracauer's thesis about Expressionist anti-Semitism begins to sound convincing. Read in light of the next 20 years of German history, and especially the Holocaust, *Nosferatu* can be viewed as an argument for a "pure" Bremen and, by extension, a pure German nation, cleansed of the threatening presence of its most despised other.

Tying It All Together

We've given you a lot to think about in the preceding pages. As we said at the beginning, you're welcome to agree or disagree with any of our interpretations. But don't just dismiss them: Take them seriously as informed commentaries on this film by a couple of guys who know what they're talking about, and see if you can figure out some ways of relating them (as well as your own interpretations) to the technical aspects of *Nosferatu* discussed in the first half of the chapter. In the end, you should emerge with an intelligent, articulate, unified view of the film as a whole that you can take with you to your next interpretive project.

A Dozen Films to Compare

Below is a list of 12 "monster movies," most of them featuring vampires of one sort or another, that we've selected for comparison's sake with *Nosferatu.* As you'll immediately notice from the dates alone, our selection ranges widely, from Bela Lugosi's 1931 American classic to Werner Herzog's New German Cinema remake featuring Klaus Kinski to *The Nightmare Before Christmas* (which we like to think of as "Expressionism for American children"). Don't blow off this list: We guarantee you'll learn much more about *Nosferatu* through comparison with other films of its ilk than you would in isolation. Besides, most of these flicks are pretty fun to watch!

- *The Cabinet of Dr. Caligari* (Robert Wiene, 1919).
- *The Golem* (*Der Golem, wie er in die Welt kam,* Paul Wegener, 1920).
- *Nosferatu: The Vampyre* (*Nosferatu: Phantom der Nacht,* Werner Herzog, 1979).
- *Dracula* (Tod Browning, 1931).
- *Vampyr* (Carl Theodor Dreyer, 1932).
- *Dracula A.D.* (Alan Gibson, 1972).
- *The Hunger* (Tony Scott, 1983).
- *Vampire's Kiss* (Robert Bierman, 1989).
- *Bram Stoker's Dracula* (Francis Ford Coppola, 1992).
- *Interview with the Vampire* (Neil Jordan, 1994).
- *The Nightmare Before Christmas* (Henry Selick and Tim Burton, 1993).
- *John Carpenter's Vampires* (John Carpenter, 1998).

What Now?

The next step is to take what you've learned here and apply it to another film, whether one of John Ford's early silent films or the latest *Lethal Weapon* flick (what are we on by now, *Lethal Weapon 6? 7? 8?*). And then another, and another, and another, until you've become a master interpreter of world film, able to talk with fluency about the cinematography, mise-en-scène, camera work, lighting, psychology, and gender politics of virtually any movie you encounter! If you've followed the simple steps laid out in this chapter and this book, there's no reason you can't become a real expert over time. Good luck!

The Least You Need to Know

- *Nosferatu,* directed by F. W. Murnau, was an influential work of German Expressionism.
- The technical and aesthetic aspects of this film are mostly typical of 1920s Expressionism, but the picture does have its idiosyncrasies.
- Viewed from a Marxist perspective, *Nosferatu*'s aesthetics were clearly influenced by the material conditions of its production.
- A psychoanalytic reading reveals that the film, like all Expressionist works, is deeply concerned with the unconscious inner world of human pathology and evil.
- *Nosferatu* is also very much about repressed eroticism, though it anticipates in important ways the rise of anti-Semitism in pre–World War II Germany.
- Comparison with the century's other vampire movies, flicks, and films helps illuminate the forces at work in *Nosferatu.*

Appendix A

Other Good Books on Movies, Flicks, and Film

From the literally thousands of books on the history, aesthetics, and theory of film out there, we've chosen just a handful that we think will be most useful to you as you set out on your journey through the universe of world cinema. We've included film and video guides, massive encyclopedias, specialized studies, beginner's "how-to" guides on any number of subjects, and several quite dense history books that fill in some of the inevitable gaps in our own coverage. Now that you've begun with *The Complete Idiot's Guide to Movies, Flicks, and Film,* start expanding your library today!

Allen, Robert C. *Film History: Theory and Practice.* New York: McGraw Hill, 1985.

Baltake, Joe. *Dolly, Gaffer, and Best Boy, Too.* www.movieclub.com/

Bogle, Donald. *Toms, Coons, Mulattoes, Mammies, and Bucks: An Interpretive History of Blacks in American Films.* New York: Continuum, 1992.

Bone, Jan, and Ron Johnson. *Understanding the Film: An Introduction to Film Appreciation.* Lincolnwood, IL: NTC, 1997.

Bordwell, David, and Kristin Thompson. *Film Art: An Introduction.* New York: McGraw-Hill, 1996.

Cook, David A. *A History of Narrative Film.* New York: Norton, 1996.

Friedman, Lester D. *Hollywood's Image of the Jew.* New York: Ungar, 1982.

Gever, Martha, et al. *Queer Looks: Perspectives on Lesbian and Gay Film and Video.* New York: Routledge, 1993.

Giannetti, Louis. *Understanding Movies,* 7th ed. Englewood Cliffs, NJ: Prentice Hall, 1996.

Halliwell, Leslie, and John Walker. *Halliwell's Film and Video Guide.* New York: Harper's, 1999.

Hill, John, and Pamela Gibson. *Oxford Guide to Film Studies.* New York: Oxford University Press, 1998.

Katz, Ephraim. *The Encyclopedia of Film.* New York: Harper Collins, 1994.

Konigsberg, Ira. *The Complete Film Dictionary.* New York: Penguin, 1997.

Kracauer, Siegfried. *From Caligari to Hitler: A Psychological History of the German Film.* Princeton, NJ: Princeton, 1966.

Kupsc, Jarek. *The History of Cinema for Beginners.* New York: Writers and Readers, 1998.

LoBrutto, Vincent. *Selected Takes: Film Editors on Editing.* New York: Praeger, 1991.

Maltin, Leonard, ed. *Leonard Maltin's Movie and Video Guide 2000.* New York: Signet, 1999.

Mander, Jerry. *Four Arguments for the Elimination of Television.* New York: Quill, 1978.

Mast, Gerald. *A Short History of the Movies.* Rev. Bruce Kawin. New York: Allyn & Bacon, 1999.

Monaco, James. *How to Read a Film: Movies, Media, Multimedia.* Oxford: Oxford University Press, 2000.

Musser, Charles. *Before the Nickelodeon: Edwin S. Porter and the Edison Manufacturing Company.* Berkeley: University of California Press, 1991.

Nowell-Smith, Geoffrey, ed. *The Oxford History of World Cinema.* New York: Oxford University Press, 1996.

Postman, Neil. *Amusing Ourselves to Death.* New York: Penguin Books, 1985.

Pym, John. *Time Out Film Guide.* New York: Penguin, 1998.

Rogin, Michael. *Ronald Reagan: The Movie.* Berkeley: University of California, 1987.

Schatz, Thomas. *The Genius of the System: Hollywood Filmmaking in the Studio Era.* New York: Henry Holt, 1996.

———. *Hollywood Genres: Formulas, Filmmaking, and the Studio System.* New York: McGraw Hill, 1981.

Sklar, Robert. *Movie-Made America: A Cultural History of the Movies.* New York: Vintage, 1975.

Stam, Robert and Toby Miller. *Film Theory: An Introduction.* Malden, MA: Blackwell, 2000.

Taub, Eric. *Gaffers, Grips, and Best Boys.* New York: St. Martin's Press, 1994.

Winokur, Mark. *American Laughter: Immigrants, Ethnicity, and 1930s Hollywood Film Comedy.* New York: St. Martin's, 1996.

Appendix B

Major North American Film Festivals

The following list of accessible film festivals tries to include a wide variety of regions, venues, mediums, and festival themes in the United States and Canada. Many more festivals can be tracked down online at FilmFestivals.com (www.filmfestivals.com). We hope you find a festival in your area that you can actually attend. Enjoy.

Acapulco Black Film Festival
c/o UniWorld Group, Inc.
100 Avenue of the Americas
16th floor
New York, NY 10013
212-219-7267
E-mail: abff@uniworldgroup.com
www.abff.com/splash/splash.htm

Ann Arbor Film Festival
Ann Arbor Film Festival
P.O. Box 8232
Ann Arbor, MI 48107
734-668-8397, ext. 22
http://aafilmfest.org

The Atlantic Film Festival
P.O. Box 36139
Halifax, Nova Scotia
B3J 3S9
902-422-FILM
E-mail: festival@atlanticfilm.com
www.atlanticfilm.com

Austin Film Festival
1604 Nueces St.
Austin, TX 78701
1-800-310-FEST
Fax: 512-478-6205
www.austinfilmfestival.org/

Calgary International Film Festival
Penny Lane
219–513 8th Avenue SW
Calgary, Alberta
Canada, T2P 1G3
403-283-1490
Fax: 403-283-1498
E-mail: marrelli@calgaryfilm.com
www.calgaryfilm.com

Canadian International Annual Film Festival (CIAFF)
Canadian International Film/
Video Festival
Ben Andrews HonFSCCA,
Festival Director
25 Eugenia Street
Barrie, ON L4M 1P6, Canada
705-733-8232
Fax: 705-733-8232
E-mail: ciaff@canada.com
www.crcn.net/%7Etimber/Canadian.
html

Canyonlands Film and Video Festival
Canyonlands Film & Video Festival
59 South Main Street, Suite 214
Moab, UT 84532
435-259-9868
E-mail: canyonfilm@hotmail.com
http:/moab-utah.com/film

Chicago International Film Festival
32 W. Randolph
Chicago, IL 60601
312-425-9400
E-mail: info@chicagofilmfestival.com
www.chicagofilmfestival.com

Chicago Underground Film Festival
3109 North Western Ave.
Chicago, IL 60618
773-866-8660, 773-327-FILM
Fax: 773-327-3464
E-mail: info@cuff.org
www.cuff.org

Cine Las Americas: Festival of New Latin American Cinema
Attn: Celeste Serna Williams, Director
2215 Post Road, Suite 2056
Austin, TX 78704
E-mail: info@cinelasamericas.org
ww.cinelasamericas.org/

Cinefest Sudbury
90 Elm Street
Sudbury, ON P3C 1T2, Canada
705-688-1234
1-877-212-3222
Fax: 705-688-1351
www.cinefest.com

Crested Butte Reel Fest Short Film Festival
Crested Butte, Colorado
970-349-7487
E-mail: cbreelfest@webcom.com
www.crestedbuttereelfest.com/

Digital Film Festival
D.FILM Digital Film Festival
7095 Hollywood Blvd. Suite 1001
Los Angeles, CA 90028
www.dfilm.com/

Festival International du Film de Québec
Margarita Wolniewicz, Coordinatrice
Festival International du Film de
Québec
(In Québec) 418-534-FILM
E-mail: fifq@vl.videotron.ca
www.telegraphe.com/fifq/2000/
introen.html

Greenlight International Youth Film Festival
Greenlight Youth Festival of the Arts Society
P.O. Box 3029
Mission, BC V2V 4J3, Canada
604-852-4727
Fax: 604-852-3997
E-mail: info@greenlightfilm.org
www.greenlightfilm.org/film_festival/
index.html

Inside Out Lesbian and Gay Film Festival
401 Richmond Street W
Suite 219
Toronto, ON M5V 3A8, Canada
416-977-8025
www.insideout.on.ca/inout.htm

Los Angeles Independent Film Festival
323-937-9155
Fax: 323-937-7770
www.laiff.com/

New York Film Festival
212-777-7100
E-mail: filmmfest@aol.com
www.filmlinc.com/nyff/nyff.htm

New York Underground Film Festival
453 West 16th St.
Office Six
New York, NY 10011
212-675-1137, 212-252-3845
Fax: 212-675-1152
E-mail: festival@nyuff.com
www.nyuff.com

Planet Indie Film Festival
125 Trader's Blvd. East, Suite One
Mississauga, ON L4Z 2H3, Canada
E-mail: info@planetindie.com
www.planetindie.com

Queer Film and Video Festival
Out On Screen
Box 521
1027 Davie Street
Vancouver, BC V6E 4L2, Canada
604-684-XTRA, ext. 2014
E-mail: general@outonscreen.com
www.outonscreen.com

San Diego International Film Festival
E-mail: rbaily@ucsd.edu
http://ueo.ucsd.edu/

San Francisco International Film Festival
San Francisco Film Society
39 Mesa Street
Suite 110
The Presidio
San Francisco, CA 94129-1025
415-561-5000
Fax: 415-561-5099
www.sfiff.org/

San Francisco International Lesbian and Gay Film Festival
Frameline
346 Ninth Street
San Francisco, CA 94103
415-703-8667
E-mail: Info@Frameline.org
www.frameline.org/festival/

Thaw 00: Festival of Film, Video, and Digital Media
The Institute for Cinema and Culture
162 Becker Communication Studies Building
Iowa City, IA 52242
319-335-1348, 319-354-5536
Fax: 319-335-1774
E-mail: thaw@uiowa.edu
www.uiowa.edu/~thaw/

The Vancouver International Film Festival
410-1008 Homer Street
Vancouver, BC V6B 2X1, Canada
604-685-0260
E-mail: viff@viff.org
www.viff.org/

Women in Cinema Festival
Cinema Seattle
911 Pine Street
Seattle, WA 98101
206-464-5830
Fax: 206-264-7919
E-mail: mail@seattlefilm.com
www.seattlefilm.com

World Film Festival Montréal
1432, De Bleury Street
Montréal, Québec H3A 2J1, Canada
514-848-3883
Fax: 514-848-3886
E-mail: ffm@qc.aira.com
www.ffm-montreal.org/

Worldfest-Houston International Film Festival
713-965-9955
Fax: 713-965-9960
E-mail: worldfest@aol.com
www.worldfest.org/

Zoie Films Broadband Film Festival (Georgia)
404-816-0602
Fax: 678-560-6777
E-mail: filmfest@zoiefilms.com
www.zoiefilms.com/filmfestxprt.htm

Movie-Related Web Sites and Video Distributors

This appendix contains additional sources and resources that may help you quench your thirst for movies, flicks, and film.

Movie-Related Web Sites

The following sites on the World Wide Web provide useful and entertaining information about film and cinema. All these sites were up at the time of this writing, but the Web moves so fast that it's hard to tell which sites will be around in a year. Still, give these puppies a shot.

The Internet Movie Database
(http://us.imdb.com)
Probably the most popular film site on the Net, and rightly so. It provides complete production information for its huge database of films. It also provides local show times for current releases.

Cyber Film School
(www.cyberfilmschool.com)
Some good general information about how the production process works. Contains a rather useful "Movie School Encyclopedia."

Box Office Mania!
(www.boxofficemania.com)
Information on contemporary films. It's kind of a fanzine/ad page, but has some cool links and downloads.

The Black Film Center/Archive
(www.indiana.edu/~bfca/websites.html.)
Good links to African American film resources on the Web.

Premiere
(www.premiere.com/Premiere/HomePage/0,2054,0,00.html)
More information about contemporary films and actors.

Mr. Showbiz
(http://mrshowbiz.go.com)
Despite the name, a little more serious look at the deal-making in Hollywood, as well as news about contemporary figures in the news.

Society for Cinema Studies
(www.cinemastudies.org)
At the other extreme from most fan sites, this is the American academic film studies site. Worth a look.

CinemaZone
(http://store.cinemazone.com/index.pl/insider/facts/afi_top100.html)
Place to buy cinema-related stuff, from videos to action figures to posters.

American Film Institute
(www.afionline.org.)
Those wonderful people who gave you film preservation. Education, news, shopping, and so on—a worthy cause.

PopcornQ
(www.planetout.com/pno/popcornq)
Lesbian- and gay-oriented film site. Terrifically organized and informative.

The Silents Majority
(www.mdle.com/ClassicFilms)
Subtitled "An Online Journal of Silent Film." The title says it all. Great site.

Video Distributors

Your local Target will, of course, sell currently released popular films on video, films like *It's a Wonderful Life* (1946). Blockbuster Video will have an even wider selection. But we are really big fans of locally owned "mom-and-pop" video stores because they tend to buy and keep a wider selection of titles. But as your tastes broaden, you may want to start tracking down the following mail-order companies specializing in rare and hard-to-find titles:

- **Critic's Choice Video.** P.O. Box 749, Itascaa, IL 60143-0749. 1-800-367-7765, 1-800-544-9852. Specializing in silent films, minor studios, and films not in general video release.

- **Eddie Brandt's Saturday Matinee.** 5006 Vineland, North Hollywood, CA 91606; 818-506-4242, 818-506-7722. Specialties include silent films, classic genre films (Westerns, 1950s sci-fi, and animation), and foreign films.
- **eBay.** www.ebay.com. It's very easy to get ripped off at auction online houses, so buyer beware. The best of the online auctions is eBay, both because they tend to have the largest number of films for sale, and because they are the best at monitoring their business for fraud.
- **Facets Video.** 1517 West Fullerton Avenue, Chicago, IL 60610; 773-281-9075; www.facets.org; sales@facets.org. Facets probably has the largest video collection around, and is probably the first place you should call for a title. If they don't have it, they'll tell you who might.
- **Festival Films.** 6115 Chestnut Terrace, Shorewood, MN 55331. Phone or fax: 952-470-2172; www.fesfilms.com; FesFilms@aol.com. Specializing in foreign, classic, and silent titles. Also sells 16mm film.
- **Grapevine Video.** jbhardy@grapevinevideo.com. Specializing in titles from the 1930s through the 1950s. Grapevine also sells film prints.
- **Peter Kavel Video.** 1123 Ohio Avenue, Alamogordo, NM 88310; 505-437-6739; www.netmdc.com/~pkavel; pkavel@netmdc.com. Specializes in rare and scarce titles.
- **Kino on Video.** 333 West 39th Street, New York, NY 10018; 1-800-562-3330; kinoint@infohouse.com. Perhaps because it was originally a film distributor, Kino has successfully branched out into video as a sort of generalist company, carrying something of everything.
- **Videobrary.** 5812 Wish Avenue, Encino, CA 91316; 213-660-0187; paullisy@aol.com. Rare films from the silent and early sound era.

Appendix D

Glossary

35mm Refers to the width or gauge of the celluloid film strip passing through a camera, editing machine, projector, and other equipment. George Eastman's first celluloid strips were 35mm with four perforations per side on each frame, which remains even today the industry standard.

additive color process The additive color process mixes colors on the screen's surface itself, rather than dying the film strip.

ADR Stands for Automated Dialog Replacement, a computerized method for looping, which is itself a method for redubbing dialogue.

agitki The propaganda films made by the Bolsheviks in support of their revolution. The first instances by the Bolsheviks of an interest in using film as a propaganda device aimed at the masses. The trains used by the Bolsheviks to distribute, advertise, promote, and project the films were called agitki-trains. The word *agitki* is related to the English expression "agit-prop."

aleatory Originally used for the other arts, in film this means setting up the camera in such a way that you allow the possibility of interesting things happening without artificially preparing their occurrence.

allegory A work that employs fictional figures or characters as symbols of wider cultural, political, moral, or religious values in order to express a particular viewpoint concerning contemporary society.

anamorphic lenses A type lens that distorts images in the process of filming them but straighten them out again during projection.

anamorphosis An anamorphosis is any visual object, such as a painting, in which a certain image comes into focus from a certain angle while remaining invisible or obscure from others.

art director The person responsible for the look of a film's sets; also responsible for their construction.

art film (or ***film d'art***) This is a term generally used to distinguish more self-consciously artistic and "cerebral" films from their generally higher-budget counterparts, "commercial films." Though the term is still used by critics to separate art-house productions from mainstream Hollywood studio releases, it's often more of a convenience than an accurate reflection of a real division.

assistant director Most of the time this is an administrative position rather than truly directorial. The assistant director helps break down the script and make decisions about the shooting order.

associate producer/production manager 1. The next-in-charge of a film after the producer. Depending on the relationship with, and the working style of, the producer, the assistant producer can have a greater or lesser say in creative as well as administrative decisions; 2. The actual administrator for the daily operations of the film.

auteur French term generally synonymous with "great director."

avant-garde An avant-garde is a group of artists or intellectuals that develops innovative, experimental, or radical concepts and aesthetic changes in an art form.

benshi The *benshi,* important figures in early Japanese cinema, were responsible for narrating the story line of silent films and explaining individual scenes for their audiences.

best boy 1. A person in charge of the paperwork for administering the head grip's or gaffer's crew. Can take care of timesheets, salaries, and so on. 2. The head grip's or gaffer's gofer. An apprentice to the gaffer or key grip. So called because he (or now she) is the "best" person available for the job.

Black Maria This was Edison and Dickson's film studio; it was a hideous tar paper–covered structure that got its name from the New York slang term for a police van.

boom operator (or **boom man**) The technician who handles the boom microphone and its paraphernalia, making sure that it is in position to record sound to the best advantage. Requires a steady hand to hold the mike over the heads of the actors.

cable person This person makes certain the sound cables are efficiently and inconspicuously placed.

camera operator (or **second cameraman**) The technician actually operating the movie camera. Of course, this person is under the careful supervision of both the director and the director of photography.

carpenter The person whose crew physically builds the set.

casting director Often in collaboration with the director and/or producer, the person who actually picks the "talent," or actors who will appear onscreen. This means not only the stars, but supporting players, bit players, and so on. At one time studio employees, most casting directors now work independently, though often regularly with the same directors and producers.

cinema The motion picture industry at large; movies, flicks, and film in general.

cinéma beur Refers to a new wave of naturalistic films directed by and featuring the lives of young North Africans in France; Rachid Bouchareb's *Cheb* (1990) and Mehdi Charef's *Le Thé au harem d'Archimède* (1986) are among the most influential examples of this recent genre.

cinéma du look Is a catchword for the postmodern films of Jean-Jacques Beineix, Luc Besson, and other '80s directors who focused on the visual image per se as the overall "message" of film.

cinematograph (*cinématographe* in French) Was a combination camera and projector first widely used by the Lumiére brothers at the end of the nineteenth century.

cinematographer (**director of photography**) This is the person who literally brings the director's vision to light. Sometimes the cinematographer is almost as responsible for the look and feel of a film as the director. It is impossible to think of *Citizen Kane* without Gregg Toland, or Charlie Chaplin films without Rollie Totheroh. Other major technicians—art directors and gaffers, for example—consult with the cinematographer who, with the director, actually decides on mood, angles, and composition.

colonialism The historical relationship since at least the eighteenth century between "Third World" regions and European nations, in which the latter assumed the power to administrate the governments of African, Asian, and Latin American countries, under the triple banner of liberation, modernization, and Christianization. Sometimes sincere, this political relationship was for the most part one of cruelty and exploitation, enforced by a strong military presence.

compositor Really one of a host of computer programmers now involved in film production, the compositor creates layers and textures for the film image in order to lend it a greater impression of reality.

computer animator The computer programmer in charge of digitally creating special effects that will be transferred back to celluloid. Images can be transformed live-action sequences, or completely computer-generated.

construction coordinator Answerable to the art director, the construction coordinator is responsible for the actual construction of the film set.

continuity clerk (**continuity girl, script girl, script supervisor**) Traditionally often a woman, this person makes sure that, if an actor is walking toward the sun in one shot, he is walking in the same direction in the next shot, though the camera may be set up at a different angle. Or, if there is a cat in the room in one shot, that cat is still scratching up the furniture and coughing up hairballs in subsequent shots.

desaturated color Refers to the tendency—most pronounced since the 1960s—to remove the richness from the usual Technicolor-style shot.

detail shot A close-up of a graphic element of the previous shot.

discourse Any signifying practice, including film.

distribution The middleman of the business, distribution includes that part of the industry that gets the movie from the studio to the theatre.

divas A term originally applied to opera heroines, were the sensuous, tragically beautiful, and passionate female leads of a subgenre of Italian film that dominated the screen during the 1920s. Women like Lyda Borelli, Rina De Liguoro, Pina Minichelli, Helen Makowska, and several others made dozens of stock melodramas that contributed greatly to the qualitative decline of Italian cinema during this period.

dolly grip The technician who operates the dolly, a wheeled and motorized platform on which the camera is placed for "dolly" or "tracking" shots.

dominant Also known as the dominant contrast, it is the place on the screen where your eye first rests. The subsidiary contrast is the next place your eye goes to.

emotional memory A term from nineteenth-century European psychology, refers to the method-based idea that an actor has had certain life experiences that will allow him or her to forge a deep-seated psychological connection with the character being portrayed.

executive producer As the job title suggests, an executive, and administrator in charge of the business end of production, issues such as raising money for the budget. Rarely involved in the day-to-day operation of the film, the executive producer may be involved in the business of several productions at once.

exhibition The branch including the theaters in which films are shown; the people and technologies involved in exhibition: projectors and projectionists, sound equipment, and so on.

Expressionism A movement in early twentieth-century art—painting, music, film, and so on—that sought to make the inner psychological and emotional life of human beings its subject, rather than event-driven outer life (realism) or sensory impression (impressionism).

film A motion picture whose age, artistry, budget, or nationality distinguishes it as a culturally significant work (thus the most subjective term of all!).

film noir Literally "black film," a term used to describe a variety of picture that arose in the late 1940s featuring dark, pessimistic, stingy atmospheres, the gloomy underbelly of society, and the life-cheapening consequences of crime, corruption, and hopelessness.

flick A movie with no artistic aspirations whatsoever that's made purely for entertainment's sake.

Foley artist Invents the sound effects that are dubbed onto the visuals.

Foley stage The workshop in which the props employed to make sound effects are used.

formalism Any artistic or critical practice that privileges the outer form or structure of a work over its political, social, and ideological content; in fact, formalists will often deny such content when producing or analyzing a work of art.

frame This word really has two related meanings. The first is roughly equivalent to "screen," and alludes to the border separating the picture from the theater auditorium. Everything thrown on screen by the projector is in the frame. Everything in the dark is outside the screen: the theater stage, the walls, the popcorn, your lover's legs, and so on. The second meaning is simply one picture on the film strip.

Free Cinema The term given to a six-part series of film showings screened at London's National Film Theatre from 1956 to 1959 that launched a socially conscious cinema movement of the same name.

gaffer 1. The chief electrician, responsible for lighting the set. 2. More generally, the technician who makes the set run smoothly, from scouting locations to streamlining the set. Legend has it that the term originally applied to the European carney who herded, or "gaffed," audiences into the circus tent.

gendaigeki Modern drama films set in Japan's larger cities, especially Tokyo and Kyoto, in the present.

grip 1. A jack-of-all-trades on the set, responsible for physically moving and setting up equipment, sets, and so on. The "muscle" on the set, the grip must also be able to do a bit of carpentry. 2. The grip is in charge of all physical work except electrical.

Hays Office Shorthand for the Motion Picture Producers and Distributors of America (MPPDA); the name derived from the MPPDA's first and most important head, Will H. Hays, who was primarily responsible for the writing and enforcement of The Code beginning in 1930.

HUAC Short for House Un-American Activities Committee, a temporary panel in the U.S. House of Representatives that terrorized the U.S. film industry in the early 1950s by rooting out real and alleged Communists and attempting to cleanse the business of their allegedly seditious influence.

indie Short for independent production company, it refers to artists and their companies making films outside the Hollywood production industry.

insert shot A shot of an object that generally informs or reminds the audience of something it needs to know: the missing gun laying in a gutter on the outskirts of the city.

insider A person in the Hollywood system, either on the talent side or on the administrative or executive side.

jidaigeki The term for a period drama set in the Japanese past but always very much concerned with the present.

key (or head) grip The person on the set in charge of the other grips, or the crew of workers.

key lighting Refers to the intensity of the lighting of in the frame.

kinematoscope Invented by Coleman Sellers in 1861, employed a rotating paddle machine that showed sequential photographs mounted on individual paddles.

kinetophonograph An American invention, was a device capable of showing film and producing sound simultaneously.

Kino-Eye The name Vertov gives the camera eye, which is more perfect in recording impressions, and in moving through time and space. For Vertov, the Kino-Eye is both a perfectly objective recorder and an ideal interpreter of reality.

Klieg light A spotlight produced by the Kliegl brothers around 1914 for use on the live stage. It was imported into film by the early Lasky film company, and was the most famous arc lamp in use during the silent era.

lamp operator Person in charge of operating film lamp.

lead man The set scrounger, responsible for finding objects to make the set more atmospheric or realistic.

line producer (production manager) This executive oversees the day-to-day operations of a film's production.

location manager A person who finds locations at which to shoot.

marketing The process of getting the finished product to its audience.

method acting (often called simply **the method**) refers to the system of acting developed by Constantin Stanislavsky that emphasized the emotional and psychological bond between actor and character, the goal of which was to discover the "inner spirit" of the latter.

mickeymousing The matching of music to mood. The term probably derives from Walt Disney's early sound cartoons, whose soundtracks were almost completely indexed to the characters' and the audiences' emotional states from sequence to sequence. The term is a little contemptuous because it describes a rather easy sound technique, and because it manipulates the audience too visibly.

midnight ramble Refers to showings of late-night movies to African American audiences, who were largely segregated from whites-only daytime and evening film performances.

mise-en-scène Every visible element in the frame: lighting, costume, decor, and so on; how these elements are related to each other; and how you see these elements (that is, how they are photographed).

mixer The sound technician who assimilates, or "mixes," sounds together for each of a film's sequences, determining the relative values (volume, pitch, and so on) of the background music, dialogue, ambient noise, and so on.

model The actor filling in for close-ups of a portion of the principal actor's body; a "body double."

modeler Originally, a technician who makes the small-scale models that are photographed as if life-sized. Now more often applied to the computer programmer who creates 3-D digital images that are then transferred to film.

montage A number of shots edited quickly together in order to form a brief impression of a character, place, or time.

mountain films (*Bergfilme*) A popular genre of Austrian, German, and Swiss motion picture in the 1930s that featured dramatic, challenging mountain landscapes coupled with equally challenging human situations confronting the protagonists.

movie The general, nonjudgmental term for any run-of-the-mill motion picture.

neocolonialism The economic and cultural—rather than explicitly political or military—control of third World countries.

neorealism A cinematic movement, originating in Italy, that reached its peak in the late 1940s and early '50s; in response to the feel-good pap of the "white telephone" era, neorealists demanded a turn to natural settings rather than artificially constructed sets, "real people" instead of actors, and authentic human stories rather than stale melodrama.

nickelodeons Makeshift theaters—often set up in union halls, cafeterias, libraries, living rooms, and other public and private spaces—that became the first popular movie houses after 1905. There may have been as many as 10,000 nickelodeon houses in the United States by 1910.

nursery man The worker who provides the appropriate plant life for a scene.

Oberhausen Manifesto A petition-like declaration signed by more than two dozen young filmmakers at the Oberhausen Film Festival in 1962, was a collective vow to create a new German cinema that would resist the commercial demands of the nation's dominating film industry.

orthochromatic film stock Was used in the production of silent film from its earliest days to about the mid-1920s. Its main limitation was that it was not sensitive to yellows and reds, which then did not show up as any appreciable shade of gray at all on this black-and-white film.

outsider Someone not in the Hollywood loop. Often a term of contempt applied to people trying to get into the system.

panchromatic film stock (or **panchro**) The name given now-standard black-and-white film stock. It is so called because it is sensitive to the whole range of color in the spectrum.

phasmotrope First demonstrated by Henry Renno Heyl in Philadelphia in 1870, this invention showed a rapid succession of still photographs of dancers in motion.

phenakisticope Built by Joseph Plateau in 1832, employed a rotating disc covered in drawings and a mirror to simulate movement.

player Someone with power in the Hollywood loop.

poetic realism Is the term given to a wide-ranging group of films from the 1930s and '40s that feature working-class milieus, pessimistic ambience, and a gritty workaday feel that reflects the mood of the realist novels and plays on which many of these pictures were based.

postcolonialism The historical moment in which ex-colonies have to deal with the repercussions of colonialism.

postproduction The technical portion of filmmaking that turns raw film into finished product.

preproduction All the technical matters that can be settled before shooting.

producer The chief administrator for a film, whose duties can vary widely. The producer is at the beginning of the process: buying the rights to the original book on which a movie is based. He considers various "treatments" of the original "property," selects the director, and consults on creative aspects and budgets. Sometimes the producer leaves have little visible effect on the product. Other producers, like Arthur Freed at MGM, are almost auteurs themselves.

production The actual shooting of a film. That part of the moviemaking industry that actually cranks out the product. In the golden age of Hollywood, production was principally associated with the big studios.

production designer The person who decides how the film is going to look, based on the needs and vision of the director and the script.

prop man (**property master**) The property man keeps track of, cares for, and places the props on the set.

publicist Promotes films and stars through press releases, publicity events, contacts with newspapers, distribution of publicity stills, and so on. This job overlaps with that of the public relations executive. The "unit" publicist publicizes a particular film.

quota quickies Low-budget, low-quality films that English studios shot, edited, and released in record time in order to satisfy the strict requirements of the Cinematograph Act of 1927.

race movies Feature-length silent films with all-black casts that were made specifically for African American audiences, becoming the standard fare in early black cinema.

repertory system An English network of local and national theater companies that has turned out most of the country's foremost acting talents.

revolutionary realism The term coined by Mao Tse-tung to describe the peasant worker-oriented films that dominated Chinese cinema throughout the post-1949 era.

saturated color Refers to those color films in which the color is rich and bright.

screenwriter The craftsperson who writes the scripts. The writer may adapt a literary work, produce an original script, or revise ("doctor") an already-existing script. Like most of the rest of filmmaking, screenwriting tends to be a collaborative effort.

second unit director The director of the "second unit." The second unit is the film crew that photographs sequences for which the director and principal actors are not required.

sequence A number of shots edited together and unified, either through the plot, the character(s), the time and/or space, or the theme.

set decorator On instructions ultimately from the art director, the set decorator actually furnishes a set with the items that create the appropriate atmosphere and ambience: rugs, lamps, and potted palm.

set dresser Related to set decoration, set dressing is the art of making the set look as if it has always been inhabited rather than new and artificial.

The Seventh Art A phrase that was coined by critic Ricciotto Canudo in the 1910s to connote film's status as a new and powerful rival to painting, music, sculpture, and the other fine arts. Though Italian by birth, Canudo established the "Club of the Friends of the Seventh Art" in Paris in 1920 to promote to the French intelligentsia the aesthetic possibilities and philosophical challenge of the emergent medium.

shot The basic temporal unit of film photography and editing. A shot consists of the celluloid used from the moment a camera begins rolling on a scene to the moment it stops.

shot-reverse shot A series of two shots, the second of whose angle is approximately 180° opposed to the first. Generally used to show two characters speaking, or to show the relationship between a character and the object of his gaze.

socialist realism Included not only film but all the arts. Derived from the realist aesthetic in the novel of the nineteenth century, it was a blend of realistic setting and ideologically correct plot and message in which the proletarian hero wins against great odds over the enemy of the people.

sound crew The technicians on the set responsible for audio recording. This crew is sometimes a single person: the sound man.

sound designer The production designer for sound, the sound designer oversees all aspects of sound recording for a film project.

special effects supervisor The special effects team is now most often an independent company rather than a division of a major studio, so the effects supervisor can be either an administrator or a supervisor of the day-to-day operations of the special effects team.

stand-by painter The set's "touch-up" painter who makes any last-minute adjustments in the set's color and sheen, subduing glare or changing hues when necessary.

stand-in Chosen for their physical resemblance to the main stars, stand-ins are the people who substitute in place of the stars during the often time-consuming process of readying the set for actual photography.

star system The cinematic practice that fashions a select number of actresses and actors into box-office sensations by constantly giving them leading roles, which in turn inspires a massive fan base that perpetuates the system.

story analyst/reader This is the person who considers whether a script or a literary property is worth considering as a film.

stunt coordinator Determines where, in the film script, stunts will take place.

stunt person The stunt people take all those falls, dives, crashes, and punches that making a film "action-packed." The stunt person can either play a distinct, if minor, character: the yeoman in the landing crew on the original *Star Trek* series you know is going to die upon landing on the hostile planet. Or she can double for the star in the automobile crash that no one could actually survive in real life.

subtractive color process A process that involves dying the film itself, subtracting some color from each of two or three strips of film that, when projected simultaneously, mix to give a wider and more naturalistic experience of color. This was the final form classic Technicolor took.

supervising editor The person in charge of film editing, this technician works closely with the director and, if budget allows, supervises a team of editors.

swing gang The grunts who fetch and carry props and other equipment to and from the set.

talent Vernacular expression for the people in front of the camera; the actors. Occasionally used ironically.

Third Cinema This term derives from an Argentine political manifesto titled "Towards a Third Cinema: Notes and Experiences on the Development of a Cinema of Liberation in the Third World." Third Cinema has gradually become the preferred expression for critics in the know for national cinemas not a part of the ex–Soviet Union or of the Western, industrially developed countries.

trick film Perhaps the earliest true film genre (and mastered by French musician-cum-filmmaker George Méliès), trick film was a form of stop-action animation in which one figure (say, a horse) was switched for another (perhaps a lion) between frames, creating the illusion of shape-changing.

typage The term given by Russian director Vsevolod Pudovkin to the practice of casting nonprofessional actors in motion pictures to create a heightened sense of realism.

unit The designation for the technical crew actually working on the set.

unit photographer The still photographer who takes publicity photos on the set for the film.

vertical integration The move of one industry into related industries; for example, block booking was part of a larger move in the industry to bring all three segments of the film industry under single ownership.

visual effects supervisor The person who oversees the team that actually creates special effects.

white telephone (*telefoni bianci*) films One of the predominant forms of motion picture during the Mussolini regime. The elegance of these films' glamorous settings was embodied in the image of the "white telephone," a symbol of their opulent refusal to comment on contemporary affairs.

wrangler (animal wrangler) The person responsible for the animals acting in front of the camera, whether dogs, horses, mice, or fish. Cares for the animals. Job can overlap with that of the "animal trainer," who actually owns and prepares the animal for movies.

zoetrope A Victorian drum-shaped toy with sequential drawings or paintings around the inner surface, invented by William George Horner in 1834. The drum was spun around as the user viewed the images through a narrow slit.

zoopraxiscope Eadweard Muybridge's device for viewing his hundreds of sequential shots of animal movement.

Index

Symbols

A

B

C

D

E

F

G

I

J

K

L

M

N

O

P

Q

R

S

T

U

V

W

X-Y

Z

About the Authors

Mark Winokur teaches film, popular culture, and American literature at the University of Colorado at Boulder. He has written a book on American film comedy called *American Laughter: Immigrants, Ethnicity, and 1930s Hollywood Film Comedy*, published by St. Martin's Press. He has also published in *The Velvet Light Trap, Cinema Journal, Sight and Sound,* and other important film journals. Praise, sinister notes, disagreements, cavils, snooty remarks, wisecracks, and nonconstructive criticism may be sent to him at zaphod@myrealbox.com. But no spam.

Bruce Holsinger teaches medieval literature and culture in the English department at the University of Colorado, where he has worked since receiving his Ph.D. in English and comparative literature from Columbia University in 1996. His interests in literature, music, and sexuality in the Middle Ages converge in his recent book *Music, Body, and Desire in Medieval Culture* (Stanford University Press), and in numerous articles and reviews appearing in academic journals as well as magazines such as *The Nation.* His current work focuses on religion and literature in medieval and early Reformation England, and he's completing a second book on the influence of medieval studies on modern critical theory. Bruce lives with his wife, Anna Brickhouse, and their new and insomniac son, Campbell Thomas, in Boulder, Colorado.

U.S. $18.95
CAN $28.95

Get the "reel" truth about the movies you love!

You're no idiot, of course. There's nowhere you'd rather be than at your local multiplex. From action-packed to animated, comic to creepy, you've seen and loved 'em all. But when it comes to understanding the history of cinema or terms such as *film noir* and *auteur,* you feel like you should be rated "I"—for Idiot.

Don't yell "Cut!" *The Complete Idiot's Guide® to Movies, Flicks, and Film* will help you understand why you like what you like—and give you interesting facts about great filmmakers, classic flicks, and important moments in the history of cinema. In this *Complete Idiot's Guide®*, you get:

- A fascinating glimpse into Hollywood's "Golden Age."
- A whirlwind world tour of foreign films—from Europe to India, Russia to Asia.
- Incredible facts about the world's greatest directors—and their contributions to film.
- Helpful hints for honing your interpretive skills.

MARK WINOKUR and **BRUCE HOLSINGER** teach film studies and English at the University of Colorado. Their credits include books and articles on topics from medieval music to monstrosity in Hollywood science fiction—and they are eager to share their love of film with a mainstream audience.

You'll learn ...

- How studios, producers, directors, and actors created the fabulous films of the '30s and '40s.
- The many ways films are financed.
- What best boys, gaffers, and Foley artists really do.
- What makes silent films so special.
- The influences of European directors on the culture of American films.
- How directors and cinematographers decide what to leave in—and what to take out.
- The basics of sound, light, and editing.

988-X
51895
9 780028 639888

Cover image © Stone/Paul S. Conrath

Visit us online at: www.idiotsguides.com

alpha books